The House of Yamazaki

THE HOUSE
OF YAMAZAKI

The Life of a Daughter of Japan

Laurence Caillet

Translated from the French by Megan Backus

KODANSHA INTERNATIONAL
New York • Tokyo • London

Kodansha America, Inc.
114 Fifth Avenue, New York, New York 10011, U.S.A.

Kodansha International Ltd.
17-14 Otowa 1-chome, Bunkyo-ku, Tokyo 112, Japan

Published in 1994 by Kodansha America, Inc.

Printed in the United States of America

94   95   96   97   98   6   5   4   3   2   1

Library of Congress Cataloging-in-Publication Data

Caillet, Laurence, 1947–
[Maison Yamazaki. English]
The House of Yamazaki : the life of a daughter of Japan / Laurence
Caillet ; translated from the French by Megan Backus.
p.   cm.
Translation of: La maison Yamazaki.
Includes bibliographical references and index.
ISBN 1-56836-007-X
1. Yamazaki, Ikue, 1918–   2. Beauty operators—Japan—Tokyo—
Biography.   3. Yamazaki Ikue Biyōshitsu—History.   4. Japan—Social
conditions—1926– .I. Title.
TT955.Y35C3513   1994
646.7'2'092—dc20
[B]   94-14726
CIP

Book design by Sara Stemen

The text of this book was set in Bembo.
Composed by Graphic Composition, Athens, Georgia.

For Wan-sheng

Preface

The life of Yamazaki Ikue is an exemplary one. Her history encapsulates that of her times: it is the story of the mutation of a rural society into an industrial power, the story of the obvious success of a nation, due in large part to the labor of the middle class. As the daughter of a wealthy rural family opposing the will of her parents, a young woman in revolt against her mother-in-law, and later a successful businesswoman, Yamazaki Ikue clearly belongs to that middle class. In a society in which democracy is commonly associated with relative material equality and the possibility for each citizen to develop his or her capacities, her own success appears to her to mirror that of Japan. She was neither an attentive witness to nor a conscious critic of the evolution of her country but an anonymous participant in its economic development, a passive spectator of the political upheavals to which, like most of her contemporaries, she submits without thinking of questioning.

But Yamazaki Ikue is as exceptional as she is typical. In spite of having been educated to be retiring (the lot of most Japanese women of her generation), she has fully succeeded in a business world in which male authority remained uncontested until very recently. Such is the most original character trait of this entrepreneur, who, breaking with traditional gender roles, largely sacrificed what we would call her womanly life (a life the Japanese define as motherhood) for the realization of her professional ambitions.

A symbol of the success of modern Japan, Yamazaki Ikue also personifies the uncertainties that success engendered. If the fervor of her beliefs seems unusual to some, her religious itinerary (typical of the merchant and working classes, who have little intellectual education) is a testimony to both the difficulties of her life and the constant necessity for reworking of traditional values. It is only the adaptation of those values in the service of a new way of life that has made possible the preservation to this day of an ongoing Japanese cultural identity otherwise threatened by Westernization.

Modern Japan is not constructed in opposition to the old; it was born of it. Japan's rural origins still mark the social fabric, both in the ways people think about the bonds of authority and subordination and in the nation's relations with the rest of the world.

Contents

A NOTE ON JAPANESE NAMES AND USAGE

Japanese names are presented in Japanese order, that is, surname first and given name second.

Japanese words are italicized, except for words generally familiar to the English-reading audience. Macrons are used to denote long vowels, except in the case of well-known place names. The possible macron in Yamazaki Ikue's maiden name, Endo, has also been omitted.

To prevent recognition of real people in the story, some minor elements of the account, as well as names, have been changed, except for members of the Endo and Yamazaki families.

I

Asaka

Prologue

On January 2 in Year 7 of the Taishō Era, 1918, the seventh year of the reign of the 123d emperor, who, according to custom, had ordained that time recommence with his coming, a fourth daughter was born in the house of Endo in the Kitai section of the village of Asaka. They named her Endo Nami. As soon as she could walk, the sun, the dust, and the wind over the rice paddies tinted and dirtied her face and hands, making her as brown as a boy. She preferred the lessons of the meadows and woods to those of school. She loved the tart taste of the wild apples she crunched on, seeds and all, in the marshes; the leaves of dwarf bamboo that tear the palm when pulled up; and the desperate song of the buffalo toad at night.

In adolescence, however, a strange ambition—that of being a hairdresser, to increase the beauty in the world—would lead her to the capital. It was there that, becoming known among her peers, she took the name Yamazaki Ikue. Yamazaki was her husband's family name. She chose the first name Ikue with the aid of a divining monk: it was made up of the sounds *i*, meaning "master of the world"; *ku*, meaning "eternity"; and *e*, meaning "mouth of great rivers." This official name change signified that a country girl had become a captain of industry.

When I met her, she was a rather plump woman of around sixty; her speech and gestures were those of Tokyo's merchant bourgeoisie. But there were also what might be called dissonances in her persona, and she appeared to use a prodigious amount of energy on luxurious whims and extravagant fits of anger. When asked about her success, she would bow her head. She would twist a white lace handkerchief in her fingers, all the while attributing her merits to the grace of the gods and ancestors. Everyone was in awe of her modesty. At other times, she would let drop that she had worked like a soul in the fires of hell. An uncharacteristic pallor would

3

cloud her features while she stared into space, her pupils turning as black as the seeds of the *hiōgi*, the blackberry lily,[1] and conversation would come to an awkward halt.

One afternoon as we were seated in the half darkness behind closed shoji screens, languorous in the humidity of the rainy season, she began to tell me her story. And then, day after tepid day, she seemed to develop a taste for what she called the game of foxes.

She said, "Have you ever seen two foxes chasing each other? You observe them carefully: You name one of them Tarō, the other Jirō. But both are red; they run back and forth, and you no longer know for sure which is which. Was that one Tarō, or was it Jirō? The sunlight dazzles you; now there is only one fox left, but you don't know which it is.

"What does it mean, to tell the story of my life? Is it to look at the old woman of today with the eyes of the little girl from Fukushima? To observe the child that was, with the eyes I have now? In this floating world where beings and things change endlessly, will I be able to describe the foam on the surface of the water?

"Surely not. But I will try; I will tell you where I was born and how I have lived until now. I will talk about evanescent bubbles, the flight of the mayfly, and cherry blossom petals—all the fragile reality of my life. I'll lie, too. And who knows? Perhaps my lies will be the greatest truth of this story."

1

Origins

三つ子の魂百まで

Mitsugo no tamashii hyaku made.
The soul of a child: the same to one hundred years.

Watakushi ga umareru sukoshi mae no koto de gozaimashita . . . This was a little while before I was born. Father was forty-one; Mother was thirty-eight, and she prayed every day to the *kami*,[1] the gods and the ancestors, that they would grant her a second son. My oldest brother, Yoshiki, was already past childhood. Two girls, Kiku and Riki, had followed him. Then a son, Yoshio, who had drowned at the age of three. And then yet another girl, Risa. *O kane ga kakaru!* The money it would cost to marry three girls! Even if it was still the most powerful house in the village, the house of Endo no longer enjoyed the splendor it once had.[2]

Of that splendor, I will speak soon. I will speak of our house, of its history. But first let me tell you about Asaka. That is the name of the village in Fukushima where I lived, near Kōriyama, in the region called Tōhoku (Northeast).

UBU-SUNA: LAND OF ONE'S BIRTH

Asaka . . . Now it's no more than one of the suburbs of Kōriyama.[3] And Kōriyama itself is only a factory town. Light industry came first, then heavy industries. Travel brochures put it this way: "The city of Kōriyama typifies the evolution of the lost regions of Tōhoku, the Northeast of Japan." That evolution devoured Asaka. Gray machines and black machines ate up the rice paddies. If you take a walk there today, you'll still see some wooden farmhouses, unpaved roads, rows of fruit trees. As child, I walked barefoot there. I made holes in the earth with my heels. Perhaps I knew that one day I would have to leave, and I was trying to put down my roots. Still,

5

later I myself cut those roots—with a vengeance, hardly realizing that I was turning myself from a living plant into a cut flower.

Today, modern houses with their blue roof tiles have spilled over the old village limits, into the rice paddies. Plastic greenhouses, shacks hastily thrown up in the middle of fields, transform the countryside into a construction site. It's all a dirty, unappealing mess.

They used to say that it was here, in Fukushima, 320 miles north of Tokyo, that the lands of Tōhoku, the most underprivileged province in Japan, began. This frontier region was linked to the rest of Japan only by the Nakoso and Shirakawa passes. To the north were the barbarian territories of the Emishi, who it was feared would come charging down into civilized provinces. It was this fear that gave rise to the name Nakoso, meaning "don't come!" And it was that fear that Minamoto no Yoriie, called Hachiman Tarō, son of Yoritomo and the second "great general charged with the pacification of the barbarians" of the North by the *bakufu* government of Kamakura, sang about:[4]

> *Kaze fuku wo Nakoso no seki to omoedomo*
> *Michi mo se ni saru yama-zakura kana!*

> The blowing wind
> that might be the pass of Nakoso
> but I wonder
> could it be the rows of mountain cherries
> fallen blossoms covering the narrow road?

Mother spoke these lines to me the night before I left for Tokyo. I would have been sixteen then. Since then, every time I go back to Fukushima, I find myself whispering, "Nakoso, Nakoso—don't come!" The road from Tokyo to Fukushima is such a hard one!

I also recall the poem of the pilgrim Nōin,[5] composed at the narrow pass of the Shirakawa (the White River), farther west. Travelers on their way through the pass, planted with dark, tall Japanese cedars, would here express their nostalgia for the city:

> *Miyako wo ba kasumi to tomo ni tachishikado*
> *Aki kaze zo fuku Shirakawa no seki.*

> The capital has disappeared in the mist
> The narrow Shirakawa pass, where the autumn wind blows.

Here, the wind runs faster than men. But it is the men who pass on—the wind never stops.

For the warriors who pushed their horses on toward the conquest of the North, and for the mendicant monks, poets, and pilgrims who followed the *Oku no Hoso-Michi*, the narrow road to the end of the world,[6] the adventure began at these walls. From here, they would follow the river Abukuma, which runs between the mountains, bisecting the two large valleys of Kōriyama and Fukushima. Then travelers would plunge northward, toward Miyagi.

All of them, my ancestors included, believed that they would come back from the end of the world covered in glory and shiny with blood. They served the lord of Itō, whose domain was Asaka, and they wanted to attain through combat the brilliant reputation of Tamuramaro, an eighth-century warrior with the eyes of a falcon and a golden beard. Some would lose their lives in the north, others their youth.

Fukushima on the road to the end of the world. Mountains covered with dark forests, perforated with volcanic lakes. Within their folds they enclose depressions in which the houses of men huddle together.

The village of Asaka is found in the basin of Kōriyama, west of the river Abukuma, exactly in the middle of a plain where on the clearest days the mountains are visible beyond the rice paddies. To the east are the mountains of Abukuma; to the west, the beginning of the heights of Ōu. About twenty houses, with gardens, faced a brook that ran alongside the Naganuma Road, which crossed the fields from east to west; all of the houses bore the name Endo. This section of Asaka was the hamlet of Kitai, meaning "North Well."

Snow doesn't accumulate here much in the winter, but a glacial wind blows for three long months. "*Homachi kaze da*, It's *our* wind, our secret treasure," the old people would murmur when, late in the autumn, the first gusts rushed up from the mountains to the west on their way down to the Abukuma. The wind dried the skin and started fires. Still, the old people of Asaka were as proud of it as they were of their own advanced age and the ancientness of their region. "This wind," they told us, "surely blew long before our ancestors settled here. It is the first master of any place. Look, the trees and grasses bend before it. Everything obeys it. But we come after it. It is we who have come."

Surrounding the houses, and to the north, were dry fields, but to the east and the south, the rice paddies stretched all the way to the river Abukuma. Periodically the river would overflow its stony banks. These brutal floods carried off bridges and frightened the women. People said, "It's dangerous to marry a man whose family lives on the other side of the water." Also, parents who married their daughters into houses upriver were considered mad. That brought bad luck.

Suddenly, then, the waters would once again be calm and smooth, the rice sprouts would mature in their seedbeds, and only the paddies, thrice plowed, would be flooded. Soon after the seedlings had been transplanted, in the fifth moon, frogs and buffalo toads would start up their cacophony in the grass. In the summer, when the ears of rice turned brown, the heat would hover, stagnant, at the bottom of the basin. The wealthy people of the village would escape toward the mountainous plateau to avoid the heat, or do *hisho*, as we called it.

Lying down on a path, I would watch praying mantises climb up stalks of wild rice. Early one afternoon I saw a dragonfly perch on a mantis's back. At once the combat began. Pincers versus proboscis. The mantis scratched the dragonfly in the face, but the dragonfly terrorized its enemy with its large, colorless eyes, riveting it to the rice stalk. The mantis churned the air slowly, more and more slowly. It no longer breathed through its proboscis, and then its wire-thin body began to rock back and forth around the stalk. It fell. I combed through the grass so I could find it and finish it off. The dragonfly's wings touched my hair, and I shuddered. In the village, people said that the dragonfly was a messenger from the otherworld and that each summer it carried the souls of the ancestors to this world on its red-spotted back.[7] I got scared and went home.

From our house, I could see the hills, which climbed in serrated rows toward the sky. Round or pointed, pink in the morning, blue-tinged at dusk. My hands cupped over my ears, I pondered the sound of the brooks flowing down their slopes, the echo of the nightingale's song. When autumn comes, I told myself, the needles of the *hinoki* cypress will make a crunchy bed. I'll deck my hair with garlands of red flowers, fragile as the breeze. And there, I will dream of the future. . . .

If I talk about the Fukushima of the past, it's not that I miss the old times. Indeed, I feel afraid, not nostalgic. When concrete covers the entire earth, I wonder if there will still be a place where man can put down roots. When I see grass break through asphalt in the summer to reach the sun, I wonder if man will one day be reduced to the same wretched fate. When I see the morning glories unfold their bluish petals in the dusty light of the cities or climb toward the roofs in search of light, I wonder if something like that will be our destiny one day. Man is often described as an animal; in Japan, we even speak of ourselves as the "economic animal." But for me, the human being is not primarily an animal. He cannot, like the bird, fly from pillar to post, from wall to fence; he cannot, like the cat, jump ten times his height. He is captive. He is a plant. That's why everyone, in the cities as well as the villages, venerates the *ubu-suna-gami*, the *kami* of the land of one's birth. Some call him the *uji-gami*, the god of lineage. The god of beginnings, he watches over the local inhabitants.[8] The land is the basis of the world.

MI: THE VEGETABLE BODY

The *Kojiki*, or *Records of Ancient Matters*, tells that at the beginning of the world, even before Japan came into being, the *kami* sprang from a reed sprout.[9] It states: "The original matter grew hard, but neither energy nor form had yet appeared. There were no names, there were no actions. . . . And then, when the young country was floating, oillike, and it drifted like a jellyfish, the name of the god who was formed from all these things, who expanded like the bud of a reed, was called Umashi-Ashi-Kabi-Hikoji-no-Kami."

This *kami* incarnated the vitality of the reed. It is from him that all things issued.

In the spring, after the rain, when bamboo shoots peek up through the soil, one might think that they are born spontaneously, out of nothing. But they have roots, and only the part buried in the earth is good to eat, tender and sweet.

Everyone knows, too, that when there is an earthquake, the place to take refuge is in a bamboo grove. The roots of bamboo are so dense, so tight, that they hold the soil. No one has ever seen a fissure open in a bamboo grove.

When a child is born, the umbilical cord attaches him to his mother. That is his root, the place of his origins. When the cord is cut, the child sets out on the path of animalness. But he is still not really an animal; he will always be partly plant. What his parents teach him, everything they give him is like the rain that makes the bamboo trees shoot up, like the water that irrigates the rice plants. The child grows naturally, with the harmony of a beautiful plant. It becomes progressively more animal . . . or more human. Plants, animals, and humans do not belong to such different realms. All of us coexist in the same world.

Sometimes people say that man governs the world, but this is only a manner of speaking and a way of bragging. Have we ever made the rice grow in winter? The body of man, his substance, is it not formed of the vegetables and flesh that nature offers? And the word "body" itself, did it not originally mean "flesh"? This is the flesh of men as well as that of animals or the pulp of a fruit and the seeds of all the grains. "Body" and "fruit" are the same word, even though we write them with different characters.[10]

In olden times, in the homes of the nobility, as soon as a child came out of the belly of his mother, a midwife would cut the umbilical cord with a metal instrument. But in Fukushima, people said that metal caused the cord to putrify, and that the body of the child would follow suit, so they used a wooden knife. The cord, preserved as precious, would be put aside to dry. If the child later fell ill, the dried cord would be ground to powder and fed to the child, so that he might recover the vigor of his origins.[11]

In *kanpō-yaku*, or Chinese medicine—our traditional medicine—the navel is an essential point on the human body. The navel of a healthy body has a vertical crease. When a person is tired, the crease will be on a diagonal, or even horizontal. Therefore, one has only to look at someone's navel to ascertain whether he is well. This is why one must take special care of the navel. It must not be washed just any old way, or the stomach will inflate and the person will fall ill. It must be cleaned only once a year, using sesame oil, because the deposit that builds up in the navel is called *goma* (sesame).

The reason the navel is so important to the human body is that this point best recalls the quasi-vegetable origin of man. The character for "navel" is written as "ears of grain," next to "the body." And long ago the five grains came into being from the navel of Ōgetsu-Hime, the great goddess of food.[12]

The land of Fukushima, my motherland, fed me. It is more than just the land *where* I was born, it is the land *of which* I was born.

RITES FOR AN EASY CHILDBIRTH

When I came into the world, Asaka was still a real village with at most 120 inhabitants. People there said that Mother was the best woman in the world. However, late in Year 6 (1917), her smiling face was altered by a mask of fear. Perhaps she was afraid of a difficult birth. Also, at the end of Year 6, there had been a terrible epidemic of the deadly Spanish flu.

At the house of Endo everyone feared for Mother's life and for my health. The death of a pregnant woman is the worst death of all: when a child is taken from a dead mother, the soul of the mother will sneak back to the village every evening to steal sweets with which to feed the crying baby. Therefore, after the child has been taken from her body, days and months of prayers are needed to appease the dead woman, to keep her from prowling about among the living. They say there are women who died in childbirth in the *Chi no Ike*, the Pond of Blood, in Hell.

Mother and the other married women of the village took part in the sorority of Koyasu, the sorority of easy childbirth. They venerated Nyoirin Kannon, the compassionate Kannon of the jewel. On the eighteenth day of each month, the *ennichi* (the "day of connection" of Kannon, when she listens more willingly to humans' requests), wives would gather at the monastery. The women settled themselves before the side chapel where the statue of Kannon was located: seated on a lotus, she held a flower bud in one hand, a jewel in another, and a wheel of the law in still another.[13] Time had so polished the black wood that it gleamed like bronze in the candle-light. The women offered her flowers and water. They stayed up late, munching squares of baked tofu called *dengaku*, rice paddy dances.

Alongside the road to the monastery were stelae representing the nine-teenth and twenty-third nights, which celebrate the last stages of the lunar cycle. The sorority of Koyasu had erected them, engraved with the figure of the monk Jizō, a long time ago.[14] Whenever Mother passed these stone markers, she would stop, bow her head, and put her hands together, asking the gods for an easy birth. She had a gloomy presentiment.

Stele of the twenty-third night.

The beginning of her pregnancy had been difficult. She had vomited for three moons. And those three moons were barely gone when I began to hammer at the door of her belly. At the same time, a black down began to grow beneath Mother's navel. By the beginning of the fifth moon, I had so inflated her belly that she was forced, earlier than was the custom, to wrap her waist with a large white maternity band.

Soon thereafter, on a day of the dog (according to Chinese astrology), because as everyone knows dogs give birth easily, Mother invited her *na-kōdo*, the go-between who had arranged her marriage, and all the close relatives to the *obi-iwai*, the celebration of the maternity band.[15] Mother girded herself with the immaculate obi that her mother had sent her and served everyone rice with azuki beans before saying her good-byes. From that time on, she would no longer go near the shrine of the *ubu-suna-gami*: it would be his assistant, *ubu-gami*, the god of birth, who would watch over her and me.

At six months, I was so big and I wiggled so much that the *tori-age-bābā*, the village midwife, came to tell my mother, "These pains indicate that it will be a boy." And all the old women of the village repeated it after her.

Encouraged by the rumors, Father showed such tenderness that he shared Mother's pregnancy sickness. He, too, became nauseated. Mother remembered gratefully how, during her first labor, he had massaged her belly for a long time. By force of his pushing, he had made my eldest brother come out. She thought, "Since it is a boy, this time, too, he will help me." And that soothed her anxiety.

CHILDBIRTH

When she felt that the time was near, Mother asked one of the servant women to prepare the *nando*. This small storage room, in the far northwest corner of the house, was converted for the time to a birthing room.[16]

In ancient times, women gave birth in the *ubu-ya*, or birthing hut, constructed within the hamlet.[17] Thus the villagers kept their distance from the defilement of the blood, which could make them ill or even kill them. Birth is where life and death come face to face, but this meeting took place apart from this world, in which the two must never mix. That is why, as best they could, people made these special places, sealed off from normal life.

In childbirth (as in all else), the practices of the nobility were extremely refined. Ladies of the court prepared a room measuring twelve tatami mats,[18] thirteen in years that included a supplementary month, because the acts of men must always conform to the rhythms of nature.[19] In Asaka, the practices were not that complicated. The village did not even have a birthing hut, and, except for their firstborn,[20] women gave birth in the houses of their husbands—especially if the houses were large enough.

In some houses, an enclosure called a *su*, or nest, was set up in the *niwa*, a dark room with a packed-earth floor located at the front entrance. It was partitioned off with planks and rush mats, and straw was spread inside. But Mother thought this practice improper; people came and went through the entryway, next to the nest, whereas women giving birth had to isolate themselves from society. So she asked that the *nando*, which was rarely used, be cleaned. It was a large room, measuring four and a half *tatami*, which served as a catchall storage space. The servant women hung white cloth on the walls. On the floor in the middle of the room they placed three round stones to represent a hearth. Next to the stones they left *soba*, buckwheat noodles, and a *hōchō*, a large kitchen knife, so that the gods might take note that Mother was consuming no food cooked on the family fire. The rules of the day required that after giving birth a woman use a separate fire, or *bekka*. In practice, however, it was deemed acceptable that three times a day she be brought dishes prepared on an old kitchen hearth that was ordinarily no longer used.

Having given the orders to prepare the *nando*, Mother left for the hill shrine of the god Hachiman-sama, in order to fetch a small pillow of white silk filled with straw as well as a length of hemp twine. In our area, Hachiman-sama was the god of the mountain, venerated in mountain passes, where the wind blows strong enough to tear the sleeves from a person's garment.[21] On the day of the birth, to obtain the aid of the gods, Mother would place the pillow next to her head and tie her hair back with the length of hemp. The part of her soul that was in pain would then exit her body to rest on the silk pillow, but her life would not leave her.[22]

When she arrived at the shrine of Hachiman-sama, Mother saw that the *torii* gates had just been repainted vermilion and stood out brilliantly against the dark green of the conifers. The sky was an almost transparent blue; the silk covering of the pillows glistened in the sun. After giving birth, every woman would return the pillow she had borrowed and offer a new one, also made of silk.

Mother, always unpretentious, chose a very small pillow; its fabric was still very smooth. She pulled her length of hemp from a skein suspended from the roof. Then, as she was bowing to thank the god, I began to bang against the door of her belly with the strength of the dead when they batter down the gates of the underworld and return to this world near the end of summer.[23] Close by, a horse began to neigh. Knowing that horses carry souls from the other world to ours, Mother went back down to the village. The horse neighed again, and Mother felt the first contraction.

Back at the house, I left her barely enough time to go and greet *Benjo-gami*, the god of latrines. It is he who makes beautiful children. In any case, that's what they say (because women urinate more frequently when they are pregnant). Like all the gods, *Benjo-gami* likes cleanliness. Mother had carefully cleaned the lavatories every day since the onset of her pregnancy, in order to please this god. Sometimes she could barely stand the acidic, stale odor of urine that assaulted her nose when she lifted the wooden cover from the pit where, summer and winter alike, foul vermin swarmed. She would toss in wormwood to drive them out, then scrub the floors, splashing full buckets of water. She didn't like this task, but she wanted a good-looking child.

At last, Mother had satisfied the requirements of all the gods; as soon as she lay down, I was born.

At that moment, the factory whistles of Kōriyama screamed. I bellowed in the hands of the old *tori-age-bābā*, who watched me cry. Noting that it was exactly noon, she exclaimed, "Without a doubt this child will become someone who everyone will say is busier than anybody! Those born in the morning are active in the morning; those born in the evening, the evening. But she who is born at noon, she will bustle about all the time."

Mother smiled politely at this presage of my fortune. Still, she was disappointed. In spite of all the pains she had taken, I was only a girl. "The fourth . . . ," she sighed.

At that moment she wished not to have any more children for a time. She decided to be sterile for a long time. She knew that Father would not like it, but, with the complicity of the *tori-age-bābā*, she took two reeds the length of chopsticks and, as soon as the old woman had cut the umbilical cord, she colored the ends of the reeds with her blood. Later, in secret, she would climb up on the roof of the kitchen and throw them as far and as high as she could. Might the menstrual blood keep its distance from her!

This practice was hardly effective: Mother had three more children—a son, Yoshihisa, and two more daughters, Kikumi and Yaeko.

ARA-MITAMA: A WILD SOUL

From the start, I was aware of the chilliness of my reception. That's why I cried so much, for months. Especially at night, when I feared that my soul, still barely enclosed within my body, would leave it. The *mi*, the vegetable body, is only the physical body; it does not constitute the entire person. It is but a receptacle, like a box, which is animated by a vital and spiritual energy, called *tama*.

When I was a little older, I asked Mother how babies are born, and she told me this story:

"In olden days, there was a carpenter in Shinshū who had no work. He traveled to Ōshū to make money. When the job was finished he set out for home, but as night was falling, he had no choice but to take cover in the shrine of a village through which he was passing. Toward the middle of the night, he heard the sound of a horse's hooves!

An unknown *kami*, who had come to seek out the god of the village, said, 'Hachiman-sama! This night, they have made a house of childbirth in such-and-such a farm of your village. A child is to be born. That is why I have come. You must accompany me there!'

"Hachiman-sama responded, 'Sorry to have put you to so much trouble.

I really did mean to go. But I have an unexpected guest tonight, so I must stay here and watch over him. *Yoroshiku!* I beg of you! Do me the favor of handling it yourself!'

"The carpenter heard this dialogue as if in a dream. At first he was terrified. Then, realizing that Hachiman-sama was protecting him, he was relieved, and soon he went back to sleep. A little later, he again heard hoofbeats.

And then the voice of the *kami*: 'Hachiman-sama, the birth went well!'

"'Ah! Thank you! But tell me, was it a boy or a girl?'

"'It was a girl.'

"'And what destiny did you decide for her?'[24]

"'Her destiny is to marry the man who has taken refuge with you this evening.'

"Hearing that, the carpenter was extremely annoyed. He was already twenty-three years old. And what? Was he to marry that baby? That would mean he could not take a wife before another twenty years had passed! He decided to kill the little girl who had just been born.

"He waited for the sun to rise. He went to the farm in the village below, where the birth had taken place. But he could not resolve to kill the baby. *Shikata ga nai!* He had no choice. He found work for a month in a nearby village. Then he returned to the baby's house. She had grown; she was lying in an *izumi*, a basket, and there was no one around. He pierced the baby's throat with a pair of scissors and ran away without a backward glance.

"Alas, twenty years passed before the carpenter found a wife. One day, as he was looking attentively at his wife's throat, he saw a scar! He asked her what had happened. The young woman told him that when she was a month old a strange man had stabbed her in the throat with a pair of scissors and then run away. *Bikkuri!* Secretly, the carpenter was filled with astonishment.

"The god who comes on horseback," said Mother at the end, "is *ubu-gami*, the god of birth. He is the *kami* who decides our birth, our marriage, and our death, and we can do nothing about it. At the moment of birth he brings the *tama*, the soul of the newborn, and he fixes its destiny. Without *tama*, there is no life. All living beings possess *tama*: gods more than men, and men more than animals and plants. Always keep your body clean so that your soul feels well in it!"

I don't know exactly who *ubu-gami* is. Some say he is *ubu-suna-gami*, the god of the place of one's birth, but that he changes his name for childbirth because of his horror of blood. Others claim he is the god of latrines, he who makes children healthy. Some believe he is *hōki-gami*, the god of the broom, a banisher of impurity who helps the mother push the child from her body that it may enter the world, and those people also think he is the god of the mountain. In Asaka, people said that he was an associate of Hachiman-sama, the guardian of the silk pillows. The soul of each newborn on its way from the otherworld would stop for a moment at his hilltop shrine before going down to the farms below. The *kami* would then point out the road to the village and direct the soul to the house where it was to incarnate.[25]

While the body, half-vegetable, half-animal, puts down roots in the soil of its birth, the *tama* itself is unstable and light, like a gas or a bird. This is true particularly with children and then, much later, at the approach of death. It is our spirit and our strength. Without *tama*, it is impossible to live. Without it, no birth is possible. That is why the birth of twins is dangerous. As soon as the father learns there are twins, he must go up on the roof of the house and cry out to the heavens, to the god of birth, that he must bring more *tama*. If there is not enough, either one twin will monopolize all the *tama* and the other will die or they will share the *tama* and think and act in exactly the same manner for their entire lives.

If Mother said that I had to keep my body clean to have a good *tama*, it was because the soul and the vegetable body are interdependent. When the body is soiled or impure, the *tama* is weakened, and it becomes wild. In the same way, when the *tama* is moved by a passion, especially jealousy, it may sometimes abandon the body, which remains on the earth like an empty envelope. That is why the god who brings the soul at birth is the same god who decides the great matters of life: marriage and death.

In spite of the lukewarm welcome afforded me by the world, I wanted to live, but my soul tended toward the wild and was unchained within my body, which it sometimes tried to quit. I cried a lot, in order to bring my spirit back to my body. Noises drive away the worst of evil forces. Mother, who slept by my side, would caress my chin and stroke my jawbone for a long time until, satisfied, I would doze off.

In fact, no one took much trouble with the little girl born the day after the new year. No one even tried to find a name for her. For Father, girls held no interest. He had fought in the Russo-Japanese War and had proven himself so valiant that he drew a pension. He wanted sons to make soldiers. "Japan," he often said, "has no need for girls."

He was by no means a bellicose man, but he thought that colonial expansion was inevitable: the country was too small and the people too numerous. There was not enough land for everyone to be able to feed his children. And who would wish to see their descendants emigrate to the city? In the big, modern cities, promiscuity was rampant; no moral life was possible. Therefore, it was necessary to seek out lands abroad, in the vast spaces of China, which were so large the Chinese by themselves were incapable of making use of them.[26]

Father had nothing against the Chinese. He even had a profound respect for the ancientness of their culture. He said, "It was they who taught us to write." Then he added, "But why must we stay crammed together on this string of tiny islands when there is an immense amount of land available, right over there within reach?"

This proximity, he explained again, was a sign from the gods. And girls were useless in the pioneering of new lands. Worse—when they married, they had to have dowries, which would cut some rice paddy or mountain off from the ancestral patrimony. Only this would assure them a good marriage, into a house whose status suited their own.

My birth was all the more unnoticed because it happened during the first three days of the year, which are celebrated with magnificent public festivities. No one wanted to interrupt the festivities for the birth of a girl. In Asaka, the second day of the first month was *hatsu-ni*; this was the day on which everyone ceremonially inaugurated the year's work, because the word for "load" and the word for the number "two" are both pronounced *ni*. Merchants made their first deliveries of the year, parading through the streets on carts decorated with multicolored streamers. In Kōriyama, stores held the first big annual sales.

So for my birth Father did not observe any of the normally imposed interdictions. He had hardly buried my placenta beneath the veranda of the house before he ran off to resume his duties as a town official, which had been suspended for the time of the festivities. He didn't even take the trouble to place a white stone over my placenta—to keep the worms from crawling on that tomb of my birth and affecting the spirit that, from then on, would watch over my growth. So the worms crawled there, and, as is well-known, this always makes newborns cry. This was no doubt another cause of my ill humor.

ENTRY INTO THE WORLD

Only Mother observed the required taboos. For twenty-one days, she ate food cooked on a fire separate from that used by the rest of the household. This was in order not to contaminate the other members of the family with the defilement of the blood.

During those three weeks, the old *tori-age-bābā* took care of me. The neighbors gave her gifts of food. I got to know her well years later. She was small, extremely wrinkled, and, near the end of her life, completely bent over, one hand dragging on the ground as if it were a cane. People said, "Her back is bent. She's been worked too hard."

Immediately after my birth, she dipped me in the *ubu-yu*, the hot, purifying water of my first bath. Scalding water in a wooden tub. Then she swaddled me in a simple piece of cloth without sleeves, like a shroud. She laid me on my back, my head resting on a sash folded to look like a pillow, a long, fine sash, that my days might be long.

"When you have a son," she said to me when I was six or seven, "if you wish him to have younger brothers, slip a pair of long underwear under his head."

Then she prepared the birth rice, the red rice which she offered first to the *kami* of birth, then to Mother and to me, so that both of us might gather strength. Of course I didn't really eat any. She had had special rice cooked for Mother; it had been sent from the home of her birth, because the vital force of any person can be reinvigorated only through a return to his or her place of blood origin.[27]

The old midwife also found my milk mother, a woman in the village who had just given birth to a son. The mother of a boy had to give me first suck to ensure that my feminine and masculine natures would be well-balanced.[28]

Mother's parents, who lived in a hamlet a little farther up the Abukuma, sent me a lightweight white garment with sleeves called the *enagi*, the after-birth vestiture. This was my first real piece of clothing. I was dressed in it on the third day after my birth, once it was assured that my soul would stay in this world. This was when the god of birth who had brought the soul went back to his hill. He went away, and I stayed here, thrown into the world of men.

The morning of this third day, the family gathered for a breakfast in my honor: rice, miso soup, seaweed, eggs, and fish. After having changed me, Father's mother took a bit of lampblack from the bottom of the pot that always hung above the square hearth, at the end of a hook sculpted in the shape of a fish's head. She rubbed some of it on my forehead so that from then on neither demons nor spells could harm me. That same day, at sunset, I crossed a bridge in her arms: she threw some grains of rice in the water and walked straight ahead, without turning back. Thanks to that, I would never die by drowning.[29] The sixth day, the *tori-age-bābā* shaved my head, leaving only a tuft of colorless down at the neck, by which the gods could catch me should I fall into the fire or the latrine.

My first week passed in that way. All the neighborhood had heard my cries, but I didn't yet have a name. It was time to decide. Again, it was the midwife who suggested that they call me Nami, a simple inversion of the syllables of Mother's first name, Mina. And it was under this name that Father had me inscribed in the *koseki*, the Endo family register. He wrote my name in *katakana*—that is, phonetically, without even thinking to

choose two Chinese characters that would give it a meaning. Written phonetically "Nami" was only a meaningless sound.

In Japan, they say that the meaning of a first name determines the nature
of a child and rules his or her destiny. Parents often consult a monk or a
wise man to have him choose an auspicious name for the newborn. But in
my family, only the boys had the right to real names. The characters used
to write the name of my eldest brother, Yoshiharu, meant joy and happiness; later, Father would name my younger brother Yoshihisa, joy and eternity. They did not go to such lengths for me or any of my sisters. Our
first names were all written in *katakana*.[30] They were nothing more than
something to put in the register. I would have to wait until I was married
to get a real name. My mother-in-law, the first to do so, chose characters
with which to write Nami: for *Na* she took the first character in Nara, the
old capital of Japan, and for *mi*, beauty.

In short, I was one week old when they named me Nami. All the
women of the village gathered at our house for a feast to celebrate my
birth. I appeared before them muffled in a padded kimono and quilted
blanket decorated with motifs of helmets and warriors. This was the style
of the age—for boys. My family had so hoped I'd be a boy that they hadn't
prepared anything suitable for a girl, such as pink peach blossoms. The
ladies enjoyed themselves over this incongruity, and I roared with shame.

Three weeks after my birth, Mother got out of bed. She left the *nando*
and rejoined family life by accepting a bowl of miso soup cooked on the
common fire. Everyone rejoiced at how good she looked and pinched my
enormous, pendant cheeks, which they tell me displeased me no end.

That afternoon, Mother brought me to her parents' house for the official
presentation. My grandparents exclaimed delightedly over my vigor and
congratulated Mother on her good coloring. They gave her eggs, saying
that she would have to eat foods that give strength so she could feed me
without overtiring herself. I had, it seems, a healthy appetite.

On the way home, I made my first pilgrimage to the shrine of the *kami*,
who protected our village. Father's mother, who had come to meet us,
carried me. Having cried so much that morning, now I wanted to sleep in
peace. When she presented me to the god, I had to be pinched to make
me cry again, so that the god would notice my presence. On the way back,
my grandmother made me wave at the passersby as she distributed delicacies to all the children I met.[31]

In this way, the circle of my social relations was enlarged little by little.
When I was one hundred days old, I took my first meal in public. I was
offered a pair of chopsticks and a round, smooth, white stone which had
been picked up within the precincts of the *ubu-suna*, the land of my birth,

all set on top of a platter heaped with rice and an entire fish. Mother raised the chopsticks to my lips and forced me to swallow a grain of rice so that I would always have a good appetite. Then she grated the stone against my gums to harden my teeth (*ha-gatame*), and to ensure that the solidity of my body would assure health and a long life. This stone was the god of my birth. I must have cried not only because the stone hurt me but also, I think, out of fear of this world which I must now enter. I had completed the first lap of my life.

The next day, Mother stopped nursing me.[32] I rebelled and continued to cry, as much as I could, to the end of the following winter. Through this racket, I attempted to impress my presence on the house of Endo.

2

The House of Endo

Hai no fukuro kara shiroi kona wa derarenu.
White flour won't come out of a sack of ashes.

IE: THE HOUSE

Ie to mōshimasu no wa, kazoku no koto de gozaimasu . . . When I say "house,"
what I mean is "family." We Japanese prefer the word "house."

For us, a house is not merely a structure that people live in. It is also a
way of living that human beings adhere to generation after generation. A
house is men and women, young and old, who sleep and eat under the
same roof. They dedicate their work to making the patrimony handed
down to them by their ancestors bear fruit. And they venerate those ancestors.

That is why in Japanese a single word, *ie*, designates both house, meaning the structure itself, and family. *Ie* signifies our attachment by blood to
our line.[1] The *ie* lives in each one of us; it is the chain of our existence
that gives it strength, while it crystallizes the sense of our passage through
this world.

 Ie, the house.

A house without domestic altars is a sad thing. The *butsudan*, the Buddhist altar, must be dedicated to the dead, and the other, Shinto altar, the
kami-dana (shelf of the gods), to the divinities that protect the house.[2] In
Tokyo today, half the homes have no altars: to me, these are no more than
poor empty shells.

We live on this Japanese earth by the grace of our ancestors. They have
given us this gift that we might perpetuate these isles for eternity.[3] For that
reason, the worst of all faults among the faults of men is *oya-ko shinjū*, or
parent-child suicide-homocide. They tell me this is a rare thing in the West,

21

but in Japan, sometimes a man forced into ruin or a woman in despair will commit suicide instead of facing up to it. And they drag their children down with them.

I understand their unhappiness, because a very long time ago I once considered committing *oya-ko shinjū* myself. I had invented a product that turned out to be harmful. I believed the authorities were going to prosecute me. So I thought about hanging myself and killing my children to wash away that shame! Then I understood that I could not so simply put an end to a line that had come through so many centuries. This affair did not concern me alone—it also involved the long line of the ancestors of our house. I did not have the right to destroy their lives' work or to exterminate, even before they were born, the children of my children. Luckily, with the aid of our household gods, I found the strength in my heart to fight.

To take lightly the ties that unite us to our ancestors is to deny Japan itself. Cut off from their lineage, people do whatever they want and become selfish. These days people talk about *kojin shugi*, individualism, but that's the same thing.[4] The young forget that they are Japanese. Soon they will confuse our history with that of the countries of the West. And so, Japan will disappear. But the gods will not allow that.

When I think in this way, the old main house of my childhood comes floating up to the troubled surface of my memory: shadows appear, faces blend in endless succession: Mother's pale silhouette, in the recess of a door. That of my eldest brother, smoking foreign cigarettes. My sisters, always noisy. Father's silence. The smiling efficiency of the servants. I see them as clearly as in a dream, because living quarters are inseparable from the faces that have inhabited them. These are the companions of the past, of the lives of generations who have been succeeded there. And in the case of our house, they made a very old history.

THE HISTORY OF THE HOUSE OF ENDO

It was at the end of the sixteenth century that the Endo clan settled in the plain of Asaka and founded the hamlet of Kitai.[5] They came from more developed, distant regions, probably in the southwest.

The memory of our ancestors goes back to that distant age of warriors with long swords. In the twelfth century, two sons of Minamoto no Yoshitomo, a descendant of the emperor Seiwa, quarreled. Earlier these sons— Yoshitsune and his older brother, Yoritomo—had fought together against the Taira, their common enemy, but it came to pass that the elder, filled with jealousy over his younger brother's military prowess, decided to kill him. And so Yoshitsune fled in great haste toward the north and came as far as Hiraizumi, a city of immense temples and flowery gardens, in the middle of the province of Mutsu.[6] A man called Kudo Suketsune followed him there and killed him through treachery. He carried his head back to Yoritomo, from whom he then received favors. Kudo took as recompense lands as vast as the sky and as rich as the sea—the entire province of Tōhoku.

Kudo's youngest son, who had received the family name Itō through adoption, settled in the Asaka plain.[7] Our Endo ancestors were among his vassals. Such is the origin of our house.

Wars followed one upon the other. In the fifteenth century, the *Sengoku Jidai*, or Warring States Period, began.[8] One after the other, noble families claimed rights to our land. The Date attacked the Itō. The descendants of Kudo Suketsune wanted to defend their lands, but Date Masamune conquered and killed them.[9] Of the Endos who served them, only one child survived, a girl named Endo Mine. She escaped and took refuge in Kitai, where she began to clear land and founded a hamlet. On the seventh day of the first month of Year 18 of the Tenshō Era (1590), at a poetic gathering held for the festival of spring herbs in his castle in Kurokawa, Date Masamune composed a poem:

> *Nanakusa wo*
> *Ippa ni nosete*
> *Tsumu nezeri!*

> The seven herbs
> Placed on a leaf
> The parsley, plucked!

What he meant by those lines was that he had united in one hand the seven domains of our region: Shirakawa, Ishikawa, Iwase, Tamura, Asaka, Adachi, and Shinobu.

That same day, they say, Endo Mine finished building her house.

I don't know much about Endo Mine. According to my elder sister, she was a very pious woman who performed pilgrimages to the three sacred mountains in Kumano and to the shrine of Amaterasu, the ancestral goddess of the emperors of Japan, who is venerated at Ise.[10] It was there, in a place called Shirako, that she met the priest in charge of the place, named Hakuō. She took him to Kitai so that he might found, on a height that marked the northern limits of the hamlet, the *Gawaba Hakuō-Jinja*, the Shrine of Our Mother and of the White Old Man. People today are amazed that in such ancient times a girl could found a village in this way, but the Endo women have always shown themselves stronger than the men.

I am sure our ancestors were not rich then, nor were their holdings extensive. People were reluctant to clear more land than they could use given the available manpower. We grew barley and millet, I think, as well as rice to pay taxes with. Luckily our soil was so fertile that Asaka rice is famous today throughout all Japan.

However, Tōhoku was so isolated that even after the Tokugawa came to power and made their capital in the east in Edo (Tokyo), the local disturbances continued. Finally, toward the middle of the seventeenth century, this is what happened: the neighboring province of Mutsu was granted to a Lord Matsudaira; Hoshina Masayuki. The son of the shogun Tokugawa Hidetada and a concubine, he was an adoptive son of the Hoshina family. Mutsu was renamed the fief of Aizu, after the large town of Aizu Wakamatsu. Aizu was an immense fief of 230,000 *koku*,[11] where commerce flourished under the aegis of the Matsudaira clan.

The Shrine of Gawaba Hakuō (drawing by Shige).

Masayuki himself was a man open to change. He attracted manufacturers to Aizu Wakamatsu, regulated the employment of farmworkers, and promoted the lacquer industry. He also outlawed widows' suicides and the cremation of fetuses. He often visited Yamazaki Ansai, the great Confucian thinker.[12] When I think that my husband is a descendant of Ansai, I tell myself that there must certainly exist an *en*, a very ancient "tie" between us.

The Matsudaira were truly great lords. They ruled over the fief of Aizu until the Meiji Restoration,[13] and it was they who made possible the prosperity of the Endo family. This was because the Endos took part in the development of this poor region: our house became rich, and we lived on a grand scale. We owned immense properties, and we needed many sharecroppers to cultivate them.

A huge crowd of servants looked to us for their livelihoods. First of all, there were the *genin*, or underlings. These unfortunates sold to us the children they couldn't feed, and these became *fudai*, or hereditary vassals, who would be employed generation after generation. And then there were the *nago*, the name children.[14] These were men whose families had worked for us for at least three generations, with the result that they were sometimes known as *sande kosaku*, or third-generation tenant farmers. We granted them the right to adopt our name and gave them land; many of them counted on us for the feeding of their children.

These servants were treated as members of the family, like younger brothers. We would lend them tools or animals (and, back then, a cow or a horse was not cheap). When a servant was sick, we paid the doctor bills. If he died, we took care of his family. In exchange, he worked for us, and he also would come to greet our Endo ancestors at both the New Year and the festival of the dead, *O-Bon*, at the end of summer. This was because our house was among the *honke*, or senior houses, the head of which is the male heir.[15]

Our house was built at the far east end of the hamlet, with only two others nearby, on a verdant mound that dominated the valley. This prominent location showed that we counted among the most ancient of our *maki*, or herd. During postwar reconstruction, the main pillar of the house was exposed; on it was engraved the original date of the building, which proved to be 208 years old. It was built well before the exploitation of the common lands, even before the rice paddy irrigation system was put in. Our ancestors "divided the wild grasses"; they turned up the brown earth for the first time. It was precisely for that reason that more recently built houses owed us complete obeisance.[16]

In the eighteenth century, with the development of a monetary system, the old industries of Aizu, lacquer and sake making, made great progress. Local lacquer, both red and black, decorated with plant motifs in a pale green, was especially renowned for its durability, simplicity, and elegance. It was thanks to rural families like ours, who invested their money in business, that a time of plenty was ushered in. And we ourselves were able to feed more and more laborers.[17]

It was only natural, then, that on the day that the emperor was restored to power, the ninth day of the twelfth moon of Year 3 of the reign of Emperor Keiō (1867), our ancestor, whose name was Heizaburō, should at first have been on the side of the Matsudaira lords who supported the shogun. They had protected us, if only for a while. But the emperor had always been our legitimate sovereign. Heizaburō must have weighed the problem again and again in his mind, the way a drop of water hesitates on the edge of a shiny leaf, until the day his son Heisuke was recruited by the government's army. Because Heisuke was the eldest son and heir, a younger son, Sukesaburō, took his place, poor boy! This was the beginning of that war they call the Boshin Revolt, after the Chinese calendar year in which it took place, the year of the eldest of the earth and of the dragon. It was a horrible massacre. Before being defeated by the regular army, the soldiers known as the White Tiger Brigade had repelled the conscripts. Pursued by the enemy, Sukesaburō passed by his own house. He went in. He told them that he was afraid and that he didn't want to go back to the war. But everyone insisted that it was his duty, and Risa, the wife of my father's father, offered him a drink of water. So he left. Three days later, he was dead. Then, because they were defeated, the survivors of the No. 2 White Tiger Brigade, twenty young soldiers of sixteen and seventeen, retreated to the Iimoriyama hill. There, while watching the castle Tsurugajō burn, they all took their own lives.[18]

Today, when any of us goes to that ancient castle-city or the ruins in the shade of giant trees, a testament to the pride of the Matsudaira, we never fail to make a pilgrimage to Iimoriyama and leave a few sticks of incense in the cemetery of the White Tiger Brigade to appease their spirits.[19]

Alas, as the proverb says, "*Nakittsura ni hachi*, A face in tears draws a wasp"—that is, bad luck never comes singly. In spite of our fortune, death was over our house. The Matsudaira had barely been vanquished when the eldest son of the family died. There was only one child left, a daughter, and the line was in danger of being extinguished. So the family looked for a son-in-law to adopt from the Kuniyoshi branch of the Endos, with whom they had maintained privileged relations.[20]

In fact, it was through my grandmother that the Endos became rich. She was the only daughter of a man who had been a candidate—albeit unsuccessfully—for the office of *tagaku nōzeisha giin*, that is, the representative for the largest taxes in the district.[21] The family was so rich that they never went anywhere except by rickshaw, even to school. Their holdings were immense. They did very well in sericulture. It was for that reason that my great-grandfather adopted my grandfather and made him his son-in-law. But, alas, he was a good-for-nothing who severely depleted the family fortunes.[22] Grandmother told how he would invite geisha to the house. He would set up a fan, releasing packets of banknotes into the wind it made, in order to amuse himself watching the naked girls fight one another to catch the flying money. I never saw this spectacle myself (because I knew him much later), but it makes me laugh just thinking about it.

A much more serious problem was that he plunged into speculation late in life. I don't remember much about it. He became friends with a shady businessman who deceived him in the hope of taking hold of the Endo fortune and got him to sign some drafts, we don't know how. On top of this came a crisis: silk wasn't selling anymore. This nearly ruined the family.[23] Luckily, Mother then made good use of the pension Father got from the war. She said, "This money was acquired by doing extraordinary work. It must not be wasted." And she bought new land with it. That meant we could sell some fields. Close relatives helped us pay the necessary fees and penalties. So the affair was taken care of without causing anyone difficulties.[24] It was then—I was sixteen—that they gave me permission to leave.

This was a bit of luck for me, like an east wind for a sailboat. But sometimes I miss the village, where the virtues of the past were in force, those of an era in which the will of the gods was respected over that of men, in which everyone was content with his lot and people gladly helped one another out.

THE VILLAGE AND THE FORCES OF NATURE

It is the gods who choose the locations of villages, because people cannot build dwellings just anywhere. There must be water, a valley or a gentle slope, wood for cooking and for keeping warm in the winter. Miserable villages are always those in which people have settled without consideration for the will of the *kami* that is written in nature.

We must bend ourselves to this plan of the gods, in the placement of streets as in all else. In Japan, houses are built close to one another. In windy regions, this can be extremely dangerous. In Asaka, in winter, when one rainless day followed another and the wind came hawking fire door to door, all the dwellings were destroyed. Finally, in the nineteenth century, people began to rebuild with more space between the houses. And they planted hedgerows from north to south to stop the wind that blew from the west.

Formerly, when a house was rebuilt or the roof redone, the wife of the head of the family would attach a large wooden phallus with testicles of straw to the roof beam. With this offering to the storm god, she hoped to keep fire at bay. *Oni-gawara* were placed at the two ends of the roof, in order to keep away evil. On these round demon tiles, artisans would mold grimacing faces or the character for water, *mizu*, which deflected thunder and put out fires.[25]

The street of Kitai (drawing by Shige).

When the dry season went on for a long time, every evening little boys would dress in short cotton jackets and parade up the street behind a lantern bearer. They would cry, "*Hi no yōjin!* Be careful of fire!" They spoke in time to the beat of wooden clackers. People would then check that their stove fires were well out before going to bed. The sound of the children's voices would fade as they rounded the corner. It reminded me of a poem by Bashō:

> *Furu-ike ya*
> *Kawazu tobikomu*
> *Mizu no oto.*

> The old pond
> A frog jumps in
> A splash.

Silence springs from noise.

But a bronze alarm bell had to be installed west of the village, and there was nary a winter night it did not ring, signaling a fire.

A PHOTOGRAPH OF THE ENDO HOUSE

Like all Japanese houses, ours was built low to the ground, along horizontal lines whose regularity, though somewhat monotonous, calmed the spirit and promoted harmony. These days, of course, we Japanese build skyscrapers—in spite of earthquakes, which are sure signs of the gods' distaste for tall structures. But our souls do not inhabit these modern buildings. Our true dwellings are still our horizontal houses. Sitting on the floor in our houses made of wood, earth, and paper, in which the original nature of the materials is readily visible, we will never forget that we are part of the world.

The old Endo house faced south, like most Japanese houses, and in winter the sun penetrated deep within. In the summer, on the other hand, the roof that extended low over the facade afforded a cool shade. A *furin*, a wind bell, hung from the roof; this made a charming, tinkling sound in the breeze, brightening the heart and banishing demons.

The essential thing in a Japanese house is the roof. From a distance, that is all that is visible. A farmhouse roof is like the sign outside a shop: its beauty and lavishness demonstrate the greatness of the family for all to see. We had what is called a *yose-mune*, a pyramidal roof, whose thatch-covered sides sloped steeply, so that water could run off easily. At the ridge of the roof, a few rows of tiles kept the straw solidly in place. They were of thick, gray ceramic, and their luster bore witness to the status of the house of Endo. Tiles were once a great luxury.[26]

So I was proud not only of our gabled roof but of the gable on top of it as well, which was constructed the same way. Through the windows beneath this small raised gable, sunlight came into the highest part of the house, where we raised silkworms.

The house was long and rectangular, spanning east to west. The outside walls, which had a white coating, were of ordinary *shinkabe*—a latticework of split bamboo, covered with clay mixed with straw and sand. Slender wooden pillars were spaced at large intervals. The largest part of the south facade had shoji windows, with divided paper panes that let in light. Almost in the center was a heavy wooden sliding door. It was kept open all day, but in the evening, a smaller door, the height of a man, hinged in the Western fashion, was left open to allow sleepwalkers a way back in.

It was a true country dwelling, imposing but very simple. Out front, there were always a few large, white daikon radishes hanging from a pole attached to the eaves. How much they had dried showed how far into autumn we were. In the winter we ate them fermented, with rice. After the harvest, a few clusters of rice would also be drying in the garden on wooden racks. Once those were up, visitors could see that there was always plenty to eat at the house of Endo. We had white rice every day, and it was never mixed with barley, as was the custom in poor homes.

However, the house of Endo is no more. After the war, we lost half of it. Nothing is left of the old house but a bad photo taken just before it was torn down. It is blurred and yellowed. All things pass in this world, evanescent foam on the surface of the water.

THE LUXURY OF THE ENDOS

When I think of it today, I know that the Endo fortune did not reside in several rows of beautiful tiles, but in the barns and granaries, the scale of the house, and the number of people who lived there.

Next to the main house (or mother house, *omo-ya*), just on the other side of the windbreak hedgerows, were two freestanding wooden structures made of daub, also with thatched roofs. These were the retirement residence (*inkyo*), and the quiet residence (*kankyo*), where grandparents and great-grandparents lived in leisurely retirement. In this way four generations could live together in the house of Endo, and that was our true wealth.[27]

Beyond the residential buildings, the garden was enclosed by a row of fruit trees—peaches, plums, and cherries. Here and there, one could see rows of camellias, Japanese bush clover, and azaleas. West of the house was a large orchard, where after the war twenty rows of grapevines were planted. To the north were two huge granaries made of white-coated earth, which were filled each year with the bales of rice the sharecroppers paid in annual tribute. We also stored our reserves of fermented soy and the farming implements there.

These granaries were so big that the army requisitioned them during the war, as well as the barns, to use as airplane hangars. In order to escape the bombings in Tokyo, I took refuge in Asaka myself, where I saw those war planes that we called "the Milky Way"—as if they were something pretty. As for the soldiers, we thought they were dirty and disgusting, but we had soldiers in our family, too, so we couldn't say anything.

In the old days, there had been a third granary, between the main house and the retirement houses, across from the front entrance. There we'd kept farming tools and the *kahō*, the family treasures. But everything we put in there went bad, because this granary had been built in a bad direction. It had to be torn down. Although we didn't know it at the time, it turned out that a granary in which the family treasures are kept is a very important place, whose location must not be chosen haphazardly. The almanac says that a granary must be built in the direction either of the dog and boar, the northwest, or of the dragon and serpent, the southeast. If absolutely unavoidable, north is allowed, but northeast and southwest, and, by extension, east, west, and south, are strictly forbidden. It is in these directions that the two demon gates are located, the front, *omote kimon*, and the back, *ura kimon*, through which bad influences sweep down upon people.[28]

Our granary was built to the south, so naturally everything went bad. It had to be torn down, which was an enormous job. There were several days of noise, with trucks coming and going to haul away the debris. All this goes to show that when you infringe on rules, your luck falls apart and leaves you.

Being one of the richest families in the village, the Endos had four barns, lightweight buildings where each year's harvest was stored. Located on the other side of the road that cut through the garden, they were to the west, beyond the latrines, which, to me, seemed far enough away, as it was.

The latrines were in a wooden shack: the color of a chestnut polished by the weather, it was a humid place filled with awful smells, and I was afraid to go in there in the dark. I ventured in with my elder sister. We spoke loudly to scare away the shades that, along with the insects, prowl around these places. The noise roused some hens, the grotesque silhouettes of which we could see by the light through the windows. We had long been sure that these birds made fun of us; we threw fistfuls of dry dirt at them, which made them cackle all the more.

Our family also owned many fields and rice paddies. When the season came, we planted a sign in the mulberry field that read, "Mulberry Leaf Picking for the House of Endo." People came to work from all around, soon hauling their baskets full of green branches to the house. We set up big scales at the doors of the granaries for weighing the leaves, rice, or whatever. Then we paid the workers and stored the harvest inside. Especially in the fall, the carts lined up for several days at the entry to our courtyard.

Harvesttime was the most lively period of the year. The sky would be very clear, the trees tinged with blue, and the men laughed loud. When their loads had been put away, they came to the house and sat themselves down on the vast beaten-earth entryway we called the *niwa*, chatting and drinking sake. People were joyful, and that frightened me.

Mother heated alcohol in large, grayish earthenware flasks called *binbō-dokuri*, jugs of the poor, which were covered with long, cursive writing in brown or black. My older sisters helped her. Mother herself had a polite word for everyone and would bow, smiling. She never neglected to send her regards to the old people at home or to inquire about newborns. She remembered the first name of every child in the village and had a small present for each: a few pieces of petty change pierced with a hole, skewered on a little bundle of straws, which we said bristled like a *yashōma*, the tail of a skinny horse. The men went away satisfied.

One day, in the courtyard, one of them stroked my head and asked me, "Are you one of the Endo girls?"

"Yes."

"Your mother is a very kind person."

I turned toward the house. There was Mother on the doorstep, bending slightly, somewhat stiff in her kimono of gray fabric printed with a delicate black-and-white motif of cranes flying toward the heavens. She was thin and fragile, her face as white as a fish's belly. The roughness of the man brought out her grace.

I was seized with terror, and I ran all the way to the doorstep to cling to Mother. It seemed to me that something more than the weight of that man made me afraid. Removed from the noisy procession of baskets and carts, I set out to observe the workers with their wrinkled clothes. Seated on rough mats spread out directly on the ground, they spoke in loud voices and laughed, showing their loose teeth. An old woman with her shirt falling open, her chest uncovered, smoked a long pipe. Occasionally, she would turn it upside down to empty it, and a powder of ashes would fall on her sagging breasts. This disorder and filth upset me, and I passed the rest of the day clinging to the skirts of Mother's kimono, my heart fluttering like that of a scared rabbit.

Everyone agreed that harvesttime was great fun. We ate "festival" rice (rice with azuki beans), and the smell of hot sake filled the air. In the entryway, the sharecroppers prepared *mochi*: sticky, elastic white cakes of rice gluten eaten on special occasions.[29] After the rice was steamed, they would put it into a heavy wooden mortar. Three men with large pestles would array themselves around it and take turns beating the rice. A woman would turn the ball of paste between blows. Everyone laughed and sang:

> *Goitcha! Goitcha!* It's sticky! It's sticky!
> I pull, I pull myself away!
> Oh, the mortar! It's heavy!
> *Goitcha! Goitcha!* It's sticky! It's sticky!

The men's eyes were too bright. The women, as if upset, wiped the corners of their eyes with the ends of their sleeves: but these were tears of laughter. The peasants came and went between the entryway and the kitchen. I didn't understand why the men suddenly had the right to invade these precincts, which were usually the realm of Mother, my sisters, and the female servants. Men, they used to say, must not hang about in the kitchen. When they were there, they spoke in loud voices, and I ran away.

All this struck me as vulgar and brutal. These people were unworthy of the grandeur of the Endo family. How could Mother, so refined, take pleasure in their company? Secretly, I resented her gracious airs.

SHADE AND LIGHT

Around this time—I must have been six or seven—everything in our house became foreign to me. I didn't understand how I belonged in the house of Endo. My dreams were of distinction and beauty; I hated the land. I wanted the world to bend to my whims.

The house itself became frightening. It was a cold building, too large to heat, and the sliding doors didn't meet very well. It appeared to me like a dark labyrinth, a universe of imprecise contours laid out in zigzags, a world of arbitrary rules and regulations that wouldn't make sense to me until much later. The primary sensation of my childhood was, I think, bewilderment.

A short veranda ran partly along the south facade of the house, and a little light came in through the shoji. But the dark wooden partitions and the walls the color of chestnut sable mixed with quartz sparkles gave me a sensation of enclosure or vertigo. The rooms closest to the entryway had no ceiling, and your eyes could get lost, like the smoke from the stove, traveling past the joisted beams to the underside of the immense roof. Suddenly, rays of sunlight filtered through the frame structure, making the little clouds of dust dance like maleficent insects. Once in a while, in all that dark, an object would catch the light and scintillate madly.

One evening a female servant originally from the house of Yashimada, in the village of Azuma, told me the story of the phantom cat, a monstrous creature that appeared at nightfall.[30] It happened near the monastery of Shimono in Noda-chō, in a well-respected house belonging to the biggest distiller in the district.

"Long, long ago," she said, "on an evening when the wind blew over Azuma, the master of the house of Uesugi, who was still a young man, took in a kitten that had been abandoned in an obscure part of Fukushima. He took it home with him. The entire household looked after the cat, and the family grew wealthy as the cat grew bigger.

"One day, the master of the house died of a sudden illness, and his son succeeded him. But he and the rest of the family forgot about the cat. The house declined, and the animal ran away and returned to the wild.

"That same day, the most beautiful girl in the village, who was named Oshin, disappeared also. However, almost immediately thereafter, a traveler reported having seen her on the Fukushima Road.

"A few nights later, a young man who had taken that road saw a beautiful young woman beckon him to follow her. He obeyed and had his gold and all his belongings stolen from him. Another time, it was a warrior, apparently, who attacked and robbed a passerby.

"An accountant named Tanji Shōzaemon, who was in the employ of the house of Uesugi, called on Yasuda Shigeru, a man renowned for his skill with firearms. In the evening, as night fell, the two of them went to the Fukushima Road. They hid in the shadows and waited. Soon, the beautiful Oshin appeared. Yasuda Shigeru, who had the gift of foreseeing what people would do, raised his gun and took aim at the beauty who was walking toward them. He fired. Oshin fell with a dull thud. When they looked at her in the light of the moon, there, lying on the ground, was nothing but an enormous phantom cat.

"But," our servant continued, "the phantom cat was not really dead. From that day on, he unleashed himself on the countryside every night, terrorizing the people who, to no avail, carefully locked their rain shutters.

"The real corpse of the beautiful Oshin was found. Her wounds were inspected: the phantom cat had killed the young girl for the use of her form.

"And so every evening the phantom cat, its eyes bursting with a strange light, prowled through the village. The people no longer dared go out. They decided to put it in the hands of a seer who had the title hōin, seal of the law.[31] He told them to pray to the merciful Kannon, and the phantom cat's attacks stopped immediately. Soon, he died.

"The villagers buried the cat, and over his grave they built a pavilion dedicated to Kannon of the Phantom Cat. It is also said that on the road where the cat had made his attacks, they put up a stele with the head of a cat."[32]

That story terrified me for several nights. "If you don't go to sleep quickly," the servant woman threatened me, "the Phantom Cat will come and take you away." I sensed the presence of the horrible beast crouched in the shadows of the old house, ready to spring at me and tear my throat out. A ray of sunlight glinting on a metal container, a reflection on water— everything was the eye of the phantom cat to me.

This made me hate the dark, which had given rise to these frightening glimmers. I consigned darkness and shadows to the category in which already resided dirty clothes, evil intentions, grains of rice left uneaten in a bowl at the end of a meal, and characters written with a runny brush on raggedy paper. Later, I would have to add death, but at that time I didn't know death yet.

Since then, I have always preferred small, sunny rooms where the mind is not in danger of losing itself in unknown corners like the recesses of the heart but squarely faces the walls in the open light of day.

Still, I have many a nostalgic memory of that house. I loved the wood floors, polished by repeated washings, smoke, and time—the floors at our house always gleamed. There were always at least three servants, and everything was very clean.

In our *tabi* socks,[33] we would slide on the darkened wood planks, which would sometimes squeak like the song of a nightingale. I would imagine myself the lady of one of those old noble mansions in which the floorboards were specially designed to betray the slightest living presence by their creaking.

In Japanese aesthetics, there are two opposing, or complementary rules: *sabi* and *kirei*. *Sabi* originally meant "rust," the wearing of time on objects that, little by little, acquire a sort of soul. It suggests flat tones, muffled reflections, a sense born of history and a kind of beauty borrowed from melancholy. We see the word *sabi* in *sabishii*, which means lonely and sad. On the other hand, *kirei* means "pretty and clean": clear, sharp forms, light colors, the prettiness of young people, the brightness of new things. The most beautiful Japanese dwellings are without a doubt those in which *sabi* and *kirei* have been merged successfully. Because of the terrors of my childhood, *kirei* attracts me more, but darkness exerts a sort of ambiguous fascination on my spirit, perhaps because I look for glimmerings of the past in it.

When I was a child, there was so much shadow within me that I couldn't bear that uncertainty around me. No doubt that was the reason for my hatred of the old house. I know today that it didn't make sense. We should work on domesticating the shadow that lives in us, because to think that we can change the world is just illusory desire. We have no power but over ourselves.

THE INSIDE OF THE HOUSE

The *niwa*, the vast entryway with its black earth floor, was where the rice was shucked. Even in my own childhood, there was still a *senba-koki* suspended from a pillar—this was a wooden plank to which was affixed a row of rusty iron teeth, between which the peasants would wedge handfuls of rice to shuck the grains from the stalk. It was there, too, that our workers crushed the flour and met in winter to weave straw and reeds. Seated on mats, they would make baskets, cords, and straw sandals, whispering and spitting all the day through. Our servant women passed through the entryway constantly, on the pretext of watching the soybeans used to make miso that were often simmering there on the cookstove; they chattered ceaselessly with the peasants like frogs in a pond.

To the west, the stables adjoining the house always harbored five or six horses. To the right of the *niwa* was a large kitchen with a raised wood plank floor, where Mother spent most of her life. The hearth—at our house we called it the *hodo*, which means "vulva"—was hollowed out of the center of the kitchen. A blackened metal pot was constantly over the fire, suspended from the pothook ornamented with the head of a fish, which was supposed to keep the flames in check. Mother, who was in charge of the upkeep of the fire, told us nearly every day that Kōjin, the god of fire, lived in the pothook and that women in particular must show him respect. On the day that, for the first time, the moon—that is, their period—appeared on my older sisters' undergarments, each had to offer some grains of white rice mixed with azuki beans at the edge of the hearth. They thereby won the right to tend the fire themselves, without supervision. Later, the wife of my oldest brother would succeed Mother by the side of the god of fire.[34]

The family had to respect a strict order of precedence around the hearth. There was no common table; we ate from individual trays. The place called *yoko-za*, which was reserved for the head of the family,[35] was at the foot of the main pillar of the house, the pillar of Daikoku. That pillar, erected on the border of the kitchen and the inner room, was decorated by Father every month with a branch of green leaves. He said it was to honor the god Daikoku, Great Black, who made the house stand up.[36] And we at our house, like everybody else, promulgated the adage that outside of Father, only the cat, the village idiot, or the town monk would ever dare to sit there!

To the right of Father's place, on the same side as the sink, was the *kā-kā-za*, the place of the mistress of the house. To Mother's left was the *kyaku-za*, the seat of the guest. My oldest brother sat there when there were no guests. His wife would sit at Mother's side, somewhat behind. We, the girls and the younger brother, were placed across from Father, in the place they called the wood end, because it was from there that logs were put on the fire. The servants ate seated on mats that were spread on the beaten-earth floor in the entryway.

Because the inner room, with its tatami mat floor, was the warmest in the house, I slept there with the other girls on futon mattresses. Every autumn, after a good harvest, we would replace the rustling straw inside our futons, which, night after night, we had soaked with our sweat. In the evening, we would run to pull our futons from a cupboard in the boys' room, at the far east end of the house.[37] To get to that cupboard, we had to cross the tea room, which contained the household altars dedicated to the gods and buddhas. At the first one, we prayed to the Shinto gods, and at the second, we venerated the dead.

Father was often in that room, reading by the light of the snow and the fireflies.[38] He would hold the book at the end of his outstretched arms,

Cookstove in the entryway (drawing by Shige).

Irori hearth (drawing by Shige).

rocking gently as he sucked on a long wood and metal pipe. When we would enter, riotous as puppies, he would stop rocking and then, without raising his eyes from his reading, fire at us, "Only women and children run!" That made me laugh, because I could not imagine Father running.

Sometimes on winter afternoons, the tea room was off-limits to us, because Father would be ceremonially receiving distinguished guests. Before they came, we would open the shoji doors that faced the garden, in order to sweep the tatami with moist green tea leaves. When there were several guests, we'd also have to take out the partitions that separated the tea room from the adjoining inner room; there would then be one room, so vast you could do judo in there. These were the only two rooms in the house with tatami floors. In other rooms, when necessary, we would put down simple straw *mushiro* mats on the wood floor.[39]

Father and his colleagues spent many hours in the tea room, seated around a low cherry-wood table. They drank and blew big smoke rings, gazing out at the garden. Generally they spoke little, except when they were drunk. So we had to keep quiet in order not to disturb them.

But every evening we ran through there like a flock of swallows in the spring, noisily slamming the sliding wood doors. We would skirt the hibachi, the white porcelain brazier with a blue landscape design, always filled with glowing red ashes. Two long metal sticks were always buried in there. Then we would go roughhousing into our brothers' room. We would pull out our futons and drag them willy-nilly to the edge of the hearth.

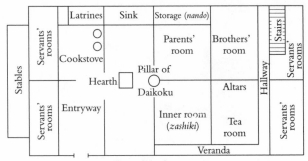

Plan of the house.

In that part of the house, the north side, there were two bedrooms. One was our parents'; the other was our brothers'. In the northwest corner was the *nando*, where Mother brought nine children into the world. My older brother stayed there for a time after his marriage, before he and his wife set themselves up in the retirement house, which the deaths of my grandparents had left empty.[40]

Behind the tea room and my brothers' bedroom were a hallway and two or three small bedrooms left to the servants. It was from one of the servants' rooms that a little stairway of wood, steep as a ladder, gave access to the attic, where we raised silkworms.

Our house was designed on the classic plan, in the form of the *katakana* サ (*sa*).[41] It was surely bigger than average.

Even though Father, who worked at the mayor's office, and my brothers, who were busy with their studies, were not often home, the house was always full of people: workers in the entryway, Mother and my sisters in the kitchen and the inner room, the servants, who came and went everywhere. As many as twenty-three people sometimes lived in that house. There was always the sound of voices. Solitude was a luxury in the country, they said.

1. Beaten-earth entryway   4. Cookstove
2. Hearth   5. Altar
3. Daikoku pillar   6. Porch roof

Plan of a traditional Japanese house.

WAR AND DESTRUCTION

After the war and the subsequent land reform, everything changed. How sad that was, when one thinks of the troubles our ancestors and Mother took to enlarge and keep our lands! But the new laws imposed by the Americans restricted ownership of land to those who cultivated it themselves.[42] Because of agrarian reform, our properties were reduced to 3,500 *tsubo* (a little less than three acres, not counting the garden). That would barely assure the subsistence of what was left of the house of Endo.

In truth, no one in our family had actually farmed for generations. Father had been totally absorbed in his municipal functions. After an idle adolescence, my older brother did his studies in Tokyo, before returning to teach in a neighboring town. Had it not been for the war, he would have succeeded Father. As the eldest son and heir of the house of Endo, he did not feel he had to know anything about agriculture or sericulture. When, after the reform, he was forced to work the land in order to keep a portion of his property, his body revealed itself to be so fragile, so little made for labor, that he fell ill. Luckily, my sisters secretly helped him to farm the fields so that he could remain the master of the parcel that the new law had apportioned him as landowner-farmer.

But I wonder if all that was really fair, if the ways of our ancestors were not perhaps better. They tell us that it's democracy, and democracy must be a good thing, since it put an end to the war. But, as Mother said, not a single one of our servants or sharecroppers thanked us. After the mobilization, moreover, most of them stayed in the city to make money.

It came time to rethatch the large roof. It used to be that the families would help one another in re-covering roofs. But very few men had come back to the village since the war. The young settled in Tokyo. There weren't enough people left in the village. And, in any case, the war had destroyed the virtues and solidarity of the old days.[43] To hire outside contractors would have cost too much. In addition, the house itself had lost many of its inhabitants. The house of Endo was quite simply too big—only my older brother, his wife, and my youngest sister still lived there.

Exterior view of a traditional Japanese house (drawing by Patrick Mérienne).

Because of financial problems and his distaste for housekeeping tasks, my brother decided to cut the long building with its bronze-colored roof in two. He kept only half of it; the other half was torn down. The new house was covered with a modern roof of gray ceramic tiles. In the postwar world, tiles had become cheaper than thatch.

I remember that the walls crashed to the ground in clouds of dust that day. My childhood fears lay in pieces at my feet, in those beige and gray earthen blocks coated with crackled lime. Suddenly I felt a poignant nostalgia as my heart narrowed. I had belonged to the house of Endo. To be sure, I had left it long before, for marriage, which is the destiny of women. But I had always known that it continued to exist. And now the house of Endo, like so many others, was ruined.

Today, far to the east of the new house, one gray stone still flattens the grass. Like a fox, I prowl around it sometimes. It reminds me of the dimensions of the old edifice, the former splendor of the Endos.

The retirement houses have also been rebuilt. These are villas, neat and small, like dollhouses, with delicate verandas of blond wood.

MEMORY

As the gods would have it, the only building to survive the war intact was the most fragile of all. It was the minuscule shrine of Inari-sama, the god of the land upon which a house is built.[44] It had been built in an appropriate direction, that of the dog and the boar (the northwest), and it faced southeast, the direction of the dragon and the serpent, where the house stood. As was true for the granaries, this was the most favorable direction for houses. That is why our house prospered for so long before everything changed, because of the war and the errors of men.

When I was a girl, the chapel was nothing but a three-foot-high shelter, its lightweight wooden armature supporting a little roof of straw. On the platform, in the center, was a holy receptacle, a box made of gray planks, faded by the rain. Within it was the *shintai*, the body of the god: a perfectly round white stone that had been handed down for generations.[45] Because Inari, the god of rice, was venerated there, two little foxes carved of gray and pink stone were placed on the doorsill. In Japan, foxes are the messengers of the god of rice.[46] Every year, at the beginning of the harvest festival, on the ninth day of the ninth moon, Father would change the straw on the roof and he would place a dozen *mochi* cakes in front of the shrine, along with pure water and sake, salt and some green branches.[47] He taught my oldest brother the rules of how to place the offerings, in anticipation of the day when he would take over the cult of the ancestors of the house. And of course it was our ancestors who watched over our land and the growth of our rice from this shrine. To express the gratitude in our hearts, my older brother finally covered the shrine with a real roof.

Even when all ephemeral constructions fall away, a house is never dead as long as the generations succeed one another and keep the memory of the past. The gods and ancestors outlive human edifices. They harbor our entire history. It is through them that our houses, all of what we remember, exist.

3

Childish Knowledge

亀
の
甲
よ
り
年
の
劫

Kame no kō yori toshi no kō.
Better than the shell of a tortoise: the experience of age.

Taishō jidai wa odayakana shōgatsu no sora no yō ni . . . The years of the Taishō
(Great Correctness) Era were serene as the cloudless sky of the first month
of the year. When the Shōwa Era began, everything changed. It was late
in 1926 by the Western calendar, on the twenty-fifth day of the twelfth
moon of Year 14 of Taishō, that the new emperor Hirohito decreed the
commencement of his era.[1] He called this time Shōwa, light and harmony,
because people dreamed of a peaceful and prosperous life. But that first
year, beginning at the end of December, lasted only a week—which always
means bad luck—so their hopes were dashed.

I was six years old and had just started school in the village, and I participated for the first time in the rites of the *kodomo-gumi*, or children's group,
with the elder children from the east gang.[2]

I was not robust. At the beginning of Year 13, I contracted such terrible
pneumonia that they feared for my life. Mother had called to my bedside
six doctors, who, one after the other, said, "Her fever is too high; this little
girl is done for." An ordinary person would have been resigned, but she, a
mother of eight, knew far more about it than any wretched doctor. Having
heard that horse meat would lower a fever, she got some from who knows
where and placed it on my forehead. She went out to the fields to pull up
taro, which she grated and mixed with vinegar and wheat flour. With this
she made poultices, which she applied to the soles of my feet. Because my
fever was high, they dried quickly and she had to change them often. Then,
for six hours, with the help of my older sisters and some neighbor women,
she rubbed my body all over. Next, she called in a seventh doctor, who
looked at me and said, "She'll live."

And I did. Because I remained weak, Father and Mother took me to a
mountain hot spring so I could breathe the good air. Hot springs weren't

43

as expensive then as they are today, and we stayed for three or four weeks in a simple inn where Mother cooked our food. I took two baths a day and slept a lot. Nevertheless, for months after our return to Asaka, everyone still said that I was white as a ghost and would have to rest.

So I didn't have a responsibility in the world—all that Mother and my sisters asked of me was that I gather sticks to burn in the hearth. And of course I was far too young to know life.

I did know, though, that poor children had to work. First, I saw our *o-mori*, babysitters who had left their homes, where there were too many hungry mouths.[3] They would also help out with the plowing and feed the farm animals every morning. After the harvests they ran through the fields, cutting the overlooked heads of grain. Two times a year, at the New Year and *O-Bon*, the festival of the dead, they would return home. Going into the bushes was the name given to their holidays, since they were going back to those forgotten regions where the wild grasses grew taller than men. They would wear a kimono and new clogs. We would see them, then, hanging around in gangs on the streets of the town. They would smoke on the street corners, purchase gifts, or go to the movies before taking the train home.

Their sophistication impressed me—I myself never went to the movies. Their lives astounded me. They knew all kinds of terrifying things. They talked about girls twelve years old, or even younger, who worked in the mills. They hummed a song in vogue at the time:

> *Kago no tori yori, kangoku yorimo*
> *Kishukusha-zumai wa nao tsurai*

> Harder than a cage is to a bird, harder even than prison
> Is living in the dormitory.

They also said that there were walls around the factories, so girls could not escape.[4]

At the beginning of the Shōwa years, after the drop in the price of rice, poor people posted signs on the walls in Kōriyama near the train station, advertising their girls for sale. One girl was worth a good 400 yen, thirty or forty years of my allowance.[5]

I suspected that a sad and dirty world existed. That world was not my own. But I knew that in that world every gesture might provoke confrontation or even death, so sometimes I would find school, games, all that was my own life, to be utterly dull.

STARTING SCHOOL

In the spring of 1926, I started school. They dressed me sumptuously, in all the trappings: a *hakama* pants-skirt in silk moiré, dark with a red underside, which Mother's mother had given me. The soft silk rustled as it brushed my ankles. I left for school very proud but with a nervous heart. Perhaps it was an after-effect of my illness, but I remember that my legs were heavy and that I had trouble walking. Father carried me halfway on his back.

Primary school (drawing by Shige).

And then we were there. The teachers all wanted to feel the underside of my skirt. They lifted the bottom of the *hakama* and said they had never seen one so beautiful. "For a child," they exclaimed, "this garment is an extraordinary luxury!" This irritated me.

A girl whispered to me that my red underlining was indecent, worse even than an old woman in a youthfully bright garment. "It's not until after puberty," she said, "that girls can wear red under their clothes." So I began to sob with all my might. No one understood why. From then on, I would sulk on principle whenever they tried to dress me in the moiré *hakama*.[6]

Aside from that incident, I remember nothing about my first day. But I did not like school. Because our teacher was the husband of Kiku, my oldest sister, I felt ill at ease.

THE TWO KINDS OF LEARNING

I quickly grasped that there are two kinds of learning: *gaku*, studies by the mortar, and *shū*, knowledge with white wings. "To study at school" is written with a character that can be read either *gaku* (a noun) or *manabu* (a verb). It represents a mortar which two hands grip tightly, a roof, or a canopy—we don't know for sure—and underneath, children. It means "the learning of the truth by children ignorant of it under the roof of a school." The mortar and the hands, of course, mean effort. The roof seemed to me like a barrier, which hid the world from me. I couldn't believe that knowledge resided in a closed-up place. *Manabu*: this was to repeat tirelessly what our masters taught us, to trace each character eight thousand times, the way one strikes a pile of glutenous rice in the mortar to make *mochi* cakes.

Manabu, to study,
"studies by the mortar."

I hated the character *manabu*. No matter how many times Mother told me we must never step over either books or people, I felt no respect for studies, and my mind was closed to writing.

Every morning at school, we would gather in the courtyard, in rows, by ages—exactly like they do today. We had to bow before the emperor and the empress, whose photos were hung in a frame above the entrance of the wooden building. To one side, there was a photo of Ninomiya Sontoku, the great peasant pioneer of the Edo Period. And then the director of the school would read the Imperial Decree on Education.[7] I still remember it:

> To our subjects,
> Long ago, our ancestors founded this country and they implanted here the virtues of the goddess Amaterasu. . . .
> In order that our subjects show proof of filial piety to their father and their mother, and friendship to their brothers and their sisters; that harmony reign between man and wife, and trust between companions: Be respectful and modest, show your goodness to all, consecrate yourselves to the acquisition of the sciences and the practice of the arts. . . .
> In this manner, you will not only be acting as splendid and loyal subjects, but you will illustrate with brilliance the traditions handed down to you by our ancestors. . . .

The text of the decree was posted on a little platform at the rear of the class, and every day we offered it water and green branches.

The director gave a discourse on our country and on education. Next was the physical fitness class, broadcast nationally over the radio. Still later in the day we would have to climb rib stalls. It was Father who had insisted that these be installed, since children, he said, must have straight backs.

Father was able to do this because he was an important man. At home he spoke little, and I knew nothing of him. But at school, on the day of the festival of the land army, the school director told of Father's great deeds during the Russo-Japanese War and read the list of his decorations. I was very impressed, and I was not the only one—the villagers always valued his advice.

In any case, school sports were important. The boys played baseball. In town, little girls jumped rope, but we did not, because we had no Western-style school uniforms. It's just not possible to jump rope in a kimono.

In a country area like ours, the entire village got involved in the annual sports festival. Like cultural or other gatherings, this festival was of far more concern to the villagers than to the students. So the mothers of the village and the other women prepared rice balls and all kinds of good things on which to feast. The ladies came, under their arms their rush mats, which they would spread out to make a camp. This affair was both a pleasure and an important time. The cherries were in blossom. All was right with the world!

At my primary school, there was a giant courtyard in which they held sporting events and other gatherings. We jumped and we paraded. I wasn't much good at anything, but I didn't like to lose. Once, in a footrace, I grabbed the collar of the girl ahead of me to keep her from winning!

The surface of the courtyard, which sloped down to a row of trees and the river, was bare earth. We did our exercises barefoot. Then, our clogs in our hands, we would go to the river. We'd wash our faces, hands, and feet, dry them off, and go back to school. We'd also go to the river after our calligraphy lessons to wash our writing boards and brushes. The river, which we called *otonashi-gawa*, soundless river, was perfectly still.

We had the school, the soundless river, a bridge over the river—and, on the other side, a mountain. To us, this was a magnificent place! A true country school.

From our classrooms, hidden behind the covers of our wooden desks, we would watch the trees grow green at the beginning of spring. Then we would run in the courtyard. We would make holes in the snow so we could see the black earth; breathing in its pungent smell and uncovering the pale shoots that announced the return of warm weather.

It was a happy school. In Year 2 of Shōwa (1927), I was given a doll with blue eyes and blond hair. As a sign of friendship, the people of the United States had sent at least fifteen thousand dolls to the schoolgirls of Japan. I told mine about the adventures of Norakuro, the little black stray dog who was the heartrending hero of my favorite comic strip.

Of the classes per se, I don't remember much. Like children everywhere, we studied history and geography, arithmetic, writing, and *shūshin* (ethics).[8] I think I was not too bad in arithmetic and composition. I wrote a piece on a cat that was rather well received, but I'm sure it wasn't on a very high level.

Our exams, however, were more difficult than they are today. We didn't have true-false tests, where you answer with a circle or a cross. They would ask us things like "Give the names of all the emperors you know of who, in history, showed particular proof of compassion." The teachers kept monthly scholastic report books on each of us. My own weren't good enough for me to remember what was written there. I recall only the maxims written on the first page:

> That which you can do yourself, so do.
> Respect the rules of politeness.
> Do nothing that might bother another.
> Perform all things correctly.
> Study well and play well.

But the smells of the water and the woods came in through the windows and exerted a pull on me. As soon as the bell had rung, I would escape to eat mulberries on the banks of the rice paddy footpaths. My little sister Kikumi and I would stretch our hands out to catch the tiny loaches that swam in the irrigation ditches, and we would come home encrusted with mud that tasted of iron.

I preferred the character for *narau*, also read *shū*, to that of *manabu*. It is written with the characters for "wings" and "white." "To learn," this character whispered in my ear, "is to put on the wings of a bird. They flap gently in the air, and you rise up effortlessly." *Narau* reminded me of the word *nareru*, which means "familiar, daily habits," as well as *narasu*, the peaceful motion of leveling the ground of rice paddies for planting.

 Narau, to learn,
"knowledge with white wings."

So I rejected knowledge by mortar for the familiar pleasure of knowledge by white wings.[9] I learned that in the mountains one must never pronounce the word "mouse" but rather call these rodents brides, because mice, so numerous in the holes of rocks and earth, are the favorites of the mountain god.[10] I also learned that in years when crows are numerous, there is a greater chance of want, because they, the messengers of the god of the mountain, would mistake our sown seeds for offerings. I learned that when the fox calls "*kon kon*," it is auspicious, and that when he says "*guai guai*," it's inauspicious. The spider is a harbinger of good luck: you must put one in a one-*shō* rice measuring cup and offer it on the altar of the household gods.[11] I soon learned that, when you see a snake in a brook where there are many fish, you mustn't fish that day, because that's the god of the waters' day to fish. And you must never start building a house on a day determined by the Chinese calendar to be a fire day, lest it be prone to catch fire later. If you point at people with your finger, you must then moisten that finger with your saliva, to keep it from rotting.

AGE GROUPS

In Asaka, in addition to all the mutual aid associations, there were five *kumi*, or age groups.[12] The *kodomo-gumi*, the children's group, included all those between seven and twelve or thirteen, the girls on one side, the boys on the other. Like the gods, children surprise adults by what they do, because, only recently arrived from the beyond, they live on the border of the human and celestial worlds. That is why they are given charge of the rites of *sai no kami*, the gods of the town limits, which protect the village from intrusions by evil forces such as pestilence or flood.[13]

The *seinen-dan*, or youth group, the young unmarried men, would pitch in for all difficult jobs. They would build a festival pavilion as quickly as bamboo grows in the spring and would rethatch a roof in less than two weeks. At that time, they still took the place of police in the village, and they would catch vagabonds who came to steal from us. They trained themselves in firefighting by climbing ladders. Officers taught them the rudiments of the military arts.

As for the group of heads of households, the *koshu-gumi*, they met frequently at the mayor's office to take care of village administrative duties. The fourth group, the *yome-gumi*, included the wives who, hoping to conceive boys, would pray together once a month to Jizō-sama, as well as to the other gods who granted children.

Finally, there were the grandparents in the *rōjin-gumi*. This group was also known as the *nenbutsu-kō* or brotherhood of Amida Buddha. The Amida Buddha reigns in the paradise of the Pure Land, located to the west of the world. For their salvation and that of their descendants, the old people would invoke the glorious name of Amida for hours on end: "*Namu Amida Butsu!* Hail, Amida Buddha!"[14] Some of them had never traveled farther than Kōriyama or Aizu, but they often said, "What good does it do to roam all over the world if you don't even know Asaka?"

That was what they taught us in the children's group. There I learned that human will is nothing in the face of nature but that the correct performance of the rites and rules confers a power equal to that of the gods.

SEASONAL RITES

At the New Year, when the Buddhist bell that banishes the 108 life-enslaving passions had sounded 108 times, we went to the monastery to fetch the new fire on cords affixed with a spongy, inflammable mushroom used as a fuse.[15] And when *toshi-toku-gami*, the god who renews time,[16] went away, we would build a *dondo yaki*, a woodshed on the bank of the brook on the way out of the village. Each family would then come and toss all the decorations from the altars for the new year and the entire preceding year onto this hut of straw and bamboo. It would be set aflame, and the god of the new year would leave on the smoke, and with him, all pests, birds, and animals who eat the crops. In a circle around the fire, we, the children's group, would call as strongly and as loudly as we were able: "*Dondo! dondo! dondo! yaki! dondo!* It's burning!" *Dondo* is the roaring sound of the flames. Then we would grill *mochi* cakes as white as ivory on the ends of long sticks over the fire. I would bite deep into those hot, stretchy cakes, in order to prevent upset stomachs and insect bites for the coming year.[17]

Then we would run through the fields, expelling moles. We would kick all the molehills we found and stir up the black earth holes with the end of a stick. We would sing to them, saying that we were sea slugs. People said moles hated sea slugs, because their name is written "water mole." The song went, "*Mogura-don*, noble mole! Here we are! *Namako-don*, noble sea slug! Here we are! The sea slug is coming through!" To frighten the moles, we called everything "sea slug," including the stick with which we struck the dirt, the brush we dragged along the rice paddy walkways at the end of a rope.

Next, it was the birds' turn. We would beat metal buckets with wooden ladles and call out "*Hoi! Hoi!*" like fox hunters.

Sometimes we would run into children from the west gang. We'd jeer at them and hurl clods of dirt at their heads to chase all the snakes, moles, and evils, which had surely come from the west, back to their side. Tradition demanded that the encounter end in a brawl.

When the melting snow traced the image of a deer on the side of the hill of Hayama, the time had come to prepare the seedlings.[18] At our house, which was a main house, we were responsible for the germination of seeds. We kept them underwater in a seed well, for a month. People said that seeds, like mothers who have just given birth, must stay one moon in bed. Then, the seedlings were wrapped in balls of straw for about ten days. There they would germinate, and when the spring equinox, which marked the time to plant them in their seedbeds, came, we distributed them to all the houses under us. At our house, Mother stuck a little bamboo measuring stick in the middle of the first seedbed. Then she attached a *goō* amulet—a piece of paper with magic formulas written on it, which she had purchased at the temple in Kōriyama. This was to keep off devouring insects.[19] Near the mouth of the irrigation ditch, she offered a very dry ball of *mochi*, one that she had saved from the new year, with some fried rice and wildflowers. We children would chase away swallows by hitting our knocking sticks together directly over the rice plants.

Again, about the time of the equinox, *higan*, the day when the sun sets exactly in the west, the dead come back from the other shore of the world.[20] So the old people would say, "Let's go pick flowers in the mountains."

The gang of children would follow them along the paths of the hills. On nice days, we would cut down the high grasses with sickles, terrifying the animals that had hidden there since the beginning of winter. We picked multitudes of flowers, paler than those that grew on the plain. At the top, while we ate our rice balls filled with pickled vegetables, a grandmother would always complain: "This is the seventy-second time I've climbed this mountain. One more time, and I won't be able to go back down."

And we would all answer, "Yes, you will! We'll carry you on a litter of flowers!"

We walked home taking small steps, our arms full of branches. The flowers we had gathered were then affixed to bamboo poles that we mounted in our gardens. They served as a sign to the dead, so they could find their way back to our houses.

Every spring, on the third day of the third moon, like all little girls in Japan, I would make a straw basket in the shape of a bird's nest. In it I would place two dolls made of paper, a man and wife, to whom I would offer pink and white sweets on a half sheet of velvety white paper. I would release this little boat into the river, and, squatting on the bank, watch it flow away: it would take the defilements of the previous year beyond the borders of the world and the sea, to the place where the ancestors lived. In imagination, I followed it; in spirit I was on the little boat as it made for that calm world where there is neither night nor day.[21] Staring at the water, I wondered what the other world must be like.

At last, it came time to transplant. So Mother would remove the bamboo measuring stick from the seedbed. She would bend it in half until it broke: if the two parts were of equal length, this was a good omen for the harvest and the prosperity of the house. I remember the stick broke exactly in two the year my older sister married.

But this fifth-moon transplanting was primarily the business of the young. Groups of *yui*, those who are allied, would band together to transplant all the rice in the hamlet. The boys pulled the seedlings from the beds; the girls replanted them. They began at the rice paddy of the shrine of the tutelary god, where *kannushi*, the master of the gods, made the glutenous rice that was used for festivals grow—and always without chemical fertilizer.[22] The priest placed a stick right in the middle of the rice paddy, and the rice maidens, as we called the girls, their hair covered by new scarves, turned their backs to him, fanned out in all directions, and planted the rice in lines like the rays of the sun. We'd go with a picnic lunch to hear a flute and drum orchestra mark the occasion.

In other places, the rice was transplanted in straight lines marked with cords.

In the summer, when the humid heat set in, the grasses grew even faster. They would once again overgrow the mountain paths and the tombs of the ancestors. Pests of all sorts took over the world: snakes in the water, caterpillars on the plants, and worms in the bellies of men. It was up to us, the gang of children, to chase them away. After having put insects in a paper bag that we attached to a stick, to the sound of drum and cymbals, we would run and throw them in the brook that flowed out of Asaka, that they might get lost farther downstream, in Abukuma. We sang:

Inesashi mushi okuru yo!
Hasuppei mushi mo okuru yo!
Ao-mushi okuru yo!
Mushi dara nandemo okuru yo! Okuru! Okuru! Okuri okuru yo!

Away with the bugs that bore through the rice!
Away with the stinkbugs, too!
Away with the green caterpillars!
Away with any and all pests! Away! Away! We send them away to get rid
   of them!

Toward the end of summer, before *O-Bon*, I pressed my ear to the ground.[23] The earth vibrated with the rumbling of the dead as they left their subterranean abode to come to this world. Anyone who has heard this sound even once will never forget it. From then on, no matter where he is, he has only to cock an ear to hear the quaking from the beyond. He knows that that ground to which he pressed his ear is none other than their flesh, none other than that of the dead who stir within the earth; it shivers with the ancestors' impatience to revisit the world of the living.

For the *mu-en-botoke*, those dead without descendants, Mother set up a very simple altar in the garden, a lightweight bamboo frame on which we placed their mounts, horses and cattle that would carry them to the homes of living people: these were eggplants and cucumbers in which we had stuck legs of wood and tails of straw.[24] Inside the house, on the Buddhist altar, far more abundant offerings were presented to our own ancestors: summer vegetables, cubes of agar-agar, flowers, and five-colored streamers. The entire family would meet at our house to pray for their deliverance and obtain their protection.

The young people built a two-tiered dance platform in the schoolyard. The drummer was on the higher level, above the girls, the best dancers of the village, dressed in starched cotton *yukata* (summer kimonos), hiding their overly flushed cheeks under new hats. Everyone knew that the girl who looked prettiest of all on the nights of *O-Bon* might look homely again in the morning—the excitement, slightly magical, showed them off to advantage. For three evenings, the villagers, all decked out in beautiful clothes, danced to the flute and the singing in order to amuse or console the dead. They mimed the acts of sowing, transplanting, and harvest, as a polite way of explaining to the dead what we expected their help with. I danced very badly myself, but I clapped my hands much louder than anyone.

When we neared the 210th day after the point of departure of spring and storms were raging, we would drive a big stalk of bamboo into the dirt, into which we would stick a knife blade, the cutting edge facing northwest, source of the great winds. We said this would cut off the roots of the wind.[25]

The adults had little faith in these rites—which were in fact no more than games—so they met at the Buddhist temple and gave money to the monk to perform ceremonies to stop the wind and bring rain. But we children continued to strike the soil to make it fertile.[26] We beat the drum and imitated the croaking of frogs, to call the storm.

And then it was harvesttime, on the ninth, the nineteenth, or the twenty-ninth day of the ninth moon. When I was born, rice was still cut with a sickle. After that, they used machines. The first heads of the grain were for *ta no kami sama*, the god of the rice paddies, who resided on our altar with the other family gods. The workers again hammered glutenous rice to make *mochi* cakes, which they asked the frogs of the rice paddies to carry to heaven. With the approach of winter, the frogs would go back to the otherworld with their master the god, not to accompany him on his return to the village until spring.[27]

The harvested rice was laid out to dry on wooden props before it was piled in stacks, the heads turned to the center to keep the animals from eating them. Then the rice had to be beaten, husked, and milled for flour, and all that before the snow came, which kept sensible people tightly closed up in their houses, around their hearths.

Particular joys corresponded to each season. In the spring, we picked mountain flowers. In the summer we caught cicadas. When *O-Bon* came, we listened to the reptiles that hissed and slid through the grasses. I enjoyed frightening the little ones with stories of poisonous snakes that, once the season of the dead had passed, went mad and attacked passersby. In the winter, we would run on the frozen earth. Sometimes, if a rice paddy near the house had not completely dried up, it would freeze; our parents would attach blades to the bottoms of our wooden *geta* clogs, and we would slide across the ice.

There were kites in winter and during the fifth moon, tops and yo-yos for the new year, streamers painted with calligraphy for the seventh moon, fireworks during the hot months, and paintings on stelae of Jizō-sama at the end of the feast of the dead.[28] In the village I learned a calendar that was not that of school. As I speak to you now, I can smell the light scent of wild azaleas, the slightly swampy odor of the rice paddies, and the sugared breath of summer breezes.

AGRICULTURAL CALENDAR

The old names for the months teach us that time is a succession of landscapes: *mutsuki*, the moon in which the grains of rice are set to germinate; *kisaragi-zuki*, the moon of the swaying buds; *yayoi*, the time of germination; *uzuki*, the moon of deutzia flowers; *satsuki*, the moon of transplanting; *mina-zuki*, the waterless moon; *fumi-zuki*, the moon of the heads of rice; *ha-zuki*, the moon in which the leaves fall; *naga-tsuki*, the moon in which the nights grow long; *kamina-zuki*, the godless moon; *shimo-tsuji*, the hoarfrost moon; and finally, *shiwasu*, the moon in which monks scurry from house to house, reading the sutras.[29] How much more poetic than the numbered months, one, two, three, of the official calendar!

In the wave of modernization that swept the country during the Meiji Era, of course, we adopted the Western calendar, where the months succeed one another, each just like the last, named with simple numerals like those on the Western clock on the wall.[30] But we in Tōhoku far preferred the old lunar-solar calendar invented by the Chinese—this living year in which we sometimes had to add a supplementary month, so that the moon's time might catch up to the sun's. The time of the Westerners seems empty, whereas that of the true life is a series of images.

THE TEACHINGS OF THE COUNTRYSIDE

The countryside around Asaka—mountains, plains, rivers, and the sky beyond—is like a summary of the destinies of men. The god of birth brings the soul from the mountains. Man lives on the plain, and then his spirit, following the water or the wind, takes off once again for the other world, for the sky or perhaps the sea. I believe in the truth of landscapes—unlike men, they do not lie.

I ran wild over the countryside; I got my lessons in all kinds of marvelous places. That's how I made the precepts of the old people of the village, our living ancestors, my own. They said, "When a human being acts, he sees only the corner of the world in which he moves his own arm. But for someone with eyes that know how to see, the landscape contains all the principles of wisdom."

First, there were the mountains that touched the sky, our mountains, inhabited by gods. If springs do not flow from their summits, that's because the gods didn't mean for men to live there: their sacred realm is above the springs. Men cannot go there, except to welcome and venerate the gods in great solemnity.

There was a spring coming out of the side of the Hayama hill, and the pure water that flowed from it was extremely sweet. People said that the saint Kōbō had passed by there one day, and the villagers had welcomed him hospitably. So he stuck his walking stick into the ground, and, all of a sudden, water came out. That was how he thanked the villagers.[31]

About two-thirds of the way up the hill was a recess in the rock, so narrow that a child could barely slip through. People called this the weaver girl's abyss. On moonlit nights, you could hear the lapping of the water coming from the bottom.

The old people said that long ago a father and his three daughters lived nearby, alongside a pond. One day, the father saw a snake about to devour a frog. He said to the snake, "Let the frog go, and I'll give you whatever you want." The snake immediately released the frog and laid claim to a daughter. The father was very vexed. The eldest girl refused to obey, and the second also. Only the youngest girl agreed. Then, as time passed and nothing happened, they forgot all about it.

One night during a spring thunderstorm, a youth came to ask for the youngest girl in marriage. This was the snake in disguise; the girl went with him. Luckily, as they were getting ready to cross the river together, thousands of frogs attacked the reptile. He died. Alas, the young girl, already pregnant, threw herself into the river, which was connected on the upper end to the hole in the mountain and below to the palace of the dragon king. That is why even now, if you lend an attentive ear to the hollow, you will hear the voice of the young girl from the palace of the dragon king, singing as she spins her silk.[32]

In front of another rock grew a giant camellia. A large tree, it spotted the rocks with its bloody petals at the end of winter. This camellia, a flower of life like all red trees, had its story, too.

Long ago, on the Sea of Japan, the daughter of a fisherman once accidentally ate the flesh of a mermaid, which made her immortal. Not knowing what to do with her time, she became a nun and set out on a journey across Japan. She walked for two hundred years and got so old she had to lean on a walking stick of camellia wood by the time she got to Tōhoku. Then she began to get irritated. Was it really true that she could never die? She waited and waited, but nothing happened. Finally, she felt so weary that she decided to close herself up in a mountain rock. She went into a grotto and carefully pulled the stone behind her.

Since then, no one has heard tell of that eight-hundred-year-old nun. But the old people say she still lives in the rock. So that she would be remembered, she stuck her camellia rod into the earth in front of the place. It took root and flowered each year to announce the springtime.[33]

The entire countryside was inhabited: women closed up in mountains, gods who blew the winds on the edges of the passes, gods of slopes and springs, gods at crossings of roads. Even on the banks of rice paddies foxes, the messengers of the god of rice, lived. In all honesty, I never saw any prowling around the fox mounds, but, from time to time, we would find a hen with its throat torn open by an animal of unknown origin. Whatever it was had not eaten its prey.

Everything in nature had its history, divine or human. This or that river, this or that mountain had been in the family for three generations. Another one for only two. A tree, struck by lightning twenty or thirty years before, was called the Lord of Thunder. There wasn't a single place that didn't have a name. And I knew all of them, because Asaka was my village.

THE ORIGIN OF THE WIND

In my seventh year, the day the *hagi* (Japanese bush clover) bloomed—it was in the autumn—the *tori-age-bābā*, the old midwife, took me to Hayama. The delicate mauve flowers swayed like stars on their background of light greenery.[34] Cotton wool clouds floated in the sky. In the middle of a bamboo thicket, a nightingale sang, to which the echo of the *hinoki* cypress replied with a hollow sound, like the circles made by a stone dropped in water. On the base of a five-story tower (*gorintō*), a snake lay sleeping in the warm rays of the setting sun. I looked at it, and I struck the ground with the end of my stick. It left.

"It was on a fine day like today, that he left the village," began the *tori-age-bābā*.

"Who?" I asked.

"The young man who never came back . . . the third younger brother of my great-grandfather."

"What happened to him?"

"We don't know. Or, rather, we do, he is dead, he became a nightingale."

"Tell me."

"But you know the story."

And then, of course, she told it:

"It was a day like today, when the clouds run through the sky as fast as a woman changes moods. The young man said to himself, 'This morning, the weather is fine. It's been a very long time since I went to work in the mountains.' And he walked to the foot of the mountain. There, in a bamboo grove, was a hidden thicket of dwarf bamboo. He heard the nightingale, and, guided by her song, he entered the thicket. The *hagi* flowers were gently blooming there. And at the foot of the *hagi* bush was a little house.

"In the back, *gotan gotan!* a waterwheel was turning, *gotan gotan!*

"In the house was a beautiful young girl. The young man thought that he would like to go into the house for a moment's rest. And then, as that house was very pleasant, without even having thought about it, he'd moved in.

"One day, the young girl said to him, 'There is something I have to do, and I'm going away for a time. Do not go into the thirteenth room.'

"Once his wife had gone, the young man became bored. So, he went into the first room.

"Inside, a dwarf was sowing seeds. The young man visited the next eleven rooms one after the other, and in each he saw dwarfs harvesting rice and doing all kinds of work. This reminded him of his own work and made him wish to return to the village. He said to himself, 'Since I'm leaving anyway, I might as well see the thirteenth room before I go.'

"So, finally, he went into the thirteenth room.

"It was the nightingale's room. Sheltered by the flowering white and mauve *hagi*, the bird was laying eggs.

"The nightingale, who was the young woman, returned to her human form and said to him, 'Why can't humans keep their promises? Had you not seen this room, you could have lived a rich man, into old age. . . . I gave you thirteen children.' She gave him a box. 'This is my separation gift to you. Good-bye.'

"Then, the woman turned back into a nightingale and flew into the sky.

"He continued to stand there, troubled and dazed: He said to himself, 'What have I done?' When he looked around him, the house, which had looked like a palace, had disappeared. He found himself standing once again in the middle of a thicket of dwarf bamboo.

"Just then, he smelled a delicious odor: in the palm of his hand was a *jūbako*, a layered box with thirteen tiers fitted one on the other, filled with thirteen *mochi* cakes.

"He said to himself, 'Why did I break my promise?' And then he thought, 'I'd better get going. My work is to farm the fields and burn forests to make new fields.'

"He went down the mountain, consoling himself in that way. But at the bottom, when he looked around him, he was stunned! His house had been torn down, and even the village had changed.

"And so, thinking sad thoughts, the young man ate the *mochi* cakes, and then, all of a sudden, he turned into a bird. Filled with happiness, he went back to his young wife, the nightingale, and the two of them flew, with a great beating of their wings, to a far country. At that moment, the wind was born, of the movement of their wings."[35]

I said, "That's not true. He wasn't the third younger brother of your great-grandfather!"

She shrugged. "If you don't want to believe me . . . "

"And anyway, how would you know, because he never came back?"

"At my age, a person knows a lot of things," retorted the *tori-age-bāba* with a look of annoyance. She looked at me and said, "You're a big girl now."

I had the feeling of having betrayed her. We got up and went slowly down the hill, smoothing our clothes, disheveled by the wind.

Every year, when the rice was harvested, came the *kami are*, the storm of the gods. The Asaka wind would suddenly begin to blow, and the gods would fly away to Izumo, on the coast of the Sea of Japan, to the sanctuary of Daikoku-sama, who decides human marriages.[36] There they would arrange all unions for the coming year. They would say to one another, "So-and-so from such-and-such a village must marry so-and-so." Their decisions were irrevocable. In the village of Asaka, only *Yama no Kami-sama*, the Mountain God, did not go. But Ebisu-sama, the god of fishing and of fortune, would take over for him around the middle of the month. People said that *Yama no Kami-sama* had had his face burned and therefore no longer dared to appear in public. Ebisu-sama hadn't any bones, so he couldn't undertake such a long journey.[37] Because they took turns staying to guard the village, people offered them special festivals to thank them. They would get rice with azuki beans and sake in bamboo vases. Then, at

the end of the tenth moon, the wind would again begin to blow fero-
ciously, and our gods would all return.

The wind is first among the elements. It destroys trees and crops. It
carries off roofs, and then, once the pollen of the flowers is distributed, it
suddenly dies down, and nature teems with life.

What is the wind? I have often asked myself. Mother said the northwest
wind was the *tama-kaze*, the soul wind. "When the wind blows from the
northwest," she told us, "fishermen don't go out, because the gods themselves are fishing. No one must go near them, nor encounter them, or
terrible things will result."

When the soul wind blew, extraordinary events took place at our house.
The *tori-age-bābā* told me that children who are born when the northwest
wind is blowing are unusually strong, because *tama* (souls) rush into their
bodies. On the other hand, if someone of a fragile constitution is exposed
to that wind, he will grow weaker—his head will become heavy, his limbs
will grow numb, he will tremble and die. That's why in Japanese we still
call a cold *kaze*, the same as we call the wind.[38]

Of all the elements, wind is the only one we haven't been able to tame.
We know how to make fire and channel water in bamboo, rubber, or metal
pipes. But the wind . . . no matter how much you blow through your
mouth or inflate your cheeks like the mask of O *Kame*, the woman of
abundance, your breath will disappear without ever turning into wind. The
wind is the ultimate force of the world.

GORINTŌ: THE FIVE-STORY TOWER

Near the base of the Hayama hill, a *gorintō*, a stone monument with five
sections, marked the site of an ancient tomb.[39] The five stone sections are
the five principles of physics that make up the world and govern changes.

The bottom section is earth, which contains the forces of fecundity, gen-
erators of beings and things.

Next is water, come down from the mountains, where the gods reside,
which irrigates the plain. Washing away the impurities that over time whit-
tle away at their vital energy, it regenerates bodies and souls. Our gods hate
what is dirty. People must rinse their hands and mouths every day, and
wash the body, in order to satisfy them. It is also for that reason that we
provide hollowed-out basins at the entrances to shrines, through which
clear water flows. We dip it out with a ladle of metal or wood, sprinkle our
hands with it, and take three mouthfuls before we greet the gods. The
religion of Japan is that of purity.

The five-tiered tower.

The third section is fire, the complementary principle to water: fire, which we keep in our hearths to heat our homes and cook our meals. Its flames consume uncleanness, while its smoke forms a bridge between these islands and the heavens.

Above that is the wind, just before the void at the apex.

As a child, I learned how to make the earth fertile, how to honor fire and call the rain. But the wind always gave rise to peculiar sensations in me. When the *homachi* blew, it would sweep into my nose, my mouth, and my ears. No matter how tight I'd pull my sleeves closed, it got in, to flutter on my skin like a hen. I was cold, but I knew that the wind revitalizes the life force, just as breath will rekindle the embers of a dying fire.

Around noon, a snake would often be found sleeping coiled around the base of the stone tower of Hayama. "Look at him," the old people of Asaka would say. "He lives under the earth and is found in water. His tongue is as rapid as flame, and he slips through the grass with the sound of the wind. That creature is holy!" And they cited his molted skin as proof of his divine origin.

At the beginning of the sixth moon, which marks the renewal of time, no one was allowed to go into the mulberry fields. "Today," people murmured, "the snake is molting in the shadow of the leaves."[40]

First he would curl up very still, as if sick or overcome by the heat. Carnivorous insects would approach him, ready to devour the prey they thought dead. But when he shuddered, all would recoil. The snake would inflate himself until his skin cracked, and he would slide away from it, slowly leaving at the foot of the tree a lightly gilded, transparent slough. According to the old people, human beings must never see him in that state, because they are not sufficiently pure. If a human had the misfortune to spy a snake in the act of molting, he himself would begin to molt, and his spirit would leave his body, which would remain on earth like a useless envelope, hanging from the branch of a mulberry tree.

I have often seen snakes molt, and it didn't kill me, but I can't help but think that these stories have a kind of truth to them. The gods are present in all the manifestations of nature—the sound of a spring, the song of a bird and that of the wind, or the dark color of rich earth, as well as the hearts of men.

But the supreme realm of the gods is the void at the top of the five-tiered tower. That is the place of awakening, according to the teachings of Buddhism, the place where the wisdom of a man detached from the passions that enslave the world is completed. And since the word for "void" is written with the character for "sky," it is also the place in which dialogue with the *kami* takes place, the place where true and effectual speech, which humans receive from the gods, resonates.

In fact, the order of the five elements is not simply defined by their material weight but also corresponds to their disposition in space and in the successive stages of life that lead men of the earth to the divine world.

The spirits of the dead are classed under air and wind: they prowl for a time around houses, susceptible to the whims of seasonal breezes, then they leave for heaven. It does the living no good to call to them; nothing can hold them back. Later, catching sight of a bizarrely familiar butterfly or a flower swaying silently, people sometimes think that it is the soul of an ancestor, purified by the wind and visiting them in that form. They dream that that beauty is the emanation of the spirit that flew away.

Born of the earth and smeared with blood, in the end men become delicate flowers or evanescent butterflies. And that is how, raising themselves from earth to wind to void, they play their appropriate roles in this world.

4

Intimate Memories

親
の
心
子
知
ら
ず

Oya no kokoro ko shirazu.
The heart of the parent: to the child, unknown.

I think of my childhood nostalgically. I know for sure that I was happy, but forgetfulness or the monotony of the rhythms of village life may have swept away the events; they have nibbled at my memories, whether great or of no consequence. I have but a vague memory of happiness, a few images floating like the tops of Japan cedars over the haze, impressions as fragile as soap bubbles.

I would climb one of the fruit trees that surrounded the house and stay hidden up there, observing the yard below. The servants rushed about like insects, always carrying something. From the bits of their conversations that reached me, I learned, in the language of the common people, how the world worked.[1] Their gestures, their motivations, the too-vivid flush of their cheeks—no, I thought, I could never lead the life of a common woman.

MY OLDEST BROTHER

One bright fall morning, straddling a branch, I sank my teeth into an apple. I said to myself, "No one has ever touched this apple, it belongs to me alone. To me alone." It was acidic, and it burned my lips. A crow went by. *Kā kā!* He was making fun of me. I dropped the apple and fell to the foot of the tree. I wasn't hurt in the least, but I cried. My oldest brother picked me up. He took me in his arms, and I buried my head in the hollow of his shoulder. His smell was strange, the odor of the city, of luxury perhaps, which clung to his clothing. He was dressed in Western clothes. He carried me all the way to the house.

I didn't often see my oldest brother, because he was engaged in difficult studies, far away. In fact, everything about him was special.[2] He smoked American cigarettes, which encircled him in bluish vapors. He often looked pale, and he played the violin. One time—I must have been about twelve—he came back from Tokyo, and after we had all gathered in the garden, he taught us the Charleston. For the rest of the day I forsook my cotton crepe kimono for the blue skirt and blouse of my school uniform, thinking it more suitable for those modern rhythms.[3]

The female servants pulled up their kimonos in order to lift their legs. *Ichi, ni! Ichi, ni!* "One, two! One, two!" They told me I had a talent for it. The gaiety of the Charleston filled my heart with joy. All that activity frightened the hens, who ran about flapping their wings. For a few weeks, the yard resounded with the sounds of the foreign dance. And then my oldest brother went away, and I didn't see him for four or five years.

FATHER

Although my oldest brother lived far from us and was fifteen years my senior, he was far more familiar to me than Father. Father had a large body, with immense shoulders when he put on his military jacket with its decorations, too many medals to fit on one row. He was a man so stiff that we didn't dare address him directly; all communication was via Mother. When I think of him now, I don't believe he was a hard man—only serious and honest. Severe and taciturn at home, outside he was dedication itself. He worked like a demon in the service of the village. When there was a funeral, he took food for everyone. He would tell Mother to cook three *shō* of rice to make little *musubi* balls with seaweed. He took these to the funeral, saying, "Here—eat as many as you can."

He was also concerned with the youth of the village, who had to pass our house to get to the high school. He'd had a basin made so they could drink and wash their hands and faces, and he insisted there be a fresh towel at all times. Once a year he'd have the basin cleaned out to make sure the water was pure for the students.

No, it's true, a man so thoughtful of others could not have been a bad man. But he was of that era when fathers had no room in their hearts for any child save the eldest son, the treasured heir. We girls held no interest for him. In fact, he made me ill at ease, as did most adults.

In old photographs, I look very glum. I didn't like people looking at me. Had I been a bird, I would have turned toward the sky above our house, *kuru, kuru,* and flown with all my might to the sea. But I was not a kite, nor even a sparrow, and I had never seen the sea. Sometimes my own wildness pushed me far from the family home; then again it held me back and kept me by Mother's side.

MOTHER

Mother was the great heroine of my childhood. Everything about her seemed admirable.[4] People say she was beautiful as a young woman, which is what saved her. Married at fifteen, she soon had one son, but then she was barren for such a long time that, had he not been charmed by her grace, Father would undoubtedly have sent her away.

In fact he loved her. I learned this from reading the letters they had exchanged during the Russo-Japanese War. In Year 37 of the Meiji Era (1904), Father was sent to Manchuria, where he knew fear and cold. In December, he wrote to Mother that his battalion would be the next to be sent to the front. So many soldiers had already died; he was sure he too would die there. He wrote to Mother, "You are still young, and you have only one son. After I am dead, leave him with the Endos and remarry."[5] Mother wrote back with photos of the house and the family to reassure him.

It turned out he wasn't sent to the front that time. Soon he wrote, "I was astonished and happy to receive the photos. They didn't send me to the front after all, and I'm sorry to have caused you so much worry. It's so cold here that when I wake up in the morning, my body is white with ice. It's terrible. I would like to get sick so they would send me home, but unfortunately I'm just fine—not so much as a runny nose!" So he reassured her. Nevertheless, one day he was wounded. The three little flattened bullets they took out of his body were kept for a long time as souvenirs of his courage. I think my older sister may still have them.

But, for me, Mother was a woman of forty—slight, with a very straight back. She wore kimonos in soft, pale colors, decorated with small motifs, the elegance of which suited her delicacy. She had a calm grace, a pleasant face, a smile always hovering at the corners of her mouth. Her very black eyes shone like two seeds. She was never ill, at least as far as I recall, and never angry. I believed her to be unchangeable.

Her fine white hands were busy all day, with great skill. When she folded a piece of fabric, it fell easily into place, with impeccable corners. When she gave orders, with a tranquil ease, we all obeyed her without a murmur. Sometimes she would advise Father on his work. He would pretend not to hear. He would grumble that it was no business for a woman. "Look at the animals," he would say. "The females keep a low profile; they mind their young. It must be the same with people. So don't bother yourself with such thoughts!" But, secretly, he appreciated Mother's clear-sightedness. She always knew the appropriate gift for a situation. She gauged men with fairness and knew exactly what to give to one, what to ask of another.

Mother detested superfluous words and showed, in her speech as in all else, absolute order. She herself spoke little, and, truly, until her death, a very small number of words passed her lips. "What we say," she would tell us, "has as much weight as what we do. You don't do whatever you please; so, likewise, don't speak without rhyme or reason." She wanted to teach us strictness: "Never leave even a single grain of rice in the bottom of your bowl. Think of how the peasants sweated for it." Or when we went to bed: "Don't let your arms and legs go every which way. A bed is not a field decimated by a storm. Keep your legs together, and stretch out in the shape of the hiragana sa [さ]."

Mother had a sober respect for education. When she saw my older sisters dallying before the mirror, she would reprimand them: "It's not by adorning yourselves that you'll build the Japan of tomorrow. You must work, my girls. Study that you might embellish your mind, and that will decorate your body." Reminding us how highly the women of Japan had always esteemed culture, she held up Murasaki Shikibu, author of The Tale of Genji, and the Bluestocking feminists as examples.[6] She was in complete support of the modernization project, in which the nation had been engaged since the Meiji Restoration.[7] And in that, education must play an important role. Like many of those in authority at the time, Mother was betting on knowledge to, in the oft-repeated phrase of the day, "create a modern state, forge a national consciousness, and educate citizens." She encouraged all of us in our studies. "Do not be lazy," she would warn us, "or your life will be as empty and soft as the shell of a river crab."

In fact, in her era, there were no happy women. It was the age of danson johi, as they said, "men exalted; women scorned." But she hoped that our lives would be better. She wanted us to have enough learning to make good marriages. In contrast to ordinary mothers, who tried desperately to keep their daughters with them, she wished for us to leave home as soon as we could. In the meantime, she never allowed us to miss a day of school, even carrying us on her back when fever or exhaustion rendered us unable to walk.

I was very flighty myself. I'd leave my notebooks and brushes all over the place. She admonished me: "You must have respect for writing." And I would pretend to pick up my things. But, for her, the written word was sacred. Her father had been a man of letters, and she herself had a taste for reading. She was interested in the sciences and read thick tomes translated from foreign languages.[8] Although she had no education, her handwriting was lovely, firm and square.[9]

CALLIGRAPHY AND MARRIAGE

Every Saturday, Mother placed in my hand a calligraphy brush wrapped in a *hanshi*, a half slip of white paper and bound with a little cord of finely rolled paper. She said, "Go and offer this at the shrine of Tenjin-sama. Ask him for a good *hanryo*." Tenjin-sama was the same as the historic figure Sugawara no Michizane;[10] he was the god of calligraphy and knowledge. But as to what a *hanryo* was, I hadn't a clue. The other children also went to pray at the chapel of Tenjin-sama, on the edge of the village. We bickered among ourselves and pretended to swipe one another's brushes before we set them before the god. The god was a very black statue, with a high hat like those worn by nobles in the olden days, hidden at the back of a shack overgrown with moss. I clapped my hands before this Tenjin-sama and asked for a good *hanryo*, as Mother had instructed. On the way out, I picked up a brush from among those we had offered the preceding week.[11]

When I was thirteen and had for a short while been allowed to offer rice to the god of the hearth, I asked Mother about the *hanryo*. She looked at me gravely. "A *hanryo* is a companion, a spouse. Pray to the gods to give you a good husband, because your life will be sweet or harsh according to the house you enter in marriage.

"The brush that you give to Tenjin-sama signifies your desire to perform everything you do correctly. When you can form good characters with that brush, you will be an accomplished girl, ready to be married. A brush is a sacred object: never throw it on the ground, never tread on it, never step over it."

I understood for the first time that I would have to leave the house of Endo one day, to marry and enter another house.[12] That discovery made me afraid. So I told myself that perhaps I would not marry.

Since the age of six, every summer morning I went in a group to the shrine of *ubu-suna-gami*, the tutelary divinity of the village. It was a pretty wooden shrine; the wind and rain had turned the vermilion coating on the outside to brown. There we studied calligraphy under the direction of the master of the gods of Asaka.[13]

First, we placed before the altar a few grains of uncooked rice wrapped in a *hanshi*; then we clapped our hands three times to attract the attention of the gods to our offerings. Next, we had to sweep the veranda of the shrine before we sat down there, in the shade of the great thatched roof with its hair of wild grasses and flowers growing as heaven would have them. Brushes dedicated to Tenjin-sama, paper, ink sticks, inkstones, and water were all unpacked. The oldest girls drew large black characters on padded sheets. They would hold our arms to guide us in our first exercises.

The white gravel enclosure was surrounded by *asunaro*, trees that look like *hinoki* cypress.[14] *Asunaro* means "become tomorrow." People said that every night the trees sighed, "*Asu, hinoki to narō*, Tomorrow I will become a *hinoki*." When we wrote misshapen characters, the master of the *kami* would yell at us: "Try harder, girls! Don't be 'become tomorrows'!"

The master of the *kami* taught us that learning calligraphy is contained in its entirety in the character for "eternity." He told us that this word brings together the eight gestures of the way of writing. The first stroke, called *soku*, "the side," is the dot at the top, written with a slightly inclined brush. The second, *roku*, "the reins," is the horizontal stroke one makes by pulling the brush the way one reins in a horse. *Do*, "the crossbow," the third, is the vertical stroke that one pulls toward oneself with the gesture of a crossbowman. *Teki*, "the wing," or the fourth gesture, finishes this vertical stroke by leaping up to the left. Next comes *saku*, "the whip," a short horizontal stroke, which one performs as brusquely as if giving a horse a touch of the whip. To compose *ryaku*, "the caress," which extends this whipcrack toward the lower left, the brush must barely touch the paper, the way a woman smoothes her hair. *Taku*, which is written on the diagonal, from right to left, is "the pecking"; the movement is like the way a bird pecks at its food in the dirt. The last of these strokes, also called *taku*, but this time meaning "disunion," moves left to right, leaning casually like a body in defeat.

Ei, eternity.

"Later," the master said to conclude the lessons, "you will study the character *ichi*, because the learning of calligraphy culminates in the ability to write this single horizontal stroke, which means the number 1. It is the most difficult of all Chinese characters, the one that most exemplifies the perfect mastery of calligraphy."[15]

I loved calligraphy. The hand was never to rest on the paper but had to hold the brush in a gesture that involved the arm and, in fact, the way one held one's entire body. The student would trace a character eight thousand times, concentrate his mind on the movement that made him one with the paper, and, through repeated attempts, one day a stroke would come to be on that paper. And no one could say that he was not the true author of that stroke. To do calligraphy is to give birth to a sign that preexists some-where and that at last one has been able to uncover.

Unfortunately, I believed that lovely handwriting would force me into marriage. I didn't want to be marriageable. We called girls who were good marriage prospects *hako iri musume,* "maidens in a box," meaning that they would be sheltered until their wedding day. I didn't want to be closed up. People said in those days that the destiny of girls was to obey: first, their fathers; next, their husbands; finally, their eldest sons. I didn't want to obey. I told myself again and again that I would not marry. After I learned of the connection between calligraphy and marriage, I refused to go back and study calligraphy at the Shinto shrine. And I never again offered a brush to Tenjin-sama.

Mother looked sad. Even I envied my older sisters, who were turning into young women with small, very white hands and tapering fingers. Be-fore going to the shrine, they did their hair in the *momo-ware,* or split peach style, making a center part and rolling the hair high up at the back of the head, puffing it out at the temples. They would smile dreamily as they traced their Chinese characters. I myself refused all the trappings of girlish charms and still wore my hair tied at the neck with a rubber band. But, secretly, I collected hair ribbons.[16]

In fact, the softness of women horrified me. It suffocated me. Theirs was a world lined with felt, made of whispers, laughs repressed behind hands raised to the mouth, the sound of rustling fabric. My first menstruation terrified me. An unbearable violence lay in wait in the belly. Although they tried to hide it with elegant manners, it was ready to gush out through all the poorly sealed orifices of the body.

I took it out on Risa, my older sister by two years.

RISA

This sister, who was tender and fragile, never made any noise. She had skin that was as white and soft as a city girl's, and quarrels terrified her. When a fight would start, I would always stand in front of her. That gave me a sort of power over her life. Everyone believed that my older sister had a calming influence on my thoughtless behavior. But an incident that hap-pened while I was in my first year of middle school revealed the perverse nature of our relationship.

It was August, several days after *O-Bon.* The susuki trees were blooming along the roads,[17] and the wind chased the clouds across the sky. From the song of the morning nightingales to the song of those of the evening, I disappeared with my older sister, no one knew where. We came back that night cheeks aflame, vague looks in our eyes. No one would have noticed had the same thing not happened the next day, and the next.

Hidden away in the heart of the sacred woods, we played school. This in itself was not unusual, but I, the younger sister, played the teacher, while Risa played the student. This was abnormal. Informed by a female servant, Father called us to him and told us to switch roles immediately, in respect of our age difference. I feigned submission. But the next day, on the pretext that my sister played the role of teacher badly, I resumed my place behind the bundle of bamboo that served as a desk. From time to time, I pulled out a branch and pretended to beat my sister with it. That is how I scratched her cheek—a drop of blood trickled out and she screamed. They claimed I did it on purpose. Perhaps I did. But I defended myself by wailing louder than anyone. Finally, we were solemnly forbidden to play school.

It is not impossible that this prohibition secretly comforted me. My own daring frightened me: I had struck an older sister, yet the gods had not visited upon me any of those terrible skin diseases that are said to mark infamy. In fact, nothing happened. Or almost nothing: I wondered vaguely whether the order of the world was of so little importance that it could be trespassed without danger.

STARTING MIDDLE SCHOOL

The end of my childhood was difficult.[18] In my last year at the village primary school, I decided to become a teacher, because everyone said I would. To do that, I would have to study for four years in the Kōriyama middle school for girls in the upper grades: two more years than were required for ordinary children. After that I would have to go to the girls' high school. All children who had reached the age of eleven went to middle school, but, after the first year, some establishments were reserved for more gifted children, those who would continue their studies in specialized schools.[19] For me this entry into middle school was therefore of great importance. Besides, with my older sisters already engaged in that elite series of trials, I could not permit myself to fail. The shame alone would have killed me. So I worked at my studies like a soul in hell.

In Asaka, four of us, two boys and two girls—me and one of my cousins—were preparing for the entrance exam at the Morioka middle school in Kōriyama.

It was about an hour's walk to that school. The day of the test, I got up early. All I ate was one bowl of hot rice with a raw egg mixed in and some *nori*, then I waited for my cousin. She was early, too. Because she was in her school uniform, while I was dressed in a pink and white kimono, I wondered if I should change. After thinking about it, I said, "Too bad, I don't have time." And I slipped into my *geta* sandals, ready to leave the house. But Mother held us back, saying, "Remember last year, when your sister left too early. She waited in front of the school longer than she would have had to, and that tired her needlessly."

Mother poured us some green tea and gave us two quarters of an apple each. My cousin took *o-te-dama*, little beanbags that you juggle while singing, out of her bundle of possessions. And we became so absorbed in the game that we forgot everything else.

In the end, we got off to such a late start that the exams had already begun by the time we got to Kōriyama. They wouldn't let us in. So we stood and cried in the street for a while, then went back to Asaka. It was Father who met us, back at the house of Endo. He scolded us for laziness. He said that Mother had run all the way to Kōriyama as soon as she realized how late we were, and here we were, back again.

So we set off once more for the school, sobbing all the way. When we got there, we wandered around in the hallways. They were deserted. We didn't know what to do or where to go. Then, we heard Mother's voice. She was pleading with someone. We went closer. Dressed in the peasant garb she wore for housecleaning, not having even taken the time to untie the *tasuki* (the cord that kept her kimono sleeves tied back out of her way for housework), Mother had forced her way through the door of the director's office. She said in a loud voice that she was ashamed, that it was she who had kept us back! She said she didn't know how to begin to beg the forgiveness of two little girls who had studied so hard, for months, for nothing. Mother implored him. She bowed very low, that they might allow us to take the exams! That alone would assuage the shame she felt before us. She said, "I have come to prostrate myself to you, in the hope that you might hear my request. I don't dare ask that you give the girls grades, or that you accept them into the school, since the rules of the exam must be respected. But if you could just let them take the test, that would give some meaning to all the work they have done."

With my cousin, I stood in the waiting room outside the office. In there, an adult drama was going on of which I understood very little but which nonetheless concerned me. Mother was wailing on my behalf, but I felt nothing. Nonetheless, I knew that it was all my fault. I began to weep: gray, mechanical tears. Then Mother began to cry. I had never seen her shed a single tear. That upset me. I ran away, up the hall. They caught me and sat me down in a chair, offering me a handkerchief perfumed with musk. I disliked the scent.

The supplication went on a long time. Finally it was decided that all the teachers in the school would meet to decide how to handle the problem. One teacher, Mrs. Hakozaki, took Mother's side and pleaded her cause. She said, "What we want to do in this school is to educate women to be good wives, and not to force-feed knowledge that would be useless to future mothers." Mother was a model of this ideal, and they could not discount the exemplary character of what she had done.

That same afternoon we took the test. We were fairly unnerved by it all and could not have done very well. Like every year, the results were posted the following week, but we were not to be graded, so we didn't bother to look. Several days later, though, a letter came which Mother read to me, flushed with pleasure: because there had been dropouts, my cousin and I were to be accepted into the girls' school in Kōriyama. I jumped for joy and ran to announce the news to my teacher at my primary school in Asaka.

My teacher spoke only of Mother. She admired her courage. She asked me to thank her for what she had done. But no one said a word about my own success. I went back home annoyed, resolved never again to speak to that teacher at her little school.

The entrance ceremony took place some weeks later, at the beginning of April.[20] For the last time I was dressed in the *hakama* with the red lining. But that day I was so happy I barely noticed. They lined us up in the yard of the middle school. The teachers were introduced, and then, one by one, we said our names and bowed, and asked that others be kindly disposed toward us. People pointed at me, because I was already famous for the lateness incident. It seems that parents of children who were not accepted had protested, even demanding that the Endo girls be turned back. But the authorities stuck to their guns. As for me, I was pleased with this notoriety, which facilitated my entry into a world where the name of Endo meant less than it did in the village.

In spite of this remarkable beginning, I was not a good student. Having been born in January, I was one of the youngest in the class, and I was immature.[21] So my grades were mediocre. After four years, I left. I never went to high school. In any case, I had long before chosen another path.

The way middle school had started had left a bitter taste in my mouth. Mother was not the all-powerful Kannon I had thought her to be. She had debased herself, pleading with the authorities. She, usually so calm, had run down the road like a peasant woman, with her *tasuki* still binding the sleeves of her kimono. And she had wept. That day, I had a foreshadowing of a fragility that I wouldn't know in a definitive way until much later, during the war, when I came back to Asaka from Tokyo.

The middle school at Kōriyama (drawing by Shige).

That time, when I saw her again, she seemed thinner. Her eyes were sunken, and her chin jutted out. I thought, "Mother is an old woman." And it was as if my own body became detached from hers. Maybe it was simply that I had grown up.

At that moment, too, I understood that Mother had loved me very much. In Tokyo, during the long years of my apprenticeship, every month she sent me one yen that she took out of her secret savings, savings that we call hidden in the navel. When I fell sick, she cried. I felt indebted, perhaps guilty, for her struggles in my behalf. The money she had sent me, the tears she had shed for me: were those not the causes of her current fragility? Her body was lost in its dark gray, silver-threaded kimono. Had I destroyed Mother's body?

As time wore on, she grew still thinner, while my own body thickened with three pregnancies.

Mother didn't die like other people. She lived a very long time, and her body grew so small, she disappeared. They buried her on a windy, foggy day, under a gray sky. The news made me sad. I furtively thought that there was no one on this earth to cry for me now, no one before whom I would be capable of shame.

But I had run away from Mother, I had refused to study calligraphy and the pleasing arts. "And so you will be a teacher," she had said to me. But I always traveled the fantasy road of childhood dreams.

CHILDHOOD GAMES

I took refuge in games no longer suitable to my age. I would spend several hours each day with the group of little children from the east hamlet where we lived. But by the age of ten or eleven, I should have left their childish amusements behind.

I still played *take-uma*, "bamboo horse," or stilts, with the boys, and I worked a top with far more passion than I did a calligraphy brush. With the girls, it was hopscotch. I didn't much care for playing house, but I was very adept at making cat's cradles: I mastered Shinto shrine gates, pine needles, and the fish and the river. Sometimes we would swim half-naked in streams. In the village, we would await the little bell of the sweets merchant, who carried a great platter full of candies and paper pinwheels on his head. He would go everywhere, making a great noise and fuss, striking his drum and moving his large fan in every direction.

In Kōriyama, where we went for the *ennichi*, the festivals of the gods and buddhas, when the the fair stalls took over the streets around the monastery, we would buy blue or red demon masks and firecrackers, which we'd set off at night on the verandas. Here we found both large and small *hōzuki*, those Japanese bladder cherries filled with black seeds that I would plant later, for my own pleasure, in a corner of the garden. When their fruits became ripe, I would pick them one by one and stuff them in my mouth. When I bit down on them, they made a funny noise. I also liked *kamishibai*, the paper theater: a traveling showman would call us to come and watch by knocking his wooden clackers together. Enthralled, I would watch the most furious battles of our history unroll before my eyes. I would eat grilled sweet potatoes, which the vendor handed over burning hot, wrapped in a piece of newsprint. Their skin was blackened; their flesh melted in my mouth.

By the age of twelve, all that had ceased to interest me. Nonetheless, as soon as I got out of school, I would throw my uniform aside and slip into my cotton crepe kimono. I would go outside, barefoot. My older sisters said that I had passed the age when I could parade around in bare feet. They spent two hours a day sewing their trousseaux, and they changed clothes for every occasion, thereby demonstrating their charm and aptitude for marriage. I watched them secretly, a little forlorn, and then I went out into the fields to adorn my ankles with slimy brown mud.

RITUAL MOTHERS

Sometimes my milk mother—the mother of a boy baby of my exact age, who had given me my first suck—would see me in the village. She would call out: "Nami-chan! You're too big, listen to me! Haven't you offered rice to Kōjin-sama by now?" I stopped. My cheeks would become very red. She would invite me to her house, and I would follow without a word. She would serve me tea with pink and green sweets. Then out of a drawer of her *tansu* dresser, she would take hair ribbons, with which she would tie up bouncing piles of curls in my shiny, thick hair. Holding my hair at the top of my head, she would say, "You have a well-made nape. You will be beautiful!" I was flattered; a fine nape and beautiful hair were the greatest signs of beauty. I would laugh, shaking my head to make my hair fall back down, and then I would scream at her, forcing myself to get angry: "I will not! *Otoko onna da!* I'm a tomboy, I should have been a boy!" But I would always take the ribbons home with me and bury them in a drawer. I especially loved those that were the color of water, because their cold pallor helped play down the unsuitable tan of my skin. From time to time, my older sisters would find my ribbons, but I always refused to lend them out.

During that period, the end of childhood, I often went to visit the *tori-age-bābā*, the old midwife who'd brought me into the world and not only on days when I was expected to, like the New Year, but whenever I was bored in our big house. She would give me grilled flour cakes wrapped in *nori* and tell me strange stories. Although she must have told me the story of my own birth a hundred times, I asked her to tell it again. "You were still all dirty from being born, when the factory whistles of Kōriyama began to scream. You were a girl. So your mother, whose belly you had deci-mated . . . "

"And then?" I asked. She spoke of blood and births. She said that a woman who had cheated on her husband once gave birth to a snake.[22] The husband pinned it to the ground with the point of his sword. The woman cried out in despair for hours and then died. Another woman screamed for three days and three nights, because her child was trying to come out of her mouth. They had to open her belly up and pull the breech baby out by the feet. I said, "That's not true!" She said to me, "What if it is? You'll see, when it's your turn to be a mother."

But, in my heart, I had decided not to become a mother. I wanted to escape the horrible destiny of women. "I'm not going to get married. I won't have any children!"

I told her so one day. She said, "But who will make *kuyō* offerings for you? Who will pray for you after you die? Your spirit will never attain enlightenment. You will become a wandering soul, a *mu-en-botoke*, a 'dead one without ties'! A *gaki*, a starving demon! And you will cling to the living to feed off them."

When I was ten or eleven, I realized that she herself had no children. And from that day on, I never really believed her stories. Still, like a moth captivated by a light, I would say, "Again!" And she would tell me, one after another, about all the births in the village.

THE O-MORI: THE GUARDIAN

I stopped seeing my *o-mori*, my guardian, when I was twelve. At our house, each of the children had his own personal guardian, an adopted child nine years older than he. Since the house of Endo was rich, people from the area often came to borrow money, land, or seeds. As a pledge for their debt, they placed one of their children or the child of a relative even poorer than they, who wished to reduce the number of mouths to feed, in the big house. So at the age of about nine, these children came to live with us. These were called *yori-ko*, the brought children.[23]

In Asaka, people said that it was from the age of nine that children have the strength to work, since the number of years of their life is then equal to the number of teeth in a harrow, as well as the number of pillars in the Imperial Palace in Kyoto. And it takes nine months for a child to come into the world. All of which makes it obvious that nine is a sound number.[24] The harrow was attached to a horse's nose and connected to a guide pole: a child would walk two steps in front of the animal, holding the pole in his hand. It was a task that a nine-year-old could easily perform. In a time when there was a such a dire need for hands, they might have enlisted the family cat for his paws! He alone stayed home and grew fat for nothing.

Ma-guwa, harrow.

At our house, the brought children didn't work in the fields. We had plenty of labor without them! But as we couldn't refuse all the people who counted on us to take care of their children, we adopted them so they could watch over the newborns of the house. That is how each one of us received, at the moment of birth, an *o-mori*. Today that seems like an extraordinary luxury, but, at that time, we all thought it worked out fine.

I myself was raised by a boy—not a girl, as is the custom. If I was a tomboy, perhaps that is because, as they say, children bear a closer resemblance to their *o-mori* than they do to their parents.

My *o-mori*, whose name was Toshirō, came from the region of Sendai, in the north, some weeks after my birth. He was a tall, skinny boy with eyes too round and hands too long. But he knew how to do everything. He would make me little sailboats of *sasa*, single dwarf bamboo leaves, which we would set adrift on the rice paddy canals. He carved me a jointed doll, also of bamboo, which he named Take-chan, which means both "bamboo" and "valorous." I dragged Take-chan around with me for three months. And then, after I had worn him out completely, I offered him on the grave of a boy who had died at the age of six. Where he was, it no longer mattered whether the doll was whole or not.[25]

The *o-mori* taught me how to catch bell crickets, grasping them by the middle of the back. We would put them in reed cages and feed them with little cubes of eggplant. "You have to take eggplants with spots on them," he would tell me. "They belong to the gods, and people can't eat them." This was thriftiness, of course, but he explained everything that way, very poetically.[26] And the bell crickets would sing for several evenings in the autumn before I would wake to find them lying on their backs, their abdomens caved in and covered with filth.

I was eleven when he brought me back a pair of *geta* clogs with leather thongs from the city. He said, "Now your sisters won't make fun of you anymore." I bowed politely to thank him. The other children had *geta* with straw or bamboo-leaf thongs, and even the adults had cloth ones. I was so proud of those *geta* that I never took them off. I would run down the stone walkway of the garden in them, clop, clop. The leather was a little stiff; it rubbed blisters on the tops of my feet for a long time before a callus formed.

Until they reached adulthood, the brought children received a small salary, which was deducted from their families' debts. Of course, they were fed and lodged as well. In principle, military service would mark the end of the contract between the house of their birth and their adopted house, but in fact we weren't so uncaring as to abandon the brought children in that way.[27] Father wasn't *mizu-kusai*, one of those people, as we said, whose hearts smell cold and metallic as water.

Once they had finished their service, the *o-mori* would return to the house of Endo. They would bow to the altar of our ancestors and to Father, and ask him once again to become their *oya-kata*, like a parent. We would find them good wives and give them money to build houses. When they were established, they would continue to work for us as sharecroppers, and, to thank us, they would give us several days of free labor a year. We treated the o-mori like younger brothers.

At the New Year and the feast of the dead, they would put on clean clothes and come to the house to greet Father. They would bow before our gods and our ancestors, and we would serve them sake. For festivals, they would help pound and form mochi cakes in the form of mirrors. In the spring, they would work for us during plowing time and then again for transplanting and the harvest. They also gathered mulberry leaves for the silkworms.

But my o-mori, Toshirō, was very intelligent. He never became a share-cropper. Like my oldest brother, he went to Tokyo to pursue higher studies.

Before that, until I was ten, we were almost never apart. He would carry me on his back. We would visit relatives of his who lived in the neighboring village. I always greeted them politely. We would sit by the hearth in a small, dark room in which voracious flies swarmed noisily. The mistress of the house, the wife of his father's older brother, would serve us tea with a few slices of pickled radish arrayed on two white saucers on which the brine left yellow traces (we amused ourselves by interpreting these like auguries). That thin woman with her pointed nose had skin as wrinkled as a dried-up winter radish.

One day, I brought her a gift of white sugar from the big house; we sometimes ate it at the house of Endo. She went to fetch the grandmother. She told her that they were going to give her a taste of white sugar, because she couldn't have had any very often. Broken by overwork, she dragged herself in, leaning on one pointed elbow. The orbs of her eyes were filled with the darkness of the house, which she never left now because she was blind. The old woman stroked my hair with her hand, deformed like a chicken claw, and she told Toshirō that he must be sure to take good care of me. We sucked on the white sugar while drinking tea.

The grandmother died a few weeks later. My parents sent a little money to Toshirō's family. I went and left some white sugar on her grave, because she was nice. At least she had eaten it once before she died. She had liked that.

By the time I was twelve, I hadn't needed an o-mori for some time. Besides, since Toshirō was pursuing studies, and in the evening worked the fields; he didn't have time for me anymore. Nonetheless, that was the year of our last outing together: we went fishing.

It was the beginning of summer. When the sixth moon came, the god of the rice paddies went away and the season of fishing followed that of sowing and transplanting. From that day until the 210th night after *risshun*, the first day of spring, fish abounded in the streams. On the 210th night, there would be a great wind, which would bring back the *kami* of the fields and announce the beginning of harvest. Fishing would be ended. And so the world was well planned; the seasons and the gods succeeded one another harmoniously.

In general, it was women and old people, who no longer worked in the fields, who went fishing. But at our house, no one had the leisure for it. Mother did not have six hands, and our grandmother suffered from rheumatism. As for my older sisters, they were far too busy with their hope chests. But in the streams up in the hills, at dawn or dusk, there were salmon, char, crucian, trout, and carp for the taking.

One day when the Abukuma River had overflowed its banks at the bottom of the valley, Toshirō woke me early to go fishing upstream, in a mountain brook that flowed into the Abukuma.

The weather was gray and heavy. Toshirō walked fast, and my *geta* hurt my feet. I was panting. He took me on his back as he ran on the walkway. Then he suddenly dumped me on the ground. I twisted my ankle. But he sat me down gently by the edge of the stream. The water was full of the yellow mud of the rainy season. From a bag Toshirō took some small pieces of silvery fish that he had stuck on fishhooks. And he showed me how to hold the line between my thumb and forefinger. We caught some char with yellow fins, spotted with foam and rust.

As time passed, I got bored. I kicked off my *geta* and dipped my feet in the water to attract all the trout in the stream. None came, but the water froze my calves like the bite of icy jaws, and they turned as red as red spider lilies. They burned when I took them out of the water. Toshirō called me a rotten brat, then began to rub my legs with a rag. The rag stank of fish, and I screamed that it was disgusting and hit him with my fists. He grabbed my wrists and tied them together with the dirty rag. I felt stupid. I made the face of Butchō-zura, the surly expression of Amida Buddha like that which appears at the top of Kannon's hair. That got on his nerves. He threatened to throw back the fish, to give them to *suijin-sama*, the god of the water. I screamed he should do it: "Go ahead! *Suijin-sama* will give them back to me in gold!" He tossed one fish in the river. But no matter how I begged all the gods, they gave me nothing.[28] I felt ridiculous, as one does at such times, and I forced myself to laugh so it wouldn't show so much.

We brought back the wriggling char, and that evening we grilled them on sticks over the hearth. Grandfather and Grandmother, the family and the serving girls: everybody ate some.

At the New Year, we would have salted salmon. In the spring, sardines.

The latter we also used year-round, once they were dried, to make broth with soy sauce and floating *konbu* seaweed. Sometimes, instead of *konbu*, we'd use *kajime*, which grows on the northern coasts: this long, brown seaweed, spotted like a snake's skin, has the consistency of new leather. But fresh fish was rare in Asaka, even in a house like ours. Not to mention those poorer houses where they ate rice with daikon or sweet potatoes three times a day with nothing but miso soup and pickled vegetables.[29]

That evening, as usual, the workers were seated in the entryway on the earthen floor, while the family was next to the hearth. The serving girls had taken out the *hako-zen*, box platters on which everyone's place settings were arranged. We silently turned over their covers, which served as plates, and on them we placed bowls, saucers, and chopsticks. Two maids brought rice, soup, fish, and salted vegetables, which Mother served to everyone. She ate very little and kept a close watch on the girls' good manners. My older brother ate two bowls of rice. Father slurped his soup noisily, his large back hunched over; he held both his bowl and his chopsticks in one hand. Then he rested his chopsticks with a clinking sound on the cover of his bowl, cleared his throat, and, without looking at me, said, "You're becoming useful. We can marry you off soon." And those words, which normally would have made me crazy, flattered me instead. I blushed; I felt important.

Later, as my sisters were sleeping, I watched the light coming in through the partially closed shutters. It formed a pale band on the translucent paper of the shoji screen. I got up, careful not to step over my sleeping sisters, as Mother had always forbidden that, saying, "Never step over books or people." I gently opened the shoji and fixed my gaze on the opening between two rain shutters. It was a clear night, without stars. The moon shone like a pearl. For the first time, I felt I had a destiny.

5

Exclusion

女は三界に家なし

Onna wa sangai ni ie nashi.
Woman is without a house, in all three worlds.

Haji wo shiranai kodomo wa nonki na mono de gozaimasu . . . Children are care-free, because they know no shame. Tightly bound in their carrying har-nesses of cloth, they go from hand to hand, from back to back, then from shoulder to shoulder, and, even before they can walk, they discover the ground. Adults guide their movements by example, until the day the little ones try the gestures of their elders on for size, lips pursed in comical in-tensity.

From the moment I began to toddle, my *o-mori,* Toshirō, stuck a rag doll on my back. At that time of day when spiderwebs still hang across the roads, I would run, stumbling, through the shrine of *ubu-suna-gami-sama,* the god of the village. My hair in tangles, I would play there, watched over by gods and men. Advancing on the road of life without a regret or a thought, ignoring the existence of pain and sadness in the world, I simply grew, rich in the freedom of having no tasks to perform.

I think I acquired a vague sense of the importance of the Endos very early. When children from other families called me Endo Mame, which means "bean," because I was small and round, I told them that they were morons and that the Endos were the greatest family of all. They made fun of me: "Look at the little bean, blowing on a conch shell and bragging!" So I would shrug and—never one to hide the slightest thought I harbored in my heart—say that one day I'd show them.

CONFORMITY

When I was about seven, I felt a true pride in living. The joy of being born an Endo ruled my behavior, which I wished to be as straight and true as the blade of a sword. I had a sense of the absolute rightness of conformity

81

and spared no effort to scrupulously perform what people seemed to expect of me. The slightest gestures of daily life filled my spirit, and the correct order of things afforded me a feeling of personal perfection. In Kōriyama, I bought a large notebook in which I noted all my activities in minute detail, day after day.[1]

I kept the journal throughout my childhood. Over the years, I set up three categories, one for each of the settings in which my life took place. I described first of all the activities of the family, how they dealt with one another under our roof, the names of our guests, domestic incidents. That intimate sphere constituted the kernel of my existence; it was a closed reality, solid, incontestable, in which everyone's glances crisscrossed without end, forming a soft, cushioned barrier around me. Every morning, I would carefully fold my futon in thirds, so it would slide into the cupboard without having to be pushed with either knee or foot. When I knotted my belt so that the two ends were absolutely equal in length, when I filled the cast-iron kettle just exactly enough, or when I bowed to my oldest brother just a bit lower than I would have naturally, I felt approving looks fix on me. So I said to myself, "You do things the way they should be done." This filled me with an exultant sense of peace.

But outside the house, the network of eyes on me seemed to slacken. I often went to visit my milk mother, the old midwife, and others. But still, in spite of my known status as an Endo girl, a feeling of ignorance, a kind of absence, ripped gaping holes in the space around me. There, life was mutable, like a reflection in water. Troubled, I forced myself to define the rules for the outside by creating a personality.

The contemplation of nature seemed to me particularly worthy of the status that had been conferred on me by my birth. And I was more than willing to take the time to meditate on the delicacy of a peony moist with dew, or the form of a bicolored cloud, to listen at twilight to the rustling of the *higurashi*, the evening cicadas. Sometimes I would compose verse for such occasions, lines so poor that they couldn't even be called poems.

> *Yama e itte,*
> *O Jizō-sama no mae e itte . . .*

> Going to the mountains,
> Going to see Jizō,
> The backs of the ferns are bent . . .

Those words came to me one spring day when I was in the mountains, when the leaves and the grasses were still yellow and pink. I gathered young ferns that had overgrown a stele dedicated to Jizō-sama, the bodhisattva who, always dressed as a monk, watches over dead children. The ferns' tender crosiers looked to me like the faces of the poor innocents in profile. Moved, my song on my lips, I added a stone to the top of a collapsed pile of stones by the side of the stele, which depicted the smiling Indian monk. But the next day, when I put these words down in my notebook, I realized that they were the first stanza of a fern-gathering song I had learned when, with my sisters, I had gone to gather a basketful of wild herbs for pickling. Then I remembered the rest of it:

> *Warabi, warabi, naze koshi kogonda?*
> *Oya no hi ni zeze kute*
> *Sore de koshi kogonda!*

> Fern, O Fern, why is your back bent so?
> On Parents' Day, you counted your pennies
> That's why your back is bent!

It was just a common song! I crossed out my poem, for a moment cursing the gods for not having made me a poet, one of those great poets who write of a world in which vulgarity is unthinkable.

The last category of my journal had to do with school. In that world—for I was then in middle school, where the name Endo had no particular significance and the chance looks of others moved over my body without seeing me—my breast filled with a horrible sense of unreality, which then rose to my lips. Only the flat sentences I wrote in my green notebook made it all bearable.

For a long time, I kept that journal as a souvenir of those happy years when I believed that my name justified my presence in the world.[2] And then, when I understood that the name of Endo and all other names were reserved for boys, I threw it out.

It was as if the world had become detached from me.

OTOKO NO SEKAI: A MAN'S WORLD

We girls and women had no decision-making power whatsoever. To make pronouncements was a male prerogative. And leadership was conferred on only a few of the very best men at that.

Twice annually, at the beginning of the year and at the end of summer, when the living dance for the dead, the heads of all the households in the area would gather at the shrine or elsewhere to plan the future of the village. Father always sat in the choicest seat, beside the mayor. He was the leader chosen from among the houses of Kitai to represent them at this assembly. Should we extend the rice paddy irrigation system farther west? Rethatch the roof of the eldest Tanaka son's house, or that of the house of the younger Tanabe? That was the sort of thing they talked about. Often, Father's opinion swayed the group.

It was his task to bring everyone into agreement. He would invite the masters of the houses of the eastern part of the village to our house. They would spend hours in the *zashiki* (inner room), smoking and drinking as they drew up the plans for the future. Mother would heat sake from Aizu, her ancestral region, which she served in priceless cups of Kutani ceramic with green and chestnut brown designs. She would bring in dried fish, salty fresh-boiled soybeans on the vine, and preserved vegetables arranged on delicate plates.

That kind of hospitality was not cheap, and sometimes the courtesy of an expensive gift was needed to attain someone's consent. Father would call to Mother: "*Oi!* What happened to the seaweed from Sado?" He would make a show of looking around for it. Mother would enter discreetly; at each step the front panels of her kimono opened slightly with a gentle rustling of silk. She would bow several times, smiling; then she would kneel and, rolling back her sleeves with their gray and blue striped linings, place a box before Father, wrapped in a *furoshiki* of violet-colored silk. Father would take the package from the fabric without even untying the knot. With a brusque movement, he would slide it across the table in front of everyone, until it reached the place of the guest. The latter would have no choice but to accept, and then to accede to Father's will.

But when the matter was more difficult or the guest too important to force his hand in that simple way, it was Mother who would offer him the gift when he turned around to face her. She would say to him, bowing deeply, "This is for your wife. Tell her that this seaweed comes from Hokkaido. It is rich in vitamins." To that end, we always kept boxes of fresh or dried delicacies in the *nando*, the storeroom, ready to be given as gifts. The other houses in Asaka could afford to give only local products, or those from Kōriyama. These rare gifts were another sign of the power of the Endos.

At our house, as everywhere in the hamlet, Father had authority over everyone under the roof. During meals, he sat at the *yoko-za,* and Mother would prepare special dishes for him. Only Father would get to eat the large beef steaks they sometimes sold in Kōriyama.[3] And he would swallow them in great gulps, smothered in butter. The stench of the meat nauseated me, while Father would wolf it down, licking his chops. That sight made an impression on me. For days afterward I would be afraid to go near him, and when it was my turn to have a bath after he and my older siblings had

had theirs, I would examine the water for the drops of blood which I was sure would be clouding it.

As heir to the house, my oldest brother, Yoshiharu, was educated with special care. Father wanted him to study German, but at that time that was very difficult because there were so few books. One time, Father told Mother to serve my oldest brother meat, too. He must have been around twenty, because I remember a light down covered his cheeks. Mother cut the meat in thin rosy slices and handed him a pair of Chinese chopsticks made of precious wood. My oldest brother contemplated the plate for a long time, then, without looking left or right, he ate the meat, chewing a lot. A yellow sweat came out on his forehead and temples. As soon as he had finished, he pushed his plate from him and cried out, a little louder than necessary, "*Gochisō sama deshita!* It was a feast!" Then he drank sake for the first time in his life. His eyes became a little red, like those of the peasants at the end of those long winter evenings when the cold has etched white lines around their eyes and mouths. The next week, Father took him, alone, to Kōriyama. My older sister told me they visited some geisha.[4]

Mother always told me I had to speak politely to my oldest brother. I was never to speak to him on the run but should stop and softly address him: "*Onī-san*, Older Brother." It's true he was much older than I. When Father turned sixty, he would inherit the house with its altars, and he would wear our crest, the Chinese character for "strength," 力 adopted by our family in memory of our esteemed ancestors. In that way, through him, the life of the house would go on unchanged from generation to generation, like the waters of the Abukuma, which will flow forever.

MURA NO SABAKI: VILLAGE JUSTICE

During one summer, which I remember very clearly because the trees had turned a shockingly intense, dark blue, a violent quarrel arose between the Sugimoto brothers (who had such a name because their house was near the stump of an old Japanese cedar, or *sugi*, on the road out of town). The younger brother, who was called Tasuke, was thin and ugly, with a very dark face and pale, empty eyes in which everything was reflected, even the colors of the earth. People said he was argumentative and jealous, incapable of being content with his lot. The skin on his hands was blistered, as if he had just escaped from the caldron of hell.

When Tasuke had married, his father had given him a house and a parcel of land to the west. It was more than enough land to support his family, if he worked at it. However, when the boards of his house came unjoined, he did not find it in himself to hammer a single nail to fix them. What's more, as he refused to help the other members of his work group, or *yui*, weeds overgrew his roof, his field came to be badly farmed, and if he fell sick no one came to his aid.[5] Because men cannot live without others, he had little by little dragged his family down into misery, sadness, and dearth.

During that summer of maddening heat, the village assembly decided to build a road which was to encroach on Sugimoto Tasuke's field. They proposed to give him a new parcel in exchange, one far from the village but bigger. He refused. The older brother tried to bring him to reason, but people said that they quarreled, and that it went from words to blows. The older brother had two of his fingers broken. Harvesttime was imminent; he wouldn't be able to work for days, and his son wasn't old enough to help.

The affair was brought before the village leaders. In the old days, the younger brother would have been condemned to village ostracism (*mura hachibu*), the worst of punishments (which was reserved for those who don't respect the rules of life—stubborn people, thieves, and arsonists). In those days, almost all relations, all ties of mutual aid with such offenders, would have been cut. The two exceptions to this rule would have been if their houses caught fire, since the fire could spread to other houses; and funerals, because death is the beginning of a new life in which the faults of the old life may be forgiven. And, besides, an unburied body could bring bad luck.

While the village leaders could have ostracized him, his brother had suffered only two broken fingers. Anyway, ostracism was already outmoded, since by that time people changed houses, or villages, the way they used to switch to lighter clothing on the first days of summer.

Father summoned the younger Sugimoto for a talk. The latter remained standing in the entryway of our house, because a man this stripped of honor didn't have the right to come into the rooms where we received people. I saw him from a distance. He stood there immobile, stiff, his chin held defiantly high. Meanwhile, seated next to the hearth, Father spoke. His lips moved more than usual. I couldn't hear what he was saying. I later learned that he had proposed a compromise: the offender would perform twenty days of labor for his older brother, and he would treat the assembly of village leaders to sake. Also, for one whole year, he would dig all the graves for the village.

I saw Sugimoto Tasuke only once more. He was working in one of his brother's fields. I started to approach him and say hello, or some pleasantry, when I saw that half his head was shaved. His head was very long, bullet-shaped. He looked at me as if he didn't recognize me. Frightened by his air of bewilderment and rottenness, I beat a quick retreat.

He died three months later. The gods finally took pity on him. His wife was taken back into the family of her birth, along with the children, except the oldest boy, who was adopted into the family of the older Sugimoto brother. But he too turned out badly, so true is it that families have a destiny and that that of the younger branch of the Sugimotos was nearing its end.

Father lamented the affair for a long time. In the evening, after he had been drinking, he would say, "That decision about the road was wrong-headed. One must never make a decision that is not unanimous." And people blamed the heat, which drove everyone mad.

This story frightened me greatly. I thought that if I refused my fate the way the younger Sugimoto did, they would cast me out of society. Then, as a sign of my infamy, my face would turn as dark as his. My skin would be covered with blisters, like that of a toad.[6] Everyone would see at first glance that I was a bad girl. And that was terrifying.

ONNA NO SHIGARAMI: THE DESPAIR OF WOMEN

I knew by then that, like all girls, I would have to leave the Endos. But the day of my departure was still so far off that I didn't yet feel I had to think about it. Then, all of a sudden, the door of my childhood slammed shut with a bang.

The way it came about is very strange. At the beginning, it was only a tiny incident, a stupid blunder.

One morning when I was bored at school, daydreaming, I began to nibble on *senbei*, salty little shrimp-flavored rice crackers I had bought on the way to school. My teacher, Mrs. Hakozaki, asked me to hand them over. Without thinking, I stuffed a fistful into my mouth before I stood up. And, my cheeks puffed out like those of a squinty-eyed baby at the breast, unable to speak a single word, I deposited the half-empty package on her desk. That was all.

Mrs. Hakozaki looked stunned. She said, "You must have left the house without enough to eat this morning," and sent me home.

I dawdled all the way home, but I still arrived earlier than usual. Mother asked me, "Are you sick?" I said nothing for a moment; then, mumbling stubbornly, my eyes darting left and right, I told the pitiful tale.

Mother served me tea and cakes. While I ate, vaguely disturbed by her calm, she went into the room where we honored the gods and buddhas. There, in a voice that was only slightly sad, monotonous even, but loud enough for me to hear, she reported my misdeed to the ancestors. She said, "Nami-chan doesn't understand that she is grown now, although all her sisters have understood it. I must have raised her badly, since she throws shame on our name. Forgive me, it's all my doing!"[7] And in an instant I understood the vileness of my behavior. I knew that there was nothing more odious in this world than the parody of innocence, and I felt shame. It was like something that had long dwelt within me. I hadn't seen it, I had thought it was a sort of parasite, and I had wanted to rid myself of it. And then, heavily, that shame and the fear of that shame settled together in my heart. I'd already heard it a hundred times: I was a big girl now. Everyone kept saying to me, "Don't play so much with the boys. They have work to do and must study so they can succeed." Or "Don't just chatter on about nothing. Say only things that are beautiful or useful." And "Stop squirming like a child."

I had never paid attention to the meaning of these phrases I heard daily. But here they were, suddenly gathered together like a flock of migratory birds at the end of fall, swirling and squawking in my head: "You're grown now, yet you don't conform to your destiny." I knew very well what that destiny was. I had known that I could not remain an Endo because I was a girl, but now the time for that separation was coming without my having spent a single day in preparation for it.

The fate of my younger brother seemed terribly enviable. He would receive a small plot of our land, just as Father's younger brother had. Even though he would have to leave our house, he would keep our name. And his separate house would remain tied to ours for as long as he wished, because, even when they became independent, separate branches still belonged to the *maki*, the same group of houses. If he wouldn't be rich, at least he would remain near his ancestors, whom he would come to honor in rain, storm, or sunshine, whenever he wished.[8]

But for me everything was different, since I was only a girl. Of course, when I married, my new family would form ties of *shinrui* with the house of Endo. But those ties would never have the strength of blood ties. They would be but temporary attachments, destined to be extinguished with my own existence. The chains of life created by women disappear when they die.[9]

I wondered if the Endos had ever really wanted me. I had been a whiny baby. Because Mother hadn't had much milk, I had been cut off from the breast at three months and nursed on rice water. Was it that which had made me unhappy, or did I feel a need to train my voice? Whatever it was, I had screamed every day. That was how I learned to talk.

In my second year, I already knew quite a few words, but I still had no desire to walk. My *o-mori*, Toshirō, tried to teach me, but I preferred to totter, just missing tumbling into the fire and breaking my neck. One day, he tried to get me to sit on my heels. I fell backward and screamed louder than the rooster of hell. Of course, my *o-mori* should have stood behind me to keep me from falling over, but I was unharmed, and nothing justified that inglorious racket.

My grandmother decided to take me to a physician-monk in Kōriyama. He massaged the crown of my head and burned moxa on my wrist, which warmed me up a little. Then he rested his hand on my mouth. I grabbed that hand, trying to bite it. All of sudden, he said, "It is over." And he showed my grandmother a *mushi*, a little white worm that had come up from the bottom of my insides. He explained, "There, the evil has left. From now on, she won't cry anymore." And from that time, apparently, I began to look, and act, more like a girl.[10]

"That was lucky," my grandmother often said to me later, "because if we hadn't been able to purge you of your anger in that way, we might well have given you away. You wore out your parents' ears so, they thought about adopting you into another family. If I hadn't been there, no doubt you would not have been an Endo."

Now, sitting in front of my tea and hearing my mother greet the ancestors, tears mounted from my chest to my throat and eyes, tears such as I had never cried before; they flowed effortlessly. I thought they wouldn't stop until I died. I felt my cheeks with my fingertips, then I licked them. These tears seemed sweeter than ordinary, almost sugary, nauseating. I wanted to vomit from sadness.

Mother returned to my side. She said, "There really is nothing to cry about. Just be aware that you are beyond the age when you may behave like a child. Stop running around so much outside, and think about us a little more."

I stayed there, seated in front of my bowl of tea.

It was at that moment, just after the autumn equinox when the ancestors came from the other side of the world to ours, that melancholy settled in my heart. Like a fragile bird, it made itself a nest there, that it might grow and remain for a long time.

In winter, I asked Mother if I would be buried in the Endo cemetery. She told me no, that I would go with my in-laws.

"But that would be as if my life didn't count for anything! I don't want death to cut the ties of my life, not ever!"

She explained to me that it wasn't like that: "Your real ties will no longer be those that unite you with the house of Endo, but those that you will make with the house of your husband. You will venerate his ancestors, who will become your ancestors. And you will perpetuate the ties that have been granted you in that way, in your children."

"Then I won't be anything to you anymore?"

"Of course you will. We'll visit each other often. I'll look after your children."

I told myself that, since I had to die, there was no use in living. Only eternity had any meaning. Maybe it would even be better if there was nothing at all, because the rest was trickery, a terrifying illusion of happiness. The only eternity for me was that of our line, which would continue forever through the sons and their sons. But we girls belonged to other lines. Once we left Father's house, we'd never have another, ever. A woman had no more existence than those mayflies that live for three days, just barely enough time to reproduce. They are noticed only by chance, like the transparent insects that gather in clouds around lamps on summer evenings, singeing their wings. The next morning, there is nothing left but a fringe of tiny gray cadavers on the ground, like seaweed abandoned on a rocky shore by the highest wave. People sweep them up with wet tea leaves, so their bodies don't spot the tatami—to make sure not a trace is left of them.

Once a month, the little girls of the village would gather with the old women from the sorority of *nenbutsu*. The eldest among us would question them about our destiny. The old women, their Buddhist rosaries tangled in their knotted fingers, would say to us: "When a girl marries, her parents break her rice bowl on the doorstep of the house of her birth, as they do for the dead. Their daughter is dead to them; she no longer belongs to any but her husband's house.

"When there is a birth," they would cry, "we have to ask the parents, 'Is it a girl?' In that way, if the answer is the unfortunate one, they can respond simply, 'Yes, you are right,' without having to pronounce the word 'girl' at all. That relieves them of the embarrassment one feels when one has to announce sad news."

They taught us songs, too:

> *Gogatsu hitotsuki naku ko ga hoshi ya.*
> *Aze ni tatasete koshi sarasu!*

> I want a baby that will cry all through the fifth moon.
> I'll prop it up on the rice paddy walkway, and rest my back!

Throughout the fifth month, which is the month for transplanting the rice shoots, women are constantly bent over for days and even weeks in the flooded paddies. At that time, only a crying baby is a suitable pretext for standing up straight for a moment.

"A wife," the old women would say, "is no more than a beast of burden!"

We would protest: "But we'll often go back to our birth houses!"

They would answer: "Your first visit back will be seven days after your wedding. Your sisters and mothers will ask you how you are without even daring to look at you. As for your fathers and brothers, they will make it clear that after all you've cost the family, you've left none too soon. And that you should leave again even sooner. They'll be thinking, 'Good riddance!' You'll come back next for the New Year, the equinoxes, and at *O-Bon* to greet the ancestors of the house of your birth. But you will never spend the night, because the rules of marriage forbid you to sleep even one night under the roof of your blood ancestors. And so, you'll be gone from there quick! Quick!"[11]

The old women laughed at our fear. They said, "*Onna no yo da*, That's the world of women, that's life!"

When I asked Mother about it, she murmured that I was well-born and didn't have to worry; what the old women said applied to poor people. She reassured me: "*Kakaku no takai ie ni.* We'll marry you into a good house.[12] We'll spend whatever it takes. You'll go with enough pretty kimonos to last you at least ten years. When you come back here after your wedding, I'll unpin your married lady's chignon; I'll wash and smooth out your long hair. We are not so poor that the marriages of a few girls will ruin us. And besides, when you have children, I will give your sons warrior dolls and *koi-nobori*, carp banners.[13] I will give your girls emperor and empress dolls, complete with all their musicians and serving women."

I told my friends, "What the old ladies say applies only to the poor."

One of my friends' older brothers succeeded his father. The night before the parents were to move into the retirement house, before the evening meal, the mother called the daughter-in-law to her. She solemnly stated, "You have adapted yourself to the *kafū*, the customs of the house. Now your miso soup is as good as mine." She placed a new rice-serving paddle on top of a new rice pot. The daughter-in-law bowed, and, her forehead pressed to the tatami, she thanked her and accepted the pot and the paddle. And since, from that moment on, she had the right to manage the household as she saw fit, she had miso brought from Nagano, her native region. It was a miso as red as the earth west of the village, and as thick as rice gruel. My friend's oldest brother laughed a lot that night and drank more sake than usual. The house had become very joyous.[14]

While that story reassured me, I still sometimes told myself, "If I never marry, they'll have to keep me here, in the house of Endo. I won't take up any room. They'll forget about me." And other times I thought the opposite: "I'll leave home, I'll succeed in the world, and I'll amaze them all." But in the end, the joy slipped from my heart like water through my fingers. I said to my older sisters, "But how can one be born an Endo, and then change?"

They answered, "Is that any way to thank the Endos for all they've given you, by clinging to them forever?"

No doubt they were right. I would have to become what the Endos wanted me to be.

But still, the reproaches of my older sisters, who accused me of selfishness and hardheadedness, left me at a loss. They said that my difficult character tried their patience. But that wasn't what I wanted—I simply wanted to remain an Endo, as I had always been. They were trying to exclude me from the only world I had ever known. So I wrapped myself in solitude. Then, little by little, my face grew as ugly as the faces of stubborn, sad girls who refuse to leave childhood behind always do.

6

The Sages

Ushi ni hikarete Zenkōji mairi.
Led by a cow, a pilgrimage to Zenkōji Temple.

Ningen no tenmei to, hito sorezore no tenmei . . . Every human being has two
destinies, one personal, the other common to all. The first, forged by the
deeds of the past that create the future, justifies the moment of birth as well
as one's status among men. It defines the kind of life possible. It is about
that future, or *yo*, that the old women spoke to us.[1] For generations they
have submitted to regulations hostile to them. Knowing that no one may
interrupt the chain of causes and effects without the aid of the buddhas,
they bent to the will of men, which they attributed to the gods. For them,
the life of a woman was necessarily a miserable existence. Surely they
mustn't have known about the other destiny, *unmei*, which is the working
of the world: for those who observe the principles, it makes life better, but
for those who scorn them, it is a source of troubles. That was something I
would not learn until much later, in Tokyo.

Unmei is the movement of the stars, the play of the five elements that
make up the universe, the orientation of beings and things according to the
compass card: the totality of all causes, natural and invisible. It determines
the conditions of the existence of beings and things in the world.

Long ago, the Chinese discovered how the entire universe is composed
of five elements, the combining of which forms nature, space, life, and
time. These elements give rise to one another in a circular order: wood
makes fire; fire, earth; earth, metal; metal, water; water, wood. At the same
time, wood is in opposition to earth, earth to water, water to fire, fire to
metal, and metal to wood. That is how wood produces fire, metal rests in
the earth, and water and fire destroy each other.[2]

The strength or weakness of each of the five elements governs the life
of the glowworm as well as the movements of the planets. Women born
under fire signs have vivid complexions, lively minds, and changeable

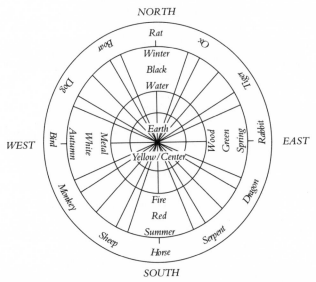

Compass card and the sexagesimal cycle (drawing by Patrick Mérienne).

moods.[3] Those born under earth signs have dark hair and are hardworking, patient, and courageous. Nothing can change this.

If our acts are not in conformity with natural causes, they lead us into failure. People today all dream of heroism. They want to perform magnificent acts, which will have instantaneous repercussions in this life. And they puff themselves up with pride with no more thought of the fruits that will result than of the initial seeds. Thinking they are gods, they all want to remake the world around them to fit themselves alone. And look at the result: the air we breathe has become smog, and the water that the gods have granted us in abundance is dirty. Soon we Japanese, too, will buy water in bottles.[4]

Families who respect traditions, by contrast, venerate the ancestors who founded their lines, those who settled territories, who farmed them for the first time. But we forget the other, the unnamed links in the chain who assured the continuation of the blood and handing down of the land![5] We neglect the loyal intermediaries who, following the wishes of the founding ancestors, kept or enlarged the patrimony. Still, the order of the universe is a tightly stretched fabric; the pieces of it that we cut to our convenience are but rags.

When we look at the characters that designate the animals of the zodiac, we see that *ne*, the rat, is in the north. That is the place of winter, of black, and of water. The character for the rat looks like that which signifies "end," because everything comes to completion in the north. The pillows of the dead are pointed north. And it is to the north, also, that births take place, because things start over where they finish.[6]

The tiger, the character for which resembles that meaning "exhibit" or "develop," is located in the east-northeast. Acts undertaken in the north (that is, on a day of the rat) develop in the east-northeast, on a day of the tiger. In the east is the rabbit, which is written with the same character used for *u*, deutzia flower. It means blossoming. In the south is the horse, which presides over the balancing of yin and yang. And in the west, finally, the rooster, whose name is written with a character that evokes the idea of maturity. The west is the direction of autumn, of white, and of metal.

Look at the colors of the earth: in winter, the rice paddies turn black, spotted with puddles. Winter, like the north, seems to be a place of cold and death. But at the very moment that the ice rends the crust of the soil, the plants are secretly germinating, and men are contracting their pacts of abundance with the *kami*. The peasants sweep away the snow to lay bare a small patch of earth, and on this they scatter seed rice to call the crows. They cry, "*Pō! Pō!*" Then they go away. So the crows, who are the messengers of the god of the mountain, come down and eat the seeds: if they are satisfied, the harvest will be good.

Long after everything begins in the north, autumn, the season of white clouds, arrives. We cut the heads of grain with metal tools, because the promises of winter must be kept in autumn.

Everything in this world bends to this development. If a person acts in harmony with other men, with things, and with nature, if he observes the universal rhythms, his life will develop smoothly. But if he acts counter to the precepts of order, he will have to resign himself to failure. It's like the saying He prunes a cherry—the fool! He doesn't prune a plum—the fool! Neither one will harvest fruits, because nature has decided otherwise.

It takes seven years for a newborn baby to become fully human. And with death, too: if it is from natural causes, the dead person will become a buddha on the seventh anniversary of his death. But, if he dies in some other way, it takes much longer, because people must die at a correct age and under appropriate circumstances. For the dead as for the living, everything must be performed at the right time.[7] And no one can change that. The primary virtue is that of respect for the principles that govern the universe. That is why our ancestors attached so much importance to an understanding of times. That is why they call sages and saints *hijiri*, they who know the days.[8]

MORALITY, RELIGION, AND KNOWLEDGE

In ancient Japan, the word "virtue" didn't exist. They used *makoto* instead: truth of word and deed. *Ma* expressed integrity, totality, that which is true, complete, and superior; sincerity. *Makoto* suggested the efficacy of truthful speech, the speech of the gods and that of the emperor. And then, under Chinese influence, the virtues came to be named. The highest were *akashi*, clarity; *kiyoshi*, purity; *tadashi*, correctness; *naoshi*, rectitude; and *isoshi*, application. This is because the soul must reflect the rules of the world with the clarity and purity of a mirror; because the mind must be limpid, free from preconceived ideas that would be in contradiction. Correctness and rectitude refer to the adherence of the mind to the statutes dictated by the *kami* and the emperor. Finally, application is the attention that a person brings to the other four precepts. All these qualities were adopted in the same way as the titles of nobility that the emperor Tenmu granted the aristocracy.[9]

Unlike Westerners, we do not think that good or evil per se exists. Instead, the acts of people, according to the circumstances, awaken the good or provoke the bad. Believing in good or evil in themselves would be like trusting to an imaginary destiny. There would be nothing, then, to do but let things happen, the way superstitious people do, based on the pretext that all is predetermined.

In the same way, morality and virtue cannot be personal creations, since they come out of the universal principles that the ancients taught. Filial piety and respect for knowledge are the *zengon*, the primary roots of the good. What is most important of all is to study the rules of this world. That is what education, and especially religion, are for.

Shūkyō, religion. According to the dictionaries, this word means "teaching common to all those who share the same origin." But at the top of the character *shū* there is a dot or a circle, which represents the sun; in the middle, the earth; and at the bottom, the character for "show." *Shū* means "the sun which shows the earth." Religion is the teaching revealed by the light of the sun falling on the earth. It is the primordial knowledge, the understanding of the causes behind the infinite succession of days and nights.[10]

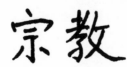 *Shūkyō*, religion.

That is why, when doubt assails the heart, one must first consult religious people. In the northeast region, we consulted both children of the *kami*, or *miko*, and children who transmit the word, *noriwara*, for this purpose. Of course, they were not really children, but they spoke with the gods as easily as children do. There were also great specialists called seals of the law, *hōin*, who had studied Buddhism.[11] When we were fearful we might do something counter to our destinies, we would ask one of these to consult with the gods and nature for us.

THE MOUNTAIN, PLACE OF
MEDIATION WITH THE GODS

The true religion of Japan is communication with "great nature," *daishizen*.[12] Some call it Buddhism and others, Shinto. But in any case, beyond words invented by men, there is but one sacred reality. Today we think of Buddhism and Shinto as separate, but it was the Meiji government that decreed the separation of the two cults.[13] Such machinations make no sense; the veneration of nature has no need for names. All of our prayers pass through men whom the gods have chosen to receive them. They fly out of pure hearts, over the mountain, the domain of the dead and the gods, and from there to the beyond.[14]

In Asaka, it was the winged mountain, Hayama, that united heaven and earth. That verdant hill was very close to the village. It was covered with great *hinoki* cypresses that grew, swaying, up to the sky. I often climbed it.

I would cross a stone bridge over Sai no Kawara, the bed of the river of hell that flowed at the foot of the mountain.[15] There, the villagers piled gray stones in small, irregular heaps, dedicated to the children who had died too young to engage in the cycle of transmigration. Condemned by the law to wander indefinitely on the banks of the underground river, the children, hoping to accumulate merits for their grieving parents, endlessly build towers of the stones thrown down on them—out of sheer malice—by horrible demons. In spite of the help afforded by men, the stone towers remained, half-collapsed, as numerous as wild iris, and, like them, abandoned. The air smelled swampy there.

Once I had crossed the river of hell, I would climb another eight hundred steps to the shrine at the summit. The wind blew a golden light through the gigantic trees. Flowing in waves over the earth, the light continually cradled the spirits of the dead children, which roamed by the thousands around the funerary plaques of white wood, about eight to twelve inches high, that were stuck into the earth here and there in jagged rows, like a miniature army. Baby bonnets, bibs, tiny shawls, little toy vehicles made of tin were placed on the graves, at their feet. The wind scattered the offerings, turning them into ridiculous, lugubrious trash, a carnage of red and white objects. Like bodies left behind after a battle. A little windmill made of multicolored paper turned noiselessly, stirring up the sweetish smell of death.

It is often said that we Japanese do not fear death. That may be true, but we certainly deplore the deaths of children. We don't really know what becomes of them—especially when they die before the age of seven. Some say that they build towers on the banks of the river of hell, to help their parents. Others, that they go directly to the world of the *kami* and that their souls reincarnate in the same house, or the same village, as soon as the next child is born. That may be true . . . anyway, it reassures us.[16]

At the summit, the wind always blew among the clouds, alternately glacial or burning, cool or caressing. In summer, the trees grew so thick with foliage they blacked out the sky. In winter, when everything was as white as the far-off country of the bears, snug in my *kanzen-bōshi*, a cape of straw with a pointed hood, I would look down, toward Asaka. I would throw snowballs. I said to myself, "If these snowballs reach my uncle's house (the house of Father's younger brother, which was the house closest to the mountain in the village), all my wishes will come true." But they always crash-landed far short of it.

In the spring, from the heights of Hayama, I contemplated the green, smooth rice paddies, where yellow and gray shadows played like waves, at the mercy of the wind, in the mulberry trees. There were darker groves where gods resided. Low stone walls enclosed the orchards. And rows of tiny houses, hidden by their large roofs of straw, were bronzed by the weather. It was a gentle countryside that stretched to the mountains on the horizon; for a moment, I felt I could hold it in one hand.

It was at this summit that the gatherings of gods and ancestors on their way to the village took place, at the beginning and the end of the season of agricultural work: on the eighth day of the fourth moon of the year, for the deutzia flower months, and for the full moon after the harvest.[17]

Every autumn, then, we celebrated the gods of Hayama. We would question them about the prosperity of the coming year, and they would answer through the mouth of the *noriwara* of the village. Our *noriwara* happened to be a man, although most were women—but he was very good at it. Ordinarily, he worked just like the other villagers. From time to time, though, the *kami* of Hayama would take possession of his body. Then, like it or not, he could not disobey.

Sometimes, when he had too much to do, the *noriwara* tried to evade his calling. He acted as if he had forgotten the ceremony, staying too long in the fields. But the *kami* of Hayama wouldn't allow it. The day before a festival, as night was falling, they would go to look for him. They would find him in the most unexpected places, even when he was on the toilet, where one has no defenses. They would force him to dress himself properly. They told him to rinse his mouth with clear water and to wash his hands. Then they would make him run to the shrine, where the assembled villagers were waiting for him. The *noriwara* would collapse at the foot of the altar, and cry, "*Tsuita! Tsuita!* They've attached themselves to me! They're possessing me!" And then, in a very low voice, he would recite the names of the gods that were clinging to his body. They were the gods of Hayama. Also the *kami* of the Dewa Mountains in the district of Yamagata: the god of Gassan, the mountain of the moon, its sides covered with gray marl dotted with star-shaped flowers; the god of Haguro, the black-winged mountain, where Japanese cedars grew clear to the middle of the sky; the god of Yudono, the red rock, cinnabar, which the ascetics of ancient times tied with a sacred cord.[18]

The Dewa Mountains were too far away even to glimpse from Asaka. Our ancestors had designated three others in the Abukuma chain as stand-ins, which we venerated from afar at festival times.[19] But for a long time, I believed those were real sacred mountains.

ORACLES

Our *noriwara* actually spoke the language of the gods of the mountain. I can attest to this myself, as could all the residents of Asaka.

During a festival of the tenth moon, he announced that the *kami* of the water would be angry the following year. He said, "The twentieth day of the sixth moon will be a day of disaster." However, perhaps out of defiance, a large village gathering was planned for that day. It was a picnic lunch on the banks of the Abukuma. The sky was cloudless, completely blue all the way to the horizon. The rainy season had just taken a breather. People laughed at the predictions of the *noriwara*.

"Hey! *Noriwara*! See that blue sky?" one man said.

The *noriwara* shrugged. "I merely transmit what the *kami* say. If what I say is wrong, there's no use keeping me around!"

We opened our picnic boxes and sat down on the mats we had spread on the ground. The blue water of the Abukuma drifted along peacefully.

The man who had taken the *noriwara* to task drank a lot of sake. Soon he was drunk and began to insult the prophet. The discussion turned ugly, and people were afraid it would come to blows.

Then there was a great thunderclap in the sky, which turned dark as a stormy sea. Clouds filled the air with the color of lead. Frogs croaked. And it began to rain, *zā zā!*—a downpour. It rained for three days without cease; the walkways in the rice paddies were washed out; the storm carried off one family's roof. Then, suddenly, the sky was as blue as if nothing had happened.

After that, the *noriwara* was consulted on everything. As soon as a child fell sick or an object got lost, he was called in. He would find out the cause of the trouble. Generally it would be an error committed in observing the cult of the gods or the ancestors: an unclean girl who got too near the *kami*; a dead snake stuck in someone's roof tiles.[20]

Little by little, our *noriwara* acquired a great reputation, and people came from surrounding villages to consult with him. He was a very gentle man. He never gave up his peasant work, because he wouldn't take money for his calling. Still, he'd accept little gifts, those that showed the feelings of the heart. I liked him very much. He was a man all made of bones, with very light-colored eyes, like those of my *o-mori*, of a brown that was almost green, but I found them beautiful. One time, I had lost a book or a writing brush (I don't remember which anymore), and I asked him to get it back for me. He agreed. Unfortunately, Mother found the lost item in the court-yard of the house before he had a chance to consult the *kami*. I was disappointed.

In fact, Mother didn't have much faith in the motivations of the *noriwara*. She thought that, when proposing to communicate with the gods, it is difficult to know whether one is dealing with someone who is serious. "If he is a good fortune-teller, then things will be fine," she would say. "But if he isn't, one is at a loss after that." She told us the wise choice was to go to someone who had studied, who truly knew the rules of how the world works: "In that case, the quality of the individual man is of little importance; objective knowledge guides his words. A learned man doesn't practice divination; he knows how to interpret the signs."

THE SEAL OF THE LAW IN KŌRIYAMA

And so, when it came time to decide about the marriage of my second oldest sister, Riki, Mother chose to consult a *hōin*, a seal of the law, in Kōriyama, a man who understood the truth of Buddhist teachings. He was a famous exorcist who had studied a lot and bore the title *gon-sōjō*, vice rector, of the monastery of Fudō-myōō, the immobile king of wisdom.[21]

My older sister was still young—I don't think she was eighteen yet—but a proposal had come from Narita, Mother's home village. The prospective groom's father had been the mayor there for almost fifty years, and the Endo family was favorably known there, which allowed us to harbor the highest hopes for this marriage. In fact, it meant marrying Riki into Mother's own family. The new mayor of Narita was quite willing to act as a go-between in the transactions. Additionally, because the prospective groom was an eldest son (and therefore would inherit the house), my sister would not suffer the usual material difficulties.

At that time, girls of good family were not often allowed to choose their husbands. Above all, marriage meant establishing relations between two houses of the same status. While a girl was not usually forced to marry against her will, marriage was still, fundamentally, a way of establishing alliances. Perhaps Father hoped to become mayor himself, which would have been difficult, since his father had been an adopted son-in-law. So a marriage to the eldest son of the former mayor of Narita was welcomed.[22]

Mother was not opposed to the marriage, either. She would doubtless have preferred, like all mothers, that my sister marry in Asaka. But it was unlikely that she would ever find a suitable husband there, and Mother knew she would sooner or later have to give her daughter to someone outside. Narita wasn't far. Also, my sister had already lived there—right after Riki was born. Because Mother didn't have enough milk and was feeling weak, she had given Riki into her own mother's care for three years. Finally, this marriage between cousins would give Mother a chance to see her own family and old acquaintances once in a while. But she said to us, "Riki-chan is a fine, stable girl, of course. She can marry an oldest son and won't balk at the task; she'll easily be able to prepare three meals a day for her in-laws. But I know little of the young man. What if he is dictatorial, or worse, capricious? A capricious husband is a husband impossible to satisfy! What if he drinks more than he should? What if his mother is mean?" That mother-in-law had come from another village, far away to the west, so they said. Surely she didn't follow the customs of the region. And would Riki herself be able to bend to the ways of that house?

In fact, Mother was worried because my oldest sister's marriage had failed. They had found her a husband, rich and in good health, who lived in Kōriyama. But Kiku had been married only three days when she ran away. She came back to Asaka and hid in one of our barns. We didn't find her for a week. Asked about the reasons for her flight, she said, "He has the skin of a shark. Every evening, when night falls, I tremble with terror."

She was so afraid of Father that she didn't dare come back to the house. Finally, things worked out. Considering that she had been married only three days, the village schoolteacher consented to take her as his wife.

So Mother was afraid she might make another mistake. She felt the need to seek counsel. And because she was pious, she decided to consult the seal of the law in Kōriyama.

It was a colorless morning in mid-May. Mother dressed in a straw yellow kimono with a gray and mauve obi. She looked nervous, younger than usual. Riki wore an elegant blue kimono with a pattern of large pink flowers and a violet obi. As for me, Father had been promising me a new ink pen for several months, and I wanted to stop at the store and pick one out. So I went along, dressed in my simple school uniform.

Large, puffy snowflakes fell this way and that. They crashed to the ground, white flowers that soaked into the earth on contact. We called this *botan yuki*, peony snow. Surprised by the return of the cold weather, men and women huddled in their houses, warming themselves by the hearths. The road was deserted. I ran in circles around my sister, making fun of her: "Your hair is falling down!" "Stop puffing out your cheeks, you look like O-Tafuku!" (Also called O-Kame, O-Tafuku is a comical mask of a puffy-cheeked woman, symbolizing abundance.) Full of her own importance, Riki didn't deign to answer. Then, tired of playing the gadfly, I dragged my feet when we got to town.

Mother, who knew the way, knocked on the door of the temple of Fudō-myōō. A young monk opened the door and led us into a small, dark room that reeked of cheap incense. A large altar full of white and gilded offerings took up half the room. When my eyes adjusted to the darkness, I saw the seal of the law seated there, behind a low table on a cushion covered with light green silk. Although he was old, the skin on his face was remarkably smooth—with the exception of his forehead, which was very high and bore a single deep wrinkle under a skull that was circular though ever so slightly pointed at the top. His expression was melancholy, with serious but shining eyes. Most striking, his lips were very large and too defined, always moist, which made them red like raw meat. His somewhat stubby fingers fiddled with his stole.

Mother knelt on the ground, just to one side of the cushion he offered, as a mark of respect. We girls, a little intimidated, sat behind her on our heels. When the seal of the law asked her why she had come, Mother bowed so deeply her head touched the ground, all the while apologizing for disturbing his meditation. She said that word of his reputation had traveled over hills and rivers, so that even she had heard tell of the immensity of his knowledge—she must therefore be all the more muddled to think of bothering him for a trifle. Mother addressed the seal of the law in language of an extremely refined politeness, explaining to him that her problem had to do with the marriage of her daughter, who was here with her. She said, "I am not sure what I should do. I would like you to enlighten my mind."

The seal of the law asked Riki's age, then that of the boy from Narita. He asked their first names, too. He sat for a contemplative moment, then began to rub his rosary beads very vigorously between his hands, which sounded like somebody carelessly shaking an abacus. I kept my head lowered, but I tried to peep out through half-open eyes. I hoped something marvelous would happen.

The seal of the law simply muttered a formula; then he fell silent for a moment before saying in a loud voice, "I am ready. Ask me your questions." So Mother asked him if my sister should marry the young man from Narita. The seal of the law, his eyes opened wide, answered, "Yes, she may get married."

That was it. It was over, but nothing at all had happened. It was all very boring, and I thought that the *noriwara* from Asaka was at least as good. Then, because I wasn't used to sitting still for very long, my calves had grown numb and I began to wiggle. The seal of the law looked at me and asked, "How old are you?" Mother murmured that I was in my second year of middle school. Vaguely disturbed, I wondered what the seal of the law could want of me—after all, I had come along only for the ride. He said, "Even though you are a girl, you will have a profession. The ends of your fingers are finely made; you will be clever with your hands. You will be a *biyō-shi*, and you will bring happiness to many people. But, in order to do that, you must follow the best master of your day."

Biyō-shi, "master of beauty" or hairdresser—I was hearing the word for the very first time. In Asaka they spoke only scornfully of *kami-yui*, hair knotters. That word, *biyō-shi*, struck me as admirable, and my body was invaded by a sort of unbearable sweetness. I wanted to laugh, and to cry.

I saw Mother stiffen; she seemed on the point of speaking. Her lips moved. Perhaps she wanted to protest. Perhaps she didn't dare. Or else she was simply wondering if she now owed for two consultations rather than one, because this seal of the law was very famous. In the end, she said nothing.

The interview was terminated. Mother and Riki bowed very deeply as they thanked him; then they got up and bowed some more. "Thank you for your attention to us," said Mother.

As for me, I was under the spell of the language of the seal of the law. The word *biyō-shi* transported me to a universe different from all I had known since the day of my birth. I wanted to become a master of beauty, to bring happiness to men and to women! With those three syllables, the fortune-teller had turned my life upside down; he had given me the gift of a new world.

Under astonished looks, I finally got to my feet, with difficulty. I managed to bow politely to the seal of the law without jumping for either joy or sadness. When I reached the door, I saw that the air around me was sparkling magically. I cried to Mother, "I will be a *biyō-shi*!"

She shrugged, murmuring between somewhat tight lips, "We'll see about that later." Then she turned to my older sister and said, "Are you pleased?"

My sister blushed. I understood that meant yes. Then the two of them began talking absorbedly. They discussed Riki's trousseau and the ceremony. The marriage of a rich girl was no mean affair. Visits with the in-laws and the exchanging of gifts would have to be arranged long before the couple would exchange three cups of sake in a Shinto shrine, as dictated by the Taishō emperor. Afterward, the bride would travel to the home of the groom with all her things—and those things would have to be impressive, a public testimony to the grandeur of the house of Endo. A new carriage would be purchased, and a new paulownia wood chest of drawers. Either that or a cherry dressing table.

Their conversation bored me, and I plunged into daydreams that little by little changed to irresistible desires.

On the road home, I imagined a crowd of women all dressed in white, like pilgrims going to a shrine. They climbed in a line all the way up to a chapel at the top of a deserted mountain. The chapel was a small stone hut where, all day long, the faithful would offer flowers and burn incense and candles. I stood to one side and watched. These pious women had come to thank the gods, who, through me, had brought them beauty.

I saw myself, too, dressed in a white blouse like a European lady. I reigned with an expert hand over troops of bottles radiating sweet smells, decorated with flowery labels depicting rare plants. It was all of an exquisite harmony.

A THWARTED CALLING

After we returned to the house of Endo, everyone talked of nothing but Riki's marriage. They chattered on about her wedding kimono and the furniture that she would have to take with her. I stayed quiet, my chin held high, my eyes fixed on a sublime future. I was dreaming of an easy existence, light as a five-colored soap bubble. No one paid me the slightest attention. Suddenly, I said to Father, "I will be a master of beauty!"

He shrugged and said nothing. I repeated it: "I said I'm going to be a hairdresser!"

Mother intervened to tell him what the fortune-teller had said, by way of excusing my impertinence.

"Feminine foolishness," Father grumbled.

I cried, "I will be a hairdresser!"

Father became very angry. This was unthinkable in the house of Endo.

Everyone knew how selfish and rebellious I was, but no one had ever imagined I would want to dishonor the family name!

"There will be no hairdressers in this house! You're out of your mind. You will do like your sisters and marry a young man from the area. You will be given a plot of woods or a rice paddy as a dowry. I won't hear another word about it!"

He spoke forcefully, even angrily.

"But the seal of the law said so! I will be a hairdresser!"

"That's enough!"

I dodged a blow and ran away.

Even now, when I feel tired or lose my courage, I remember that sad evening in May. Following that scene—which impressed me all the more for the fact that Father almost never lost his calm—they tried to shut me up in the *dozō*, a large stone and earth barn, my usual punishment. But I rebelled, running off to hide in the bushes, near the shrine of Inari-sama. There, I grieved over this development: Father would never, ever, let me learn hairdressing. He would try to marry me off, but that I would never allow. In secret, I asked the ancestors to help me realize the fortune-teller's prediction. Vowing to prove myself worthy, I offered them three white stones, smooth and round, which I had picked up in the grass. I implored them. Finally, overcome by exhaustion, I collapsed next to the shrine, and Inari-sama sent me a wonderful dream. In a vast house filled with golden clouds floated long, silky locks of hair. They stuck to the fingers like the spiderwebs that block the roads at dawn in summer.

They found me a little while later, at the feet of the sacred foxes. Mother said perhaps I would actually become a hairdresser; but that would only be a mediocre life, which would bring me little enjoyment. If I was destined for such an existence, it meant that the undoing of the house of Endo—perhaps even its ruin—was near. Was the seal of the law indirectly announcing that fall by his prediction for me? Mother looked pensive. Then she told me not to torment myself, to forget about it all. They put me to bed. Everyone, after that, avoided talking about it.

But from that day on, I knew that I would not be someone ordinary. My destiny would amaze people. I never spoke about it to anybody, except once, to my *o-mori*. Toshirō was living by then in Tokyo, pursuing his university studies. One day when he was back for a visit, I told him that I would create beauty in the capital. He didn't understand what I meant. "You want to live in the city?" he asked me.

"No, that's not it. I want to make beautiful things."

"But you can do that anywhere! The city is not beautiful, you know. People there aren't living in golden clouds but in filth, grayness, and promiscuity. You wouldn't like that!"

I knew that, to become a hairdresser, I would have to follow the greatest master of the day. And that meant I would have to leave home. I had bothered my *o-mori* so much that he sent me, from Tokyo, the brochure of a beauty school. He walked past it every day; in an area called Ochanomizu.[23] He had inspected the place and seen pretty girls in kimonos with large, flowery patterns coming and going through the door at all hours: they were obviously not a bunch of miserable hair knotters, but nice young ladies, who studied there for a few years before they married. It seemed to him that they were being instructed in the rules of aesthetics for the modern woman.

I immediately knew that was the school for me. For months and years afterward, I kept those printed sheets tightly pressed inside my obi. I reread them countless times. Surely the day was coming when I would be able to realize the prediction made by the seal of the law. That was the only way I could see to the accomplishment of my *toku*, my virtue.[24]

7

Waiting

えてに帆をあげる

Ete ni ho wo ageru.
Raise your sails before the wind that's blowing.

THE THIRTIES

Hōin-sama wo o-tazune shite kara, mitabi haru ga otozuremashita . . . Three springs had passed since our visit to the seal of the law. Three times, the sharecroppers had gone to the mountains to cut grasses: they had put them in water to rot, along with oak and willow leaves, and had spread the mixture over the sacred rice paddy. Three times the glutenous rice had ripened there, and we had made stacked balls of *mochi* for our festivals. Three times, too, the *yamabuki*, breath of the mountain, had colored the valleys with its yellow blossoms.[1] The frogs had croaked for three seasons and the bell crickets taken up their songs three times in their houses of reeds. In Asaka, timeless events played out again and again.

But strange rumors reached the house of Endo, weakened echos of an excess of warlike fervor that excited men and frightened women. In Tokyo, they had assassinated the minister of finance, the general administrator of Mitsui Bank, and then the prime minister. Father said, "Will you look at these parties! The Minseitō and the Seiyūkai! They cannot even manage to form a stable government! With all that infighting, they let the power slip through their hands."

On the continent, the Russians and the Americans were inciting the Chinese against us. So the Chinese despised us; they were killing Japanese in the streets and derailing the trains. Only the soldiers could reestablish order.

Father said, "What good is having power by right, if we don't have it in actuality?" Like many others, he came to hope for a military government.

In the eighth year of Shōwa (1933), the great powers spoke out against Japan because we were threatening their monopolies. But hadn't the Western countries themselves once forced us, by threat of arms, to open our doors?[2] Besides, Father thought that there was no shame in the bad opinion of countries that refused to admit that Asians were the equals of whites. Finally, Japan left the League of Nations.

The economy was not healthy. Everyone was complaining of one thing or another. Everyone felt that sooner or later the military factions would take over.

Father had important responsibilities at the mayor's office at that time. He was in charge of preparation for the elections and of all official receptions. He also belonged to Asaka Sosui, the irrigation company, and to Kyōiku Iinkai, the education committee. He was involved in the road system and the electrification of the region. All that cost money and brought in almost nothing.

"The world must change," said Father.

At school, all the textbooks had been modified. They now spoke of nothing but the emperor and the army.

Patriotism, they told us, was as natural as the attachment we feel to our villages and our affection for our mothers. To be Japanese was to love the land of our birth and the emperor, descended from the gods who created these islands. I once again learned the names of all the emperors since the beginning, and the dates of their reigns. The history of the Imperial Line was that of the country; we owed them everything, as we did our ancestors. Our sovereign held the supreme moral authority. He was Japan incarnate. He was completely different from the politicians, who, qualified or not, wanted to seize power for their own selfish ends.[3]

Secretly, I dreamed of the emperor, who lived in Tokyo.[4]

Finally, the acts of violence and the assassinations brought the nationalists to power.

THE END OF SCHOOL

The confused din of history, however, did little to disturb the even march of time.

The wait was by turns impatient and monotonous. I thought, "Something will happen soon that will give some meaning to my boredom." My hope was ebbing. It left in its place a void: a sort of sad beast, incessantly prowling my guts with its pointed teeth. I hated it for a time, then gave in to its bites without a struggle. They lessened with the mournful passage of the seasons.

Years passed. I was fifteen. The end of my school years had come.

There was a ceremony. It was cold. The sky was gray white. They had us line up in the schoolyard. The principal gave a speech. He spoke to us of our futures, of the country, of hope and duty. I understood that an era was coming to an end, but I had the feeling that nothing awaited me outside the walls of the school. It was like a death, with nothing to follow.

I gathered my things. A notebook, two brushes, some books. Not much. I was getting ready to leave when Mrs. Hakozaki called me into the kitchen, where she was making green tea flavored with puffed rice.

She was my favorite teacher. A tall, strong woman, the complete opposite of Mother, who was so tiny. She was imposing. Her skin was so white as to be almost transparent, and her hair was light, nut brown (she must have had Okinawan blood). Though still young, she had a wise understanding of the human heart and always told us marvelous things.

That day she asked me what I was thinking at the exact moment that my school days were ending. I began, "I want to become . . . "

But that was not what she wanted to hear. "Do not think of yourself, but of others, who have guided you to this day."

I tried again: "I'm grateful to all the teachers. They have taken pains with me and been very patient, though I wasn't a good student—"

Again she interrupted me. "They were only doing their jobs. It is of your mother that you should be thinking. The fact that you're leaving school today is due to her having insisted we accept you, Nami-chan. Another mother might not have done what she did, might have given up or deemed it unsuitable."

Hakozaki-Sensei explained to me that Mother's attitude carried a double lesson for me, in both courage and humanism: "You, too, on the road of your life, must conduct yourself bravely. If you wish to accomplish great things, you must always forge ahead, without fear of failure. Your will shall come from the bottom of your belly; in your actions, you will be like an arrow let fly without troubling yourself about the odds, great or small, of accomplishing your ends. And so, as long as you act with sincerity and honesty, all will be well. Because there is nothing that will stand in the way of good faith and a good heart. Your mother's second lesson is that one must act not for oneself but for others. It was Endo Mina's respect for you children that moved us to admiration. When one keeps good relations with others, his acts will naturally find their true path."

Although I didn't really understand the meaning of all that, it awakened in me a kind of hope, like a cool wind blowing through the fog.

At home, when I dragged my feet and yawned, Mother looked at my forehead and placed her hand there. Then, leading me outside, she said, "The air we breathe today is our life of tomorrow."

My listlessness left me; it remained there, suspended over the wild grasses that lined the road. I felt something of the joy that I had taken in the words of Mrs. Hakozaki. "*Attate kudakero*, Throw yourself face first at what you do." To risk everything, that is what it took.

Attate kudakero
(calligraphy by Yamazaki Ikue).

I stayed in touch with Hakozaki-Sensei for the rest of her short life. Long after I had left for Tokyo, whenever a student from the school came to the capital, Mrs. Hakozaki sent her to me bearing letters sealed in beige envelopes, in which she included a flower of the season. All the girls at school had loved flowers.

Hakozaki-Sensei died, just before the war, of lung congestion. When I went back to Asaka during the war years, I scrubbed her gravestone every week. There I recited the Hannya Sutra,[5] left flowers, and burned incense. One day when I returned from the cemetery, there was a bombing attack. Someone cried out, "Hide!" Slowly, I moved behind some close-cropped bushes. I wasn't afraid, because I knew that the spirit of my dead teacher was watching over my life. For years, I went back regularly to visit her grave. But today I no longer have the leisure. It's been more than fifteen years since I went there. That negligence numbers among the sad facts in my life.

So I was going on sixteen. School was over. Encouraged by Mrs. Hakozaki's advice, I once again spoke to Father. I told him again of my plan to go to Tokyo and study hairdressing.

He answered that I had ten fingers and ten toes, that I was made in the normal way, and that he saw no reason why I should become a hairdresser. Mother supported him. "It's impossible," she said. "Because of *seken*, of what people will think. A hairdresser from the house of Endo! That would destroy your father's relations in town." She also told me that she had found a husband for me, a rich man, a rice wholesaler or something like that.

Secretly, though, I wrote to the school in Tokyo. I asked them how one could study without spending any money. An answer arrived, written in elegant calligraphy on very fine paper. It said, "There is a way. You may become an *uchi-deshi*. But it is highly unusual for a young lady who has completed four years of middle school to become an *uchi-deshi*. Well-educated girls constitute the bulk of our paying students. You see, the disciples of the house must do the cleaning, the cooking, and the laundry to pay for their studies. We will be frank with you: it is a hard way of life."

I paid no attention to the details of the letter. I simply said to myself, "If I have to become an *uchi-deshi*, well then, that's what I'll be."

But above all, that letter instantly gave form to the existence of the school in Ochanomizu. It made a bond between us. Now I was sure of it: I would go to Tokyo, whatever Father thought of it. All I had to do was retrace the route of the letter they had written me.

Did that certainty make things less urgent? I had memorized both the hairdressing school brochure and the letter word for word, and I carried .hem folded on my breast. Reassured of my destiny, I once again surrendered myself to waiting. My dreams and my impatience had given way to a vague sadness, like the plaintive notes of a *hichiriki* flute, which resonate in the mind long after the playing has stopped.

To pass the time, I read. The lives of famous men, told simply. I especially remember a book on George Washington, the founder of the United States. I found it admirable of him to have known how to unite and lead men of different origins.

Then, I decided to do something with my time.

THE MOLTING AND METAMORPHOSIS OF SILKWORMS

In country houses, it is the women who raise the silkworms.[6] The larvae are housed under the roof beams on the upper floor of the house; this attic is partitioned off to maintain an even temperature. At our house, it was the servant girls who fed the silkworms, under Mother's direction. That year, in the spring, I sometimes filled in for her.

As a child, I had almost never gone up to that floor, because it is forbidden to all who are not involved in caring for the worms. They said that was bad luck. In fact, too-frequent comings and goings caused variations in temperature. Paper charms bearing the name of Okonko-sama, the goddess of silkworms (who can drive away mice and silkworm diseases), were affixed all over the partitions and especially on the beams. The worms are susceptible to terrible diseases after their fourth molting.

In the spring, when the mulberry buds burst, we would line paulownia wood boxes with thick paper on which the eggs of the larvae had been placed. These were pearly white seeds through which one could see the shape of the larvae: a black dot, the mouth; and a dark crescent shape, the body, already hairy. In the heat of the fifth moon, the eggs would turn yellowish, then gray-brown. Next, the worms began to migrate all over the paper in their shells, in order to hatch. From mid-May on, we would regularly inspect the paper, to check the color of the eggs and determine when the worms would be born. If they all hatched at the same time, we could lay out all the larvae at once. When one paper seemed too far ahead, we would place it in the path of an air current: that way, hatching was delayed.

Then the young larvae would be born. They were barely one sixteenth of an inch long, and covered with fur. We called them *kego*, hairy children. We arranged them on large, flat baskets made of thin sheets of bamboo, the bottoms of which were lined with pieces of matting. We then stacked them on shelves.

Almost as soon as they were settled, the young larvae would begin to move their mouths, funny mouths the shape of horseshoes.[7] They ate the tender young leaves, buds almost, of the mulberry tree.

Feeding them was an awful job. New mulberry leaves were needed constantly, thicker and harder ones as the worms grew. We would chop them with a kitchen knife and put them in baskets. The worms ate enormous amounts. In order to produce a single gram of eggs, it took about sixty pounds of leaves, and to feed the larvae while they spun their cocoons took a good deal more! They fed incessantly, not stopping to urinate or defecate. So the baskets became filthy and moist. From time to time, we attached cords above the baskets; on these cotton cords, toughened with wild *kaki* (persimmon) juice and covered with straw, we suspended mulberry leaves. The worms climbed up into them, and, when they reached the upper level, we changed the baskets.

Five or six days after they had begun to eat, their jaws would relax their chewing (before each of their moltings, the larvae stop eating and their mouths cease to move). It was strange. Ordinarily, on entering the attic, you would think you were in a humid aviary. If you closed your eyes, you could hear the noise of crunching leaves and the moist-sounding commotion of the worms' mandibles, a gurglinglike rain beating against the trees. But before the molting, suddenly all would go silent. The worms ceased their munching and sputtering—they did nothing but move slowly over the leaves, which were as worm-eaten and torn as those of chrysanthemums. Then, the larvae would expand themselves and contract the rings of their bodies, and their skin would split up the length of their backs. This was their first molting.

Some began to form their cocoons four or five days after the third molting. People said that that was lucky. I myself took these first cocoons to the goddess Okonko-sama and hung them on rosaries from the wooden trellis of her shrine.

The seventh day after the final molting, the larvae once again stopped eating. They became yellow, shiny, and transparent. One by one, we shut them up in their cribs.

As they did so, the servant girls would hum a song from Kiso:

> *Kuwa no naka kara, kouta ga moreru*
> *Kouta kikitaya! Kao mitaya!*

> From inside the mulberry grove, I hear the strains of a little song
> I want to hear that song! I want to see that face!

All the girls, surely, dreamed of a handsome young man, whom they would someday marry.[8]

The larvae had come up. It was the time of the year when there was the most work to do. Elsewhere, women helped their neighbors, but we had many servant girls, so we didn't need anybody. Nevertheless, that spring, I lost weight from fatigue, and purple circles appeared under my eyes. This gave new meaning to the saying "*Niwa oki no yō da*, It's like after the fourth molting of the silkworms," which people use to mean they are very busy. In the village, traveling merchants came in greater numbers, because women no longer had time to do their shopping in town. They brought salt, oil, everything.

After that, the worms began to slobber out their silk threads. Their bodies became transparent and as wrinkled as the skins of old people. Bent in the shape of horseshoes, their backs to the inside, their feet outside, making oval circles with their heads, the worms wrapped the fibers around their bodies.

A few days later, we threw out the sick worms—those who hadn't had the strength to eat, those who had eaten some kind of bad fungus—and the yellow ones who had puffed up and died. We got rid of the dead ones first, because they were contagious.

We continued to change the mats in the cribs regularly. The larvae continued to eliminate water from their bodies, making the straw moist. Because the water would impregnate the silk fibers and dull their shine, we had to change the mats twice a day. It took six or seven days to make a cocoon. At the end, the fibers would have to be perfectly dry to the touch.

That year, the best cocoons were sold to the factory in Kōriyama. Most of the others were sold to a traveling merchant. Mother kept the profits from the sale to the factory in Kōriyama; I kept those from the traveling merchant. The lowest-grade cocoons were used to make silk waste and rough silk.

To do that, one had first to kill the pupae: we steamed the cocoons, covered with green leaves. When they changed color, that meant the pupae had been suffocated. I looked at them: they were a waxy white, their wings no more than undeveloped wing shapes, gray on the males, white on the females. I pondered them for a long time.

I had watched these strange creatures spit out the water from their bodies and dribble on the crumpled, cracked, salty mulberry leaves. These frightful little beasts seethed like worms on a putrefied cadaver. Then, at the end of two months of molting and metamorphoses, behold, the larvae spun silk, the most beautiful of fabrics. And they became butterflies, the most beautiful of insects.

I thought about the mystery of molting and metamorphoses. Perhaps beauty is a possibility that exists in each of us. To bring it to the light of day, it must be necessary, week after week, to molt and to rid oneself of useless skins. To die, finally, that beauty might appear. To lose oneself in order to reveal the best that exists within: that sacrifice must be one of rejoicing. I had the feeling of having helped put my own body to death.

Finally, we scalded the cocoons to unwind the fibers. A single fiber could be up to a thousand yards long.

THE LEGENDARY ORIGIN OF SILKWORMS

Silkworms are mysterious creatures. In Tōhoku, it was often said that the worms were the marvelous avatars of a horse and a young girl who, long ago, loved each other.

The father of the girl, filled with rage over her extraordinary love affair, killed the horse. He put out its skin to dry, stretched tight between two mulberry trees. Then, when the girl came to view the skin of her lover, it rolled itself about her. She was taken up into heaven, where the horse was. One year had passed when two insects, one black and the other white, came to light on a mulberry tree. The black insect resembled a horse, the white, a young girl. The two of them began to spin silk threads.

The father of the young girl gathered that silk. Then he grew richer and richer.[9]

In our region, we offer a woman's hair, or skeins of black hemp that look like hair, to the goddess of sericulturists. Horses' manes and human hair: they are at the origin of silk. That is why the silkworm's mouth looks like a horseshoe, and its body does, too, as it bends to spin its cocoon.

Mother told us that silk came from China, and before that, from India.[10]

"Long, long ago, there was, in the north of India, a country called Kyū-chū. In this country, there was a king, who was called Rini, and his wife, who was called Kōkei. Their union produced a princess, whom they named Konjiki.

"But her mother, the queen, fell ill and died. Her father remarried, and the stepmother, like all stepmothers, hated the young girl. She visited upon her one hundred miseries. First, she abandoned her in the Shishika Mountains, which were infested with wild boars. But a boar took the princess home to the court on his back. Next the stepmother abandoned her on the mountain of Ōgun, which was infested with falcons. And so, a warrior on a falcon hunt found her and saved her again. Next, the stepmother, feeling her hatred grow and grow, took advantage of the temporary absence of the king to abandon the young girl on the mountain of Kaigan, where, so that nothing could save her, she had her buried alive.

"Later the king, her father, filled with sadness, was walking in the garden of the palace admiring the flowers, when he saw a light bursting out of the ground. He commanded that they dig on that spot: the princess emerged from the earth, and she was once again saved.

"But the king understood that the princess could not forever escape the queen. So he had a boat hollowed out from the trunk of a mulberry tree, and in it he placed the girl. Then he sent it off at the edge of the water. It headed for the open sea.

"The king had a hermitage built in a mulberry woods which grew by the water, and there he retired from the world. That is why they called that hermitage the Hermitage of the Mulberry Plain, and why, since then, we call monks *sōmon* (mulberry gate).[11]

"The boat, however, floated all the way to Japan, to the bay of Toyoura in the province of Hitachi.[12] A man named Gondayu found it there. But the girl died, and immediately her body turned into a silkworm. Gondayu fed the worm with mulberry leaves. And so the princess taught him, in dreams, how to raise the silkworms, and another hermit came down from Mount Tsukuba to show him how to weave a marvelous fabric from the threads of their cocoons. Gondayu passed his knowledge on to the world, and he became richer and richer.

"And do you know," Mother told us, "that the daughter of King Rini was none other than Kaguya-Hime, the daughter of the emperor Kinmei? When she came from India to Japan, 'Konjiki' became 'Kaguya,' and 'Rini' became 'Kinmei.' That is the true origin of Okonko-sama, the goddess of silkworms. Finally, from Mount Tsukuba she came to live on Mount Fuji, from which she gives her oracles. In fact, the *kami* of both Tsukuba and Fuji are but one—they are both the bodhisattva Seishi, who reigns with Amida Buddha and Kannon in the Western Paradise."[13]

I dearly loved these stories, which told how silk is a woman. The character for silkworm, *kaiko*, for which the Sino-Japanese reading is *san*, shows an insect under the sky, and the sound *san*, which means "dive into" or "bury oneself in," recalls the way the silkworm envelops itself in its cocoon. But *san* also means "give birth," because, like women, the worm does that.

Kaiko, silkworm.

When the silk-raising season was over and I once again found myself unemployed, I didn't know what to do but go back to waiting. And when the larvae began to spin their cocoons the next year, all that had long since ceased to interest me.

BOTSURAKU NO TOKI: RUIN

As the New Year was approaching, cold once again settled in the village along with the god of the mountain.[14] When evening came, men and women hugged themselves, gathered around their hearths, and warmed their fingers over porcelain braziers.

Father often got angry. The children's noise got on his nerves. At dinner, he drank more sake than usual. Now it was the wife of my oldest brother, Yoshiharu, who poured it for him, out of a white decanter decorated with delicate gold lines. My oldest brother was back from Tokyo. He taught school in a neighboring village and helped Father with his municipal duties. He was married to the daughter of the Endo Kiyosaburō and Tori families, who were vaguely related to us. She was a gentle and quiet woman, with round cheeks and fingers. Her steps made no sound. Sometimes, I would be sure I was alone, and there she would be, smiling her witless smile, and I would feel guilty for no reason.

Riki also was married. We hardly saw her anymore. She had visited from Narita two or three times with her son. He was a strapping big baby with deep red cheeks who laughed very loud.

My sister Risa was a good girl. But one of our servant girls, who had come to our house very young, chased after boys. Word of it reached Father's ears. He screamed all night because she hung around with young people of low birth, and that was no example for us. Once when everyone in the house was in bed, she got up, as was her custom. I saw her pass near our beds. I moved a little. She put a finger to her mouth before she slipped outside. She didn't return until after the moon had set.

Father's moods worsened. Mother told us that he had worries. I felt that danger was prowling around our house like a starving animal. Walled in by my melancholy, I secretly waited for the worst to strike and turn my life around. And then the catastrophe for which I had hoped in my heart finally came.

I've already said the Endo family had been rich, so much so that my great-grandfather was once a candidate for the title of *tagaku nōzeisha giin*, "member of the House who pays large taxes." My grandmother had never gone to school but by rickshaw, and our own educations had been paid for in parcels of land rather than money. We had so many fields and forests! But, as I also said, my grandfather was a terrible spendthrift. That wouldn't have been so bad had he not let himself become entangled with a bad adviser. The man promised him he would make a fortune in the silk business. I don't know how it happened, but my grandfather ended up signing over bank drafts, and we were ruined.

He had been swindled, but there was nothing we could do about it. We had to pay, one way or the other. As we were favorably looked upon in the community, things were not difficult to arrange. Father sold the land that Mother had bought with the pension he received for having been wounded in action, and thanks to guarantees posted by close relations, we were able to arrange a time payment plan and pay the penalties. The affair was taken care of without causing anyone great trouble. But with that, suddenly, our situation had changed. The New Year festivities were celebrated without display. They were morose gatherings, without much merrymaking.

This ruin revived my hopes. I remembered Mother having, four years earlier, associated my leaving with the fall of the house of Endo. Our ruin was a fait accompli; the time seemed to me to have come.

I begged my oldest brother to let me go. I told him that I wanted to leave for Tokyo, that it wouldn't cost a cent. He smoked a cigarette and said nothing.

THE DECISION

Enveloped in a padded coat, I stayed every day, for hours at a time, seated outside, at the edge of the garden, on a low stone wall. I waited. Nothing happened. Perhaps this would be my life: waiting. Time was gently suffocating me. I would be like those sick larvae that refused to spin for some unknown reason. They were tossed out. I looked at the countryside, thinking how it was hemmed in by hills, just as was my existence by Father's will. On one of them, there were brown speckles: the melting of the snow would soon etch round patches there, like those on the skin of the fawn that had always announced the beginning of spring.

One day as I sat daydreaming like this, a cry interrupted my misery: "*Onē-san!* Big Sister!"

Someone was calling me. It was my little sister Yae-chan: "*Onē-san!* Big Sister! He's agreed to it! You're going to Tokyo!"

My breast split in two, bringing my old wound to fresh life. Yae-chan said, "Tokyo! Tokyo!" And then, "Father is waiting for you." I got up mechanically. A thistle scratched my leg. Yae-chan was chattering at top volume, an agitated jumble of words I didn't understand. I followed her into the house.

Father and my oldest brother were seated next to the hearth, facing the inside room. They were wearing Western clothes—city suits. They looked me over without speaking a word. I kneeled and bowed all the way to the ground; then I sat up very straight. I didn't dare speak. They still said nothing, so I apologized. "I kept you waiting."

I bowed again.

Father tapped his delicate *kiseru* pipe on the edge of the hearth. He put it down, sighed slowly, and said, "In view of the circumstances and of your attitude, it has been decided that we will send you to Tokyo. Thank your oldest brother, who argued your case, and your mother, who intervened in your behalf. Your oldest brother will give you the details."

I thanked him, and he got up in silence, stiffly, and left the room.

My oldest brother seemed to relax. A gleam, like a little lightning bolt of high spirits, flashed in his eyes. He began a long speech:

"Nami-chan, our circumstances have changed, you know that. Grandfather has acted unwisely. He signed some bank drafts, and we had to pay them. We have sold land. It will take years, and much work, before we regain our former stature. And so it might be best that you have a profession. That is why Father is allowing you to go and live in Tokyo. But understand this: you will not have an easy life. We will not pay your way. You will enroll at the school in Ochanomizu, not as a student but as an *uchi-deshi*, an in-house disciple. That means that you will have to work to pay for your room and board and your studies. And know this well, too: you must not come back home, complain, or ask anything at all of us. If you come back to Asaka, you will never again be allowed to leave. There, that's all I have to say for now. Think about it. Do you want to go or not?"

My heart was beating like that of a fox caught in a trap. The fox that gnaws off his own foot to escape. I looked to the back of the room. My little sister had stayed there, standing in the corner. She looked at me with very wide eyes. I noticed for the first time that she looked like me. I had no choice but to go. If I didn't, no one would respect me. To leave home . . . I was scared. But I wanted it, too. Anything would be better than those interminable days staring out over the uniform countryside.

I said, "I will go to Tokyo."

He became solemn. "Very well. If you are firm in your resolve, no one will try to hold you back. But if you come back here, you will never be able to leave again. Such is our agreement."

Tilting his head a little to one side, he continued, "Perhaps our reversal of fortune will work in your favor. You're still young; it will allow you to live as you wish. But think sometimes of our parents, who must rebuild their lives in order to return the house to its former glory. Think, too, of me, who has never imagined an existence other than the one I was raised for. You are lucky."

His face took on a severe expression, with two brown lines at the corners of his mouth. "Be careful, however. Remember that in the city, life is dangerous. Here, you were raised in luxury. Do not seek luxury in Tokyo. In the country, there is a natural limit to foolish expenditures, but in the capital, there is none whatsoever. Do not heap shame on the name of Endo: we will have you struck from the family register."

I wanted to thank him, to ask his forgiveness for those months of black moods, perhaps to cry—but his severity stopped me. I couldn't speak. I bowed profoundly as a sign of obedience and respect. My forehead touching the tatami, I mumbled a standard polite phrase. Then, I stood up. I didn't know where to go.

Wandering from room to room, I ended up in the storage room, the *nando*. Mother was in there. She was unpacking old kimonos. She had spread all around her the vivid colors of her youth. The vertical sunlight that came in through a narrow window high on the wall shone on the fabrics. I knelt next to her.

"*Okā-san*, Mother . . . "

"I know."

Mother was bent over the kimonos, both hands buried in the wrinkled cloth. "I've been looking over what you can take with you. There, you'll need bright clothes, since you are still young. But nothing too showy. That would be unseemly for an apprentice."

She showed me a kimono whose fabric was faded by the sun. It had a pattern of large blue diagonal stripes with little pink bouquets, over a cream-colored background. "With this pink and beige obi, it will be gorgeous."

We chose three kimonos. The edges of the loose, flowing sleeves were well-worn, but my arms were shorter than Mother's, and they could be taken up. I wouldn't be leaving for four weeks.

Mother carefully folded the three kimonos. She looked at me briefly.

Her nostrils trembled. I remembered an old horse of ours that had died the year before. He had lain on his side on the ground. His large, useless legs had rubbed the earth convulsively. His nostrils had trembled for hours. And then they hit him. When he was dead, he looked terribly calm, with a wise smile on his lips that melted the heart.

"*Okā-san . . .*"

Mother wouldn't let me continue. "You won't have any money, you know. I myself am not rich. I have often tried to put aside a secret savings, *hesokuri*, savings hidden in the navel. But there are so many of you, and you all wanted so many things, that I wasn't able to keep any of it. Of course, I didn't think we'd ever really need it. The night before you leave, I will give you five yen. And every month, I will send you one yen. Like the allowance we used to give you. But don't spend it foolishly. One day, that money may save you."

She looked at me again. "Leave me now. You have much to do. Go and greet your teachers, your milk mother, your girlfriends, and all your uncles and cousins. Thank them properly for all they've done for you. I have put together packets of tea, which I've left in the kitchen. You will take them as gifts for everyone you visit. They will give you money as a going-away present. Thank them politely, and don't forget to write down all the amounts in a notebook. Because when you come back, you must bring each of them a gift worth at least half the amount they have given."[15]

Those last weeks, I shopped. My second eldest sister, Riki, taught me how to do my hair in a full chignon that showed off my earlobes and helped make my rounded face look longer. I felt very busy. But, actually, I wasn't doing much of anything.

I had wanted to go to Tokyo, and now it was to happen. The very fact that my desire had come to pass astonished me. Was wishing for things all it took to make them happen? I felt powerful, I existed. I was will itself, I was pure existence. But at the same time, my desire to leave home abated. Sometimes there would be waves of impatience. They submerged me. I was to leave! I was happy! But there was a hard little point at the bottom of my insides: "Leave for where?" I was filled with anguish. I would make such tight fists my nails dug into my palms. I looked at the hills. I told myself that in a few weeks, a few days, I wouldn't see them anymore. I didn't know whether that was for the better or the worse.

The day of my departure arrived. I dressed in a pale gray kimono with a delicate red pattern, intertwined like grasses. Mother tied my yellow and ocher obi for me. She said it was in exquisite taste. In my hand I carried a large bundle of clothes, and on my breast was hung a pretty, gold-embroidered purse. It held thirty-six yen, twenty-two of which I had saved since primary school, which represented a small fortune, five yen from

Mother, and nine that my relatives and the neighbors had given me. At the bottom of the purse was a tiny wooden frog my little sister, Yae-chan, had placed there for me, because the word for frog, *kaeru*, also means "come back." The frog would make money come back to me, and bring me riches.

THE DEPARTURE

About a dozen people in all—the family and others who were close to us—climbed with me onto the cart that would take me to the train station. Everyone was lighthearted. We made jokes.

"Hey! Nami-chan! You're fat enough as you are; you're taking up all the room. Don't eat too much in Tokyo. If you do, you won't even fit into the car when you come back!"

"No matter, I'll come back in a sedan chair! Or, better yet, in a carriage pulled by a team of oxen!"

Or "Don't marry a Tokyo man, will you! They don't know what to do with women!"

"I certainly won't marry you. If I did, I'd have children as mushy as rice gruel!"

Those are the kinds of things we said. Everyone laughed. Only Father looked grim. He grumbled, shrugging his shoulders, "But why are you all going on like this—she's nothing but a *mikka bōzu*, a three-day monk. She'll be back in less than a week." And I heard him say to Mother, "And she'll have to pay back all that money." That made me want to stay.

We got to the station. On the platform, I bowed before the little group and made a speech: "You've all been so kind to me! And in the future, too, please remain well-disposed toward me: *Yoroshiku*. Life in Tokyo will be hard, but I will often think of you and try to be worthy of your faith in me."

They gave me a great round of applause. Then I got on the train. I went to the window, my head turned to the right. I waved my hand wildly. Soon they became a blur. I sat down on the wooden bench. My body was stiff. I felt that my lips were frozen in a stupid smile, like that of a corpse. I tried to return my face to a natural expression, but my skin hurt. I couldn't do it. The train was almost empty. I thought, "I could cry now; no one would see me." I looked at the countryside without seeing it. I no longer had any sense that I existed.

The Endo house the day before it was torn down. *(All photographs are the property of the author or of the Yamazaki collection.)*

The Endo family. Standing, left to right: Riki, Kiku, Mina, Yoshiharu; seated, left to right: Risa, Kikumi, Yaeko, Yoshihisa, the eldest daughter of Yoshiharu, Nami.

Father Endo.

Endo Nami at the age of sixteen.

School trip in 1933 (Nami is fourth from the right, in the first row).

The school at
Ochanomizu.

The *hōin*, the sage, who revealed to Endo Nami her vocation as a master of beauty.

The wedding portrait of Yamazaki Tatsuo and Endo Nami.

Yamazaki Tatsuo, 1931. A self-portrait, taken on the day he acquired his first camera.

Yamazaki Tomekichi.

Yamazaki Naka.

The Yamazaki family the day before the parents' departure for France. From left to right: Mitsunobu, Motoko, Ikue, Ryōko, Tatsuo.

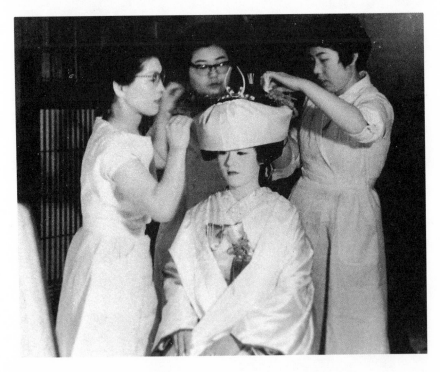

The creation of a bride's chignon.

The old beauty salon, Kanōya.

A public relations brochure for the present-day salon in Bunkyō.

Family dinner in the
living room in Bunkyō.
From left to right:
Mitsunobu, Ikue, Tatsuo,
Hitoe, Kyōko.

Statuette of the divinity Daikoku, whom
Yamazaki Ikue equates with the Great
Master of the Country, Ō-Kuni-Nushi.

Yamazaki Ikue bowing
before the domestic Shinto
altar.

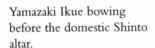

The staff of the old salon in Bunkyō celebrate the New Year.

Shinto festival at the Hakusan Shrine in Bunkyō, Tokyo: participants posing before the portable shrine of the gods. Tomekichi stands just to the right of the drum surmounted by a phoenix.

Yamazaki Ikue studying hair under a microscope.

Yamazaki Ikue reading the newspaper (1990).

At the request of Yamazaki Ikue, an employee recites the morning salutations for Laurence Caillet.

II

Tokyo

Prologue

It was in the spring of Year 9 of Shōwa, 1934, that Nami arrived in Tokyo. There, she would pass eight years of austerity and humiliation, filled with a secret anger that would exhaust her spirit and ravage her body. Illness brought her back to the village. There, the countryside, the sky, and the air of her childhood gave her the strength to return to a capital destroyed by bombings and the courage to build, in the ruins, a new life.

At first she did not want to talk to me of that bitter time. "*Omoshiroku-nai*, It's not interesting," she said, closing up in a silence that felt like a reproach. My curiosity, having become indiscreet, struck her as grotesque.

Still, one morning when the cicadas suddenly ceased their buzzing, over-come by the white-hot heat of summer, the sight of a dwarf maple in a pot made her face light up with a happy memory: toward the end of the seventh moon of Year 10, a cousin of her mother's, who worked for Mitsubi-shi in the Nihonbashi section of Tokyo, had taken her to the tree fair. This bit of nostalgia for old Edo was held every year before *O-Bon*, the feast of the dead. Everyone came to take the cooler air by the edge of the Shino-bazu pond in Ueno, this one to buy a tiny cedar tree, another a giant paulownia with its roots bundled in straw, another the bulb of an eight-colored iris.

After they had walked around the pond and Nami had filled her nostrils with the scents of wet grass and wind, the uncle bought her a firefly trapped in a wire mesh cage. They sat down under a kiosk equipped with a refresh-ment stand, in the middle of a bridge that stretched over the calm water. Sipping ices flavored with red syrup, they contemplated the blooming lotus flowers. Filled with a peaceful joy, Nami thought that her soul left her body and slipped into a lotus bud, to be reborn that instant on the pond of the Western Paradise, home of the Amida Buddha. By nightfall, when her uncle had escorted her back to the beauty school, she had a transitory feeling that happiness had come at last. After they parted, the little cage hidden in her sleeve, she climbed the stairs leading to her room. There, late into the night, she confided in the firefly, spreading out before it her riches—three kimonos—her hopes, and her winged dreams.

The next morning, the firefly was dead.

Each morning, in that nearly empty room on the top floor of the Yamazaki Building in Bunkyō, after Yamazaki Ikue prayed to the gods, she would tell me the story of her life for three or four hours. But she would not speak about the rest of that time. It was only later that, in the Western-style living room on the floor below, she agreed to tell me about her difficult apprenticeship, her forced marriage, and the procession of bitter experiences that followed. Sunk deep into the gray plush sofa, she spoke in a louder voice than usual, constantly interrupting herself to demand that tea or some luxurious tidbit be served immediately. However, little by little, these interviews, which had begun in such a foul humor, turned into melancholy murmurings. Her hand rose less frequently to her mouth to hide staccato laughs. And then, one day, she declared: "*Ashita no koto wo iu to, oni ga warau zo!* . . . The demons laugh at us when we speak about tomorrow. But the gods and buddhas must be amused when we talk about the past." That same day, she gave in to the pleasure of confiding.

Her husband, Tatsuo, an indiscreet eavesdropper on our conversations, would interrupt from time to time. In sarcastic tones, he accused her of lying. She shrugged and asked him if he had nothing better to do than hang around the house all day, circling us, but a vague disquiet clouded her look. Tatsuo snorted like an old animal in the sun and shot back with a defiant tone, "All right then, go ahead and make up stories while I take a walk!" She waited for the noise of the door slamming behind him as he left the apartment before continuing her tale.

BOOK ONE

Biyō no Michi:

THE WAY OF BEAUTY

8

Beginnings

Isogaba maware.
When in a hurry, take the roundabout way.

IMAGES OF TOKYO

Shōwa kunen shigatsu no koto de gozaimashita . . . It was April, in the ninth year of Shōwa (1934). After nine and a half hours, the train pulled into Ueno Station. It was very dark, like all train stations of that era. More than anything, I was struck by its size—I had never seen a building so vast. The roof was far higher than those on the Buddhist temples or buildings in Kōriyama. There were more people in the crowd than came to the festivals in Fukushima: pale creatures with dirty-looking circles under their eyes, swarming like clouds of yellow butterflies over fields of colza. But when you took a good look at them, they all seemed to know exactly where they were going. Those who were hurrying to meet incoming passengers waved their arms, then bowed, mechanical smiles on their faces. Others pressed firmly toward the exit, toward lives that I imagined to be regulated down to the slightest details. Only a fat woman surrounded by children showed any hesitation, before handing her bags to a porter, who (even I knew this) was recognizable by his red hat.

I myself was still on the train. Afraid of getting lost in the crowd, I waited anxiously by the window, looking for my oldest brother, Yoshiki, who was passing through town at that time and was supposed to meet me. Then, fearing that the train would start up again and go on to somewhere else, I picked up my bundle and found myself on the platform. I didn't know what to do. It reminded me of the time I had gotten lost at an *ennichi*, a small fair held during a religious festival, in Kōriyama. I had bought some goldfish. They swam about in a little bowl, which I clutched to my breast, unmindful of keeping it upright, not seeing that the water was spilling out and the fish gasping for air. When I was finally found, their gills were

129

pumping up and down very fast. Standing in the station, I told myself that if my oldest brother didn't come, I would die. My legs were like jelly.

And then there he was. Like the others, he waved his arms in the air and smiled. He spoke—he must have been inquiring about my trip and the train ride—but I was so worked up I didn't understand what he was saying. To be on the safe side, I answered him, yes, it was fine, just fine.

I followed him to the exit, but he walked very fast, and my bundle was so cumbersome, I didn't see anything until we got to the street. There, the sky appeared to me a blue I hadn't known existed. A brutally clear light etched each object before me in exacting detail. At first I didn't know whether I found that beautiful or vulgar, but perhaps because I hadn't expected it to be that way, disappointment made my throat tighten. At that moment—if not for my fear of the busybodies of Asaka, and had I known how to negotiate the trains—I would have headed straight back to the village, the ends of the earth, or maybe the sky even. But, in fact, I followed my oldest brother to the tram stop.

Ordinarily so taciturn, he waxed astonishingly eloquent, constantly blinking his eyes to show his satisfaction with or approval of the order around us. He seemed proud of his knowledge of Tokyo, which made me feel totally foreign. He said that while we could have taken the subway, we would see the capital better from the tram. The subway was very convenient, he explained, but sometimes it went on strike.

I knew the word: *sutoraiki*. In Kōriyama, too, the silk mills sometimes went on strike. One year, the factory girls had demanded higher wages and shorter hours. The silk trade had been disrupted for several months, and the association had had to lower the price it paid for cocoons in order to pay the women. That cost the farms dearly. I thought it was shocking and indecent to force someone's hand by refusing to work.

My oldest brother told me that during strikes, workers would leave the workshops and factories; immense crowds would parade in the streets with white banners, as on festival days.[1] Both men and women did this. During these demonstrations, he said, you would even see mothers with children on their backs. As if that were any way to raise children! He hoped that I wouldn't pick up city ways, that I wouldn't become one of those shameless girls, always demanding more than their due.

We had to stand because the tram was packed. It jolted along, a cacophony of colliding wood and metal. I raised my voice above the din to answer that I would be careful to avoid the wrong sort of associations.

At each stop, the ticket inspector, a woman, led a small troop in and out of the tram. Uniformed, wearing narrow trousers like a soldier's, she went from passenger to passenger, punching their tickets. She smiled; she looked happy.

In the street, people walked with larger strides than in the village. I saw some *moga*, short for modern girls. There were three of them, and they laughed loudly, without covering their mouths. The tallest played with a yo-yo. Her hair was cut short, and her skirt showed a good portion of her calves. She looked unbelievably sure of herself, no doubt because of her elegance. All three wore round hats pulled down very low on the head. I thought how very much I would like to have a hat like that someday, but I didn't dare admit it to my oldest brother.

Modern Girl, Ozaki Saburō, 1933.

As we approached Ochanomizu, my oldest brother explained that there was a spring in that district which produced water so pure that a great many masters of the tea ceremony, the best as well as the worst, had settled there. He knew a young lady who had paid for twenty lessons in advance, only to have the master disappear with the money before she had taken even one.[2]

After getting off the tram, we walked up an avenue where the red-brick buildings alternated with wooden shacks, mostly shops. There was a river, with beggars on the banks. I thought, "So that's all it is, this Tokyo." I no longer knew why I had so much wanted to come.

On the sidewalk to our left, at the corner of the second street, my brother stopped in front of a two-story building. Above the door was written in gilded characters on a black background: "*Ochanomizu Biyō Jogakkō*, Ochanomizu Beauty School for Ladies," and under that: "Recognized by the National Ministry of Education." At that time, the brochure had informed me, it was the only hairdressing and dressmaking school to be officially recognized by the national authorities. That was precisely why I had chosen it. The sight of that placard reassured me a little.

AN APPRENTICE'S WELCOME

My oldest brother called out, "*Ojama itashimasu!* Sorry to trouble you! Is anyone there?" A tall, slender woman soon came to the door and welcomed us, in a whisper. We bowed deeply and removed our shoes, donning the beige indoor slippers she had taken for us from a closet with sliding doors. My stomach hurt a little, but as there was an odor of fresh tuna floating in the air, I didn't know whether it came from worry or simply hunger. Whichever it was, I had the impression that I was joining a good house. In fact, from one second to the next, I felt the most contradictory sentiments.

That woman was Yamazaki Naka, the wife of the younger brother of the school's director. I noticed that she had rosy hands with smooth, transparent skin, through which blue veins were clearly visible, as well as curved, ridged fingernails. That worried me a little, because they said in Asaka that streaks on the fingernails were a sign of evil acts committed in the past.

Yamazaki Naka had us sit down in a three-tatami mat room with a low table in the center. She pulled from a great pile of cushions a green silk *zabuton* for both of us to sit on, and she served us green tea to keep us happy while we waited. My oldest brother engaged her in conversation, saying that the rains were late. She asked if I had come from Kōriyama, and how the harvest was going. As if, in April, we could possibly know that yet!

Yamazaki Seikō, the director of the school, received us next in a vast room in the Western style. He was seated behind a desk covered in red morocco leather. Before it were two guest chairs decked in white lace. I had to sit down in one of them, but I didn't know what to say. In any case, the director didn't seem to be interested in me. He talked only with my brother. They spoke quickly and used words I didn't know. I must have been very tired, but I heard my brother say, "If she causes you any trouble, let me know, I will come and get her."

Then he left, and Yamazaki Naka introduced me to the principal inhabitants of the school. She called me Nami, without adding the honorific *san*. Up to then, no one outside my family had ever addressed me with such familiarity. This brutal act of *yobi-sute*, discarding a name, made me understand instantly that in becoming an *uchi-deshi*, I had renounced the social rank of my birth.[3]

Yamazaki Nobuko, the wife of the director, a tall woman with a grim face, then led me to my room. If you could call it a room—it was dark as a rainy, moonless night and so tiny that I could barely stand upright. A cupboard took up the entire upper half of the left wall.

Yamazaki Nobuko spoke coldly: "As you are an in-house disciple, you will work at the housekeeping tasks. We have two hundred students here, of whom forty-eight live in. You will attend hairdressing classes when you have no other work to do." Then she left, and I was alone.

In that little attic room, I felt a sort of shame over my sudden loss of status. Panic bruised my heart the way a spring rain strips the peonies of petals. To keep from crying, I tried to convince myself that it would not last, that soon I would be living in a place as big as a castle, with birds singing outside my windows. From the bottom of my heart, torn by loneliness, I forced myself to think, "They'll see. I'll show them." But at the same time, I wondered vaguely what it was I could show them.

THE LIFE OF AN *UCHI-DESHI*

The next day, for the first time in my life, I cooked a pot of rice. The grains were soft and sticky, with an unpleasant burned taste. The paying students made faces and looked at me scornfully. I swore to myself it would never happen again, and I set to work like a soul in hell. In a week, their sarcasm lessened, and within a month it stopped altogether.

Every day for my entire apprenticeship, after I had served breakfast, I had to do the laundry and hang it out to dry on the terrace. This was followed by the housecleaning, lunch, tea, shopping, and dinner. The winters were the worst, with days of hard, blue sky I came to hate; the cold water made my hands red. In the evenings, as I made the rounds of shops, when I passed the street-corner shrine devoted to Inari-sama, I would stop a moment to implore him to make it rain. That gave me courage. Then I would walk toward the river to look for the coming of the frogs, which meant spring. The river, which reminded me of Asaka, was my favorite place in all of Tokyo. Still, because of the beggars gathered on the banks, I never went all the way down to the water.

NEW IMAGES OF TOKYO

Curiously, it was an additional unhappiness that brought me my first joy in Tokyo. Even though I often wrote home, the Endo family had serious doubts about the rectitude of my activities.

After my departure, Father had sent a cart to the train station every day to pick me up. After three weeks, he stopped assuming I'd come home. I imagine he must have grumbled about it, pretending not to care that I was making a fool of myself in Tokyo. Mother must have come to my defense as usual, but one day a rumor gave her pause. It happened that following a bad bout of the flu, she went to a blind masseuse in Kōriyama, and the woman told her—no doubt in the sententious tones adopted by those who think themselves well-informed—that the school in Ochanomizu was known for the severity of the life it dealt to apprentices. She had heard that they had stopped taking apprentices after the suicide of a young woman several years earlier.

Mother decided to have someone check up on me. She contacted Naganuma Yūzaburō, a cousin of hers who had lived in the United States before returning to Tokyo. Perhaps the idea of having to squire a child about town bored him or the responsibility unnerved him; in any case he enlisted the aid of a relative of Father, a man named Endo Isaji, who also lived in the capital. They decided to visit me once a month and then to relate to Asaka the smallest details of my life.

The last Sunday of every month, Endo Isaji would take me to stylish haunts under the pretext of teaching me manners. When Naganuma Yūzaburō came along, the three of us would visit a temple, a monastery, or a museum. Then my "uncles" would take me to a restaurant, where they showed me how men and women of good society conducted themselves. I learned how to eat Western-style, how to hold a knife and fork, how to sip my soup from the side of a spoon, without gurgling or slurping.

Both men had traveled abroad, and they amused me with their tales of how foreigners were very tall, with pink skin and ungainly long arms and legs, which they waved about in all directions, like Senju Kannon, the Kannon with a thousand arms.[4]

They also said to me, "Now, you are nothing but an in-house disciple, but later, if you wish to succeed in the world, you will need the manners of a city girl from an important family. You will have rich customers, and you will have to show evidence of an education superior to theirs. You must study the techniques of hairdressing, of course, but you must also beautify your heart, your mind, and your body. Because if your mind is less beautiful than your body, or your heart less refined than your mind, you can never possess the harmony that is the source of true beauty. You must never lose an occasion to enrich your personality."

This talk enchanted me.

For our outings, I dressed in an elegant cream-colored kimono, with a pattern of roses and delicate stems without thorns, or a light green one with white birds and bright yellow spots. My uncles congratulated me: "You're as beautiful as a young bride!"

I felt myself blush. "These are the kimonos Mother sends me."

"She must think you're looking for a husband."

"I told her to give me plainer ones."

"When a girl leaves home, parents always think it's only to find a husband. You really haven't found anyone?"

I took care to look embarrassed, but I felt a secret satisfaction in being thought marriageable in a city like Tokyo.

Sometimes, with my uncles, I would take walks around the moats of the Imperial Palace. In the clear water, at the foot of the curving, slanted ramparts of gray stone, birds would settle on the water lilies. They took me to Asakusa Temple, too, where it was impossible to judge whether the crowds of pilgrims outnumbered the merchants. We visited the monastery of Jindai, on the far west side of Tokyo. There we were served iced *soba* noodles on bamboo racks.

In that way, little by little, I developed a taste for Tokyo. Undeniably, the city was not beautiful, since after the Great Earthquake of Year 12 of Taishō (1923), which had caused the wooden houses to burn like torches, it had been rebuilt catch as catch can, with graceless shacks. But my uncles taught me to read a secret history infused with radiant beauty behind the poor facades of cracked cement or the roughly cut planks. They said, "Long ago on this spot was the house of a samurai, a beautiful house of brown wood. And over there was once a teahouse frequented by young, wealthy patrons. Here was the hovel of an old *shamisen* player who had been driven mad with fear when the earth shook. On summer evenings, he would sit out in his long underwear on the veranda. He would scratch at his instrument (a sort of three-string guitar strung with cat or dog hide), singing of screaming crowds in the midst of blooming flames and bluish wreaths of smoke, desperate flights, and wounded children."

I was discerning behind the reality another, more subtle truth that filled me with love for the past and for humanity. It was at that time that I came to understand that true beauty resides as much in hearts as in forms.

From time to time, when Endo Isaji went back to Kōriyama, he would stop by Asaka to take them news of me. The first few times he did this, Father apparently refused even to hear my name pronounced. Happily, however, through his indefatigable amiability, my uncle succeeded in procuring my forgiveness. After that, each time he came, Father would invite him to drink sake with him next to the brazier filled with warm embers. Days later, the echo of those peaceable interviews reached me via Mother's letters. It made me homesick.

In her letters, Mother always said I must apply myself seriously to my work, in order to show my gratitude to the Yamazakis, who were allowing me a chance to realize my vocation. She told me all the news about this one and that one. My *tori-age-bābā* had died. A cousin had left for Manchuria. A new cinema had opened in Kōriyama, and everyone had gone to see a film that featured shots of the young working girls of Tokyo. How well-dressed they were! According to my uncle, she added, I had put on weight, which became me. He said that my gestures had become more gentle, which gave me the allure of a real city girl. "The water in Tokyo must suit you," she wrote. Then, she always added the same flattering parting line: "It seems you've become quite a solid girl."

These compliments pleased me, of course, but I didn't feel I deserved them. I worked harder, and harder still, so as not to give Mother reason to be ashamed of me.

RESIGNATION

About four months passed in that way, and winter had come without my having done anyone's hair but my own. Like the vagabond who contemplates the moon, I watched the elegant girls who talked of curls and scissors with grave, gentle looks. From time to time I would grumble: "In their eyes, the future of an apprentice doesn't count." I saved up bitterness in my heart, like an evil fortune from which I drew a strange sort of comfort. Overwhelmingly fatigued and torn between dreams of revenge and my shame, I sometimes thought, "I'll show them all that I'll succeed." Then, as time passed, the pain of daily life annihilated my desires.

Such was my state of mind when Yamazaki Nobuko summoned me into the director's office. She brutally pulled up the left sleeve of my work smock: a gold watch glittered on my wrist.

"This is a Swiss watch."

"Yes, it was a present from Father for my twelfth birthday."

"The band is of leather."

"None of my brothers and sisters ever got one so nice."

"Are you the favorite?"

"Mother forbade my older sisters ever to step over my body or my head."

"We'll have no favorites here. That watch is not suitable to your position. All the girls at the school have noticed that you are careful to remove your servant's smock before you go outside in the street, as if you wished to hide your circumstances from the world. You'd do well to give up such airs."

Yamazaki Nobuko spoke in an even voice: "You came to us after having been accepted as an in-house disciple. Therefore, stop leading a double life, stop constantly reminding yourself that you are well-born. If that's really what you think, you prove yourself disloyal both to us and to yourself, because that is your actual condition. Are you really dishonest, or is it merely a matter of unthinking youthfulness in your heart? In the future, give up subterfuge and ruse. You cannot be both in and out at once. As long as you conduct yourself in this way, you will never be able to immerse yourself totally in your chosen work. And your acts will never bring the proper fruits."

I was humiliated. That very day, I wore my work smock when I went out. However, rather than take off the watch, I wore it well above my elbow so that no one could see it.

A few weeks later, the watch disappeared. True, the band had been worn out, and I may have lost it myself. Or perhaps I left it behind that morning in my room, and someone took it. I didn't dare ask, and I never heard it mentioned again.

I understood then that Yamazaki Nobuko was right. Having no other luxurious possession, I also lost my fine airs. Rather than smiling by spreading my lips, which made me look superior, I forced myself to raise the corners of my mouth shyly. Rather than work out of pride, I came to respect my masters.

I began to study how to do my work, saving a second here and two there. I learned how to grab and hold a spoon without hesitation, so evenly that not a drop of liquid was spilt. I would place the bag of uncooked rice close enough to the kitchen table to be able to dip from it easily. I learned the exact amount of water needed for cooking it: when I placed my index finger perfectly straight up in the water, it should come exactly to the first joint. I figured out how to waste nothing, in either time or materials. I called this economy of movement, a science that was to render me great service later in my work as a hairdresser. As my movements became surer, I discovered the pleasure of a job well done. In cooking, harmony of gesture satisfies the mind as much as a splash of sunlight on a wet rock or the royal song of a bird after a rainstorm. I took a legitimate pride in my skillfulness, which also informed my body with the reassuring feeling that I could live any kind of existence.

TEST

One morning, Yamazaki Nobuko led me into a small room that was used as a dressing room for brides. There was no furniture on the tatami floor except a freestanding mirror and a low table, on which lay implements unknown to me. Yamazaki Nobuko ordered me to sit, left the room, and soon returned with a ravishingly beautiful girl dressed in a simple under-kimono of white silk. She looked like one of those beauties out of a story-book: she had astonishing black hair, glittering with bluish highlights, which rustled on her shoulders. A fine perspiration pearled up in round drops, like dew, on her temples, lending her flesh the transparency of marble. On her delicate neck, she carried her head with the grace of a hollyhock bent by the May rain.

She was the most beautiful woman I had ever seen. I never learned her name, nor where she had come from. I understood only that she was to marry that day—the day I would receive my first hairdressing lesson. It seemed to me that our simultaneous entry into new lives created a special bond between us. I tried to smile at her, but she didn't look at me. Nonetheless, to this day, I am grateful to the gods for having permitted me to begin learning my craft in the company of such a beautiful person. By showing me that woman, at that time, the gods were telling me: "Look what heights human beauty can attain. Let this girl be your ideal. Guard this marvelous perfection in your memory."

Yamazaki Nobuko interrupted my reverie: "After I have oiled her hair, you will hand me the instruments spread out on the table as I ask for them. While waiting, do not bother me."

Yamazaki Nobuko worked in silence. From time to time, she would whisper through her thin lips the name of a comb or a kind of hairpin. It was not explicitly an order, just a word. My heart pounding like that of a sparrow terrified by a storm, I awaited these words that, for the most part, I didn't know. There were straight combs and curved combs; combs for hairdressing; ornamental combs; spatulate ones made of wood, of horn, and of tortoiseshell; hoops for holding up loops of hair and metal headbands; simple hairpins, twisted hairpins, with pointed or rounded ends. Giving myself up to chance and the gods, I chose the instruments. My head down, I would crawl on my knees across the tatami and hand them to Yamazaki Nobuko. She would grab them without a look. If I got it right, she would continue silently, but if I handed her the wrong thing, I would see her jaw tighten slightly before she threw it to the ground. It would bounce violently and hit the wall, or it would slide with the rustling of a bird's wings over a pond. When the floor was littered with them, I wondered if I should pick them up, but I didn't know if I were allowed to move. I decided to drag myself as discreetly as possible over the tatami mat, draw them toward me, and put them on the table.

This lasted for two interminable hours, during which a sense of the indignity done to me grew continually in my heart.

When the hair was done, the two of them walked out without a word. I bowed respectfully, then didn't dare raise my head. I understood that I had been put to some kind of test, and I thought I had failed. I had been there for four months already. And what had I learned? How to make rice properly, how to hang up a coat so it would dry unwrinkled. But hadn't

I forgotten the reason for all that? Seduced by the pleasure of promptly accomplishing my tasks, I had abandoned my plans and lost sight of my destiny. Now that they had trusted me to do something else, I had proven myself incapable of it. Should I not have been reading textbooks on hairdressing in the evenings, poring over the encyclopedias I had barely cracked, in which appeared the names of all the tools of my trade? For the first time since my moment of panic in the train station, I thought seriously of going back to Asaka: I would go home, beg their forgiveness, and agree to the humblest occupations without complaint.

I was overcome by a melancholy as plaintive as the cry of the owl through the weeping willows.

Yamazaki Nobuko gently slid open the *fusuma*, the sliding screens. I lowered my chin to my chest, so she would not see my eyes filled with fear, like frozen puddles. She brutally jerked my chin up, but then, for the first time, she smiled at me. She said, "Starting tomorrow, you will have one free hour every day, to study hairdressing."

I wept. They had forgiven me. I was awash in gratitude. I wanted to throw myself at her feet, to tell her I would never again play the spoiled, selfish child, that I would work hard, that one day I would be worthy. Since there was no one word with which to express that, I stammered, "Thank you. I will obey you in everything."

"Good," said Yamazaki Nobuko. "I hope that your fine words will not slip away as quickly as water over rocks."

BIYŌ NO MICHI: THE WAY OF BEAUTY

From then on, for one hour a day, I attended the classes taught by Yamazaki Seikō, the director of the school, alongside the paying students.

At that time, the master's beard was still black, and his mouth, like his eyes, smiled benevolently. He wore little round glasses, which made him look like a great scholar, and on holidays he would pin to his chest the decorations he had won in the Russo-Japanese War. He was kind and gentle, always affable. Later, long after his beard had grown white, when Japan was at war with the United States, I watched him grow sad and silent.

But before the war, he was always cheerful, and he told us marvelous things. He said, "If you wish to become good hairdressers, use the best instruments. As for wooden combs, the Japanese are the finest. Buy ones made of satsuma wood, that is a strong material, and very soft to the touch. When it comes to metal tools, get the German, because it is in Germany that they make the strongest steel." Indeed, at the school, all the metal instruments were German-made. He also advised us: "Do not hesitate to buy expensive tools. This is never a superfluous luxury, as one can accomplish fine work only when one has the most trustworthy instruments. And those of you studying here will be called upon to create the most noble hairstyles."

Yamazaki Seikō taught the *Biyō no Michi*, the Way of Beauty, a way of living that placed beauty at the center of each thought. Just as the autumn moon pierced the shells of the clouds, he opened the eyes of each of our hearts. Even now, it pleases me to repeat to my own disciples the words of the master. As they rise to my lips, these words heard long ago rewarm my throat and my mouth: "I cannot tell what your work will be like in ten or fifteen years, when people will recognize you in your turn as masters of beauty. The world is endlessly changing, and so are techniques. Today I teach you the flowering of our art, but never suppose that you possess perfect knowledge. You must continually study and search, increasing your know-how in accord with the times in which you live. In that way you will assume your responsibilities toward mankind and arrive at excellence."

In these early years of the Shōwa Era, teaching hairdressing was a difficult matter, because styles seemed to change faster than time itself. The era when married women washed their hair with *funori* (a seaweed glue) or with wheat flour—and then only on visits to the homes of their birth— was long past. So was the age when women counted on camellia oil to keep their hair black, and on plum blossom oil to increase their allure. Modern girls no longer swore by anything but *pomādo kosumechikku*, pomade cosmetics from the West, and they perfumed their hair with walnut oil, indiscriminately.

How women did their hair no longer bore the least relationship to age or social position. All fashion-conscious ladies, thinking themselves original, wore the same hairstyle: they would demand that their hair be cut very short, and the only variation from head to head was the position of the fine strands they took from the temples and piled up in front of or behind their ears, according to the vogue of the day. By contrast, the traditionalists kept the bun at the nape of the neck, consulting their hairdressers only on where to part the hair—left, right, or center. There were no more rules, but in the end anarchy led to monotony. It would take the invention of the curling iron for some to decide on a semilong, wavy style—sometimes held back with a headband, because at that time, no virtuous girl would be seen in the street completely bareheaded.

If they wished to become true masters of beauty, hairdressers had to establish principles that would lend new meaning to their art. Only imbeciles would continue over the long term to spend their money on things that made no sense. The greatest skill consisted of drawing inspiration from

Traditional hairstyles.

the past and applying the rules flexibly, in order to create good taste. And so, the basic, long-established rule for hair ribbons on a chignon was applied to modern headbands: violet for a great lady only, red for a young girl, and pale colors for older women. The rules of decorum would not be infringed.

Besides these rules, I learned the names and uses of combs and ornaments. First, one had to use a *toki-gushi* (a detangler), a large-toothed comb held with the hand; then wash the hair and smooth it out using a *suki-gushi*, a short comb with a thick back and fine teeth that caught the dust which could dull the shine. Or one could substitute a Western hairbrush for the *suki-gushi*. The ridges in a traditional chignon were made using a *kesuji kushi*, a long-handled comb with tiny teeth, which was also used to return escaped strands to their places. The fine hairs of the temples and forehead were smoothed with a *bin-toki-gushi*, a long comb with short teeth that was also useful in creating the puffed-out loops of classic chignons.

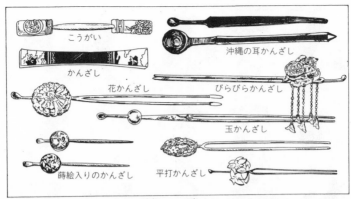

こうがい

かんざし

花かんざし

沖縄の耳かんざし

びらびらかんざし

玉かんざし

蒔絵入りのかんざし　平打かんざし

かんざし
簪のいろいろ　近世につくられた笄の先に耳掻きをつけたものが簪になる。
はじめは脚一本だったのが，その後，
耳掻きのない花簪，さらにびらびら簪
があらわれた。金銀銅・真鍮・錫・べ
っ甲・漆塗りなどがある。

天丸形　　山高形

鎌倉形　　利休形

京丸形　　高原形

牡丹形　　魚　形

寛政形　　品川形

〔上〕　櫛の形　櫛は形だけでなく，蒔
絵などの飾り模様にもさまざまな工夫
がこらされた。
〔右〕　櫛の種類　①はとかし櫛，②は
びんかき櫛，③はすき櫛，④⑤は毛す
じ立て櫛，⑥はびん出し櫛，⑦はびん
あげ櫛，⑧はびんかき櫛。

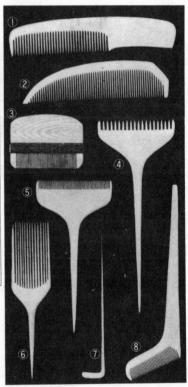

Traditional hairpins and combs.

Ornamental hairpins were all derived from the *mimi-kaki*, the ear stick. Used since antiquity to hold the hair, this was a slim stick of wood, ivory, or glass. One of its ends was rounded like a drop of water; light ornaments, balls of agate or green jade, or dangling ornaments shaped like flowers or butterflies were attached to that end.

One day Yamazaki Seikō showed me something indispensable to beauty from the era, already long past, when married women blackened their teeth.[5] An outer box of paulownia wood was decorated with a hollyhock-and-indigo flower design. Inside was another black box, finely encrusted with metal, protected by a piece of fabric in a pale sea color, and embroidered with lotus buds, and tied with a violet cord. That box had an upper and a lower compartment. The first contained fine combs; the second, instruments used for blackening. Each of these objects was covered in layers of Japanese paper tinted various colors: the first was black, with a light gold design showing cranes, tortoises, pine trees, bamboo, and *tachibana*, all animals or plants that serve as harbingers of happiness. The tortoise symbolizes longevity; the crane, which goes back and forth from the world of the sky to that of the earth, brings the spring. Bamboo grows straight in spite of its knots; the needles of the pine tree fall in pairs, inseparable as an old married couple;[6] and finally, the *tachibana*, a mythical orange that the emperors of old believed to exist in Korea, is the fruit of immortality.[7] The next seven papers bore the colors of the rainbow: red, the orange of the Seville orange tree, yellow, green, light blue, indigo, and dark violet, the imperial color. On the final sheet, which was unbleached and undyed, plant motifs were etched in many colors.

Like a nightingale perched on a cloud, I was as happy as one can be in this world. I worked ceaselessly, but my domestic duties left me two hours of leisure each day to devote to my studies. In the evenings, I read a history of hairstyling. Bent over the fine engraved illustrations, I dreamed of bringing back curls, loops of hair, headbands, ponytails tied with ribbons, curl papers, French twists or old-fashioned upswept chignons, of giving life to the long, black tresses that swept across the pages.

It was probably these foolish dreams that won me first the indulgence and, later, the friendship of the Yamazaki family. Charmed by my obstinate dedication, each brother independently conceived a plan to marry me to his son. This did not sit well with Yamazaki Nobuko, who thought me too far beneath them.

Yamazaki Tomekichi, the younger brother of Yamazaki Seiko, the director of the school, knew nothing of hairdressing. When I confided in this man (who would one day become my father-in-law) my utopian dreams, my imaginings of splendor, he burst out laughing and teased me: "Will you look at the girl from Tōhoku who thinks she's a goldfish with indigo fins!"

He often asked me, "Don't you miss the country?"

"No! I have so much to learn."

"Well, I do—when I look at pretty girls like you! They don't make them like you anymore, except in the country."

This made me explode in a puff of laughter, blushing, my nose in my handkerchief. It was true I had put on more weight. But the color in my cheeks, once imbued by the fresh air of the open fields, had faded. Sometimes I almost glimpsed a kind of distinguished charm in the mirror.

Yamazaki Naka, the wife of Yamazaki Tomekichi, was especially sweet to me. She consoled me about my blunders: "Even monkeys fall from trees." And she would encourage me to start over.

That simple life went on for about two years, until April of Year 11 of Shōwa (1936), when I obtained my first hairdressing diploma.

I wrote Asaka to tell my family that I had received my elementary certificate, and that I would like to pursue my studies for another two years, to get my professional diploma.

FAILURE

An answer soon came: my third oldest sister, Risa, was to marry into the Nakamura family, who were wholesalers in sweets in Kōriyama, and she asked that I come specially to do her hair for the wedding. I would lose some school time, of course, but I hadn't been back to Asaka for two whole years. Surely the Yamazakis would give me permission.

At the end of Mother's letter, Risa had added a few lines. They had bought a wedding kimono in the best store in Kōriyama, choosing a red fabric with large white and gold flowers and a white obi. "You'll see," she wrote. "I shall look very pretty, and even you, sophisticated city girl, will be amazed."

Reading that, I suddenly recalled the tone of our childish arguments, when Risa would go through my dresser drawers and steal my hair ribbons. It made me smile with pleasure. Risa had asked me to buy ornamental combs for her, giving me the address of a store in the Kanda district, very near Ochanomizu. She also said how happy she would be to see me: "I think the only reason I'm getting married is so I can see you again!"

All of that made me very happy, of course, but it also made me aware of the changes that had taken place in me. I found my sister's handwriting unpolished, without distinction. The very fact that she was marrying a wholesaler in sweets struck me as common and dull. She would be happy, no doubt. She would raise a scarlet-cheeked brood, and, although normally so sweet-tempered, she would rage at them. She would hold them tight in her rosy arms; her breasts would grow heavy and soft. I thought all that seemed desperately sad. But, at the same time, that vision reassured me. My sister was marvelously normal. Next to my hazardous existence, life as it had always been went on, immutable, and that certainly was a good thing. From Asaka, like a peahen spreading her wings to protect her children's dinner, Risa watched over me.

I was contemplating the different destinies that govern us when it hit me full in the chest that I had never done a bridal hairstyle. Nobuko had styled the hair of the beautiful bride before my eyes, and I had studied the technique in books. I knew in what order which pins and combs must be inserted so that the various loops of hair built one upon the other in delicate balance. But would I really know how to make sure such an edifice would stay up? I couldn't very well ask them to teach it to me now, because a bridal chignon represented the highest art of Japanese hairdressing, and no one studied it before going up for the professional diploma. Such a request would be deemed impudent.

But I didn't want to give up on this chance to revisit my village. Asaka! I so wanted to see its green hills, its houses with their grassy roofs again! When I thought about the pink and gray sunsets in spring, it seemed that the blood flowed quicker in my veins. So, in secret, I studied a book on bridal chignons, assembled the necessary arsenal, and went back to Fukushima.

From the minute I arrived in Kōriyama, I knew that this trip would bring me nothing but disappointment. Finding myself back in the big city of my childhood, I thought, just as I had on arriving in Tokyo, "Ah! That's all it is." And my heart felt pinched. The house of Endo seemed sad and cold, like unclaimed cargo abandoned on a dock. Mother's face showed age spots; Father's bearing was less noble than in my memories.

On my older sister's head I built a large-looped traditional hairstyle for the first time in my life. I hid my mistakes beneath the *tsuno kakushi*, the large white silk band we tie around a bride's forehead to hide the horns of jealousy, which are so quick to sprout on the brows of newly married girls.[8] Thanks to the gods, the hairstyle looked as it should when the family hoisted themselves onto the truck that would take us to the Shinto shrine where the ceremony was to be performed.

Alas, no monkey can pass himself off as a tiger for long. With the jolting of the rough road, the hairdo suddenly gave way. One escaped tendril slid, rustling like a piece of green seaweed, down Risa's neck. The structure collapsed when the bride bowed to the gods before accepting the cup of sake tendered by the groom. By the time my sister entered the home of her in-laws, there was nothing left but a hairy mass which called to mind the wet straw they spread on rice paddies in winter. The catastrophe was so complete that no wedding pictures were taken that day.

For days, I had prepared myself for that failure, but the words of apology I had rehearsed would not issue from my mouth. I didn't move a muscle. My head and shoulders pressed against the doorjamb of the house; I no longer knew what it was I should have said. And so, without a word, I went back to Tokyo.

Some weeks later, I received a letter from Asaka. When I opened it, a photo fell in a spiral dance to the floor: there was Risa, her hair in a bridal chignon, smiling modestly at her husband's side. Behind them, a placard read: *Nakamura Kashi-Donya*, Nakamura, Wholesale Sweets. A note from Mother informed me of the name of the Kōriyama hairdresser they had used, as well as that of the photographer. Risa, she wrote, had brought the photo at the time of her first visit back to the village. Gently she explained that they should have understood and not expected so much of me. Worse than the photo, her kind words struck me like a slap in the face. Moreover, Risa looked incredibly beautiful in that picture. I remember chewing the sleeve of my kimono to keep from crying in vexation. I threw myself to the floor of my room and stayed there, prostrate, my mind wandering, lost as a baby bird whose nest has been swept downriver in the rainy season. I was suffering from jealousy.

THE FIRST SALON

As months passed and no one spoke of the affair anymore, I tucked it away in the back of my heart. My domestic duties, my lessons, and time itself forced me to forget my humiliation.

Two years later, in February of Year 13 of Shōwa (1938), I received my professional diploma. One month after I had finished my studies, the Yamazaki family entrusted me with a salon in Bunkyō Ward, in Hongō-ni-Chōme. I was to be the sole employee there. The salon had been a branch of the school where young graduates did their internships. But after the manager passed away at the end of Year 12, they had closed up the house and weren't using it for anything. Since the Yamazakis found it stupid to pay rent without the place bringing in a penny, and they figured that a beginner was better than nothing, they handed me the keys.

When I opened the door, I was exactly twenty years old. To my horror, before long I realized that I didn't know how to do anything. I was no more than a *biyō-shi no tamago*, an egg of a beauty master, and one that would take months or even years to hatch. If the shop was always filled with new faces, it was not because I was making the least success of it but rather that we had no return customers.

The daily receipts soon declined, and I was overcome with shame, fear, and despair. Still, the quality that everyone had reproached me for so often in the past, my hardheadedness, served me well: rather than admit my failure, I determined to hide it by resorting to a stratagem.

Since coming to Tokyo, I had carefully placed the one yen pieces Mother sent me monthly in a cardboard box, which I hid at the back of my closet, behind my futon. By the time I received my professional diploma, I found myself in possession of a small fortune: 100 yen—enough to acquire, had I so desired, a complete wedding trousseau.

I began to dip into my nest egg, taking out one yen every evening, which I added to the receipts before remitting them to the Yamazakis. During the day, without anything to do, I would pick out and redo the girls' dressmaking assignments (which I'd brought from the school to keep my hands occupied), all the while vaguely on the lookout for a customer. I said to myself, "Tomorrow, at least four will come." Or "Tomorrow, I'll do exercises to sharpen my skills." Or else "Tomorrow, I'll confess all." In the morning, when I opened the shop, I would announce out loud that, today, customers would come. Prattling away, I would set out the brushes and combs. Then, as no one had yet come, I would stop my babbling and silently check the cleanliness of the curlers and pins. An hour would pass in that way. I would sit down, look at myself in the mirror, and plunge headlong into depression: "I am nothing. Why would anyone want to come and see me?" And sadness would veil my eyes like autumn mist.

When I had used up almost all my money, I resolved to spend my last few yen in having my hair done in neighboring salons, to see how they did it.

My savings melted away without any increase in clientele. Still, the terror that lived in me day and night kept me from giving up my little game. Driven mad as a spider caught in her own web, I wrote to Asaka. I told Mother: "For four years, I have scrupulously respected our agreement, and I have never asked for your help. But today, for very good reasons that I may not divulge, I find myself in dire need. If you agree to help me, I will never ask you for anything again for as long as I live. That is a promise. But just this once, help me! Save me!"

That letter sowed dread in the hearts of the family Endo. "What could she possibly need? Haven't we sent her all the necessary clothes? Is she not fed and lodged? And isn't she working in a hair salon?" My lack of money could be explained only by associations with bad company, some shameful straying from the straight and narrow, or some ill-conceived foolishness.

That is what they thought, and they quickly dispatched my oldest brother to Tokyo to investigate. When I saw him, I begged him for money. My forehead pressed to the tatami, I implored him, trembling like a puppy. But my groaning, my words so tiresome as to grow mildew in the ears or moss in the mouth,[9] did not convince him. Finally, to get on with it, he said, "Swear to me that you have done nothing to discredit the name of Endo."

I swore.

"Then I will give you the money. But you must tell me what you need it for."

"You'll give it to me, no matter what?"

"Yes."

Having imagined thoughtless expenditures, exotic perfumes, luxurious clothes, and questionable acquaintanceships, my brother had a good laugh when I explained it! But he reproached me for the deception in which I had embroiled myself. Then he laughed again. That made me cry all the harder, my mouth wide open, teeth exposed. He seemed to be moved. He put a gentle arm around my shoulders and pulled me to him over the low table. "Cry now, we'll talk afterward." I was reminded of the time I had fallen from the tree as a child. He murmured, "Could it be that you have no talent for hairdressing? Maybe the seal of the law was wrong after all. You should come back to the village. We'll forget about it all, and life will start up like it used to be.

"Remember how the water sounds as it flows through the bamboo piping after the snows melt? Spring clouds blown about by the wind? And the gentle shade under thatched roofs?" He said it again: "You may come home. I will help you, I am the head of the house now." And "If you decide to stay, there is nothing I can do for you, because I don't come from here. But it is not by taking money from the Endos to give to the Yamazakis that you will prove yourself worthy of either. On the contrary, you'll always know that your existence was vain. If you stay, you must accept the loss of that money you have unduly handed over to the Yamazakis."

To return to Asaka would be to acknowledge the failure of all my struggles. And besides, in Asaka, my life would be decided for me as it had been for the others, and I had wanted mine to be different. I knew that that desire would fade away as I married and had children. But in Tokyo I felt like one of those rootless clouds torn apart by the winds at dawn. In the end, I decided to stay, in order to be able to decide on my own destiny.

As we parted, my oldest brother said, "You're stupid, but your pride will save you!"

FIRST SUCCESSES

The following week, I was granted the title of teacher at the Ochanomizu Beauty School for Ladies. Every night, Yamazaki Nobuko instructed me in hairdressing, and early every morning, before opening the shop, I had to give the same lessons to the paying students. As I still ran the shop in Hongō, I had double duty.

My few customers, all old ladies, were soon expressing amazement over my progress: "What quickness! What dexterity! You look like a real hairdresser now!"

I learned to turn quickly on my heels without the front of my kimono coming open, as I had seen Nobuko do. I felt that gave me an air of authority. The customers said: "What elegance! You look like a real lady now!"

Then, I began to give out compliments and advice, copying an attitude I felt suited a great personage of the world. And the customers were beside themselves: "What wisdom! You've become a god!"

At last I dared to hang my diploma on the door, along with a card on which my grade of teacher had been written in calligraphy, after my name. Slowly, business began to flourish in the house in Hongō-ni-Chōme.

At that time, I worked from ten to twelve hours daily. I wore my hair pulled back into a small, severe bun at the nape of the neck. That made me look older, which I thought inspired confidence. Soon I was given an assistant, then two, and finally three. At the same time, since I hated to spend the school's money unnecessarily, I scrimped on everything, even pins and heat, so that I acquired a reputation in the neighborhood as a frightful miser.

Today, when I look back on what I was then, I see a mechanical thing, incapable of thinking of anything but success. My nerves were so taut that the skin on my cheeks and under my eyes was stretched to the splitting point. When people say to me today, "You must have been beautiful when you were young!" I don't contradict them, but it makes me smile. Sometimes it makes me want to stretch myself and look at the sky. I stifle a laugh behind my hand and then, adopting a devilish look that makes them think I'm lying, I say, "Not at all. I was ugly, I tell you, ugly as a skinny horse in the fall."

9

Marriage

Nagai mono ni wa makarero.
To the powerful, submit.

THE ORACLE OF ONTAKE-SAN

Watakushi wa, hatachi, toshigoro de gozaimashita . . . I was twenty, the age to be married. The salon in Hongō-ni-Chōme was prospering, and life flowed on like clear water, without care, like a river in spring.

From time to time one customer or another, impressed with my ardor for my work, suggested she might like me for a daughter-in-law. That flattered me more than I cared to admit to myself, but, convinced in my foolish pride that my life had attained perfect completion, I declined their offers: "A wretched affair that would be for your son! A wife more devoted to her work than to him!"

At that time, I wanted just one thing: to prove to Yamazaki Seikō and his wife, Nobuko, that I was worthy of all the pains they had taken with me. I felt extremely grateful to them. Since childhood I had sought success in vain in the fields, at school, and in sericulture. They had offered me one more chance to succeed; I knew I could never repay them, for all my life. It made my heart beat faster.

Nevertheless, when my attachment to the Yamazakis was put to the test (through divine oracles), I resisted at first. Then, like a poor little column of smoke hurrying straight up to the sky that gets caught in a western wind, I had to give in to their demands.

For the last four years, Yamazaki Seikō and his younger brother Tomekichi had continually, each on his own, insisted he wished me to marry his son. I had continued to decline these propositions politely; not believing they could really want a simple apprentice in the family, I didn't take them seriously.[1] I forced myself to bow gracefully, murmuring that I must first become a great lady!

In any case, the wives of the two brothers didn't seem to take their hus-

151

bands' competing claims to my future any more seriously than I did. No-buko, who in her heart of hearts had already decided that her older broth-er's girl would marry her own eldest son, was quick to resolve the problem. She invited her niece to live with them and encouraged intimacy be-tween the two young people, so that nature took its course: the girl became pregnant. The marriage between the cousins was celebrated with the wholehearted joy of all concerned, because everyone said they made a very well-matched couple. Both were born in Tokyo, both were tall, both had finely wrought hands and feet. Their families listed the ways they resem-bled each other as proofs of the harmony of their union.

Tomekichi's wife, Naka, was also busy at work on the marriage of her son Tatsuo. Amused by her husband's naive machinations, she preferred to put the question of a daughter-in-law to the gods.

Yamazaki Naka had belonged for some time to the brotherhood of On-take-san (Mount Ontake), the sacred mountain of the Hida chain, in the center of Honshū. Each year, during the seventh moon, with others of the faithful from Tokyo, she would make a pilgrimage to the summit of the mount: perched ten thousand feet over the world of men, they would scan the horizon to the west, toward the paradise of the Pure Land beyond the sea. Then, through their guide, a man named Uchida Kamekichi, who knew in what terms one must address the gods, they would question the divine soul of the ascetic founder of the group, Kaigen Reijin, who had opened the mountain for them.[2] That summer, Kaigen Reijin agreed to answer Naka's questions on the subject of her son Tatsuo's marriage. She submitted to him the names of twenty-seven students from the school whom she felt would be suitable, but the god rejected them all. So she gave him the twenty-eighth name—my own. She had put it last, little dreaming the gods would require her to marry her son to a fortuneless girl.

The god responded that Tatsuo would marry me, Nami, or no one. He finished the oracle by specifying that I would be difficult to convince, but that he, Kaigen Reijin, would keep watch over all the good people who climbed the mountain.

Back in Tokyo, Yamazaki Naka announced to whomever wished to hear that the gods had chosen me to marry Tatsuo. It was Year 13 of Shōwa, 1938.

GIRI: INDEBTEDNESS

No one asked my opinion. It was unthinkable that I would refuse this privilege, with which my benefactors were distinguishing me above all oth-ers. I didn't dare tell them that as a child I had sworn never to marry. I still believed keeping that vow would lead to my success. This marriage would not force me to abandon my profession, as hairdressers customarily worked up to the birth of a second or third child, or longer. But I feared that my dreams of great achievement would be dissolved in the service of my husband, since no wife may surpass in renown the man who shares her bed, no matter what their separate professions. And he would doubtless prove a good-for-nothing. The expression we use to designate men who live off their women, *kamiyui no teishu*, hair knotter's husband, says it all. I thought that this union would condemn me to obscurity, to a dull life, smelling neither good nor bad.

But I didn't know how long I could hold out against this new proposal. The many years of my apprenticeship had engendered an obligation that would tie me forever to the Yamazaki family. I possessed a *giri*, a debt owed to them. My work, far from paying it off, further indebted me daily: a *giri* contracted with persons of superior rank could never be repaid, since repeated exchanges do not break the bonds but rather reconfirm them endlessly.[3] Master-disciple relations, I felt, were like a sticky cobweb.

Only by sacrificing my dreams, or my life, could I escape that obligation. Since I didn't especially feel like dying, I had no choice but to capitulate. Doing so would settle my old obligations but would create new ones. Last, this marriage would permit the debt to put down roots in my very body. I would go from disciple to daughter-in-law. And my duty toward my in-laws would grow even more over the next ten or twenty years, until I myself became a mother-in-law.

Sometimes I felt resigned to it. At other times, I determined to flee. I would change identities and hop a ship bound for some far-off country. For a moment, I mused, "What name should I use? I'll wear a Western-style dress and take one of those names so in style now, where they add *ko* to the end, like famous ladies from history. That would be nice. I'll call myself Mari-ko. I'll do foreigners' hair . . . blond hair, and chestnut-colored hair."

And then reality would grip me by the throat, the way a fisherman seizes a fish by its gills. I remembered the words of the old people, when someone had been driven out of Asaka: "He knows no *giri*." To be a good person meant to be *giri-gatai*, strict in *giri*. "Ungrateful people," said Mother, "are not human beings. One day or another, they will die abandoned, far from everyone, like seaweed drying on the rocks."

MEDIATORS

I decided to call my oldest brother to the rescue. Sure that he would consider my request nothing more than a whim, I went all the way to the village to convince him. But to my happy surprise, he did not argue with my resolution and promised to intercede for me at once.

He made a special trip to Tokyo, and, when he went to visit the Yamazaki brothers, they welcomed him with ostentation. They overwhelmed him with little attentions and presents. They gave him sake, pear apples, and an antique treatise on agronomy. They invited him to a banquet where sumptuous shellfish, meats, and fish succeeded one another. Their welcome was such that he couldn't find the words to reject the marriage offer, which, if truth be told, had never really been in question.

As Yoshihiki left for home, he told me that a country bumpkin like himself couldn't muster the gumption to refuse these city people anything. He suggested that I go to Endo Isaji, one of the "uncles" who had shown me around Tokyo at the beginning of my apprenticeship. Endo Isaji had often pled my case to the family, and claimed to hold me in astonished admiration for what he called my courage. He often said, "I'll say this, for a Tōhoku girl, her ears are no colder than her feet!" By that he meant I was fearless.

Endo Isaji was then director of the Otemachi branch of Mitsubishi Bank. My other "uncle," Naganuma Yūzaburō, had once worked for Mitsubishi Trading—the same firm, it so happened, that employed Tatsuo. Endo Isaji asked Naganuma Yūzaburō to get the goods on this Yamazaki Tatsuo person. Naganuma informed him that in eight years of employment, Tatsuo had never once been absent or even late. After learning this, instead of intervening in my favor, Endo Isaji urged me to marry him. How could a slip of a girl from the country think herself above this healthy young man who was serious in his work? Was I a feminist, perhaps? Or did I want to live alone, in order to hide my actions from the world?

To be sure, I was no feminist. And I had nothing to hide. I would certainly have liked to live like a child under the protection of the Yamazakis, and to think myself innocent, accountable before the world for no one's actions but my own, free as a nightingale in spring before she lays her eggs. But it was something else entirely that frightened me. One time when Yamazaki Tomekichi was in his cups, his wife, Naka, begged him to go to bed, and he grumbled that she should have more respect for him, because the Yamazakis were of ancient and noble stock. "There are great men among my ancestors!" he roared. I had a presentiment of terrible things, whose shadow hovered weightily over the destiny of the family. If there wasn't some secret defect in the family destiny, why would such eminent persons have chosen an impoverished apprentice as a daughter-in-law? I would have to become part of an unknown history; this horrified me, not to mention the thought of the body weight of that man I had never seen but whom I would soon be obliged to call *shujin* (master or husband).

MIAI: MEETING WITH AN EYE TO MARRIAGE

Badgered from all sides, I agreed to see Tatsuo, stipulating only that he mustn't know. He claimed to have seen me at school, whereas, only the gods know why, I had never seen him. Nobuko, who told people behind my back that I didn't want to marry Tatsuo because I would have preferred her own son (since he was the heir to the main, or inheritor, branch of the family), tormented me. "Just agree to take a look at him," she said. "That won't obligate you in any way."

After I agreed, she was quick to arrange the matter. On a bright, overcast day, Tatsuo was having lunch in the dining hall with two friends. Nobuko invited me to peek at him through a window. I had to stand on a garbage can to see: in the half darkness, three boys turned to look at me. What I could see best were their white *tabi* socks: two of them had dirty *tabi*. Only one wore clean ones.

Yamazaki Nobuko said, "He's the one with the clean *tabi*."

This information reassured me a little, and I agreed to meet him publicly.

The official meeting, the *miai*, took place the next day.[4] I showed up wearing my servant's work smock, my hair uncurled, my face bare of makeup, hoping that my ugliness would disappoint him and he would turn me down. But it wasn't until years later, long after we were married, that I learned he really hadn't liked what he saw! The fact was he had no use for a fiancée like me at the time. He was a good-looking man, with fine features and a mocking expression that lent him charm. He was seeing a young lady, whom he would have liked to marry. He had raged against it for days, screaming he would never embarrass himself by marrying a hairdresser! But his mother held firm. We must, she said, scrupulously respect the will of the gods. In the end, he had to break with his girl to marry me.

Today, when people see us together, they exclaim: "Surely you two were a love match!" We have to laugh to ourselves, because the truth is neither of us wanted to marry the other.

MARRIAGE

It was in Year 14 of Shōwa (1939), a year of the rabbit, that they forced us to marry. Endo Isaji and Yamazaki Nobuko, particularly pleased with this alliance, of which they considered themselves the architects, served as *na-kōdo*, go-betweens. At that time, as today, when two families allied themselves, the trusted intermediaries were chosen by common accord. Their role was to vouch for the future marrieds and to lead negotiations should any litigation arise down the road.

Tatsuo had studied at the Christian school, Aurora—so that made him a Christian.[5] The ceremony was performed in a church in Aoyama. Yamazaki Seikō gave us a painted scroll depicting a rabbit gazing at the moon.[6] Three characters—*ai* (love), *kei* (respect), and *shin* (trust)—were written on it in calligraphy. But in my heart I disdained those words. I thought they had no other role but to force women into obedience. Like the virtuous words and the beliefs of Naka, they were nothing but ruses of the rich to constrain the poor. When I read them, I felt a hatred that began to eat away at my breast.

At the banquet given by the Yamazaki family in a hotel, Endo Isaji toasted both me and Tatsuo. He emphasized that my stubbornness had become as legendary in Tokyo as it was in Asaka; he detailed the virtues of Tōhoku and the audacity of Tokyoites. I listened to him, laughing as I would have at my own funeral. When the banquet was over, I burst into tears. Everyone said that was normal: just as night follows day, storms follow heat, and old age, youth. They said it was fatigue and emotion, and they urged me to retire for a few minutes to recompose my face with creams and paints. Then, we, the newlyweds, *shinrō shinpu*, left to settle into the apartment which they had furnished for us over the salon in Hongō. Two weeks earlier, Yamazaki Tomekichi and Naka had moved from Ochano-mizu to Hongō.[7]

On the narrow wooden staircase, as I stumbled with each step, Tatsuo took me by the waist to help me walk.

Japanese women often claim to have been ugly and bad-tempered in their youth. It's not that they're any worse than other women but that their entrance into the homes of their in-laws imposes on them new manners at an age when their minds are no more docile than those of children. The usual result is an exhausting lack of harmony. Today, the magazines advise young brides to continue the customs of their native provinces in the homes of their husbands. But back then a wife was not supposed to be original—she had to bend to the ways her mother-in-law taught her. That is why a daughter-in-law was never given charge of a household before the day she could cook miso soup according to the ancestral rules of her husband's line. Her skill in conforming attested to what amounted—after ten or twenty years of life together—to no less than a revolution in her eating habits, and therefore of her entire body. By that, people knew that she had broken with the rules of her old family and could be trusted to apply and perpetuate those of her new house without aid.

But that long instruction period darkened women's lives. As for myself—someone who had always lived by her own lights—I experienced the greatest difficulties in submitting to my husband, my mother-in-law, and my destiny.

AI OR KOI: LOVE OR PASSION

Tatsuo proved himself a correct husband in all things, even though I wasn't much of a wife. Of course he had mistresses, but, as for that, the gods have to allow it, because there are more women than men on this earth. There's nothing wrong in that. Anyhow, I can confess it now that I'm an old woman: men have never attracted me. Except perhaps as a child: Toshirō, my *o-mori*, had excited me a little when he rubbed my feet to warm them. Or my oldest brother when he took me in his arms. In fact, I think that amorous feelings begin with people very close to us. Sons are in love with their mothers, girls with their brothers. Then, when the circles of their acquaintance enlarge, they come to love others.

I've heard that in the West people meet and fall in love instantly. That happens in Japan, too, but these are only passing attachments. True love comes after long months or years, when time has remolded beings who live side by side to suit each other, after they've shared troubles and worries. Just look at what happens when the young people of today make love marriages. Barely two or three years pass before they go their separate ways. For marriages arranged by meeting, it's exactly the opposite: one or two years pass and love develops, so that then the couple find it difficult to part.

There have always been two words in Japanese, *ai* and *koi*, which must not be confused. *Ai* means the love one feels for parents, siblings, and spouse. *Koi* applies only to those disorders of the heart provoked in women by men, and in men by women.[8]

In Asaka, we learned very early that *koi* is a violent emotion that we must each satisfy as we see fit, whether it takes two weeks or three years. However, *koi*, which springs from individual desire rather than from the social order, must stay hidden in order to ensure the proper workings of the world. On the other hand, *ai* reflects the official ties of blood or alli-

Ai, love.   *Koi*, passion.

ance. Mother sometimes said that she had felt a violent passion in her extreme youth and that she had thought she would instantly find happiness
through it. She added, "Taste passion if you can, but do not allow yourself
to be drowned in it, because it will destroy you." Then her eyes filled with
clouds that made her look a stranger to us. Perhaps because of that, passion
has always terrified me. The fact is, in any case, I have not experienced it.
Unless you could say that my passion for work has taken the place of happiness for me.

AKIRAME OR YAMAI: RESIGNATION OR ILLNESS

After a couple of years of marriage, I became pregnant, but my soul was
souring, and my shoulders grew narrower as my belly grew round. I
coughed a lot. The doctor was called in. He diagnosed pleurisy, and, while
I was being treated, a girl came into the world. After having once again
consulted Kaigen Reijin, via the guide Uchida Kamekichi, my mother-in-
law, Naka, decided to call the girl Motoko. *Moto* is the Japanese reading for
the character read *gen* (Sino-Japanese reading) in *Kaigen*. It means "origin."[9]
"Motoko," said Naka, "is a child of Ontake-san." That made me want to
detest the baby who had ripped apart my belly and who nevertheless did
not belong to me. And in spite of the medication I was taking, I coughed
ceaselessly.

In the end, I went back to Asaka in the spring of Year 17 (1942).[10] I don't
remember anymore whose idea that was. Perhaps it was mine, because I
wanted to escape. Or else Naka's; she was sick of having me around and
would gladly have been rid of me. In any case, that was of no concern to
me. To leave my husband was no sacrifice. Besides the excuse of my illness,
there was the war, which showed no sign of coming to a quick conclusion
and which made my move to the country only natural. In Tokyo, it was
becoming difficult to find good quality rice. If the fighting went on, Tatsuo
would be mobilized and sent to boot camp. Whatever happened, Naka
and her husband would stay behind to guard the house.

The morning I left for Asaka, Naka went with me to the train station to
carry Motoko. On the way, she told me to stop my useless struggling and
to come back *akirameta toki*, when I had resigned myself to my condition.

Akirameru, to renounce, to resign oneself: another word whose meaning I refused to understand. What I suffered from was not so much my illness as the impression that fate and the gods were toying with me. Once I had finished my years of apprenticeship, I had thought that my difficulties belonged to the past, that the time had come for me to bring beauty into the world. Now marriage had cut off the wings of my dreams—it tied rocks to my ankles and weighted my belly with children. *Akirame*, the capacity for renunciation, said Naka, is the greatest quality of the Japanese woman. But I revolted against this, because I didn't know that out of renunciation grows a luminous inner peace that gives true strength, the capacity for discernment.

And so a terrible anguish weighed on my lungs, and I coughed in order to expel this evil from my breast. When I arrived in Asaka, my parents were obliged to apologize to the Yamazakis for the trouble their useless girl had caused them. At the same time, they wondered quietly what was happening to me: never before had anyone in the family had an illness like that. I myself hadn't had a fever since a bout of pleurisy at the age of twelve. It all seemed very odd to them. As I closed myself up in my sufferings, they asked themselves what horrifying fate could be connected to associating with the Yamazakis.

SEIMEI NO JISSŌ: THE REALITY OF LIFE

So I settled back into the house of Endo, now headed by my oldest brother, Yoshihiki. The first thing, I sat down on the veranda. I rested my elbows on my knees and ate a persimmon. I gazed at the landscape. I recognized the hills with their lazy slopes, their green coats spotted with snow like a fawn's skin; the misted-over grasses, where tiny bluish stars secretly flourished; the sharp scent of the first days of spring. My anguish softly vanished, but with it went my vitality.

Every morning and evening, I took the tuberculosis medicine prescribed for me by a doctor in Tokyo. I coughed less, but a slight fever persisted, which weighed down my movements and my thoughts. Anything was an excuse for depression. Motoko, the child consecrated to the gods of Ontake-san, smiled at me in my distress. I felt incapable of cherishing this happy baby girl, because the gods and my mother-in-law had appropriated her for themselves.

The spring birds emerged from the clouds, their eyes filled with scenes from the south, chirping like the laughter of tropical islanders. I compared my condition to theirs; I, the caged nightingale, envied the eagle of the mountain peak. My woman's destiny had clipped my wings. In neither town nor country was there a place where I could have freedom—I was merely a wife.

I read only scorn into the gentleness with which everyone treated me. I said to myself, "Happy are those who have never tried for anything, and who therefore have never failed!" There is nothing more morbid than a dream annihilated by the duty of obedience.

Taking refuge sometimes in my childhood, on sunny mornings I would dig my toes deep into the warm earth. I pretended that I had never left home, that happiness and glory still awaited me. My sadness was no more than the fruit of an unpleasant thought, the kind one has on nights of full moon. But when the illusion was gone, a resigned torpor filled my spirit, allowing free reign to the fever that gnawed at my body.

I had lived like that for a month or two, my illness dogging me like a demanding servant, when my older sister Risa's husband came from Kōri-yama for a visit. Although he was nothing but a wholesaler in sweets, Mr. Nakamura brought me a book entitled *The Philosophy of the Reality of Life*, an inspirational work by Taniguchi Masaharu.[11]

Taniguchi Masaharu was born on the night before the harvest festival, the twenty-second day of the eleventh moon, in Year 26 of Meiji (1893), at an hour when the full moon still illuminated the western mountains while the sun already feathered the eastern clouds. The balance which at that moment governed the movements of the heavenly bodies conferred on his mind a sense of truth so just that the gods decided to grant him the additional gift of incomparable wisdom. You see, if the instant of our birth determines our innate qualities, it is the gods who, through those qualities, dole out our measure of intelligence.

I read marvelous things in this book. Master Taniguchi wrote: "The god of the land of my birth, my *ubu-suna no kami*, is that of the shrine of Ikuta, where the younger sister of Amaterasu Ōmikami, Wakahirume no Kami, also called Wakahimegimi no Mikoto, is venerated."[12] And a bit further on:

> Half of a man's destiny is fixed by the sum of doings which took place in lives lived by preceding generations. The other half is determined by the attitude of his heart, which is manifested in his struggles and actions in this life. And [there is a third half,] the last half:[13] this is the destiny set by the gods of the land of his birth and other spirits of high rank, who reside with the god. I say "half of his destiny," but it is impossible to make an exact mathematical calculation. The general direction of destiny is fixed by the *ubu-suna no kami* in conformity with the merits accumulated in past lives.

My brother-in-law explained to me that the gods had chosen Taniguchi Masaharu to reveal to men their divine origin, because he was a person of great learning. He had read all the foreign thinkers and the Chinese and Japanese classics. By the grace of that revelation, Taniguchi Masaharu had founded *The House of Progress,* a magazine whose philosophy surpassed all the religions in wisdom, because it united them all.[14] The master also said that everyone must live in union with the gods who are the source of his true life. And that Japan, situated between Asia and the United States, between East and West, enjoyed an exceptionally favored position as mediator. Taniguchi-Sensei said,

> But what, then, is Japan's vocation? What is Japan to do for the world? Egypt and Babylon are the founders of human culture. The Jews added to this an admirable system of morality. The Greeks refined it. The Phoenicians, through their voyages, spread that culture throughout the world. The Romans preserved it. The Germans evolved it. The English strengthened it. And the Americans have put it into practice. Can it be, then, that there is nothing left for the Japanese to do? Could it be that Japan is to simply assimilate this civilization elaborated in foreign lands and satisfy itself so easily with that? Surely not. Japan, like the other great powers, must bring its contribution to mankind! I am sure that we will magnificently develop the work of those who came before.

In addition, Taniguchi-Sensei declared with blinding clarity that the world of heaven, the High Plain, residence of the gods of Japan, the Beyond of the Christian believers in Jesus Christ, and the paradise of the Pure Land of the Buddhists were to be realized on earth. It was toward that end that the Japanese must work. "The name of Jesus and the name of Japan both start with J. This is not an accident, but a divine sign of universal will," he said. "Christianity, Buddhism and the Shinto of old will all be united in the 'House of Progress,' in which souls, at last, will blossom freely. And that 'House of Progress' will be the matrix of a harmonious universe in which Japan, situated at the root of the sun, would accomplish its vocation: to bring happiness to the world."[15]

The master also taught that there were two great movements of unification in opposition to each other. The communists had tried for some time to make the world uniform in terms of the material, and even in Japan, in this country of the gods, certain individuals adhered to those beliefs and wanted to abolish the imperial system.

The other movement, fired by the ambition to unify the world through the power of the spirits, hoped for the creation of a universe in which all beings would be united under one light: that was the House of Progress.

RELIGION AND HEALING

My brother-in-law was the local delegate of the House of Progress in Kōri-yama, where he distributed the magazine that Taniguchi Masaharu had founded. When he gave me the book *The Philosophy of the Reality of Life,* he asserted that this work possessed extraordinary virtues: men and women, after having merely read the title in a newspaper column, had been known to renounce plans for suicide. Others, semiparalyzed, had felt their pains disappear. Thanks to the master's teachings, peace reigned in homes that had previously been divided by strife; both the bodies and the hearts of good people had been saved. In fact, I had already heard of "The Reality of Life," having read an ad in the magazine *Shufu no Tomo,* "The Housewives' Companion."[16] But my mind was so obstinately mired in bitterness that no light had dissipated the fog in my heart. Could it be that the gods were finally taking pity on me that day? Or that, in my pain, I was ready to take hold of any form of solace? I don't know. But the need to believe and the thirst for knowledge had seized me.

The book said that mistakes, troubles, and illnesses were signs of an im-perfect understanding of the filial relationship man has to the gods. To leave unhappiness behind, I had only to return to that "true life" which all of us, as children of the divine will, should lead.

My brother-in-law showed me that I had been struggling to turn back the boat that was the life in which I was engaged, with no hope of ever returning to what had been. These attempts, which were doomed to fail-ure, were at the origin of my troubles. He said, "It is not the gods who wish you to have such an illness. The fever comes from your own bad feelings, from your dissatisfaction. Throw away that thermometer, that worry stick, and take your medicine not with hatred, but with gratitude in your heart."

At first his words made my body stiffen with revolt, like a worm hidden deep in a piece of fruit, who squirms when cut in two by the knife. Then, the truth of this man's words was as astounding to me as the young foliage of the maple in spring. Feelings that were so heavy that I could not have admitted them even in dreams came into the full light of day. I understood that I was prolonging my illness in the absurd hope of not returning to Tokyo. And so, the eyes of my heart opened, I ceased to struggle.

I decided to get serious about my recovery. I smashed my thermometer, scattering funny little balls of mercury in all directions. After gathering up the bits of glass, without a word to anyone, I left for the open fields. I went far, to the crossing of those roads where years ago the gang of children had driven back the pests that ate the crops: there, I dug a hole and buried the pieces. As I tamped down the earth with my feet, I sang softly: "May illness be banished from me, like this worry stick!" Returning to the house of Endo, I hid the boxes of medicines bought in Tokyo in the sleeve of my kimono and took them to the brook that flowed at the edge of town. There, I released them to the current and hummed a song about the sending back of the ancestors, which I deemed, with some amusement, fitting for the situation: "Thanks for coming, don't come back too soon."[17] Recalling that little girl with her feet dirtied by the mud of the rice paddies, I laughed in a way I hadn't laughed for ten years and felt the eight hundred strings that bound my breath begin to untangle.

After that, knowing that nothing but the force of my soul would bring about my recovery, I read several hours a day, in order to gather mental energy. The household was surprised, then alarmed. They said to each other, "Look, she's gone mad now," and they increased their offerings at the temple. Finally, I resolved to walk to Kōriyama and visit Risa. My oldest brother, Yoshihiki, was very concerned about my tiring myself, but, powerless before my determination, he let me go. I returned with my eyes shining like laurel leaves after the rain and stated my intention to go and stay with my younger brother, Yoshihisa, who lived near Fukushima. They again became worried, but they soon chose to see in my stubbornness a presage of the recovery to come. I went by train.

The countryside outside Fukushima was not the landscape of my happy, vanished childhood. There, my heart at last was free from my foolish attachments. Walks, fishing, and reading—I led a wholesome life. I counted the many good fortunes that destiny had given me, which in my vain folly I had repulsed. I thought, "I will not ruin my life over love of shades of the past. I will leave the path of *shura*, that of those doomed by their own pride to fight themselves endlessly."[18] After two months, I felt strong enough to live the name of Yamazaki—a name the worthy gods had seen fit to grant me—as it should be lived.

APOLOGIES TO THE GODS, THE ANCESTORS, AND MEN

I returned to the house of Endo to announce my recovery. I wrote letters of confession to my husband, Tatsuo, and my mother-in-law, Naka. I admitted having refused the fine name of Yamazaki, to the point that my health had been affected. From now on, I wrote, if they still wanted anything to do with me, I would conduct myself in a way befitting that name. After almost two years apart from him, I promised Tatsuo to be his wife in my heart.

He came to get me immediately. He told me he had never considered divorce but had awaited this moment since the evening we were married. I marveled at his patience, his confidence, and his generosity.

On the train back to Tokyo, he had me read from the Bible he had kept since his graduation from school. Before, he had often left pious books on my doorstep, to urge me to live better, but I had refused to look at them. I hadn't wanted to surrender myself to the abusive coercion of beautiful phrases. That day on the train, I discovered that what I had taken for the urgings of an *akuma*, a demon, were in actuality the words of the gods. I understood how important a role mental attitude plays in the way one perceives and receives all that comes one's way.

As we approached the capital, I had a vague impression that the color of the air had changed, that the trees had become gray. Through the train window, very near Tokyo, I saw an immense hole in the ground. "That's where a shell hit an onion field," said Tatsuo. At the next stop, a young man got on the train. He was so pale one could almost see tiny blue veins under his skin. But in my desire to forgive myself and to start a new life, I looked away.

As soon as I arrived at the house in Hongō, I went to greet the Yamazaki ancestors. I bowed before their altar, the *butsudan*, and I left presents for them there: a can of pickled eggplants and tea sweets filled with red bean paste, which I had brought back from Fukushima.[19] And then I apologized to them: "I came into this family because the gods felt that only I must do so. Rather than showing them gratitude, I fought them, in refusing to venerate them. And so they sent that illness, to open the eyes of my heart, and I learned true discernment. Here I am before you. From now on, recognizing the good fortune you have granted me, I will serve others as the gods wish me to."

Having expressed my regrets, I looked around me and saw that the world had been turned upside down.

10

The War

腹が減っては軍は出来ぬ

Hara ga hette wa ikusa wa dekinu.
You can't do battle on an empty stomach.

Iiyō no nai fuan, ōinaru kibō, sasaina fubensa . . . sonna sensō wo Tōhoku de wa wasurete orimashita . . . The war, with its indefinable ill-ease, its outlandish hopes and trivial inconveniences . . . in Tōhoku, I forgot all that. On the morning of December 8 of Year 16 (1941), when the newsboys screamed at the top of their lungs, "*Gōgai!*" and "*Sensō!*" ("Extra, extra!" "War!"), at first I was terrified. But I knew that Japan had to drive the Westerners out of Asia. Pushed by their ambitious arrogance, they had conquered our brother countries. I knew that Japan fought for the glory of the emperor. Then suddenly we heard the news: American ships, the mainstays of that proud nation's flotilla, reputed to be invincible, had been destroyed. The gods were watching over Japan. Nothing could resist the imperial army.

After that, like everybody else, I got used to hearing the bulletins of victory which marked the advance of the army to the south, toward those tropical isles where, it was said, the people were happy all the time. We were certain nothing bad could happen under such skies. Still, as months passed, my pride was worn thin by the everyday worries of life in wartime. Very soon, soap, matches, and dishes were scarce. Our having to resort to the black market seemed in direct contradiction to the exaltation of the courage of the soldiers of Great Japan.[1] I was slowly taken over by indifference.

There were two additional reasons for my detachment: one personal, the other, no doubt, shared by many in Tokyo. At first the war—or at least talk about the war—was just background to real life. For several years already, the men in my family had been speaking of battles on the continent, in China. In the women's magazines, I read official propaganda: wives were sought for the soldiers and colonists who had left to settle far-off lands. Since my childhood, Father had assaulted our ears with tales of his prowess in the Russo-Japanese War, eternally deploring the fact that Mother had not given him more sons to make soldiers of. War was a boys' affair. It did not concern me.

The second reason was that the military operations took place far from our eyes, in empty seas. And no one I knew had yet had to count their dead, or see them in dreams.

In April of Year 17 (1942), when the American planes flew over Tokyo, I saw them from my house without knowing whose they were.[2] Later, under the direction of the neighborhood association (tonari-gumi), I learned what to do in an alert: to bury myself under piles of futons and wait for the roaring of engines to stop. But the planes did not come back, and life resumed as it had been. In fact, had my coughing not begun, I would even have felt a sort of joy at the early arrival of spring that year. Then I left for Asaka.

It was in the spring of Year 18 that I began to wonder how long the war—which we were told we were winning—would go on.[3] Even in Fukushima, we no longer had good rice to eat. The daily rice ratio was so meager that we had to mix it with barley, oats, or even potatoes; some evenings we had to make do with bean soup or soybeans. Fortunately, clothes were not a problem. From time to time, people from Tokyo or other places would come to the rural black market, where they would trade the clothing of their dead for food. So while Tokyo women at that time had nothing but monpe, loose pants gathered at the ankles,[4] to wear, the girls of Asaka had never been so elegant. We had Western-style dresses, even hats. Still, since the men had all gone to the front, we had to work all the harder in the fields.

Very little, however, was required of me. The weakness of my constitution kept me confined to the house, so I did not help with the spring planting. But, toward the middle of the fifth moon, I decided to do my part. As I had slender hands, they all agreed I must have a great talent for delicate tasks. So they gave me the job of transplanting rice seedlings in a small plot. To everyone's amazement, I accomplished in one day the work of at least three people. Alas, the shoots, planted too shallowly, floated to the surface of the flooded paddy the next day, where they waved merrily, pushed by the breeze. They all laughed at my ignorance, and I resolved in shame never again to play the peasant girl. I warned myself that the war must not serve as a pretext for finding new games for myself, when, far away, soldiers were dying, perhaps that very moment. Still, I tried not to think about the war.

So when I went back to Tokyo early in Year 19 of Shōwa (1944), I was shocked at how dirty it was. Stinking filth I could never have imagined was everywhere, because there was no one to cart away the garbage. In addition, the government had ordered the citizenry to gather as many metal objects as they could with which to make steel, so the streets were blocked with useless, rusting scrap. We had little to eat. The authorities preached the endurance of thinness as a virtue and an assurance of victory. "*Hoshigari-masen, katsumade wa*! I will desire nothing, until victory!" they cried. Country women came to work, alongside their children, in munitions factories, while others fled the capital, looking for a less difficult life. The fact was that no speech on the development of war industries could replace food in the mouth.

THE FIRST NAME IKUE

It was in the midst of that disorder that I struggled to build a new life. To celebrate my definitive rupture with an inauspicious past, I followed the counsel of my mother-in-law, Naka, who was urging me to change first names. We went together to a specialist in proper names, who asked my date of birth and then chose for me the name Ikue. It was an unusual name; I'd never met anyone who had it. The three characters used to write the name—those for "master of the world," "eternity," and "mouth of a river"—resonated in my heart like the promise of success. I went back to the house in Hongō and set to work like a demon.

伊久江 Ikue.

In fact, we had considerably more customers than usual. Many hairdressers had closed up shop. And the hair grows whether one eats well or not. The previous year, the school in Ochanomizu had been requisitioned as a barracks because it had a basement. As compensation, the elder branch of the Yamazakis had been given a large shack in Shiga Prefecture; Seikō and Nobuko gave classes in dressmaking there.

I was so aggressive that some people criticized me for acting like a man. I retorted that it couldn't be helped, for even in childhood I had been a tomboy. Others, seeing me make the decisions on everything, concluded I must be older than my husband. Naka preferred to see in this the influence of my new name, Ikue, which no one would take for a man's. She rejoiced that such strength would soon resuscitate the defunct glory of the Yamazakis. And no doubt she was right.

THE BOMBINGS

However, toward midyear our clientele diminished. After the taking of Saipan in July, we began to hear disquieting rumors that we might be bombed by the Americans. People said that, on that far-off island, our soldiers had blown themselves up in the caves in which they had hidden from the invader, and that women and children, under the horrified gaze of weakhearted Americans, had thrown themselves from cliffs into the sea rather than submit to occupation. Others, to give themselves courage, had played catch with grenades after pulling the pins, until they exploded.[5]

After that, girls were taught at school to use guns so they could defend themselves against the aggressor. We imagined the dead at the front, chins and knees pointing to the empty sky, their mouths filled with dirt. All the while expressing an absolute confidence in the emperor, I wondered vaguely if I, too, would not one day experience that horrible glory.

In Tokyo, nothing was left anymore, not even water for bathing. The water at the *sentō* (the public bath) remained grayish and lukewarm, since we had to save energy. We went there only two or three times a week, instead of every evening, as we had before the war. The neighborhood associations distributed rice in progressively more parsimonious allotments. In Hongō, we had begun to know hunger. The search for food took longer every day. As I wandered far across Tokyo, everywhere was in the same state of abject want. After the first American bombings (in November 1944), the soldiers and police demolished whole streets, entire neighborhoods, to stop the fires. They dug trenches instead of shelters. In Bunkyō, there hadn't yet been any bombing, but many parts of the city had reverted to chaos. The inhabitants were driven out. Those whose homes had been destroyed by American bombs or by our own soldiers wandered the streets, their futons rolled up and strapped to their backs. In the evening, they looked for places to rest under sheet-metal lean-tos, which they had to leave when the alert sounded, obliging them to take shelter from the bombing.

In the night, the fires—the flowers of Edo, as they used to say—blossomed profusely. We would run to the hole that the neighborhood association had provided for us. This was a ditch barely two yards deep, filled with standing water, cockroaches, and mosquitoes. Silent, we would keep our eyes wide open in the dark. Motoko clung to me, while Naka, whispering the Hannya Sutra, counted off the beads of her Buddhist rosary. Tatsuo was elsewhere. Everyone secretly wondered if Japan hadn't pushed its dreams of glory too far; perhaps the gods, deciding an immoderate pride had overtaken us, now planned our downfall. Then, when the alert was over, the women clambered out of the holes, children hanging in carrying cloths from their chests. They would run to see if their houses had burned. Cries and sobs followed the uproar of the B-29 and the rattling breath of the wounded, who were tossed hurriedly onto stretchers and rushed to the nearest hospital.

Naka and I saw a baby who had lost its arms and legs. Its entire body looked like fire-scorched earth; as it screamed, we saw its pink tongue, tiny and curved. A few minutes later, it was dead. In its open mouth, one could still see its little tongue, defeated.

Its mother had left it there on the street while she rushed off to a demolished house in the neighborhood to see if there was anything left worth stealing. We considered taking the body to a monastery where it could be burned, but as we didn't know who it was, we decided against it. The next day when we walked past the place, it remained there, half-eaten by dogs.

SOKAI: EXODUS

Because Tatsuo belonged to the reserve forces of the land army, which had not yet seen action except in China and southern Asia, he was not mobilized until Year 19 of Shōwa (1944). Like over 2 million others, he was taken to a mountain camp, where he underwent intensive training in preparation for the American invasion. He would be charged with the defense of our sacred ground, which would not be ceded to the enemy in any way other than soaked with the blood of its people, immolated for the emperor.

Anyway, that was what they told him. He had never believed in victory. He explained, "I went to American movies before the war, so I know the United States is powerful. It's only the imbecilic generals who think themselves stronger!" But if he didn't go, he'd be shot.

Tomekichi and Naka, my parents-in-law, repeated every day that we must leave Tokyo. I was pregnant again. They said that fear would make me lose the child. Hairdressing, long since viewed as a luxury, was in ill favor. And besides, the tools of the trade had become unobtainable. In any case, there was a general exodus from the city. People scrambled onto the trains out of Tokyo in droves. Entire neighborhoods had been razed by the fires. We were starving and terrified. And so, less than a year after I had left, we all went to Asaka. Tatsuo's little brother's family came too.

When we got to the village, Motoko took a long, lazy stretch and, her eyes as bright as fish scales, turned around two or three times and cried, "It's nice here!" I thought how upsetting life in wartime Tokyo must have been for her—how truly horrible the war was to frighten children like that.

There wasn't much to eat in Asaka, either, and the kids roamed the hills to pull up bamboo heads (which had previously been considered unfit for human consumption). They gnawed at them morning to night, to fool their empty stomachs, which cried out with hunger. In the house of Endo, we also lodged soldiers. They had requisitioned a stone barn as an airplane hangar. I found the soldiers uncouth and dirty, but, thinking that my own husband was training in some other countryside, I couldn't say anything about their pillaging. Still, looking at them, I felt for the first time that our defeat was inevitable. People so stripped of moral virtues could never have the gods on their side.

To occupy my mind, I opened a small hairdresser's shop in Kōriyama. That brought in enough money to buy black market salt and matches. I forced myself to think only of day-to-day life. We had to live. As the proverb says, "Giving birth is easier than you'd think." I had to keep moving. Trying to forget that Tokyo and the cities of the north were in flames from the bombings, I looked at the little hills sleeping in the sun and told myself that the gods could not allow this horror to go on much longer.

SHŪSEN: THE END OF THE WAR

We were still in Asaka when, like all Japanese, we listened to the radio on August 15, Year 20 (1945), at twelve noon. Two bombs of a new kind of potency had been dropped on Hiroshima and Nagasaki. Japan had lost the war. Japan would no longer exist.

Mother cried. Naka did, too. I burst into sobs, and we clung to one another, holding on so tight we couldn't tell whose heart was whose. Still, hardly a minute had passed until I felt a kind of happiness fill my chest: it was over, we had survived. I was alive! I understood at that moment how afraid I had been of dying. We'd surrendered—that was shameful, perhaps, but we were alive.

Word soon got around that the Americans were not going to be the cruel occupiers we had feared. They wouldn't even rape our women. We consulted local people of good family who had visited the United States before the war, when everyone had been saying the Americans were devils. And, to our surprise, they all had nothing but good to say about them. Of course, they were frightfully oversized, which explained why they had won, but they were nice. They were *gentlemen*. We forced our tongues to pronounce that new word, and others, too: *Harō!* Hello! *Sankyū!* Thank you! And who could tell, maybe they would even marry Japanese women. All we had to do was show them a little respect, and they would liberate Japan from the war.

There was finally something to eat. In their haste, the Japanese soldiers left behind stores of food in our barns. I asked my oldest brother if we could use it. He said no: "The government has entrusted it to me to guard, we mustn't touch it." Then he added, "But I can't speak for the mice."

So Mother, that woman so good she had taken in all my in-laws in time of desperate want, would get up with me nightly after all were in bed. With a big key that made an awful racket, she opened the barn doors. Then I punched holes in the sacks with a bamboo pole. A nibble here, a nibble there, like mice do. The grain poured out. It was sticky rice, very nourishing. We took enough for us and the wife of Tatsuo's little brother, a woman too timid to take any herself. That rice saved our lives.

Days passed, and I heard from Tatsuo that he had been demobilized without having seen combat. He said that they had given him a few yen as demobilization pay. Since they weren't worth anything, he figured he'd buy himself and his father a drink with them. As for Seikō and Nobuko, their shack in Shiga had burned down, with all their belongings inside—they were ruined. They went back to Tokyo. Naka thought we should go back, too. But Mother said that nothing good awaited us in the capital, that it was just a field of ruins on which nothing would be rebuilt for ten or twenty years. She invited me to stay in Fukushima. My oldest brother agreed, saying there was enough in Asaka to feed everyone. I was tempted, because, in spite of everything, I felt a vague fear of the Americans, who I was sure would not come as far as Kōriyama. Anyway, things were not going so badly for me there.

When Tatsuo wrote to ask me to come back, not knowing what to do, I went to that same seal of the law who had revealed my vocation to me. This was his diagnosis: "You know too many people here. You'll do a lot of people's hair for free and give a lot of discounts. If you stay in Fukushima, you'll never be anything but a beggar. In Tokyo, you will become rich. Here, the pond is too small for you. Big fish need to swim in deep water."

So we returned to Tokyo. I took Motoko with me, and Ryōko, my second girl, only a few months old. Tomekichi was sick, and Naka, always so strong, was now reduced to a thin old woman with yellowed eyes. After we found Tatsuo, it was with relief and without ceremony that she gave over the running of the house to me.

All we had in the world were the eight bales of rice my family had given us. Since the police and the military were confiscating food on the trains, we didn't take them with us. My oldest brother, Yoshiharu, who was the director of the cooperative in Asaka, had them sent by truck to Tokyo. We gave a little rice to our landlords, but not to the neighbors, because once one starts giving things away, where does it end?

Today, when I recall those years of hardship, it seems to me that a sort of death sickness attacked the world. That sickness was war. The gods had not wanted it; it was born of the folly of men. It was in imitation of the

West that Japan got itself onto that fatal path. And war engenders nothing but more war. People start killing one another off until the day their crimes have become so monstrous that the gods themselves are terrified. Since neither the creation nor the destruction of the world can be decided by men, the gods put an end to our battles.

But I know that the Japan of today will not allow another war. Never again.

POSTWAR

And so the six of us—Naka, Tomekichi, Tatsuo, myself, and our two daughters—set up housekeeping in Bunkyō, where a poor Chinese cook agreed to rent to us, by the year, a tumbledown shack with two rooms, measuring six tatami each. It was so small that moonbeams illuminated the entire place, all the way to the back. During the day, the grandparents minded the children in the back room. The front room served as a beauty salon: we put up two large mirrors, which were all we had left from the old days. We covered the floor with sheets of *shibu-kami*, paper strengthened with persimmon juice. In the evenings, we would roll them up and shake them out.

I worked alone, and, because I was once again pregnant, it was very hard. Tatsuo was not hired back at Mitsubishi. A little too pleased to be exempt from one of those makeshift jobs people were doing then (like carrying water, clearing ruins, or pimping girls), he would occasionally organize exhibitions for his old boss. On Sundays, when we had a lot of customers, he helped me, passing me rollers and tidying up.

Tatsuo said we should start a shop in Ginza. Everything there had burned down, and we could choose our spot. Nobody owned it anymore. Naka agreed. She even thought that, in the postwar world, there would be nothing odd about a male hairdresser. But Tomekichi disagreed. He said that a man must do work that he likes, that hairdressing was only for women and homosexuals. Anyway, neither he nor Naka wanted to leave Bunkyō, so we stayed. (In any case, Ginza never was lucky for me. When I did open a salon there, much later, it brought me nothing but trouble.)

I felt we were lucky, especially when I thought of those men and women who, unable to find lodging, collected boards and corrugated sheet metal from the ruins to build themselves shacks. Entire families set up housekeeping in old bomb shelters, spreading mats on the ground. The government called on the police to put the families out and fill in the holes. Each time, this meant angry scenes and tears, as they had nowhere else to sleep.

There were also the *furō-ji*, stray children, who lived alone in sorts of dog burrows. By day, these orphans would hang about in the streets, looking for cigarette butts and shining shoes. Their faces were ferocious. They would steal, and people would chase them, kicking them as if they were starving animals.

In spite of everything, rabid crowds continued to invade Tokyo: adventurers or ruined families looking to make their fortunes in petty trafficking in the capital, colonists back from Manchuria. The war-wounded begged in the streets in their white uniforms. They would sit on the street corners playing the barrel organ. As if they hadn't lost the war! The returning soldiers chased from the factories the women who had kept them running all those miserable years, and all these women were now looking for jobs. Luckily, I had a profession.

As soon as he got his hands on some money, Tatsuo would give it away to friends in need. He explained that he could permit himself this, since I worked. But he brought in nothing. I knew very well how much people needed money then. Since he used it for good ends, I couldn't say anything.

In fact, Tatsuo was very sad. Before the war, he liked to paint. But his brushes, paints, and canvases had been sent to Shiga with Seikō and Nobuko, and, along with everything else, had burned. That robbed him of his will to laugh. So it was up to me alone to keep the household going.

Meanwhile, Tomekichi's health continued to decline. In the past he had loved the transparency of warm sake, suggestive bantering with the girls, and the animation in the streets. I think he had been bored in Asaka. The first evenings of summer, he would sit on the veranda, contemplating the toy fireworks the neighborhood children set off. Then, toward the end of the seventh moon, after *O-Bon*, he began to tell ghost stories, stories that made cold chills run up the spine and which made the air seem cooler, as he liked to say.[6] Then, when the autumn typhoons arrived, the children stopped coming around. He stayed up late one night, watching the full moon.[7] Naka found him the next morning, trembling with a high fever. He died some months later, in Tokyo.

Naka said, in a wise voice, that a man made for pleasure could not fight off all that misery. But I watched as the pain of widowhood gently creased her cheeks. Her skin became marked with gray spots, which etched two night butterfly wings around her eyes, so clearly one would have thought them tattooed there. Every night, Tomekichi came to her in dreams. He laughed like in the old days, and told her he was not dead. In the morning, Naka had once again to convince herself that she was widowed. That happened over and over, until she nearly went mad.

In the end, what saved her was the pressing need to find food for the family; there was no time for sorrow. The daily ration was barely more than a hundred grams of rice. When we had no work, we would make our way to the outlying areas to trade what we had gathered in the ruins for food. Tatsuo went all the way to the country. The Americans distributed food, but they were unfamiliar with our eating habits, so they gave us lots of corn, which we didn't know how to eat.[8] We would gnaw at it, half-cooked (fuel was in extremely short supply), with soy sauce, and for hours afterward we would break wind in sick-smelling volleys of machine-gun fire that made the children laugh. People said that at least 10 million people had died of hunger.

Frankly, I didn't know what to think of the Americans. I had been afraid of them, but they hadn't touched the emperor. Accused of starving Japan to death, they passed out chewing gum and smiles to the children, taught them to play baseball on the empty lots created by their own bombs. Even if I couldn't really criticize them, their presence caused a certain malaise. In my wanderings around Tokyo, I would chance upon signs that read "Off Limits." One time, as I watched them through the barbed wire, a soldier pointed his gun at me, screaming something I could not understand. I ran away. I felt they were stealing the land of our ancestors. In the train stations, the names of the destinations were now written in English. The same with the names of the streets and hotels. I decided to buy an English conversation textbook. But I found I had so little gift for it, I had to give up before I got beyond *sankyū* (thank you) and *demokurashī* (democracy).

To learn English, one had to learn a new way of thinking. Slogans about peace, equality, and democracy had in a matter of days displaced nationalist propaganda. The new constitution, they said, was based on "the will of the people" and not on that of the military.[9] I wondered what the meaning of this new expression could be—how could the Americans know what "the will of the people" was when I myself had no idea? They also said that the people would give up war forever. But had they ever wanted it? Was it not the Westerners who had invented firearms and bombs? Still, I also knew that democracy had put an end to the war, and that it was therefore good.

There were two things, in any case, that struck me as extraordinary in that disconcerting time. I watched children and their teachers rebuild the demolished schools: surely that was useful. And then they proclaimed the equality of men and women.[10] The Ministry of Education posted circulars on the walls: "Women are gifted with greater intuition about things, their hearts are more just and more loyal. From now on, they will have a say in all matters."

That shocked me, but try as I might to tell myself it was an absurdity that flew in the face of all decency, I felt a secret satisfaction. When Tatsuo, mincing like a girl, tried to ridicule the new law, I shouted at him that if we wanted peace, the best thing to do would be to let women run things. We women were too familiar with the suffering of childbirth to send our children off to be killed in war. It was the pride of men that had caused all the killing! In ancient times, the gods had placed empresses at the head of the country, because women are wiser than men. If, over the centuries, internal struggles had ravaged Japan, it was thanks to the men, who had wrongly usurped the power![11] Flabbergasted, Tatsuo slammed the sliding *fusuma* door so hard on his way out that it fell from its frame! Still, what I said was not just nonsense. The proof is that today women play a growing role in Japanese politics. And the men aren't laughing anymore when we talk of equality.

Business picked up at the salon, and Naka insisted more often that Tatsuo work there. He did not answer her. We needed money for our daily life. With another child coming, we would soon have to leave our shack, and a new home would cost more. As I neared my time, Tatsuo finally decided to get serious. He started a small company to organize exhibitions and brought me his profits.

I had a son, whom we called Hikaru, luminous one. Confronted with this great, strapping boy, who laughed as gaily as a summer cloudburst, I suddenly knew that, for me, the sufferings of the war had ended.

11

The Death of Naka

鬼
の
目
に
も
涙

Oni no me ni mo namida.
Even demons weep.

A MOTHER-IN-LAW'S AUTHORITY

Kono hisan-na toki wo seisan shitaku, ie wo tateru koto ni itashimashita . . . To put that miserable time behind us, we decided to build a new house and shop. We were offered a good deal on a piece of land eighty *tsubo* in size.[1] It belonged to Tatsuo's little brother, who had been adopted into a rich family; they owned a big restaurant. In addition, thanks to the gods, Tatsuo had organized an exhibition in Hokkaidō, which had brought in 6,000 yen.

I went to City Hall to get authorization. They told me that there weren't enough of us to build a house any greater than fifteen *tsubo*. I explained that the tract was huge and that I planned to hire many employees. Unfortunately, regulations were regulations, and there was nothing we could do. I resigned myself to building a house with ten *tsubo* of shop space and five for living. The building rights and everything else would cost 15,000 yen. Tatsuo's money plus our 7,000 in savings made 13,000, so all we needed was another 2,000. Naka went to negotiate a bank loan, taking with her one of my customers, a City Hall employee who knew the ropes. She told me that I would have to give up my artisan status, arrange to hire workmen, and start a company, which would make us a legal entity, a *hōjin*, or juridical person. She said that this would be more advantageous tax-wise.

The wooden house was up in two weeks. I hired one employee, then another. And at the bottom of the sign announcing the name of my new salon, *Kanōya Biyōshitsu*, House of Granted Wishes Beauty Salon, I was soon able to brush-paint the word *Hōjin*. I set to work like a demon, more than ten hours a day, and I scrimped on everything. In the evening, fatigue made my legs feel like blocks of wood, and even in the morning I was limp with weariness. I would have liked to give in to my weakness, to stretch out gently on the ground and lose all consciousness of existence, like a cherry blossom petal in the first rains of spring. But instead I just kept running back and forth, smiling as if nothing was wrong, complimenting the customers, keeping the employees on their toes.

People say to me today, "How successful you are! You've been lucky!" They do not know how I suffered for it. It was a lot, *a lot*, of work. At last, the just gods rewarded me for my efforts: after three years, I was netting a hundred yen a month.

At that point I would have liked to hire another employee, but there was no room. I said to Naka that we needed to tear down this house and build a new one, using the entire plot of land. She was against it, arguing that neither the time nor the place was propitious. At first I considered going ahead, in spite of her objections, which I found to be more tiresome than a wasp on a filet of sea bream marinated in vinegar, but she kept saying, day after day, "I myself have excellent skills. Alas, my health is poor, and I just couldn't make a go of it. I want you to have a career. For that, the strength of human beings alone will not suffice. You must base your decisions on *hō-gaku*, the 'study of directions,' geomancy."[2]

At that time, I had little faith in that science, which struck me as obscure. Still, I asked her, "What does geomancy tell us?"

"The master of geomancy says that you must wait another three years, when the direction of *daikippo*, great good fortune, will be in your favor."

It was driving me out of my mind. Eight of us were living in this five-*tsubo* house—Naka, Tatsuo, me, the three children, and my two employees, whom I had sleeping in the closets after we took the futons out for the night. I had had a shed built in the yard for storing lumber and sheet metal, but, even so, we were on top of one another.

I said to Naka, "But there are too many of us. We've got the employees living in the closets!"

Naka said nothing, but I noticed that she grew melancholy and cried when she was alone. When I asked her why she was so sad, she said, "You're going to build the house in a bad direction, and your business will never go anywhere."

Her tears moved me. I knew that except for Mother and my older sister Kiku, there wasn't a soul on earth besides Naka who would shed tears for me. I felt grateful for that, so I decided to submit to her will. And then, not because I believed in *hō-gaku*, but out of respect and filial piety, I agreed to await the great good fortune that would come along in three years.

Since it's true that hard work, along with hope, makes time go faster, sure enough, soon I found it was almost Year 27 of Shōwa (1952). Naka went to consult with the master of directions, who announced that we might build. She asked him to specify where in Bunkyō we should find the right land. He marked out for her the ideal perimeter, right in the middle of the area called Hakusan, as he slipped the card of a *fudōsan-ya*, a realtor he trusted, into her hand. Naka ran immediately to see that *fudōsan-ya* . . . only to learn that the land in question had already been rented. Disappointed as an old woman denied her final joy by the gods, she made her way slowly back to Bunkyō with the terrible news: we would have to wait another three years for the next great good fortune. This time, I would not accept my destiny; I rushed off to the *fudōsan-ya* and offered him double the rent. He agreed. I went to see the land. It was only sixty *tsubo*, but it would do just fine. More serious was the fact that there were ruined buildings all around it, and the streets were infested with geisha. It was a red-light district, a *karyukai* (flower-willow world), a neighborhood so ill-famed that people wondered what on earth we were planning to do there. But the die of fate had been cast, and construction began.

As bad luck would have it, my mother-in-law did not live to see the house finished. In the days before Naka died, she went and knocked twice more on the door of the master of directions. He refused to receive her. Later, I thought that he must have foreseen her death and, therefore, had nothing good to tell her.

NAKA'S DEATH

Naka died without fanfare. She had said two or three times that she would try to live until the house was finished. But from time to time, she would show me a *yukata*, a cotton kimono that was almost entirely white, which she had never worn. She said that she try it on as soon as she was dead.

Then one day, she fell into a strange sleep, from which we could not wake her. We took her to the hospital. There, some hours later, they told us we would have to call a monk to chant the *makura-gyō*, the deathbed sutra.[3] They told me to go and get the *yukata* to dress her in after *yūkan*, the ceremonial washing of her body and hair with hot water, had been performed.[4]

Tatsuo murmured her name into her ear to see if she really couldn't hear anymore. Then he tried to give her something to drink. He poured a little water into her mouth and placed a bowl of water near her head, because the dead are said to be thirsty all the time.[5] A woman then dressed Naka in the *yukata*, folding it right over left, the opposite of what the living do. I watched them go about these preparations, stunned to see that my mother-in-law's face, so tormented over these last months, looked peaceful now, as if she were smiling. Finally, the hospital people announced that they would keep the body for twenty-four hours. They said that by law it could not be cremated within less then a full day, to make certain the person was truly dead.

That left just enough time to organize the wake. Our house was too small for it to be conveniently held there, but we weren't rich enough to hire a special room.

So we had to close the salon for two days. I covered the altar of the gods, all the mirrors, and all brightly colored objects with white paper. Shiny or colorful things are not appropriate to sad circumstances.[6] In fact, as I had never handled a death in the family, I wasn't really sure what I was supposed to do. Luckily, the neighbors came to help, as people always do for funerals,[7] so that the *kuro-fujō* (black defilement) would not spread:[8] because family members are allowed to touch their dead, the neighbors serve as intermediaries with the rest of the world. So two people from our street went to invite the guests: the relatives who lived far away, the customers, and all our acquaintances.

Then, the undertakers brought Naka's body home. They had discreetly taken her out through the *fujō-mon* (gate of defilement), a special door of the hospital, and brought her without a funeral cortege to the house. We were trying to make things as if she had died at home.

First offerings to the dead.

They laid her out on a futon, covered her with a white sheet, and spread a small quilt over her. So the presence of the corpse would not make people uncomfortable, they placed a fine white cloth over her face. A knife was placed on her chest so that Naka could protect herself from the harmful beings she might encounter in the beyond. On a little table at the head of the bed, we placed another bowl of water, so that she would not suffer from the fires of hell; some incense; and a bowl of pillow rice, cooked rice shaped in the form of a mountain, in which we placed a single chopstick, as one must never do for the living.[9]

The first visitors came to greet the dead woman. Each bowed and put a stick of incense in the censer. I stood near Naka's head, so that if they wished to say a last good-bye, I could lift the white cloth from her face.

Up to that point I had not felt much of anything. But the compassion shown by these guests made me understand suddenly that a terrible thing had occurred. They would stay for a moment, saying things like "It's so sad, she was such a nice woman. She'll be happier now, by her husband's side." Such words have no meaning, of course, but no one knows what to say in those circumstances. It made me want to cry.

The next day, the body was put into the coffin. The undertakers set up the funeral platform in the corner of the room farthest from the main entrance. It was a magnificent altar, with five tiered steps on which to place the offerings. The coffin, left open so that all could pay their last respects, was set on top. On the steps before it we placed a large photograph of Naka next to her temporary *ihai*, a Buddhist mortuary tablet of white wood. Naka's *kaimyō*, her posthumous name which the monk had chosen, was brush-painted on a half sheet of white paper glued to the wooden tablet with rice starch; only natural materials must be used in connection with the dead. Even though the name was no more than the feminine form of the name he had already chosen for her husband, Tomekichi, this monk had asked a considerable sum for it. But this was understandable, because the choosing of the name is an important matter.[10]

Incense, tea sweets, and candles were also placed on the altar. And all around it were the flowers we had bought and those which relatives, neighbors, and others had sent, carefully signing their names.

Finally, the undertakers hung funeral wreaths mounted on black-and-white pedestals high on the walls outside so that all could see that there had been a death at the Yamazakis'.

The wake began around six o'clock. A little before that, we family members each offered to Naka one stick of incense, because, with the dead, everything must be done in odd numbers. We stood around, not doing anything. So the guests would not be contaminated, it was the women from the neighboring houses who fixed tea and sweets, which they served on our behalf to the visitors.[11] I heard them whispering and bustling about in the kitchen while the monk read the sutras. The guests arrived one after the other. They dressed in ordinary street clothes, as one does for a wake, to show that they had come in great haste, as if news of the death had taken them by surprise.

At the doorway, the neighbors had set up a table for the *hōmei-chō*, the register of fragrant names: the visitors would write their names in it and

leave their *kōden*, their incense offerings, there. This was money in an envelope addressed to the *gorei*, the honored spirit, because one never uses a
Buddhist name before the day of the funeral. In theory, these offerings are
to be placed on the altar, before the coffin. But in fact, for fear of *kōden*
robbers, the donors wrote their names, their addresses, and the amount of
their gifts on the backs of the envelopes. The neighbors emptied the money
into a large sack and placed the empty envelopes before the casket.

Along with the registry at the door, these helped us with the accounting
and helped us set up the *kōden-chō*, the register of incense offerings, to be
consulted before future burials so as to know which families to contact.
Bonds of mutual aid for funerals between houses are transmitted from generation to generation. In addition, after the burial at the cemetery, this
register allows us to reimburse each donor with a gift worth half the *kōden*
given. (In practice, we don't give something of exactly half the worth—
that would be too complicated. We classify the gifts according to four or
five donor levels and decide on types of reciprocal gifts for each class.)

Some people give sheets or bath towels (I personally find the idea of
sleeping on sheets received from a funeral distasteful). Others don't go to
much bother, simply giving money, but that is vulgar.[12] I prefer to respect
the principles advocated by the monks, which require that perishables, such
as soap or shampoo, be given. So, for Naka's death, I bought three kinds
of luxury soaps, which I gave to the guests after the service.

No matter what the gift, this custom of incense offerings is a good one:
once half the value of what is received is reimbursed in kind, there is something left over to help defray the funeral costs, even some to give to charity.
Thus funerals end up costing nothing, while weddings incur great expense
because one has to give back the entire value of the cash gift. Surely that's
why the old village custom of incense offerings has continued, even in the
cities (though to demonstrate their wealth, some families refuse the *kōden*,
or they just collect on their funeral insurance, but then people don't know
how to express their condolences).

So at the wake, the visitors gave their gifts, then came to greet the dead
woman: they would bow and place an incense stick in the holder. Then,
in the next room, they drank green tea and ate tea sweets. We served
nothing else, because we were not rich. Today, families will serve anything:
boiled tuna or even *yakitori*. However, in principle, one should serve *shōjin
ryōri*, food for the progress of the spirit, as the monks call it—that is, vege-
tarian dishes.[13] Scrupulous people sometimes serve vegetable tempura or
kinpira gobō (shaved burdock sautéed in sesame oil with soy sauce and sugar),
but it's possible to do things more simply.

People filed past until nearly eleven that night. A wake is said to go on
all night, but around eleven, the visitors usually begin to excuse themselves,

saying, "It's late, you must be tired." We gave them each a small gift to thank them for their trouble, and they left.

Because one must never leave a wake by the same door through which one entered, we left the side door open.[14] There was a breeze, and I remember thinking it was like the cold air of death.

Then we got a little sleep. The next afternoon was luckily not a day of *tomobiki*, on which the dead "pull their friends" along with them to the funeral.[15] That meant we could also perform the *sōgi*, the mortuary service, and the cremation that day.

That service took place at the monastery. The undertakers took the coffin there and reinstalled the altar in a special room. All was exactly as it had been at the wake, except that Naka's posthumous name was now written on the white wooden funerary tablet rather than on the half sheet of paper. There were quite a few of us, perhaps a hundred.[16] The monk read the sutras, everyone bowed and burned small pinches of incense three times for the dead woman, before contemplating her face for the last time. Her face seemed to me to have an iconlike grace. I thought I had never realized how beautiful she was, which wrung my heart.

It was time to close the coffin. One of the undertakers tapped the point of a nail, just one, the "last nail," into the lid of the coffin, at the head, and each of us pounded it once with a rough stone.[17] That was a terrible moment. I had the impression of doing violence to Naka, that I myself was at that moment deciding that she should die. There is nothing sadder than hammering a coffin.

Then the old people, who themselves felt near to the next world, left, as did the pregnant women and all those afraid of death. We, the close family, went to the mountain—in other words, we followed the hearse to the municipal crematorium. We had to wait for the room we'd reserved. It wasn't like it is, now that they burn fuel oil; it was a wood fire, and it took at least two or three hours to burn a body.

When Naka's turn came, the undertaker set up her coffin in front of the oven, and the monk read the sutras. Everyone had to bow again before her remains. Then the undertaker said, "*Osame itashimasu*, The last moment has come." And he pushed her body into the great fire.

While it burned, we waited in the next room, eating and chatting. Everyone looked tense, and I felt ill-at-ease. The monk continued to intone the sutras. Then the undertaker said, "*Agarimashita*, It is finished." We went back into the cremation room, and he took out the bones and put them in a sort of drawer. He slid them onto a thick slab of sheet metal about two and a half by three feet. It made an unpleasant sound, like shaking a rattle. He had us come two by two to arrange the bones in the *kotsu-tsubo*, the bone pot. This was a white ceramic pot a foot high, eight inches in diameter. The undertaker summoned Tatsuo and me, as the closest relations, and he gave us each a stick with which we grasped, together, the largest of the bones and placed them in the pot.[18] The closest relatives always put the first bones in the pot, and these must be the largest. After everyone had come through—there were only ten or fifteen of us—there were still some bones left, of course. The undertaker separated out the top of the skull and the *nodo-botoke*, the thyroid cartilage,[19] and the rest he put in the pot.

If people die without having been sick, there are many bones left unburned, and it's difficult to fit them all in. But since Naka had been feeble for so long, she didn't have many bones. The undertaker had no trouble fitting the skullcap on top, like a sort of lid, before he closed the pot. He covered it with white fabric, then wrapped it with metal. He wrapped it in another piece of fabric (brocade, I think), and placed it in a box of paulownia wood. As for the *nodo-botoke*, he put it in a very little box, so that we could keep it a long time, at home, if we wished.

We took the pot of bones and Naka's funerary tablet home. The monk came with us, along with the last guests. He helped us to set up Naka's bones on a little table next to the altar of the ancestors. Before it we placed her photograph and her funerary tablet, along with candles, incense, flowers, and sweets. To save time, he read the *sho-nanoka* sutras then and there, those for the first seventh day (after death).[20] The guests ate food containing no animal flesh. After that, everybody went home.

Then, every morning until the *shi-jū-ku-nichi*, the forty-ninth day, I offered water before Naka's tablet. This is because the souls of the dead wander between this world and the other for forty-nine days. After that, they leave for the beyond for good, and the living may bury their bones in a cemetery.[21]

On the forty-ninth day, the entire family went to Kichijō Temple, where we had paid a fortune for a fine plot when Tomekichi had died. The monk had already had the gravediggers open the grave. On top of it they pushed into the ground a square wooden pillar with Naka's posthumous name on one side and her living name on the other, along with her date of death and her age. This pillar was to stay there until it was replaced by a stone marker. But normally that marker is furnished much later, when the family is free from money worries.

A small altar was set up to one side of the grave, on which were a bowl of rice, water to put out the fires of hell, fruit, flowers (because flowers are the clothing of the dead), and sweets. Those were the offerings. We burned incense. As I had no desire to keep bones in the house, I had both boxes of remains placed in the vault.

Back home, on the altar of the buddhas, the monk set up a new tablet, painted black, with Naka's posthumous name engraved in gold characters.[22]

He read more sutras and presented some offerings. Then we ate together, continually evoking Naka's memory.

When it was all over, I felt very tired. I had been overseeing the construction of the new house, because we were to move soon. I told myself that there was nothing more I could do for Naka, that there was no point in seeking to learn what had awaited her on the other side, since her conduct had always been so virtuous;[23] and that what she would have wanted most of all was that I make sure the shop prosper.

RELATIONS WITH A DEAD MOTHER-IN-LAW

Nevertheless, I had a feeling of coming disaster. I was as lost as those waves that softly steal away out to sea, never to return. Over the years, Naka had become someone in whom to confide the problems of my profession and the worries of daily life. Although women always harp on the hatred between mothers- and daughters-in-law, I had truly loved my husband's mother. It was only with her that I could talk shop. I threw myself into work, hoping to forget my sorrow.

It was nine weeks after Naka had left this world when, for some reason I no longer recall, I went to Kamakura. After offering money to the Great Buddha, I felt very weary and took a walk on the beach. As I walked along the shore, I felt something heavy jump on my back and, viselike, grip my neck. I wanted to cry out, but no sound came from my throat. I could not even swallow the saliva that collected quickly in my mouth. Thinking I must be terribly ill, I rushed back to Tokyo. Once I was lying down on the veranda back home in Bunkyō, I again had difficulty breathing, as if a dry mud were clogging my lungs. I choked all night long, and massaging my shoulders and the nape of my neck did not help. The next day, Tatsuo said my face was as white as a fish's belly. He thought I must have some serious illness and said I should go see the doctor. I hesitated. Then, without even thinking about it, I said that that would be useless. I was convinced that what I had was no ordinary illness.

I returned to Kamakura, where the weight had assaulted me, to see a monk. He asked me immediately if my family had recently been in mourning. I told him yes, that my mother-in-law had died.

"So, it's a *gaki*," he said. "A hungry ghost. The soul of the dead woman has become a *gaki* in the other world. This is a bad retribution, and the demon is prowling around you, to feed off your energy. You must offer her the *kuyō* rites to appease her and to make her leave this sad path of rebirth as soon as possible."

It was true that I, grief-stricken and overworked, had taken almost no steps to assure my mother-in-law's repose. I had not attempted to speak with her through a medium. I had not gone to her grave to check that friends had left her *sotoba*, the small wooden plaques shaped like Buddhist towers that would help her achieve salvation.[24] And now, I thought, look what my ingratitude had brought about. Naka had strayed onto an evil path.

I gave money to the monk and ordered services for the repose of the dead woman's soul. Although the hand that was strangling me let go a short while after that, I knew that I would have to pray and pray again for Naka's repose. If I myself wished to find peace one day, I would first have to bandage that wound that rends the deepest part of the heart of anyone who loses someone dear.

BOOK TWO

Kami no Mizu:

WATER OF THE GODS

12

Searching

七
転
び
八
起
き

Nana korobi ya oki.
Fall down seven times, stand up eight.

Haha no shi igo, nanika kono yo to no en ga kirete shimatta yō na kanji ga shite orimashita . . . After Naka's death, I felt somehow that my ties to this world had been cut. Everything seemed unreal, the sharp laughter of children as much as the polite remarks of adults. Customers would say, their faces no more expressive than those of fish, "You must be all alone now," and I would answer, "Yes, I feel alone." But their words always seemed to fall into a void that took possession of me more each day. I was surprised sometimes to find I was imitating Naka's gestures, the slightly stiff way she had of prancing about, her toes a bit turned in; her respectful little bows, even her strange way of curling her lower lip when she smiled. Looking for a sort of protection in that mimicry, I would also speak in favorite phrases of hers.

Naka had stood by my side until the day of her death. She had advised me on how to stand up to others, and she had taught me the most detailed gestures of my craft. Now I found myself alone. It would take months, years, for me to acquire confidence in my abilities, a confidence that would become the source of the cold-bloodedness and audacity which would aid me in my eventual triumph over others.

In fact, I was beset with terrible difficulties. The old house, made into dormitory housing for the employees, brought in nothing. We had had to go into debt to build the new one. The area of the house and shop I had built was nearly 40 *tsubo* (1,420 square feet), but I owed 6 million yen to the bank: 3 for the construction and another 3 for the permits, the lease, real estate fees, and so on. Tatsuo had negotiated the loans, spread over seven years, because we had almost nothing.[1] At first he guaranteed them with his own company. Then, as that was not enough, his little brother's

189

family put up theirs. So I had to pay it back by the deadline, no matter what it took—if not, we would all go under.

From dawn to night, I never stopped running like a fox pursued by hunters. Since Naka's death, I no longer had anyone to look after the children. Of course they were in school, but I had to make their *bentō* box lunches and their dinner in the evening. At the same time, without my doing anything to bring it about, simply because we had the space, the business grew. I soon had twelve employees, but we didn't make any more money than before.

In Year 27 of Shōwa (1952), as throughout the postwar era, people didn't value what they earned. They didn't work; they were thieves. Twenty, fifty, or even a hundred rollers would disappear every month. I don't know whether the employees took them home to do their relatives' hair or sold them on the black market. It was always their wastefulness that ruined me. They also dipped into the cash register. The accounts would be so imprecise that the money in the register never tallied with the figures they reported.

They weren't bad sorts, really, just men and women living in a time when people got by any way they could. Closing their ears to all reason, they couldn't hear anything but the growling of their empty stomachs. And nobody—not I or anyone else—could do a thing about that. The worst came in December of the next year.

As the New Year's holidays approached, women were coming in to have their hair done up in elegant traditional chignons before dressing in their formal kimonos. We had so many customers, we could have given work to the gods and bodhisattvas! And so, on December 28, I got to the shop around three. Inside was a calm so uncanny that a passerby would have thought the place closed. Two employees were working. The others were all sitting down, swinging their feet in the air. Still others had gone out. I asked what this was all about—had they gone on strike? One boy I had hired only recently, his eyes shining brighter than a wild cat's, told me it wasn't really a strike. He said that they had had enough of working so hard and eating so little.

"The ones who aren't here have gone out to buy mandarin oranges with money from the cash register," he said. "Because we need our vitamin C."

And then I understood, and I was scared. In fact, that employee had been fired from another house for what I had been told were unfair reasons. But it turned out that he belonged to a Communist-affiliated labor union. That day, he had set the others against me and persuaded them that we, the Yamazakis, were growing fat off their labor.

At that time, my employees never ate out. We fed them all their meals. And it's true, alas, that we didn't have the means to feed them as we should have.[2] Tatsuo went to the country twice a week to buy food (because few peasants came to the capital to sell their produce), but we couldn't do any more than that. So I told them I didn't give a damn about their vitamin B, or C, or whatever.

"I'm not starving you because I'm cheap. Japan lost the war, and you've got to be content to survive in poverty. It's not as if we live in a country where we can all fill our bellies however we please. Right now, we eat what we can get our hands on. You know I had to borrow money for this business. If I'm unable to pay it back, you'll all be out of a job. I know you're suffering, but there's nothing I can do about it."

I said that those who believed what I was telling them could stay, but that everybody else was free to leave, right now. So two left, the union man and one other. Then I turned to those who had stayed. "I'm sure you all don't believe me either, since you participated in the strike. But you stayed because you have nowhere else to go."

I kicked all of them out, except for the two who had continued working—and, you know, the daughter of one of them works for us today, and she's a very serious girl. Two girls returned and begged me to take them back. I agreed, after they swore never to do it again.

So that's what happened. We had to go on with only four employees, while I still had so many debts to pay off. But, really, I would have put them all out and started from zero if it had come to that! However, the gods knew how much we needed money!

I had put aside a few yen, because the one-year commemoration of my father's death was coming up. In fact, he had left for the other world shortly after Naka did. I would have to return to Asaka to offer presents. However, the son of Tatsuo's little brother caught meningitis just then. He needed shots that cost over a hundred yen. I told myself, Better to spend money on the living than the dead, and I gave my in-laws the hundred yen. After that, I hadn't a cent to my name. Out of pride, I didn't say a thing to my family in Asaka. I let them believe that I was so wrapped up in my work that I couldn't come back. My oldest brother thought that the city had hardened my heart. It made me sad, but in my heart, I made my apologies to Father, and I'm sure he forgave me. I started to save again, this time for the third-year commemoration (as it turned out, I couldn't go that year either, because I had the flu).

The shop wasn't bringing in enough to pay back much of anything. Tatsuo couldn't help me either—his business was going so badly that he had to forgo drawing a salary, month after month, just to keep it afloat. I told him that his business wasn't serious, that he'd do better to dissolve the company and get a job with a salary. He took weeks to decide, then found a job with the big advertising agency Dentsū.

From that point on, things went a little better. I must add here that the government raised the limit on what we could charge for hairdressing.[3] I also began to give classes and speak at gatherings all over Japan. But that's another story.

THE DISCOVERY OF GEOMANCY

It's really very strange how it happened. One day when the memory of the past was so overwhelming that it blocked my breathing, without really thinking about it, I found myself standing in front of the house of Watanabe-Sensei, Naka's master of geomancy.

I knocked on his door, calling out my name. He came out but refused to let me in. He said, "I'll have nothing to do with someone who doesn't believe in geomancy. That bothersome pest—as you put it—is dead! So don't ask anything of me! Just be happy you can do as you please, now that you've killed her!"

But I couldn't give up. Three times I went back to the master, bringing gifts of fruit, seeing only his wife. I gave those presents, which were an extreme luxury in the postwar period, to Mrs. Watanabe. Since that embarrassed her, she finally got her husband to let me into the house.

He was seated behind a table piled high with papers and brushes. He sighed. "So what is it you have to ask me, that you're so insistent about it?"

I realized at that moment that I had nothing to ask him. I simply wanted to take up the beliefs of my mother-in-law. Our older girl, Motoko, had been consecrated since birth to the god of Ontake-san, and each year (as Naka would have wished) I went on a pilgrimage with her to the mount. But I didn't think that was enough.

"If I can," I said, "I would like to believe in geomancy. If you prove the truth of it to me, I will follow all the beliefs of my mother-in-law."

And so the master questioned me: "What is the eightieth night, and what is the twenty-third night of the twelfth moon?"

"I know that! In Asaka, we used to sing a song that said the smells of summer arrive with the wind on the eightieth night. We would pound rice to make *mochi*, making wishes that the silkworms would spin and not die. Also, seeds sown after the eightieth night won't grow."

"And the twenty-third?"

"That's the night when we eat pumpkin. It's called *tōji*."

"And what is *tōji*?"

I had to admit my ignorance.

He explained, making drawings as he talked, showing me that here was the earth, and here was the sun. "On the eightieth night after the beginning of spring, the sun is at an eighty-degree angle to the earth. This is the longest day of the year, when the sun reaches its zenith. The twenty-third night, on the other hand, is the longest night of the year, that on which the sun is at a twenty-three-degree angle to the earth.[4]

"There exist universal rules, which make planted seeds grow when the sun is at a given angle to the earth. Or which, if they are planted at another angle, will make them go bad. These are the laws of nature, and no one can countermand them."

He taught me that the maximal number, the *tenkansū*, the conversion figure, at which everything reverses itself and begins again, is 12. There are twelve months, twelve hours in the day, and twelve in the night. And that is why the 180-degree circle traced by the sun around the earth must be divided into 12 parts. That gives us angles of 30 degrees, which are the natural angles par excellence. These angles must be taken into account in the construction of houses, as in all else: only those houses whose upright beams form 30-degree angles to the roof can withstand earthquakes.[5]

I realized that my old reservations about geomancy had only been ignorance. These traditions I had disdained as superstitions were the laws of the universe. From that day on, I went to see the master regularly.

One by one, he taught me the principles of the zodiac. I learned that the circle of orientations runs in the opposite direction of the hands of a watch and that respecting the fundamental precepts of geomancy assures success in all undertakings.

INVENTION AND DISCOVERY

I knew that an invention was nothing more than the discovery of something up to that point unknown, something that had always existed in nature. Inventions are nothing more than progress in our understanding of the world. In fact, the only thing that humanity has really created is evil, whereas curiosity is a gift from the gods.[6]

Had I been born in former times, I'm sure I would have taken the veil like those nuns who, retired from the world in their wild mountain haunts where the eagles and vultures fly, dedicated their days to making elixir of cinnabar, a well-known source of immortality. In the middle of the night, they concocted marvelous potions for healing the body and spirit. Beloved of the gods but shunned by men, who called them poisoners, they fled from mountaintop to mountaintop, sometimes demonstrating their miraculous powers, wowing the crowds.[7]

If born into a poor family, I would have become one of those bone setters whose eyes shone like water, or fire, and whom everyone, according to his needs, either feared or revered. Raised in a bourgeois home, I would have written poems. But it so happens I was born into a wealthy rural family and received an unpolished education. Then I came to maturity in that odd era when democracy replaced love of country. Western-style dresses took over, relegating the wearing of the ordinary kimono to the poor and the elderly. The *shinki*, divine treasures, took on new names like television, refrigerator, and washing machine.[8]

In less than ten years after the war, beauty itself changed from divine gift to human artifice. With the money earned at their first jobs, young working girls had their noses lengthened or their eyelids cut open to make them, if possible, look like the American models whose images invaded the magazine ads.

Like everyone else, I added the new cults imported from the West— scientific progress and consumerism—to my old religion. Then, when I began to see that science didn't tell us anything other than the eternal principles revealed by the sacred texts since the beginning of time, I struggled to understand how physics and theology, chemistry and geomancy could exist in the same world. I came to understand the unity of all things: that to make use of the rules of science or the mechanisms it reveals boils down to following, with virtue and efficacy, the modes of conduct set for us by the gods.

THE CRANIAL SPHERE

As I was coming home in a taxi from a visit to Watanabe-Sensei one day, I thought about how the universal laws of the workings of the world must also apply to my art, the Way of Beauty.

The great problem of masters of beauty had always been to design and construct hairstyles that would stay up. Truly, there is nothing sadder than a chignon that's fallen, or unruly hair escaping every which way like wild grass; nothing more lamentable than a rebellious lock rising straight up in the air like smoke in the wind; nothing more pitiful than a head of hair more disheveled than a haystack after a storm. Our traditional techniques called for the use of an oily coating, which gave body to the hair and downplayed mistakes. However, with modern hairstyles, permanent waves, and short hair, the artisans were at a loss. Only half the hairstyles stayed in place longer than one or two days, and they didn't understand why. They would upbraid the customer for her clumsiness in maintaining the style, blame the quality of her hair or even the weather, so as not to have to question their own art. Still, they were all of them secretly searching for a miraculous process which would assure their own supremacy.

In the taxi, I reflected that the head is spherical in form, and that the hair grows around it in a more or less circular shape, the center of the circle being the top of the occiput. Who knew? Maybe hair should be rolled in conformance with the principles of the orientations of the zodiac.

As soon as I got home, I set to work. If we divided the skull into 12 equal parts and—assuming that north corresponds to the top of the forehead and south to the nape of the neck—if we oriented the strands of hair in conformance with the regulating principles of the cosmos before rolling them on rollers and pinning them in place, would not hairstyles hold better?

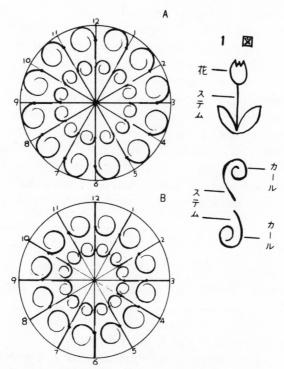

Principles of the waving of hair as defined by Yamazaki Ikue
(from the Yamazaki Ikue Manual).

I tested this first on the apprentices. As I went from trial to trial, I realized that hair treated in this new way became more manageable, the curls longer-lasting. My cheeks flushed deep with a passion hotter than a fever. Within two weeks I had developed a new theory, which I called *pin kāru* (pin curl), because, with it, a hairdo could stay in place simply with the aid of a hairpin. I called together my disciples and, with a solemnity that hid my emotion, I explained to them that hair, like plants, had a stem, and that curls were the flowers.

I added, "Knowing that no pain is felt when the hair is cut, people think of it as an inanimate thing, and of the hair left lying on the floor as trash. But in fact our hairs are living plants, because they grow. Caring for them is the business not only of chemists but also of the peasants. Like the latter, masters of beauty must follow the rules which preside over the growth of all beings and things."

After hearing these words, everyone made rapid progress in skills.

Word soon got around that I, Yamazaki Ikue, a simple hairdresser from Bunkyō, had discovered the secret of overcoming undisciplined hair. The shop was besieged with prospective trainees. But I sent them on their way, because I did not yet feel ready for them.

I applied the same natural principles to makeup: to balance a badly proportioned face, all one had to do was pencil the eyebrows so that they formed a thirty-degree angle to the base of the nose. In that way, the most disagreeable expression suddenly acquired the freshness of a fragrant springtime breeze or the tranquil serenity of the first evening of summer.

Soon I understood that we must constantly keep the laws of nature in mind. For example, we take the seasons for granted, but actually their periodic return rests on a complex mechanism that shows us the importance of relative angles. Nature teaches us all there is to know: color, form, and harmony. All beauty exists in nature. And that is particularly true of Japan.

The moment had arrived for me to reveal my discoveries to the world.

LEARNING ELOQUENCE

It came about quite simply. I had read in a brochure that NHK, the national radio and television broadcasting company, was planning a correspondence course in hairdressing. Because I had been a student of the Ochanomizu school, they invited me to a preliminary meeting.

That large gathering was as memorable for me as a wedding day is for others. For some months, by then, I had worn nothing but Western clothes, so I chose a dress of raw silk with little yellow flounces at the wrists and collar. I wore high heels, so high I had trouble walking. My hair, washed three times, reflected its bluish lights around my face.

After wandering through the halls at NHK, my heart pounding like that of a child calling for its mother, I pushed through a door: an entire henhouse of hairdressers dressed all in pink and white were wriggling excitedly on their chairs, chattering at the decibel level of schoolgirls. Everyone said that it was impossible just to talk about hairdressing, that the many techniques had to be shown, that the only way to learn it was by doing. The producers replied that they didn't see how they could plan a teaching program of any kind of satisfying cultural level if there really was no material. Hairdressing would have to be approached as a science.

Science: *gaku-mon*. I had hated that word as a child. But hearing it that day, I understood that the gods were giving me the chance to make my ideas known.

I can see myself now. I had not found a chair, so I was standing by the door when I began to expound on my theories. I said that the hair grows on the head according to rules, like those that govern the workings of the universe. I spoke about deeds that bear fruit, like trees.

I spoke in a whisper, but the hubbub receded and the room fell silent. I didn't dare stop after that.

I told of my discovery of science; I spoke about the gods who had guided me step by step and of how much joy it had brought me to increase the amount of beauty in the world. When I finally shut up—my strength gone, my mouth parched—the room was as quiet as death. I was ashamed and wanted to run away. Suddenly, a strident female voice piped up, "There's our cultural discourse!"

A few weeks later, I began to teach on television. It turned out to be a terrible trial. I felt like a leaf being tumbled downstream. Since the day I was born, I had heard it said that there is nothing worse than a talkative girl. This had made me taciturn. Here I was being asked to explain, in public, the gestures used in plying my craft, and their significance.

At the beginning, I thought only of my mouth and how I moved my lips before the cameras. Above all, I could not open my mouth too wide—that would have been vulgar. Elegant speech, at least my conception of it, involved rounding the lips (which should be carefully painted red) while using limited motions to indicate objects or to re-place the glasses that slipped down the nose with a gesture of distinguished irritation. (Since the birth of Hikaru, I had worn glasses; the frames were in the form of butterfly wings, following the American fashion.)

When I thought about my appearance, words wouldn't reach my brain but would stay hidden somewhere at the bottom of my throat, like insects at night, petrified by the light. They made me cough. So, in my heart, I prayed to the gods, to Benten-sama, the gentle goddess of eloquence and music, who plays the zither by the shores of lakes:[9] "Benten-sama, grant me ease of speech, and I will visit your shrine on Lake Biwa. Benten-sama, grant me clarity of speech, and I will offer up prayers and rice. Benten-sama, grant me speech that charms, and I will build you a chapel in my home."

And Benten-sama taught me that sincerity is the best guide. She granted

Benten

me an unwavering voice that does not betray the thoughts. Softly, the words descended from my mind to my mouth.

Finally, my honesty charmed the television viewers, who were more accustomed to the bragging of charlatans holding patents on miracle cures than to the praise of simple hard work.

In this way, things began to accelerate. The city of Tokyo asked me to plan the municipal hairdressing examinations. They were happy with the questions that I wrote, and for the next ten years I concocted problems for apprentice hairdressers. I entered national competitions, where I took prizes. When I went to large annual gatherings of masters of my profession, I sometimes heard my name whispered around me.

CHEMISTRY AND ECOLOGY

That nascent notoriety only distracted me from a nearly insurmountable difficulty in getting through the day. My head and body felt heavy. At first I thought that my mind was playing tricks with my health again. Then I realized that, among the twenty or so women who worked for me, there were always two or three who were sick. Unable to believe that some sudden feebleness had assaulted these Japanese women, each of whom had boasted of her endurance in the past, I figured it must be the chemicals we used, which made the hair as dry as a *hechima*, the loofah we use in the bath.

Several years before, we had replaced hot permanents, which gave hair the limp consistency of weeds beaten down by the autumn winds, with a chemical process. But the chemicals were more noxious than the river Sumida, polluted by industrial wastes.[10] When I forgot to use my rubber gloves, the skin on my fingers would split like ice in a hard winter. The toxins would be absorbed through the pores, poisoning the blood and the body and causing edema (which made the lips and eyelids swell), blisters or purplish blotches on the extremities, vaginal discharges, or bleeding and cramps.

So my attention to detail—to evil-smelling chemicals and all the varieties of unpleasantness associated with the use of modern hairdressing products—led me once again onto the path of discovery. Tokyo University happened to be near our shop; it always attracted the best students and the most famous professors. I counted a good dozen scientists' wives among my clientele. I approached one of them, the wife of a famous physician. "These Western products we use are astonishing," I said. "They make the hair wave like tendrils of wisteria, and, although I don't know why, they have a strange odor. Do you know what's in them?"

She did not, but she agreed to take a sample back to her husband, so he could analyze it for me in the university lab.

The following week, I went to the scientist's home to learn his diagnosis. I carried a gift of shrimp-flavored cakes, which I had wrapped in a *furoshiki*, an elegant square of fabric knotted at the top. At the door, I called out a cheery greeting. But when it opened, the doctor, on seeing me, puffed up with rage, ferocious as a cat defending its turf against a larger rival. He reviled my product: "It's ammonia! You call yourself a vendor of beauty; you're nothing but a merchant of death!"

Horrified by his thundering reproaches, I escaped through the university campus. I ran faster than I should have, like a wounded bird. Then I realized I hadn't given him the cakes. Sad, I tossed them onto a bench. I sat down. Filled with distress, I wondered why the fortune-teller of my childhood had lied to me. Then, because after all I had to make a living and this was the only profession I knew, I put my hands together and prayed silently: "I place my destiny back in the hands of the gods, who are wiser than men."

I picked up the cakes and munched them on my way home. Then I got back to work.

When the odor of the permanent wave solution engulfed the salon, I continued to feel like one of those blind fish that wash up on the shore, thinking they had been heading out to sea.

I ran around to all the seminars and speeches available to find out what my colleagues thought about the presence of ammonia in the products we used. Everyone seemed to be satisfied. I felt like a crazed weed among houseplants, but I knew that I must find a product that would not contravene the laws of nature.

MISTAKES

At one of those conferences I met a strange man, with a round nose stuck onto a craggy face and a large head that wagged incessantly on top of his bony frame. His name was Ichikawa, and he told me, "The world is packed to the gills with false scholars, whose knowledge gives them the authority to act like they own everything." He spoke of the atom, of Hiroshima, and of hydrogen ions. He explained that the human body—in fact the entire world—is made up of positive and negative particles, the balance of which gives matter its texture, its aspect, or its form. He used terms like "pH" and "equilibrium."

Obviously, most of this was lost on me. But all of it evoked the alternation of yin and yang, which the Chinese had discovered long ago.[11] I concluded from his information that only a neutral permanent wave solution would preserve the natural equilibrium of the body. Now I had to produce such a product.

So began the long adventure that was to lead me to success. But before that, again and again I would think that ruin and shame had bested me, as greedy men, one after the other, took advantage of my ignorance.

One of them prepared an acidic product that he claimed was neutral. But, rather than curling the hair, it made it stretch out. As I had bought bottles and bottles of the stuff, I decided to use it to straighten frizzy hair, because at that time girls with frizzy hair had little hope of marrying. They wore scarves all the time and wouldn't dare go to the public baths or to a hairdresser, so afraid were they of being mocked. They had no choice but to work in occupations like nursing, that are so vital people forget to look at the person.

At first, this treatment was so effective that a popular magazine, *Shufu to Seikatsu*, The Housewife and Daily Living, published an article about me which described my technique for straightening hair in the most flattering terms. It said that the product transformed the kinkiest hair into "long brown seaweed swaying gently in the waves . . . just as water makes fresh grass of dry straw." The customers came in droves, and we made money.

Alas, greed always breeds ill fortune. I soon found that the product had turned a sort of bronze color, which I hadn't seen it do before. Immediately, I asked my supplier about it, but he, oddly, insisted that nothing had changed. The sad news arrived three days later: a customer wrote to us complaining that her hair, after first turning as red as pine needles in the autumn, was now falling out like pine needles in winter. A second letter, threatening a lawsuit, came the next day. And still more letters. . . . In the end, my methods had proven more harmful than the problem they were supposed to correct. I knew that from the day I took the bait of profit the gods had ceased to watch over me.

This was without a doubt the darkest period of my life, a time that was all the more cruel for my hopes having been so joyous.

One evening just after I had tucked in my son, Hikaru, that luminous child too young to understand adult troubles, I was seized with an irresistible desire to die, and to drag my children down into hell with me. In vain I prayed to the gods to save me, repeated to myself that my children were good, that my husband didn't run around *too* much, that I wasn't destitute. But, still, I was racked with sobs of shame, my eyes wide open, my teeth exposed.

On another night, my throat became so tight I gasped for breath. When I was putting Hikaru to bed, I said to him in a low voice, "I'm going to go hang myself in front of the chemist's door."

Thinking that a soft material would lessen my suffering, I took a silk sash from a formal undergarment belonging to Hikaru. With the pretty cord rolled around my fist, I got into bed next to the sleeping Tatsuo. Once the moon had completed half its course, I silently crept to the front door.

Its squeaking woke Tatsuo. He got up and ran into the street, where he grabbed me by the arm and slapped my face with all his might. He accused me of not thinking of the ancestors. He said, "Why don't you try being a wife and mother, before you go playing researcher!" And he hit me again!

Three days later, I made another suicide attempt. I was already walking toward the druggist's when I felt the urge to urinate. I went back home, where I came to my senses. I thought, "Why should I die? I'm not really unhappy, and no one is suing me." I bowed respectfully before the domestic altar and climbed into bed.

The next day, the doctor at the hospital in Ochanomizu diagnosed me as overworked and prescribed a series of calcium shots.

BERU JUBANSU: BELLE JOUVENCE

A month later, I met a professor at Tokyo University through my oldest brother, who sometimes consulted him in his capacity as head of the agricultural cooperative in Asaka. This specialist in industrial agriculture agreed to analyze all offending products for me. He told me what they were made of, rather than blaming me for their composition, like the client's husband I'd consulted earlier. With his help and that of two young chemists, I invented a clear liquid product that made the hair healthy and shiny. This time, customers were so satisfied that they spread my reputation like the wind, far beyond Bunkyō. In less than a month, they were lining up at the door of the shop, spilling out into the street.

The money began to flow back in, gradually. Tatsuo stopped criticizing me. I felt as peaceful as an animal who has at long last finished digging her den.

This was to be the product that, years later, when it was perfected, would be called Belle Jouvence (French for beautiful fountain of youth, pronounced *beru jubansu* in Japanese). It clinched my reputation.

The components of this permanent wave solution were not so very different from those used normally, but it was of such a gentleness that its repeated usage, far from destroying the hair, actually strengthened it.[12] Over time, it was tested and perfected, and in Year 37 of Shōwa (1962), this miraculous product received the official stamp of approval of the Kōseishō, the Ministry of Health and Welfare.

It soon proved worthy of its name. Thanks to Belle Jouvence, tired hair regained the luster it had lost ten or twenty years before. Applied to the face, it made the skin glow like translucent marble. Everyone agreed that this solution really did possess the purifying qualities of *waka-mizu*, the water of youth, which the gods put into wells and rivers on the first of the new year.[13] People draw out this water with great ceremony, to regenerate their vital forces, which become exhausted by time.

Secretly I thought of my discovery as *kami no mizu*, water of the gods. I knew that only heaven could have conferred this marvelous fluid on a simple country girl. The gods were watching over me because I had never played false with anyone.

This water is a wellspring of equilibrium. It is true, just as the Way of Buddhism is the true middle path. It is as pure as the hearts of the buddhas. Its efficacy is a gift from the gods. The formula is inimitable. In the hands of money-grubbers, it turns to dirty water.

When I state my convictions in this way, some people read it as a refined form of the art of secretiveness. Others sense an ineffable mystery. As for my customers, they say, "Using Belle Jouvence is like starting a new life or adopting a new faith. After the second session, I felt so relaxed! And I have far fewer wrinkles now." My customers have skin like porcelain, their eyes as bright as a drop of fresh blood.

13

The Business World

Katte kabuto no o wo shimeyo.
Victor, strap your helmet on tight.

Shichinen no aida to iu mono moji dōri, me no iro wo kaete hataraite orimashita . . .
For those seven years, I worked to beat the devil. Every night I counted the money in the cash register, calculating and computing eight hundred times over how I could repay what I owed. Finally, in Year 33 of Shōwa (1958), all my debts were paid off. I thought that at last the time had come for me to experience joy and pleasure, have a real life.

Proud and from then on sure of myself, on the very day I made my final payment I took out another loan, to open a salon in a building that was for rent in Ginza. Ginza—that famous name fired my imagination. I hoped to get experience there with all kinds of hair: Westerners' hair, the hair of people from other Asian countries. I would expand my knowledge. I would hang a sign over the door in shining characters: "Japanese Center for Hair Care Research." That would give the right tone of seriousness. My name would be known in the fashionable quarters of the city.

A long-standing customer at the Bunkyō salon who worked at City Hall consulted a fiscal adviser from the Ministry of Finance for me. He said starting a second company would be far better than making the Ginza salon a subsidiary. That way, if by chance things didn't work out, I could close the shop without it devouring money earned elsewhere.

All these precautions made me want to laugh. I thought, "What a lot of useless trouble we're going to!" Still, because one must always do what is right, I followed their advice. It was lucky that I did, because in Ginza I once again fell prey to thieves! My manager cheated me—he watered down the product and sold it himself on the sly.

Little by little I understood that, even though the government—indeed, the entire world—was constantly talking of harmony regained, in reality the strong had never ceased to crush the weak, nor the weak to humiliate

203

themselves before the strong. Naka's wisdom, and later the fervor of my beliefs, had for a long time sheltered me from the grasp of a bunch of get-rich-quick types ruled by envy, cunning treachery, and moronic pretensions. No doubt it was naive of me, but my quest for an indisputable truth that would show me the meaning of the world and of life would now drag me into the nets of unscrupulous businesspeople. Such people may find a kind of mediocre success through the alliances they form, only to have it destroyed by their inevitable betrayals of one another. Luckily, the very traps they set for me would in the end contribute to my own success.

ENCOUNTER WITH EUROPE

My adventures began with the announcement that the 1964 Olympic Games would be held in Tokyo. I knew that Japan could not long keep its distance from the rest of the world. I had been working as if the archipelago constituted the universe, without ever stopping to consider what was happening abroad. When I learned that so many men and women of all nations were to come to Japan, I wondered whether in some other corner of the globe someone had invented the natural product I still sought. So I decided to go to France, so renowned in fashion circles, and to Switzerland, known for the robust health of its people.

Additionally, in the fourth decade of the Shōwa Era, we Japanese had begun to make a sharp distinction between those who had been abroad and those who had not. Wealthy travelers brought back from Europe fabulous tales of the lights of Paris and the grandeur of the Alps. They said that Japan was only a minuscule island, a place where a person who set out for the horizon would soon fall off the edge, whereas the world was as vast as the ocean. Their sojourns endowed them with a prestige as immense as the sky itself. I had no wish to be like those tank-bound fish who mistake the walls of their dwellings for the edges of the earth. An overseas voyage struck me as the indubitable manifestation of my first successes.

Because of my trepidation about the journey, though, I wanted Tatsuo to come with me. He asked for a long vacation from Dentsū, but his superiors refused (out of jealousy, no doubt). Hesitant to quit a job with such a reputable firm (since if he did, he would never again find suitable employment in this country, where we mistrust lunatics who change jobs the way others leave their wives), he resigned himself to staying.[1] But I said, "The hairdressing business is earning enough now that you can have your freedom back." I offered him the title of general director of the Yamazaki Company, a title he would never get from Dentsū. He accepted, on the condition that he never be required to appear publicly in that capacity. He said, "I'll be like the theater dresser in the wings of the Kabuki."

Now we had to find a way to go to France. We had to make plans hastily, and our ignorance would lead us onto a rocky road, where we infringed severely on the laws of Japanese society.

This is what happened.

Having read in a professional journal that the directors of the French Association of Hair Care Professionals were then in Japan, I requested of them an intermediary who would obtain for me a letter of invitation to visit Europe. This go-between turned out to be a tall and very elegant man whom I knew slightly and who belonged to the Japanese hairdressing world.

But as time passed and I received no response, I decided to resort to a ruse. I arranged to have a gift conveyed in secret to the president of the French association: two pearls wrapped in gold brocade. The next day, although no one had requested our presence, I dragged the now unemployed Tatsuo with me to Haneda Airport, so we could greet the foreign guests on their way out of the country.

I dressed in a kimono that was a little too showy for my age in order to attract attention, and I walked with my head held high, my chin raised more than my rank allowed for, the way Westerners do. On our arrival, Mr. Donohashi, a famous character in the Japanese hairdressing world, was already there. With his disciples and his interpreter he formed a circle around the French. Embarrassed, I started to walk around them, then I stumbled, then I thrust myself through the human rampart. I had to grab the arm of the Frenchwoman to keep from falling. When she straightened up, I complimented her on her hat, which the interpreter had no choice but to translate, along with specifying who I was. She immediately gave me the hat and handed me a note tucked into a violet-scented envelope: she said she had been honored by the gift of the pearls and suggested we visit Paris the next month, for a convention. We'd done it! We would get our passports and visas!

Realizing that our little ruse had borne fruit, the "go-between" whom I had approached now pretended to be pleasant, even to the point of helping us prepare our hastily organized voyage. However, a dishonest man does not instantly change to a bodhisattva, and wild persimmons yield only bitter fruit. So it is not surprising that as soon as the translator this go-between had found for us got his advance, he disappeared as completely as a shadow when the sun goes behind a cloud.

This put us out all the more; the trip had cost a fortune already. For the show of traditional Japanese formal dress and hairstyles that we were to present at the convention, we had acquired lavish kimonos and all the accessories. We had also bought clothes for ourselves that we thought would make the correct impression. We had entertained a crowd of respectful colleagues (as well as those burning with envy), business connections curious or sympathetic, and gossip columnists, who announced our departure in the press: "Mr. and Mrs. Yamazaki are going to Paris as ambassadors delegated by Japanese professionals, in order to take part in the presentations to the French Association of Hair Care Professionals. Our best wishes go with them!"

And so, finally, on a propitious day, a day of great peace, *taian*, carefully chosen on the calendar, we left Bunkyō for Haneda Airport with a large entourage. A mob of employees and friends carried the suitcases stuffed with kimonos, combs, and makeup to the taxis, then squeezed in behind to accompany us to the special room we had reserved at the airport for our formal send-off. I was exhausted.

Someone whispered in my ear, "Don't leave. Find some excuse. All you have to do is get your appendix removed!" It was only the grotesque nature of that proposition that gave me the courage, a short while later, to board the plane bound for Paris.

THE TRIP TO FRANCE

I have few memories of that trip to France. I visited some beautiful monuments. Paris was like a museum. But tourism is a luxury of which I barely thought at the time. I had come on business. Nothing else interested me.

As for the Parisians, they treated us as if we were toys, showed us off like exotic objects. They installed us in a luxury hotel because, they said, we had to live up to our position. When we complained that our money was evaporating, they told us not to eat so much. Finally, after two weeks, we moved to a housekeeping pension where we could do our own cooking. Western cooking had ceased to agree with our digestive systems after a while anyway.

Tatsuo and I shopped in the market. We liked that. We learned that fruits and vegetables were sold by weight, not by the piece, as in Japan. All we knew how to say was "one kilo," so we bought great quantities of everything. We were astonished at the black skin of those giant radishes that, in Asia, are as white as turnips. We bought all sorts of little presents with which to thank all our colleagues, friends, and relatives who, through a few bills slipped into envelopes, had contributed to our expedition.[2] We acquired many marvelous stories about the bizarre habits of the French, their agitated natures, and their endless chattering. Tatsuo, who had a talent for languages, enlarged his vocabulary to include "*Comment allez-vous?*" But most strikingly, in a single month, his black hair turned white from worry. That added to his distinguished air, but it made him look sad, too.

Concerned, I consulted a French clairvoyant. She said that the force of my spirit had struck her like a storm wind when I walked into the room and that I would get what I was looking for because "God" was watching over me.

"Which god would that be?" I asked.

"The God of the Universe," responded the clairvoyant.

Hearing those words, I understood that Ame no Minaka Nushi, the god who had overseen the creation of Japan and the world, had his eyes upon me.[3] That reassured me a little, as I feared that our efforts had not borne much fruit.

Professionally, in fact, the trip was only partially successful. The beauty of the traditional styles we presented awed the spectators. I demonstrated the technique of *suberakashi*, which involves lifting up strands of hair from the temples as a way of beginning to construct a chignon on the top of the head, while the bulk of the hair is pulled into a low, large loop with paper ties; I made the classic Shimada chignon, which one often sees depicted in woodblock prints, and also the *yakai-maki*, secured much closer to the head with the aid of pins. I also learned that research on acidic permanent wave solutions done in Switzerland a decade earlier had failed.

Those three months in Europe reassured me about the state of the world. Like many insular people, I had thought life outside our islands must have nothing in common with ours, and, my imagination stirred by films, I had built up in my mind phantasmagoric civilizations on which I projected both my fears and my hopes. The trip convinced me of the universality of human nature. Europe was very old, it was true, but the French had two arms and two legs just like us.

We made our way slowly back to the Far East by the southern route. Arriving in Hong Kong, it was with relief that we once again gazed upon the unexotic faces of our fellow East Asians. Back in Japan, the manners of the people struck us as so common and their preoccupations so trivial that we felt ourselves to be far superior to the bulk of our compatriots.

ALLIANCE

My newfound self-assurance soon attracted new friends. The owners of Momiji-ya, a large manufacturer of cosmetics, soon sought out an alliance with me. Their eldest son, we learned, wanted to marry our elder daughter. It is true that Motoko was a *yamato nadeshiko*, a classic Japanese beauty in the old style.[4] Tall for a Japanese girl, she had delicate, well-shaped hands

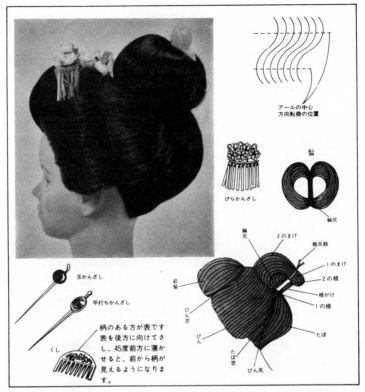

Construction of a chignon (Yamazaki Ikue Manual).

and feet, and her face was etched with an exquisite sweetness. Her extreme stylishness elevated her charms still further. This had shown up when she was only three, during the winter children's festival of *shichi go san*.[5] Dressed in a formal kimono, her face powdered and painted in the traditional manner, Motoko had refused to eat—so as not to spoil her lips, she said.

When we spoke to her of marriage for the first time, she said, "I have no need to marry." (Without knowing it, Motoko had resurrected the expression I had used years before.) Since adolescence, she had shown such a spontaneous talent for the arts of hairstyling and dress that everyone saw her as the rightful heiress to the family business. Having suffered as a young child from my absence from the home, she had decided not to have children so as not to make them unhappy. Finally, she had noticed that the family fortune attracted suitors like fleas to a cat.

However, I knew that there are no happy single people in this world. I said, "A woman who doesn't marry can never know true beauty!"

To end our dispute, we would have to visit Ontake-san, which had presided over Motoko's birth: they advised my daughter to embark on the tranquil path of a woman of the home. She resigned herself to that, nevertheless wavering between two potential fiancés, whom the gods had pronounced equally acceptable. The first was a graduate of Tokyo University employed by Dentsū. He was a gentle man, and marriage to him would assure her an easy life. The other was the Momiji-ya heir, a businessman who would never be still for a minute. After both *miai* (the official marriage meetings) had taken place, she chose the latter—for fear of being bored with the other man, she said. The family name of the Momiji-ya heir was Yamazaki, too, although he was no relation to us. So, thanks to the gods, Motoko would not have to change her last name. Yamazaki Yasuo was a tall, lithe man, with a pointed nose and wide-set eyes, who defended the cult of the emperor and the values of Great Japan (*Dai Nippon*) with heated passion.

So Motoko left our house to move to Shibuya Ward, where the family and their business were based. Yasuo got her pregnant immediately and forbade her to work until the last child's education was assured.

I felt sad at the departure of my older daughter, whose nature resembled my own. Nevertheless, unlike other girls raised after the war, Motoko soon declared her satisfaction with the arranged marriage. She appreciated living with a mother-in-law, she said, who epitomized the function of motherhood: constant attention to the small details of everyday life that give everyone a sense of well-being and security. I resented this a little bit as an indirect reproach to me, but, the truth is, a businesswoman does not have much time for family gatherings.

Even before the wedding ceremony, the Momiji-ya people had proposed that I open a shop in a building they owned in Shibuya. I couldn't refuse without seeming arrogant. Since the Ginza shop was not successful, I decided to salvage what I could of my investment there and take advantage of this chance to move without too much expense. I rented from them a space of 1,600 square feet, to be devoted exclusively to Belle Jouvence, for a good price.

From that day on, I never had to worry about finding new locations for salons. I began to get so many offers I had to turn several of them down.

The Shibuya salon hadn't opened yet when, out of nowhere, an insurance company came to me with an offer of a site in Shinjuku. The financial outlook was attractive: they asked for a million yen in security up front and after that would take a percentage of the profits. I was so honored at having been approached by people I had not even met that I was reluctant to refuse. Still, it didn't make sense—it might be years before we turned a profit on our investment in Shibuya—so I turned them down.

In spite of my respectful refusal, the insurance company persisted. I later learned that what they really wanted was to get me out of Shibuya for the sake of a cosmetics company which was getting ready to open a store on the same block. According to my source, they feared the competition. The insurance family and the cosmetics manufacturing family were in the habit of marrying their children off to each other and had formed what we call a clique of the hearth (as we had done with Motoko's in-laws). However, not knowing this at the time, I simply told myself that it would be a shame to pass up this windfall sent by the gods. (I admit I was tempted by the generous terms and the flattery.)

I didn't really know where I would find the money, until I thought that maybe Miss Nakamura, an employee who came from a wealthy family, could finance the new salon. I would manage it, so it would bear the name of Yamazaki. At my request, Miss Nakamura telephoned her family, who lived in Gunma Prefecture. She persuaded her father and her maternal uncle to lend her 500,000 yen each, which would give us the million needed to pay the security.

It seemed that the problem was solved. Then the elderly Mr. Aoki, whom I held in particular esteem, paid me a visit. When I had met him years before, he was a dresser at the Imperial Court, and he had sometimes lent me traditional costumes for fashion shows. Through his having lived among the great people of this world—he had been promoted to chief of protocol at court—there was nothing he didn't know about noble customs and virtue. He could prescribe the proper conduct for every situation.

Hearing of my plan, this old friend reproached me harshly. He said that it made no business sense and that I was foisting off my own responsibilities on a simple employee. If the problem was merely liquidity, he himself could lend me the money! I could pay it back when I turned a profit.

Just as I was pondering how to tell Miss Nakamura that I had to renege on the deal, she came to me in tears and threw herself at my feet. Her father and uncle had quarreled so violently, she said, that she no longer saw how she could get the money.

I marveled once again at the wisdom of old Mr. Aoki. I told Miss Nakamura of the shame I felt for having burdened such a young girl, with no experience in business, in that way. I apologized to her for my duplicity. She in turn apologized for her naivete. Sobbing, we fell into each other's arms, which in Japan, as elsewhere, constitutes the beginning of a happy reconciliation.

At last, on the same clear day in November, when silvery paper decorations, luminous as snow, took the place of ruddy garlands of plastic autumn leaves in the streets, two Yamazaki shops, the one in Shibuya and the other in Shinjuku, had their grand openings. One of Tatsuo's younger sisters, a simple woman whom age had rendered both voluminous and talkative, was put in charge of welcoming the customers in Shibuya. In Shinjuku the same task fell to one of his sisters-in-law, a smiling housewife, filled with joy by this testament to the confidence placed in her.

DIFFICULTIES

The salon in Shinjuku attracted as many customers in dresses from the fashionable Mitsukoshi or Isetan department stores as it did those women from the neighborhood you see chattering on the street in their workers' smocks. However, as if in vengeful compensation, in Shibuya nothing went well. I had hoped that the faithful customers from the Ginza shop would follow the move, but the inconveniences of Tokyo, the long train rides, discouraged them. Citing unusual circumstances, family problems, or financial difficulties, they first began to lessen their visits, then ceased coming altogether. To make matters worse, the entire area was gutted. After the Olympic Games, large construction projects had been undertaken near the train station and in the adjacent streets. The sound of jackhammers chased away first the birds and then the passersby. In front of the salon, where there had been a sort of empty space in which puddles reflected all the clouds in the sky after the rain, rose a building that completely hid the entrance.

After two years the situation was so bad, reason seemed to demand that we close the shop and move elsewhere. Either that or turn it into one of those ordinary beauty shops that women of the working classes frequent.

One day as I was looking over the accounts, which were even sadder than usual, I made my decision. I went to the salon dressed in a kimono, as if for a formal occasion. I called the employees together. When all of them were lined up in one unequal row of pretty and ugly girls, I announced that the shop would soon close; the girls with the most seniority would be reassigned to Bunkyō or Shinjuku; the younger ones would be let go.

Just as I was finishing this speech, whose overwhelming sadness made my voice scratch at the back of my throat like a burr, causing me to cough, a little man pushed in through the door, its bell tinkling with an indecent gaiety. When all eyes turned to him, he asked politely: What were these researches into hair care he had read about in the shop window?

What twist of chance prompted this man in his tight, civil servant-type suit to come in at that exact moment? Had he been sent by our allies, the Momiji-ya people? By the gods? Perhaps both? I never found out. It turned out he was a television producer. One week later, a local TV station showed a ten-minute story on this product, Belle Jouvence, which had transformed the art of hairdressing. The segment had barely concluded when six customers showed up at Shibuya. One month later, they were lining up out to the street, blocking any automobile traffic that wandered into the jungle of construction scaffolding.

This ushered in an era of new prosperity: Belle Jouvence was adapted for different types of hair. Large symposia were held annually, including hairdressing festivals that did very well for us. Belle Jouvence patents were registered in the United States and the principal European countries, in preparation for either selling the brand name or the delightful possibility of opening Yamazaki branches in foreign lands.

So it looked as if the boat of my life had left the tempests of springtime behind and sailed into the protective shadows of the summer rushes. Contemplating my new wealth, I waited, tranquil as a buddha. That is when a new quarrel broke out.

COMPETITION

Troubled by the growth of my family-run company, which each day grew more harmful to their competing interests, certain mediocre hairdressers dragged their organizations into a scheme. The suddenness of the ascension of the Yamazakis had at first horrified them. Realizing that we were engaged not only in hairdressing but also in the manufacture of cosmetics and hair-care products (we subcontracted production to a small chemical firm)—which meant there was no one professional category in which to class us—they privately grew more and more irritated. They shrugged with exasperation when I publicly denounced the harmful nature of the products used by most hairdressers. Finally, when we became successful, they grew fearful and decided to thwart my progress.

Quietly at first, they began to tell large manufacturers that professionals authorized to use Belle Jouvence were dangerous fanatics. They said that such professionals denigrated the actions of their colleagues (by denouncing the products they used as harmful) and that this intolerance proved their disloyalty to the association as a whole. All this amounted to negative advertising, in their view. "The use of Belle Jouvence is not hairdressing but indoctrination," they said. Another group, the Association of Permanent Wave Specialists, held a special meeting, where they resolved to discredit Belle Jouvence and to force us out of business. Four hundred of them agreed to engage me in battle.

At first their case seemed easy to plead. In Year 38 of Shōwa (1963), the Ministry of Health had authorized the use of Belle Jouvence on the skin and hair. Even though a notice issued in Year 41 had forbidden the use of one of its component ingredients on the face, the authorization of Year 38 had continued to be renewed annually under identical terms. This may have been the result of administrative oversight or the fact that no customer had ever complained. Considering ourselves well within our rights, we sometimes used Belle Jouvence as a facial lotion, which was particularly effective in the treatment of benign skin afflictions.

Another association filed a complaint with the Ministry of Health. The police then called in our subcontractor, the chemist, for questioning. A prudent man, he consulted the almanac to find a well-augured day on which to present himself at headquarters. In spite of these precautions, he was coldly received: they explained to him the grounds of the complaint and told him to go to the Department of Guidelines for Pharmaceutical Products and Cosmetics at the Ministry of Health and Welfare. When he got there, officials accused him of distributing dangerous products. He defended himself like a pike on the end of a fishing line, arguing that his sole capacity as manufacturer excused him from all responsibility regarding the usage others made of his products. He apologized. They did not detain him further.

Once the chemist informed me of these underhanded maneuverings by my adversaries, I immediately contacted my disciples—all those former employees and customers who supported my work—to solicit testimonies in my favor. Within a week, eight thousand letters arrived from the four points of the compass, in which customers described the happiness that Belle Jouvence had brought to their lives, their flourishing health, and the peace in their souls. These letters reassured me. It was in complete serenity, then, that I decided to resort to political action.

It so happened that one of my old disciples counted among her clientele the wife of a Liberal Democratic member of the Diet. This man offered to bring the matter directly to the Ministry of Health and Welfare, where he knew a man who had been his *oya-kata* (protector) in political circles, with whom he still maintained quasi-filial ties.[6] Even before the latter heard all the details, he said, "I am quite familiar with these stories of vultures who try to swallow sparrows." He made it understood that nothing about Belle Jouvence had been proven harmful and ordered his counselors to bury the file.

These awful quarrels led me to resign from all the professional organizations. My enemies forbade the trade publications to print a word of advertising for Belle Jouvence, threatening them that: Magazines in which the name appeared would never receive ads from large manufacturers.

I broke this blockade by publishing my own monthly information bulletin. Still, all wars, just or unjust, must one day come to an end. Little by little, the ad people gave in to the growing popularity of Belle Jouvence.

In the end there were neither winners nor losers. Unless the very survival of my business constitutes a sort of victory.

Even though I came out unscathed, I sometimes reflect on those insane battles. My dreams of harmony, grandeur, and beauty had engendered discord, pettiness, and ugly intrigues. I wouldn't like to have to relive that period. Why do the gods permit men to exhaust themselves in quarrels still more vain than the battles of phantoms in the next world?

14

Dōzoku-Gaisha:
A Family Business

三人よれば文珠の知恵

Sannin yoreba Monju no chie.
Three people together have the wisdom of Monju
—the bodhisattva of wisdom and intellect.

Kanemochi ni nari, kenryoku wo nigitte . . . Everyone knows those ambitious types who, seduced by the spectacle of wealth, submit to the violent nature of power and dream of seeing others kowtow before them. Free from all fears, in former times they built cities and empires; today, they put their names on a "company" and these names are transmitted from generation to generation, like titles of nobility.

But I, Yamazaki Ikue, never had a vocation for organizing great things. Having grown up fearful (if unsubmissive), I have long lived my life deaf to the requirements of society and business. Ceaselessly tearing through the world in quest of myself, I am like those seabirds that rip their own flesh as they pick through their feathers for vermin.

Nonetheless, my efforts had a cumulative effect. Whenever exhaustion depleted my courage, when failures demolished my work, I would remember those peasants on the banks of the Abukuma River who rebuilt the bridges after every flood. Then I would decide to rebuild my house even larger than before. Ultimately, then, it was the strokes of ill fortune, more than the joys of good fortune, that guided my steps.

As I've mentioned, from Bunkyō, my domain spread first to Ginza, then to Shibuya and Shinjuku—the two most fashionable areas of Tokyo. Such renowned hotels as the House of Woman and the Hotel Geihinkan put me in charge of their bridal dressing rooms. Even if my successes were uneven, the name of Belle Jouvence became known to thousands in the capital. I noticed when I entered the Hakusan branch of my bank that the employees began to bow more deeply than usual and that merchants on the grand avenues called me *sensei*, master. The business had grown little by little over the years. I now found myself overseeing eighty employees, all scurrying about dressed in pink-and-white blouses embroidered with my name. Almost an entire calendar cycle, sixty years, had passed since my birth.[1]

Still feeling like a child inside, I turned my thoughts to the past. I was stunned at the road I had taken, and I praised the gods who had brought me this far. Then I decided that I had to take my future in hand, as they say.

THE YAMAZAKI IKUE BUILDING

First I resolved to build a new headquarters, to house both ourselves and the flagship salon. Constructed out of wood in the impoverished postwar years, our old headquarters no longer suited the fame of the Yamazakis. "Living over there," said the customers, "I wonder that you don't hear the cuckoo's song!" Fashion also demanded that rich people live in new dwellings, *shinchiku*, made of stone or concrete.[2] Moreover, our house was so small that the cooking odors from the kitchen defiled the altars, which I feared would irritate the gods and ancestors. When the *biru* (building) was finished, I would be able to give them an entire room of their own. They could live there in peace, far from the hustle and bustle of daily life.

When I consulted the calendar, I saw that Year 44 (1969) was propitious for moving. The banks agreed to advance all the money we would need, because they knew we were reliable about repaying loans. We moved at the beginning of the spring, but we scheduled the demolition of the old house for the second week of the following year. The reason for this delay was that our souls might be upset by the upheaval. While we could physically move our bodies out in an instant, our souls were overaccustomed to the old shack. Fearing they might unleash their wrath—or, worse yet, refuse to leave it (thereby forsaking our bodies)—we gave them an entire year to detach themselves from those confines in which they had lived for so long.

Since business had to continue as usual, I bought a small, freestanding house nearby, which would serve as a temporary home for the salon. The employees lived over the shop.

While waiting for the new house to be finished, Tatsuo and I lived in a modern apartment in the stylish district of Roppongi. Motoko was, of course, already married. Our younger girl, Ryōko, who was engaged to be married, went to live with her future husband.

Their union came about in a funny way. Tanaka Teiichirō, the man Ryōko would marry, had come to see us for the first time two or three months before. According to a new custom, this tall, dark-complected young man, whose simpleminded air masked his intelligence only at first glance, came to see us to officially ask for our daughter's hand on behalf of one of his friends. This friend had asked Teiichirō to act as go-between, because our family was thought to be mistrustful where marriage was concerned (and I must say our affluence brought out more suitors than the night does ghosts).

As fate would have it, when Teiichirō walked into the house, he got his first glimpse of Ryōko. He said that she dazzled him with her eyes, which shone with the light of eight suns. He saw in her the plump delectability of summer fruit. So charmed that he forgot his prepared speech, he stammered out his own request for our daughter's hand.

Since the strangeness of the situation embarrassed us, we decided to consult the gods of Ontake-san. Happily, they said it was fine for the two friends to switch roles. The rejected suitor was thus charged with arranging the wedding of the new lovebirds!

After the marriage of his sisters into other families, Hikaru was our sole heir. But the master of geomancy said that the direction of Roppongi did not agree with my son, who would have to live in the north. He would have to change his first name, too, to lend firmness to his overly reticent temperament. He decided to call himself Mitsunobu, written with a character closely resembling the one used to write Hikaru, and he took an *apāto* in the north of the city. He set up housekeeping in that apartment with a girl he loved and hoped to marry. That was Kyōko, with a slender frame and distinguished air, a mild-mannered girl with whom I would later have considerable difficulties.

The new four-story building, coated with a rosy white stucco, was finished by the end of Year 46 (1971). I had a long placard attached to the building, which bore my name for all to see: *Yamazaki Ikue Biru*. The allocation of space inside has changed very little since we moved in. The ground floor and the second floor are used for the hair salon. Above them is our apartment, a duplex with a spiral staircase.

You reach the apartment through a little square entryway, where street shoes are exchanged for soft house slippers. A single step separates the entryway from the foyer, which opens to the west onto the DK (the dining and kitchen area), and to the east onto the Western-style living room. The latter continues on into a Japanese-style room. A short curtain divided into flaps—brown with cream-colored figures of cranes (those birds of happiness who fly toward the sky with stiff feet)—hides the kitchen, which itself terminates in a balcony filled with potted geraniums. The kitchen is white, modern, and functional: immaculate high cabinets surround a breakfast nook presided over by a coffeemaker in which Tatsuo makes Indonesian coffee every morning around ten. This is a very special coffee: the coffee beans are fed to ducks, after which they are recovered, washed, and ground.

Tatsuo swears this is the best of all coffees. He drinks it from a cup that he chooses very carefully according to his mood of the day. He has a collection of close to a hundred cups and teapots, including everything from one of fine porcelain decorated with the figure of a dancer swathed in diaphanous veils to a sandstone pot with a spout adorned by red-painted lips!

In a way, the kitchen is Tatsuo's office. He assumed the title of general director (as we had agreed) when we returned from France. Nevertheless—and although he sometimes fears that my whims or preposterous ideas might cause some problem or other, he shrugs over each of my audacities and screams that I'm as crazy as the autumn winds—he entrusts the workings of the business to me. He spends far more time taking walks than he does looking over files. Every morning, in the kitchen, however, he takes a leisurely look at the mail, which is brought upstairs by the employee who opens the shop.

Tatsuo divides the letters into two piles: those to be handed over to the general secretary and those he will answer personally. He gathers his tools: a brush, a calligraphy desk, and some velvety paper, with which to pen, with some satisfaction, a few elegantly turned phrases of thanks for a tasteful gift or a flattering invitation. Then he very carefully affixes to these his seal and makes his way to the post office, where his morning work ends. All of these tasks are merely the preliminaries for some stroll he invents to occupy his time and create some stories to tell me later on. Ever the boulevardier, he jokes with the shopkeepers in the neighborhood, addressing each of them in terms of exquisite politeness, which lends an aristocratic character to his nonchalance. Tatsuo knows how to enjoy, he possesses *iki*, the mark of a true *edokko*, or child of Tokyo.[3]

During the day, the residents and employees of the house encounter each other only randomly in the DK, where the television and the VCR, stuck back in a corner near the kitchen door, are usually left turned off. Idle pleasures are fine for the office worker, the "salaryman." But at our house, we're running a business, and nobody has the time. Everyone grabs a bite when he can, snacks being prepared by Satō-san, who comes in early to clean and do the cooking. Only at dinner are several members of the family together on any regular basis.

At that hour, the directors of our salons usually line up in the entryway to leave their metal cashboxes containing the day's receipts on the doorsill. It is Tatsuo who answers them when they knock at the door. From the kitchen, where he is distractedly leafing through the newspaper, he makes me laugh by calling out to them in imitation of the carnival barker accents of street merchants: "*Irrasshai!* Welcome! *Go-kuro-san!* Thanks for your trouble!"

In the entryway, the cashbox deliverer flattens himself to the floor, announcing the day's total. After he leaves, Tatsuo will bestir himself and go pick up the box.

The living room has a crystal chandelier from Mitsukoshi, which clinks in the breeze that passes through the room all summer in spite of the air conditioning; two sofas upholstered in gray linen surround a low, elaborate, Chinese-style table covered with white lace mats.[4]

It is around this table that I receive the journalists who come to interview me. This is where, cups of green tea or coffee before us, I hold my business appointments. Small glass bookcases holding beautiful albums of hairstyles line the walls. There I have hung an embroidered picture showing two young women standing on a traditional *engawa*, a veranda. An upright piano occupies one corner. But since I can't play it, I had a sort of music box installed inside. When I want to unwind, I stretch out on the sofa and listen to old-fashioned tunes like *Dōki no Sakura*, "Cherry Trees of the Same Era."[5] I prefer these old songs to today's music.

The Western-style living room.

Moving east, the Japanese room is a continuation of the living room; it is better for concentration, contemplation, and the practice of the arts. This twelve-tatami room is where our most important guests are received, where we see employees we wish to honor in the intimacy of our home, and where business decisions are weighed. It is also on the tatami that, every Thursday, I take my calligraphy and *sumi-e* (India ink) painting lessons. I have renewed my ties with the arts of my childhood. On a low cherry-wood table, I spread out large sheets of padded paper. Other times I calligraph large characters on stiff paper, which I give to all the employees as New Year's and midyear gifts. Everyone agrees that my calligraphy possesses *aji*, taste—that it is original.

The Japanese room and its *tokonoma*. Since 1988, there has
been an Oriental rug over the tatami mats.

On the south wall of that room is the *tokonoma*, the decorative alcove where I have hung a rubbing of a bas-relief of the famous bronze lantern of Tōdaiji (Great Monastery of the East), in Nara: it depicts an angel playing a flute. Below this is a floral arrangement whose three main branches evoke by their size the sky, man, and the earth. All too often it shares the space with a small junk pile of discarded boxes, wrapping paper, and magazines. People send me so many gifts and articles, I don't have time to look at them all!

In accordance with the precepts of the geomancer, whom we consulted concurrently with the architect in designing the house, the *butsudan*, the altar of the ancestors, covers the north wall. Here we venerate a statue of the infant Buddha, who, just emerged from the belly of his mother, Maya, raises his hand to the sky to attest to Buddhist law.[6] Through the smoke from the incense which is often burning before the image of this pretty, fat-cheeked baby can be seen a pile of wrapped presents, because presents are always offered to the ancestors before they are unwrapped.

The *kami-dana*, devoted to the Shinto gods who have watched for so long over the prosperity of the family, was originally suspended over the *butsudan*, on which the funerary tablets of the ancestors of our house are aligned. Some years ago, though, after Mitsunobu left home for reasons I will explain later, we moved the *kami-dana* to the top floor of the house, to his and Kyōko's old room. In any case, it's better to separate the gods and ancestors.[7]

After the carpeting was removed in that room, an old craftsman installed tatami mats, with dark green edges embroidered with gold. The carpenters covered the plaster ceiling with *hinoki* cypress panels. Around the faux granite walls is a sacred cord from which I hung *shide*, little strips of white paper cut and folded in zigzag form that mark the presence of the gods.[8] On the north side of the room, I have a lush altar which I bought in the Asakusa district: it's a miniature shrine of white wood with a *torii* gate about five feet high, also of unfinished wood. Every morning I offer fruit and uncooked rice, which I place in little white ceramic cups, or square wooden containers called *masu*, which are measuring cups for rice.

I get up around 6:00 A.M. and go to the shrine to greet the gods. After opening the windows, I sweep it with large strokes, like a sparrow spreading its wings. Then I prepare the offerings in the pantry, a little room also covered with tatami, which is between the stairway landing and the residence of the *kami*. I wash the glutenous rice so that the gods may see it must be consumed that day. I offer the food on the altar, and, my hands together, I silently recite the *Ō-Harae no Norito*, the Prayer of Great Purification.[9] Then I feel the gods breathe courage, joy, and life into me. My spirit becomes as true and sharp as a saber. I no longer fear a thing.

When I have to make a difficult decision, I retire to the pantry to meditate and plan. This room is almost bare, save for cabinets beneath the windows, which I have had covered with translucent *shoji* screen paper, so there is nothing to distract the mind. On top of those are some objects which are particularly dear to me: a pagoda of pearls, which I keep in a glass case, a Hakata doll made of boiled pasteboard, and a little lacquer box from Wajima, black with a fern design in light green.[10]

These rooms serve as a refuge for me, for I am now the president of seven hair salons, and every day I am assailed by eight hundred new ideas and a thousand questions as I rush from appointment to appointment in Mitsunobu's car or in a taxi. The atmosphere here is much more peaceful than that of our bedroom next door, where the large Western bed invites sleep rather than thought.

Besides the gods and the family ancestors, there are two more deities who preside over the house of Yamazaki. On the landing, at the top of the spiral staircase which ascends from the carpeted living room, at the edge of a stone basin near the door to the *furo*, the Japanese bath, is Benten-sama. She is the water-loving goddess of eloquence, who, following a vow that I made to her, granted me the gift of speech. And on the roof of the house, on the terrace, is Inari-sama, the god of foxes. His vermilion *torii* gates point northwest, the direction in which the ancestral divinities reside. Tatsuo and I are particularly attached to this god of rice, because both our parents honored his cult when we were growing up.

All the divinities together watch over the prosperity of the salon: on the ground floor is one room large enough to serve about twenty customers, and on the second floor are treatment booths used for time-consuming processes; the latter are also for our male clients, who prefer not to be seen from the street in the main salon.

As the business grew, the work space became cramped. We had to rent offices on the fifth floor of a nearby building. They are the domain of the three men who, along with me, keep the enterprise going: my son and two of my nephews.

THE YAMAZAKI COMPANY

The same year we built the house, the Yamazaki Ikue Beauty Salon Company, Inc., absorbed the original business, named for the first salon, Kanōya. My two companies were reunited. The name is written on an immense banner hanging over the street outside, on the corner of the lane where the new white building stands.

All the capital is held by members of the family. The Yamazaki Ikue

Beauty Salon Company is a *dōzoku-gaisha*, a family company, which means a company where members of one family group retain all the holdings. The principal shareholders are my son and myself. But among the administrators are also my nephew Hirotoshi, the son of my younger sister, and Endo Muneo, the third son of my oldest brother, Yoshiki. Everyone calls Hirotoshi and Mitsunobu by their first names, the way one does for artists. But the truth is that, for a long time now, Hirotoshi has been the real star of the company.

HIROTOSHI

My nephew Hirotoshi was skinny as a young man, proportioned like a mosquito, his hair tinted auburn, after the new fashion. He probably would have been bereft of charm had it not been for his lively eyes, his crooked smile, and his small, fine hands.

He is the only one of my siblings' children who heard the call of beauty early on. He had barely finished high school when he declared, "I want to be a hairdresser. I will be rich." He went to a special school and assumed the yoke of learning with gusto, passionately envying his masters, who, through some mysterious skill, could metamorphose human forms more completely than shadows rearrange the contours of things. At the end of his first year of study, I invited him to one of those large hair shows where the arrangement of the hair demonstrates the perfection with which the gods have created the human body. The curves, the lines, the folds, the facial features, seemed to him like celestial signs, whose meaning was revealed to him through the art of beauty. He thought, "Is it right to contemplate these things and not do anything about it?" Overcome with admiration, he was considering becoming a monk when, suddenly brought before me, he begged me to hire him.

I weighed the pros and cons of this proposition. I feared causing an envious bitterness in my own son, who, although he was two or three years younger than his cousin, would one day command and direct his actions. At least that was what I hoped. But if Mitsunobu were to refuse his birthright, in Hirotoshi I would have a ready-made successor in the wings. I thought, "Better to take action than to wear yourself out in sterile reflection," so I hired my nephew.

Hirotoshi took the last name Yamazaki, so that everyone would know he was part of the family and would understand his position. Nevertheless, he was not adopted officially, for fear that he might one day commit some foolishness that would tarnish the name of the ancestors.

Today, he is obviously proud of his skill, which early on won him prizes in both Japanese and international competitions. Moreover, he speaks to the employees in modern terms: "Taste," he says, "is the gift that the gods have bequeathed to me. Here at our house, we master traditional styles, technique, and all the chemistry. On the other hand, when it comes to contemporary fashions, the young are as stupid as ants. It's very well to construct an impeccable hairstyle where each hair stays in place, but we must also add that touch of fantasy that elevates taste—in the way one adds salt to a clear soup, to give it flavor. There you have it: it is the lack of this taste, which cannot be taught, that is our flaw at the house of Yamazaki, as it is with all hairstylists in Japan."

Then he adds, "In this era, our art must no longer be learned like the traditional 'ways'—flower arranging, calligraphy, kendo. We have entered the age of internationalization, when we must each express our personality.[11] Unfortunately, for a people like us Japanese, who fear freedom like the worst of constraints, this leads only to confusion."

His speeches thrill the young people.

MITSUNOBU

On the other hand, our heir Mitsunobu does not possess any divine gifts. Not the communicative type, he forces himself to be somewhat cheery. But with him, honesty replaces talent.

In fact, he was not very dependable as a boy. He put me through days of anguish that seemed longer than my entire life. When he was nineteen, he left home without a word of warning, to go be a truck driver in the north of Japan. The night before he left, he silently chain-smoked one Seven Stars after the other, crushing the butts out in a big cast-iron ashtray. So I wasn't really surprised when he disappeared. After asking around, I learned from a friend of his that he was alive and working for a trucker in Aomori Prefecture, but I couldn't bring myself to telephone to yell at him or beg him to come home. I waited three weeks, my insides torn apart with fear, nor did I say anything when he came back. But I wouldn't wish that suffering or that unforgettable pain on anyone.

He was already twenty-two or twenty-three when he realized that neither of his sisters would succeed me, since both had joined other families as daughters-in-law. He had entertained hopes of becoming a race car driver, but he finally decided to play the role in our house that had always been his. Partly out of filial piety, no doubt, but also because the idea of walking away from a business created out of nothing, which had grown so well in spite of all adversity, made him as sad as the thought of death—he put his Jaguar and his Mercedes away in the underground garage. He told himself that modern hairstyling made use of such a complex set of equipment that he could still satisfy his old passion for mechanics.

Although most hairdressers send their offspring to study in the shops of colleagues, Mitsunobu began as a regular apprentice in my own salon. Spoiled boy that he was (having been adored since birth), he did nothing but hand rollers to his seniors and sweep up bits of hair scattered on the tiles. Then one day a customer, whose magazine had fallen from her lap, said to him, without a trace of politeness, "Pick it up."

His cheeks flushed crimson with humiliation, and his heart split with shame like a log by a hatchet. He knew he could not continue in that way and resolved to go to France with his wife, Kyōko. She was only too happy to put an end, albeit temporary, to a difficult cohabitation with me, her mother-in-law, so she agreed to a four-year stay in Europe.

Mitsunobu apprenticed at a big salon in Paris. Soon after they arrived there, Kyōko became pregnant. She worried about giving birth so far from her family, but she wrote, and it made me laugh, "It got in there, it'll have to come out." She refused to take classes in how to alleviate the pain of childbirth through breathing techniques. In a clinic in the suburb of Neuilly, she gave birth to a large girl; two years later, she had a small boy.

They returned to Tokyo in Year 50 (1975). Mitsunobu made his mark on the business through not only his imported technique but also his managerial capabilities, which led him to computerize the stock and personnel systems well in advance of our competitors.

Today Mitsunobu is no longer a boy: his regular features have become slightly fleshy, which makes him look serious, even a little stiff. His sisters tease him, calling him a samurai who turned into a hairdresser in love with modern gadgets!

Be that as it may, he is now a man on whom I can depend, and every day I thank the gods, who kept him from straying onto an unfortunate path.

He has a faithful accomplice in the person of Endo Muneo.

ENDO-KUN

My nephew Endo is the man I trust to make business run; he's the one who pulls the strings and counts the money, the one who invents and then puts into practice the procedures. It is he who suggested the fusion of my two companies. "It's too complicated," he complained. "I've got two banks and two accounts. I'm constantly running from one to the other. Simplify all that, Yamazaki-Sensei!"

Without him, nothing would look serious around here. He is rightly proud of that. However, as he is not a hairdresser, he conducts himself like an underling. He doesn't have the right to be called *sensei*. We call him Endo-san or Endo-kun. With his simple character, his unpolished appearance, and the inferiority complex that businesspeople sometimes develop toward those they venerate as artists, Endo prefers to keep to his place, which he deems a modest one.

When he was quite young, he decided to leave his home in the country and, through relatives, found a job with a trading firm. Realizing he didn't know any more about business or the ways of the world than a fish does of the sky, he signed up for a short course of evening classes at a university, where he learned modern methods of management and sales. The diploma he earned, which he framed in black and hung on his wall, lent him such an intense confidence that, without much forethought, he started his own life insurance business. Because he adhered faithfully to all the laws and regulations, he had no problems with that side of things. But his rustic nature offended the clientele—they wanted him to talk about death, but only in terms softer than the skin of a white peach and as tender as fresh tofu.

At the age of twenty-five, Endo was earning just 3,000 yen per month (not even enough to rent a small room) and, to make ends meet, had to sleep in the hallway of the home of a man who had been an upperclassman of his at university.[12] Somehow, the latter arranged for the rash young man to be offered a job in Osaka. His future employers required a letter of guarantee.[13]

When Endo came to ask me, his aunt in Tokyo, for support, I offered to take him on with me. A wily man, though clumsy in emotional matters, Endo pledged the eight hundred thousand craftinesses of his intelligence to my service. He did so well that within a few weeks of his hiring in Year 43 (1968), I promoted him to general secretary.

Endo does not have a gift for happiness. It's as if, at his birth, the gods decided that mostly bad things would happen to him in his life. For example, he couldn't find anyone to marry him because no woman would have anything to do with this oaf who had no idea how to woo a girl, whose movements were jerky and embarrassed, with too bright eyes in a somewhat oily face. So he returned to Asaka to find a wife, bringing back a first cousin on his mother's side, a skinny, dark-complected girl with thin hair.

When they got to Tokyo, he took this girl to see our second daughter, Ryōko, who, two years after her wedding, was the formidable and beatific picture of a woman in the bloom of young motherhood. He said to his wife, "When you have children, you will be like that."

She smiled sweetly, looking abashed. But her first child was stillborn, and she never lost her undernourished look—in fact, she hadn't ever shown the pregnancy. Endo said, "I am very familiar with the anger of the gods. We must pray, perform the rites, and give the proper offerings so as not to attract misfortune. That is the religion of the Japanese."

Every morning on his domestic altar he offers water, sake, salt, and rice. And once a month he has prayers recited at the monastery for the spirit of the dead infant, now a ghost, to assure that it does not come back to haunt them.

Still, Endo is never sad. "I do what I have to do, to see that the directives of the president are carried out," he says. Thanks to him, my business grows.

THE NEW SALONS

Today, eight salons bear my name: seven in Tokyo and one in Hawaii. Two famous hotels have put me in charge of the hairstyling and dressing of their brides. That makes ten buildings on which the passersby read my name, the name of a little country girl from Fukushima.

Each of these has its own story which makes it different from the others in my eyes. These are not so much the stories of bank loans that were progressively easier to get as my success grew greater but rather of the particular paths which the gods took in granting me, one after the other, new shops. Bunkyō recalls for me the terrible struggles of my youth. Shibuya, Motoko's marriage. Shinjuku, where I now have two salons, the happy ending of a quarrel averted. Gotanda, a salon for the young people of Shinagawa, evokes for me Mitsunobu, who is sole director there.

As for Mukōjima, located in the underprivileged district whose name means "Island on the Other Side" (across the Sumida River from Asakusa), I have Ryōko to thank for that. The establishment of that salon stirred up a storm in the bosom of the family. One drizzly night, the father of an old school friend of Ryōko, an agent for the Sumamiya company, came to see me. He proposed that I open a salon on the "other side" of the Sumida, which marks the northern edge of the poor quarters where the *buraku-min*, the pariah caste of Japan, live.[14] Korean in origin, these people have for generations been confined to work in jobs considered ritually unclean: leather tanning, butchering, cremation. These are people no one wants in his family, his house, or his business.[15] And now the Sumamiya Company was going to build a luxury building there! Their agent explained that the time for class discrimination was over. In the name of democracy, the moment had come to let the most underprivileged have a taste of the luxury of the center of Tokyo.

I liked the idea, but the men in the family hung back. They said it was

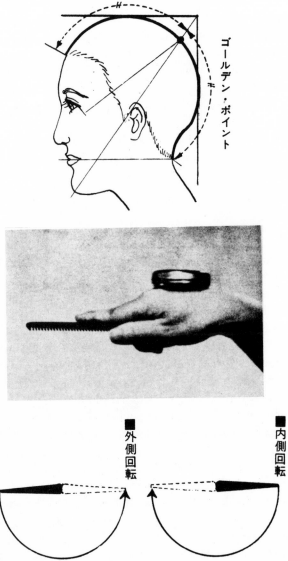

The "Golden Point." Ways of handling a comb (from the Yamazaki Ikue Manual).

madness to make an investment in a dicey area like that. It wouldn't work, or worse, the terrible neighborhood would destroy the reputation of my entire enterprise.

However, the oracles I consulted to settle the dispute approved the idea. Sumamiya offered advantageous financial conditions; they agreed to give me the space rent-free in exchange for a small percentage of the profits. (In fact, since there weren't any profits, it cost me nothing.) They also agreed to make architectural changes for my benefit—in conformity with one of the most common principles of geomancy, a hallway was redesigned with a bend in it in order to make the front door of the shop face the direction of *tatsu-mi*, the propitious dragon-serpent direction.

My stubbornness won them over.

We gave special bonuses to the employees to induce them to work in that neighborhood. After that, business went as well as it does in the ordinary salons.

In December 1988, however, following a rehabilitation of the neighborhood, the Mukōjima salon closed. I soon opened another, in a hotel farther north, but only after overcoming bargaining difficulties provoked by the differences in the ways morality is handled in the world of men and that of the gods.

When I found the new location, thinking that I would have to conform to customs that were fully accepted on earth (if not ultimately very respectable), I agreed to pay "key money": a fee of 12 million yen. I gave the landlord 7 million, promising the remainder for the following week. A vague disquiet, however, led me to question the gods. Through a medium, they responded, "We do not recognize this human custom. For the salons we have granted to you up to now, did you ever once have to submit to such extortion? If you compromise yourself in this way, we will turn our eyes from you."

Stupefied by the severity of the gods and driven mad with worry, I ran to the landlord and apologized, bowing all the way to the ground, for not being able to honor my agreement. I said to him, "Keep the money I have already given you with my apologies, but I cannot pay you the remaining 5 million yen. I will not rent this salon. Please give it to another tenant, because I'm sure there are many who will want it."

To my great surprise, he bent to the will of the gods—he okayed my moving in, waiving the rest of the fee. I marveled that the rigor of the gods has such good results in the world of men! After having thanked them in my heart for their forgiveness, I decided one more time to surrender myself body and soul to their immense wisdom.

Thanks to the gods, then, today I oversee 1,500 *tsubo* of salon space (almost 6,000 square yards)—paltry for a sovereign, perhaps, but a veritable kingdom for an ordinary woman. That is 1,500 *tsubo* where boys and girls dressed in shirts bearing my initials work every day, praising me in their hearts. I am the fourth-largest hairdressing concern in Japan! This year, the first year of Heisei (1989), our revenues will exceed a billion yen. Business is good, so good that before the year is out I will have over two hundred employees! Sometimes I repeat these figures to myself, and they make me clap my hands like a child.

I am not rich, however, for the costs are enormous. Endo and Mitsunobu often say that the profits go only for paying taxes. It's come to the point that they now insist I tear down the building in Bunkyō, take out a loan, and build a larger one.

And this is a building barely twenty years old! We'd have to move again, and that would be tiring. Sometimes I feel tired these days.

But I am far happier than all the others. I have plenty of money with which to feed and clothe myself. My business is prospering. I built a great enterprise, I tell myself. Great—the very word reassures me.

PEACE

Through my obstinacy, through wars lost and then won, I built a kingdom for myself. However, after I had left the professional organizations that owed fealty to Donohashi, the isolation caused by my lack of support in high places seemed to strip my success of all meaning. I decided to found my own organizations. Long before, I had created the Yamazaki Research Association, a professional group to which my former employees belonged. To that I added the World Beauty and Health Association, or WBHA: membership was open to all those in Japan who were enamored of beauty—hairdressers and nonhairdressers alike. Finally, one cloudy, windy day, I made the sudden decision to affiliate myself with the Federation of Bridal Hairdressers, a group over which Donohashi had little power. I soon became vice president of that organization. Then, my son-in-law Yasuo (Motoko's husband) proposed that I join an association of cosmetics manufacturers which he was going to found with his colleagues. In my capacity as president of a research association, then, I joined his Federation of the Comb.

The federation's activities center on the Day of the Comb, which the organizers have fixed as September 4 (because the word for comb, *kushi*, evokes the numbers 9, *ku*, and 4, *shi*). Because the words for these two numbers are also homonyms for the words for suffering and death and were considered unpropitious in former times, old customs prohibited the giving of combs as gifts. It was said that the comb possessed the sad capability of undoing the ties between people, just as it untangled the hair, in that way provoking suffering and death.[16] But the Federation of the Comb decided to break with these old prohibitions to give itself a modern image.

And so on September 4, hairdressers giving out combs stand on sidewalks at the intersections of stylish areas, alongside aides tossing multicolored balloons. They do the hair of the curious for free, out in the open wind, to the beat of contemporary music.

I ride around in a taxi from one corner to the next, and the crowds never cease to amaze me—they get bigger every year. It's all so lively, you'd think it was a festival from my childhood. Here and there I run into a member of the family: Yasuo, the exclusive distributor of Belle Jouvence. Motoko, who comes and helps sometimes. Teiichirō, who has become a manufacturer of hairstyling equipment. Ryōko, who handles secretarial duties for me. Even my daughter-in-law, Kyōko, who takes care of management. Today, the entire family works with me.

At the beginning of Year 63 (1988), I heard the rumor that Donohashi, one of the famous characters among Japanese hairdressers, was ill. People were saying he had cancer, and my first thought was that it was the absurd quarrels which had led to his condition. In June, even though I had not seen him in a long time, I received an invitation to the celebration of his eighty-eighth birthday, the year of *beijū*, the age of wisdom.[17] Intrigued but pleased, I went to the ceremony.

As soon as he saw me, old Donohashi rose from his armchair. He began to walk toward me, and, because he is tall, he bent low to tell me: "So much has happened. I am happy to see that you are well."

I understood then that he was preparing for death and wanted to make peace with the men and women around him who had quarrelled so bitterly. I said, "I am happy all that is over. Please take good care of your health."

I felt a calm as great as the sky settle into my heart.

BOOK THREE

The Gods of the Yamazakis

15

Fate

Oboreru mono wa wara wo mo tsukamu.
The drowning person clutches even at a straw.

LEGACY

Endō-ke ni wa, toku-ni shinjin-bukai hito wa orimasen deshita . . . At the house of Endo, no one was especially pious. In Asaka, our gods and ancestors reigned over immense and well-appointed domestic altars. But that fact stemmed more from a concern for the prestige of the house than from any particular devotion. Mother performed the expected religious rites, just as she respected human customs; she deemed some rice, water, and a few moments of prayer sufficient sacrifice to the inhabitants of the other world. We children went to the village shrines as often as was expected. We would offer brushes to Tenjin-sama, and, when summer came and we were out of school, we studied calligraphy under the guidance of the master of *kami* who lived in the shrine of the *ubu-suna-gami-sama*, the god of the land of one's birth. While playing in the cemeteries, we also learned to decipher the posthumous names of the dead written on the tombs; the familiar souls of the dead frightened us far less than the anger of Father, whose power we considered far superior to that of all the gods. So nothing, but nothing, prepared me—me, the fourth daughter of the house of Endo—to serve the invisible world.

When I entered my husband's family, I fell heir to the cults through which the Yamazaki ancestors had honored the gods for generations. There was the gentle Benten-sama, whom my father-in-law, Tomekichi, venerated privately, and who was to grant me the gift of eloquence. The fox Inari-sama was venerated in our home as in most homes in the east of Japan.[1] In the past, my mother-in-law, Naka, offered these two gods water, salt, uncooked rice, and sake every morning. On the first and fifteenth of the month, special offerings were made: cooked rice mixed with azuki

235

beans for Benten-sama; some eggs or deep-fried tofu, *abura-age*, for Inari-sama.

As for Kōjin-sama, who was represented by a paper charm next to the kitchen fire, Naka would decorate the charm, on the last day of the month, with a new pine branch.[2] She should have used branches of the evergreen *sakaki*; the Chinese character used to write *sakaki* is composed of two characters meaning "divine" and "tree." But because it is difficult to come by in Tokyo, she hoped that the god would be satisfied with a sprig of pine, with its lustrous needles.[3] When Naka gave these offerings, I would light a candle before each of the gods and bow respectfully. Because Tatsuo had been educated in a foreigners' school, I also had to pray to the god of the Christians, who requires small offerings on Sundays. Finally, like the other inhabitants of the house of Yamazaki, I was expected to honor the gods of Ontake-san, whose cult Naka had brought with her from her birth family and whom her mother before her had respected above all other gods.

Tatsuo has climbed the slopes of Mount Ontake every year since he was eleven. The customs bequeathed him by his ancestors served as the foundation for most of the ideas he had formed about life. I could not refuse to make the pilgrimage with him, no matter what I thought in my heart. I imitated his fidelity to the gods of the mountain, and I venerated Kaigen Reijin, the descendant of Kunidokotachi no Ōkami-sama (the Great God Who Stands Everywhere in the Country), who, the family always said, had made the Japanese islands.[4]

When Naka was still young, the leader of the brotherhood, he who had the title *sendatsu* and led the pilgrimages, was a sainted man named Uchida Kamekichi. It was under his guidance that my marriage with Tatsuo had been decided and that our firstborn had received the name Motoko. And because she had been in that way consecrated to the gods of Ontake-san, even after her marriage into another family, Motoko did not really have the right to change her first name.

After four years of marriage, Motoko had given birth to only one child: a son as impetuous as the wind, and she wished for a daughter as soft as the breeze. On the advice of her mother-in-law, she decided to take a new name in order to change her destiny. So she called herself Eriko. But after she had had two more children, her husband had a reversal of fortune. So Motoko gave up the name Eriko for the name Tomiko, which, according to the opinion of a master in *seimei-gaku*, the study of the propitiousness or unpropitiousness of names, would assure the success of her family and herself in the world.[5] In addition, to make sure of a favorable destiny, she pressed her husband, Yasuo, to take the name Yasunobu, threatening divorce until he complied. But as their affairs still did not improve, I went to see my daughter and said, "This has gone too far. The gods of Ontake-san gave you a lovely name which you should have kept. The first time was all well and good; you acted on the advice of Yasuo's mother, and to change names when one enters into a new life is acceptable. Didn't I once take a name chosen by my own mother-in-law? But this time! Your *seimei-gaku* and all that, it's just a lot of superstition!"

"Not at all," replied Motoko. "The master is a man of science. He made statistical studies of the destinies attached to all Japanese names."

"Consult three *seimei-gaku-sha*, you will get three different opinions. There's your science for you."

"But it's based on statistics, it's mathematical. He couldn't be wrong."

"Unlike sincere prayers, such calculations have never changed bad weather to good, and well I know it!" I said. "What's more, it's disrespectful to the *kami* who presided over your birth."

In order not to appear ungrateful to the great divinities that had kept watch over her childhood, Tomiko agreed to reassume the name Motoko, but only for pilgrimages. And her husband's affairs prospered once again. Finally, in autumn sun and spring fog alike, Motoko never again let a season slip by without ascending the mount. So I resigned myself to calling her Tomiko on most days. After all, in the past I had proven so inconstant myself that I was hardly in a position to criticize anyone for changeable behavior.

After Naka's death, for a time I abandoned the cult of the sacred mount in search of other, more powerful, gods.

RUPTURE WITH ONTAKE-SAN

During the war, Uchida Kamekichi was mobilized and, in Saipan, he offered up his life in exchange for those of the forty faithful of the brotherhood of Kaigen, of whom he was the leader. This was so effective that not a one among them was killed or even wounded during the war. After his death and Japan's defeat, the members of Kaigen dispersed, which is not uncommon when a master is gone.

Naka would not rest, however, until a group of believers was reconstituted. In memory of Uchida, she and some of our neighbors in Bunkyō gathered around a young ascetic named Shintani Kōichi. However, while this man was of true heart and mind, he was allied with his mother, who was bad. In his absence, she performed the office of *mae-za*: during consultations, she would occupy the "front seat," and when the gods spoke through the mouth of the medium with whom her son was associated—for the gods always speak through the mouths of women[6]—she transmitted the questions of the seekers. Alas, Mrs. Shintani wanted only to monopolize the master and use his talents to make money, and she acted with no respect for anything, neither gods nor men. Little by little, the faithful were driven away by her attitude. After my mother-in-law died, however, I continued to frequent the Shintanis, out of loyalty to Naka's memory.

When I was tired or simply feeling sad, Shintani's mother would interpose herself as someone who knew the depths of things, declaring that my difficulties were quite simply the result of my arrogance. She said that if I was famous, it was only by the grace of the gods, that there was nothing in that to act so proud about.

The fact was, she had it in for me because I had once refused to do her a service. Imprudently, I had once told her of my intimate connections with the Imperial Household Agency (through my old friend Mr. Aoki). Shintani's mother had asked me, "Did you know that my family has been making sake for centuries? The sake we make is very mild; we store it in vats made of Japanese cedar, and over time it takes on a smooth flavor of resin."

"It must be delicious."

"Just as you say. You know, I am sure that His Majesty the emperor would appreciate it highly."

Mrs. Shintani assumed an affected air, which she no doubt mistook for distinction.

"That's possible."

"Say, since you know highly placed people over there, could you put in a word for us? I am sure that His Majesty the emperor would not be able to do without it, if only he once got a taste of it. And think of the publicity for our house! Better than a thousand newspaper ads."

I was stunned that someone could wish to mix the affairs of gods and men in that way. Shocked at the idea of using the name of the emperor for advertising purposes, I refused to act as go-between. Mrs. Shintani reproached me for it month after month. Every time I visited, she would repeat, "It's obvious that you have no gratitude!"

That was how I learned the true nature of the master's mother. From that time on, I knew that one day I would have to break with them.

It happened in Year 45 of Shōwa (1970), during the International Exposition in Osaka. My nephew Hirotoshi had taken an international prize there. Exalted with joy, I ran to the Shintanis to give thanks to the gods. I had just told them the news, and, still under the spell of emotion, I was consulting with the master about how much to offer to the gods when the mother came into the room, carrying a tray bearing cups of green tea. In my enthusiasm, I downed the tea without having greeted her. Mrs. Shintani's face, suddenly crimson with anger, soon brought me out of my transported state. Wasn't it bizarre, she exclaimed, that a woman so crude and ungrateful to the gods should be a success! The world of hairdressing must indeed be corrupt, to make such a thing possible. I apologized for being impolite but explained that it was done in all innocence. I put down the gifts I had brought and left. That same day, I mailed 100,000 yen to the Shintanis, thereby finally breaking my ties with Ontake-san (far later than most of the other faithful of that brotherhood). By then, however, I had already been frequenting other venues for six months or so.

INNEN-GOTO: FATE

It began with a series of haunting dreams about Yamazaki Tomie, Tatsuo's cousin, the younger daughter of Yamazaki Seikō (the director of the school at Ochanomizu). Tomie was only two years younger than I. We had worked and socialized together during my apprentice days. This girl had been kind, even affectionate, to me. We loved each other tenderly. Tomie was beautiful and intelligent: she studied English and Russian. Back when I was still a poor in-house disciple, Yamazaki Seikō had proposed that I study with her. I refused, since at that time I had no intention of spending the rest of my life with the Yamazakis. At the beginning of the war, Tomie had married a manager at Mitsui Bussan. He was tall, like her, athletic, and amiable to everyone. But just one week into the marriage, he was mobilized to Manila, where he died. Tomie had worked in order to survive, first as a hairdresser and later as a waitress in restaurants and bars. It was then, in a *nomiya*, a neighborhood dive, that she met Dazai Osamu, the famous writer. He became her lover.[7]

Dazai reminded Tomie of her favorite older brother, Toshiichi, the second eldest, who had died of meningitis. The two had graduated from Hirosaki High School the same year. She began to see Dazai Osamu out of sadness and nostalgia.

Then the two of them killed themselves, in Year 23 of Shōwa (1948), on the thirteenth of June. They drowned in the canal of the Tama River. It was a double love suicide, a death that happened under circumstances so strange that it was decidedly not natural.[8] I could not understand how a young woman so full of life could kill herself in that way.

Years later, I dreamed that something heavy was weighing on my feet. I tried to move, but I could not. I realized that someone was sitting on my bed. When I looked, I knew by the designs on the person's kimono that it was a woman. I wanted to ask her to leave, but as I was about to speak, I saw that the room in which I was sleeping was perfectly closed. I said: "How did you get in here?"

"I can go anywhere," answered the woman.

She left, in an eerie silence in which nothing moved but the hem of her garment about her ankles.

I awoke with the impression of having just seen Tomie. I consulted the calendar and realized that it was the thirteenth of June of the year of *jūsan-kaiki*, the thirteenth anniversary of her drowning. That very day, at 2:00 P.M., with the family and old friends from the Ochanomizu days, I went to the *hōji* rite performed for the repose of the dead woman: we presented offerings to the buddhas and gave gifts to the monks, in order to forge roots of the good, *zengon*, which would further the progress of Tomie's soul.[9]

The dream had left in my mouth the bittersweet taste of the tea, *amacha*, which we sprinkle over the image of the Buddha on the eighth day of the fourth moon, to celebrate his birth.

After this, Tomie came to me often in dreams. I would be walking in the street, and someone would tap me on the shoulder and ask, "How many years now since Tomie's death?"

When I woke up, I would again have the strange impression of having seen the young woman, and I would look at the calendar and realize that it was, for instance, the day before the seventeenth anniversary of her death. I particularly recall the twentieth anniversary, in Year 43 of Shōwa (1968): Mitsunobu did not show up at the *hōji*. At first we thought he was just late, but as it turned out, he and some friends had gotten into a car accident. Luckily, no one was seriously injured. But hearing the news at the ceremony, I inadvertently began to whimper like a mother bird who, returning to the nest, finds her little ones gone. A woman called Shimamura who had come to the rites said to me, "There is undoubtedly an *innen-goto*, a fate, on your family."

An *innen-goto* is not a fate projected by a malevolent person. It is a destiny that results from the perpetual chain of causes and effects, one that suddenly, for some exterior reason, takes form—like the way the ringing of a bell comes from neither the bell nor the clapper but from the striking of the clapper on the bell or the way a grain of seed rice will not render heads if it's kept in the silo but will bear fruit after it's planted in the ground. More often than not, an *innen-goto* is an unfortunate destiny.

I recalled that my mother-in-law had said something about this *innen-goto* in the past. For generations, most of the Yamazaki sons had died prematurely. Tomie had had three older brothers. The eldest married a girl he met in Korea, and, perhaps because his wife was of foreign origin, he had respected nothing and abnegated the filial piety a child owes to his parents.[10] He visited his father only when he was on his deathbed. As for the other brothers, both died of meningitis, exactly one year apart, both on the tenth of April, one at the front, one at home.[11] In the preceding generation, there had been eight children, six of whom were boys. And all of them died far younger than they should have. Finally, there remained only a single heir, who had moved to Yokohama and was childless. Mitsonobu was the only other male heir left.

At this point, my son had not yet settled down; he was nothing but a source of worries. His character was weak, he loved to amuse himself, and he would have nothing to do with his future as our heir. I had often thought there must be a cause behind the continually unfortunate fates of our family's men; I knew that Naka had perceived it, too, and had tried and failed to find it in her lifetime. Hesitant to accept such a misfortune, I said to Mrs. Shimamura: "That's impossible. We've always prayed quite sufficiently for Tomie. There's no reason for it."[12]

Shimamura insisted that this sort of fate must have come from farther back and that we would have to make more inquiries. She took me to see a medium named Umeda Mariko in Arakawa ward, in the north of Tokyo. Umeda Mariko, who had the rank of *kyōshu*, master, in the Naohi religion,[13] agreed to interrogate the dead on my behalf.

THE NAOHI RELIGION

At first I was astonished that, in this religion, the dead spoke only with noises and rappings. The medium in Arakawa interpreted them like a sort of alphabet. She called it *reisho moji*, spirit writing. I thought that such a mode of expression left far too much room for interpretation by human beings and that the risk of error was very large. Nonetheless, since I had made a special trip, I told her of my problem.

The spirits of Dazai Osamu and Yamazaki Tomie appeared immediately, in a barrage of rapping noises. They were arguing, and Tomie was crying. She said that she had not wanted to die. I had the medium ask Tomie if we should pray more for her. Tomie responded that she wanted us to restore her reputation. She related the circumstances of her death: contrary to what some people have claimed, it was not she who had pushed Dazai Osamu to suicide but he who had dragged her into it. Because he was completely putrified inside; because he had no vital force. But she had died too young, when she still had much life left in her.[14]

Tomie's complaints left me flabbergasted. I suddenly understood, as if it were obvious, the existence of the *reikai*, the spirit world, and the importance of the *reibaisha*, the mediators of the dead. There was no mendacity in Tomie's words, I was certain of it. I wept for the lugubrious fate of the young woman, having found death without desiring it, tortured in the beyond by regret for her life. I silently determined to save Tomie and, with her, the male line of the Yamazakis.

In order to accumulate roots of the good for the sake of Tomie and her family, I began to frequent the Naohi sect.

Umeda Mariko's vocation as a medium had been revealed to her by Ō-Naohi no Kami and Kan-Naohi no Kami; these purifying gods had come into being at the beginning of the world, when Izanaki took his bath upon returning from the underworld, in the river of the plain of Himukai no Tachibana no Odo no Ahakihara.[15] These gods, who had given their names to the sect, were known for repairing that which is twisted and straightening that which is deformed. Umeda Mariko made two paper figurines for me that represented the lover-suicides. I took them home, placing them on the altar of the dead. For three days in a row, I gave them offerings of pure water and cooked white rice into which I stuck single upright chopsticks, as we do for the dead.

Barely three days later, a man knocked on my door. He wanted, he said, to know how Yamazaki Tomie had died. He was the manager of a Chinese restaurant in Meguro Ward, and I was sure he had met Tomie in the past, perhaps loved her, for he evinced an immense respect for the beautiful dead woman. He wanted, he said—and he used the same words as had the priestess of Naohi—to restore her reputation. I concluded that the rites of Naohi must be marvelously effective. After that, I never again dreamed of Tomie.

Still, Mitsunobu was not getting any better, and I understood that I had not yet shed light on the fate that kept the Yamazaki sons from reaching manhood. I would first have to identify the dead person responsible for this misfortune, then, through prayers and offerings, create roots of the good for him, assuage his pain, and so put an end to his ill will. Thus, I continued to frequent the medium.

At my next sitting with her, my father-in-law, Tomekichi, appeared. I politely reminded him that his wife, Naka, had once said something about an *innen-goto* that weighed on the family and asked him, very respectfully, if that fear was justified. The spirit of the ancestor bellowed that it was, but, refusing to say anything more, he disappeared. Umeda Mariko, her forehead creased with eight thousand wrinkles from the effort, called him again and again, for an entire month, but he did not deign to appear.

One day, he finally spoke again. Panting with all the force of his ghostly breath, he said that in former times, in a place called Yamazaki, there had been a great battle where, through the fault of our family, many people had perished: the Yamazakis had slain a man who could have prevented that war.[16] Having thus spoken, Tomekichi let out cries of fear and pain, which terrorized all those present; then he was gone. The following week, he again stated that it was the slain man who, tortured by his involuntary responsibility in that senseless carnage, filled with rancor and hatred for the Yamazakis, was the cause of the weakness in all the sons of the house.

"What must we do?" I asked.

But Tomekichi disappeared and never came back.

Extremely vexed not to know the name of the dead man who was at the origin of our fate, and thereby to be unable to do anything for him, I prayed to the gods and buddhas to reveal to me a place where I might enter into relations with him. I would apologize; I would rectify destiny. But for six months, I prayed every day without learning his name.

If it was difficult to call this wild spirit, that was because he did not belong to our line, and the dead, like the living, are hesitant to put themselves in the hands of strangers with whom they have no blood ties. Only ancestors appear voluntarily, to their own descendants. I finally understood that the priestess of Naohi could do nothing more for me. And because seeing her was quite expensive, and after all that we had no results, I stopped going. Besides, I had a vague feeling that the atmosphere at Umeda Mariko's had changed.

Several months earlier, my younger sister Kiku, who had often accompanied me there, had in all innocence introduced a money-grubber into their midst. The man had married Umeda Mariko's daughter in order to take over the sect. And the priestess had offered no resistance. He got rid of the old administrator and appointed himself administrative director of the Naohi sect. After that, the fees rose constantly, quicker than a monkey climbs a Japanese cedar tree.

THE RELIGION OF DAIWA

As a result, when Kiku told me that in Sendai, in the far north of Honshū, there was a master who surely could help me in my quest, because his powers were immense, I decided to go and consult him immediately.

In fact, it was my older sister Risa, the wife of the wholesaler in sweets from Kōriyama, who had first heard of him. One day she was getting a massage and was describing all her troubles in minute detail, the way women do when they are alone with each other. She said that she was lucky, because her brothers and sisters were all good people. In spite of that, they had been split apart by the matter of the inheritance, the way the sun divides north from south. According to the new constitution written by the Americans, everyone—boys, girls, eldest brothers, younger brothers—had to inherit equal parts of the family patrimony.[17] But my oldest brother, Yoshihiki, had explained that the Americans knew nothing of

Japan and that subdividing the land would ruin the house of our ancestors in an instant. Because he was obviously right, my older sister had graciously ceded her parcel; but the others had begged her not to, so the incident had a harmful effect on family harmony. The masseuse advised her to go see the master in Sendai. She said that truly strange things happened there, which made all who went understand what they must do. Risa went with my younger sister, and both of them were so stunned by what they found that they spoke to me about it.

When I heard my sisters praising the marvelous clarity of the words of that master who knew so many things, I wondered if the gods were not trying to let me know that there existed in the north a place where I could undo the fate that interfered with the happiness and prosperity of the family. Thinking that in religious matters docility is the greatest of wisdoms, I followed my sisters to Sendai.

The master from Sendai was a medium who belonged to the religion of Daiwa, Great Peace.[18] Its adepts venerate Ō-Kuni-Nushi, the Great Master of the Country, a divinity with which I had long been familiar, because he was also highly placed among the gods of the sect of Mount Ontake. The faithful submitted questions to the brothers, who in turn spoke with the gods as well as to the dead. She also performed ceremonies for the presentation of offerings to the dead spirits, which allowed for the accumulation of roots of the good.

The medium was seated behind a low table, a twisted rosary between her fingers. I first asked the gods if Naka's presentiment about a fate was well-founded; they responded that it was. I then begged the medium to call the spirit who was so bent on the fall of the house of Yamazaki. She knocked her head against the low table. Her breathing became labored, and a raucous voice, such as does not exist among the living, came out of her throat or her breast. Finally the spirit spoke. He used an archaic language, like that of the samurai in former times. He seemed to be furious that we had forced him to appear. He stuttered and shouted with anger and spite. Though disconcerted by this fantastic spectacle, I managed to maintain enough presence of mind to ask him if he belonged to the Yamazaki family. Stop, the spirit bellowed, he did not want to hear that name spoken. I apologized and said to him, "Whatever the crimes of my ancestors may be, I beg you to forgive me." His answer was an insane outpouring of filth. Not knowing what to do to appease him, I promised him offerings and made a date to meet with him on *higan*, the autumn equinox, when the dead return to this world from the beyond.

At the equinoxes, as is well known, the sun sets exactly in the west, so that the Western Paradise is briefly situated closer to the world of the living.[19]

As soon as I had made this promise, the terrible spirit gave place to old Tomekichi. At first I greeted him politely, telling him that with all the rites I had performed for the family, he must soon be delivered and must be close to enlightenment. But the old man muttered fearfully, without thanking me. He wanted to stop me: "All this is too dangerous; you will have an accident or an illness that will prevent you from returning!" He explained that he was terrified because the savage spirit that prowled around the family was destroying what he and the other ancestors had built up for their descendants.

My little sister, Kikumi, who had attended the séance, tried to hold me back. Fear overcame both of us. But I got a grip on myself. I recalled that there is nothing more shameful than a broken promise and renewed my vow to come back for the equinox. Then I questioned my father-in-law as to the best means of keeping the danger at bay. He said to pay the master to recite daily the sacred texts that distance evil and to hold an offering ceremony once a week. Additionally, I myself would have to read the Hannya Sutra every morning for a year.

When all the spirits had gone and the medium came out of trance, her brother gave me the list of charges for the various ceremonies. They were expensive, but I was so afraid for my son, Mitsunobu, whose soul was on such shaky ground, that I paid no mind. If those costs could transform my only son into a true inheritor, all the sacrifices would be nothing to me. I also hoped that the difficulties I was then encountering with Belle Jouvence would diminish as soon as the savage spirit had given up on his vengeance and that, finally, I would come into my money. And, last, I had succumbed to an immense curiosity about the world of the dead, and the fascination it exerted over my intellect kept me from renouncing my quest. So I reached an agreement with the medium and her brother about their fees.

On the train back to Tokyo, I began to recite the Hannya Sutra. Back in Bunkyō, I presented the offerings to the gods and the dead more carefully than I ever had before. And, little by little, my devotion bore fruit. During the earliest séances, the spirit's voice shook with resentment when he mumbled the sutras which, according to the medium's brother, belonged to Shingon-Mikkyō, an esoteric Buddhism practiced by sorcerers, using mantras.[20] His transports were all the more violent in that he thought himself on the verge of destroying the Yamazaki family forever. But, through my piety, I had kept him from realizing his plan.

As my visits to the master in Sendai continued, the spirit became gentler. He revealed his identity: he was a *bushi*, a samurai in the service of a great lord. Learning that, as I had often heard that our ancestors had close ties to the Court, I asked him if the Yamazakis, too, had been *bushi*. He again screamed that he cursed that name and immediately disappeared.

It was at the next sitting that he told his story: the lord of his fief had entrusted to him a message to deliver to another province. He had therefore left, disguised as a mendicant monk, or *komusō*, his head hidden under a straw hat and a flute in his belt.[21] He was accompanied by a single servant, who was also dressed as a monk. They had stopped in a shrine dedicated to Marishiten, the god of war, who agreed to watch over the success of their mission.[22] As they approached their goal, they became lost and asked for shelter in a great house, very brightly illuminated, which was used for the training of physicians. At that house was a man named Yamazaki, who welcomed them warmly and then, in the wee hours, had them both killed. Their failure to accomplish their mission then led to further deaths.

THE VISITS OF THE MEDIUM OF DAIWA

It was at this point in my voyage through the past that Belle Jouvence began to come out. My business was continuing to grow, so much that I no longer had the time to go to Sendai. Nevertheless, because I could not give up my consultations at the very moment they had become useful, I made a new agreement with the master of Sendai. Every full moon, the medium traveled to Tokyo by train, the statuette of the Great Master of the Country carefully wrapped in silk and thick Japanese paper, resting on her knees. (Later—because in spite of these precautions, this process was still disrespectful to the god—with the aid of our family, she acquired a small car that would permit her a suitable means of travel to Tokyo. She would set up the effigy, placed in a small lacquered wood box, on the backseat.) Several customers, employees, and colleagues of mine became curious and wanted to pose their own questions to her. They were invited to hear the oracle as well, for a small fee that covered the medium's travel and lodging costs.

We developed the habit of consulting her on everything, business matters as well as family problems. At that time, it was usually Marishiten who appeared. That god told me that it would take five years for the ferocious soul who was harming us to be appeased. He said that, from the world of the gods, from which he clearly saw into the hearts of men, he knew that the sincerity that motivated us—Tatsuo and me—would sweep away all obstacles. Our piety had already influenced the evil doings of the stubborn ghost.

I also learned that the spirit's first name was Kiyoharu and that he had lived three centuries before. But I never did learn his family name.

The day soon came when Kiyoharu declared himself to be satisfied: he calmly announced that he was going to forsake the black robe of mourning and hatred, and present himself before the gods clothed in white.[23] He asked that we offer him money with which to purchase the new clothes and that we perform solemn offerings for him on the tenth day of the fourth moon, the anniversary of his death.

I recalled then that the two Yamazaki sons who had died of meningitis had left this world on the tenth of April, and I knew that the fate was at last undone.

As I said, the master of Daiwa was coming every month to Tokyo, where I gathered about a dozen people, who would submit their problems to her. Still, the hastily arranged character of these assemblies made me ill at ease. When her brother, who ordinarily served as *mae-za*, transmitting to her the prayers of the faithful, did not come along, the medium agreed to receive the questions of the participants herself—to the point where anybody could converse directly with the gods who spoke through her mouth. I thought that, if the gods really were there, they would have good reason to take offense at this lack of ceremony.

Then the medium asked for more and more money, without explaining in what way the sums paid for the performance of rites would influence their efficacity. The woman's avarice became so apparent that I began to fear that I had naively led the clientele in my charge into underhanded transactions. I told myself that things could not go on this way when, for the festival of *setsubun*, which is celebrated the day before the beginning of spring,[24] the medium arrived from Sendai with a register in which she had noted the offerings in advance: across from the name of each of the faithful, the sum of 10,000 yen was written. Of course, it was no doubt convenient for her to deal with fixed amounts, but it ended up being very expensive. Even though things were going better for me, it was then that I lost confidence in the medium's sincerity. Since I knew that the gods grant their protection only to those possessing true and just hearts, I was sure that these acts would in the end lead to results contrary to what I hoped. Not daring, in spite of everything, to break with such a powerful master, I merely lessened the frequency of my invitations and, in my heart, began to seek out other gods. And then I found the gods of Ansai.

16

The Gods of Ansai

地
獄
で
仏

Jogoku de hotoke.
In hell, the Buddha.

Shōwa yonjū-shichi hachi nen goro ni natte, katsute no shūto no jiman-banashi wo omoidashimasu . . . It was around Year 47 or 48 of Shōwa (1972 or 1973) that I recalled the boastful talk my father-in-law had sometimes indulged in. Some evenings, full of drink, he would brag about his noble origins, claiming that one of our ancestors had been a scholar and physician. Knowing through the oracles that this man had lived three centuries ago, it suddenly occurred to me that this could be Yamazaki Ansai, the very famous Neo-Confucian scholar and founder of a Shinto sect known as Suika.[1]

I pressed the medium of Daiwa to ask the gods about this. They responded that it was indeed so and immediately sent me the spirit of Ansai, who, alas, refused to speak.

Stupefied, I looked through the *kahō*, the treasures of the household, where I discovered marvelous signs that I interpreted as proofs of the extraordinary history of the family. It soon appeared to me that the Yamazaki family themselves possessed gods noble enough to be able to bypass the intervention, for ordinary circumstances at least, of a licensed master.[2]

Among our treasures were two paintings which I immediately knew would be as precious to me as water is to rice seedlings. Both were mounted on silk as fine as a spider's web, which time had first soiled, then rusted. I took them to an artisan to have the fabric restored, and he told me that these rare works were at least three centuries old.

The larger, which was signed by Kanō Sozan,[3] pictured a red sun and some gods: the sun was high overhead, next to a strong and fine calligraphy of the name of Amaterasu-Kōdaijin, the sun goddess who is venerated in the shrine at Ise, which the Imperial Family consecrates to its ancestors. To the right of the sun, Tsukiyomi-Daimyōjin (the night star) is figured under a crescent moon; he is the god who, since his quarrel with his sister Amaterasu at the beginning of time, has reigned over the world of shadows and death.[4] Across from him is Inao-Daimyōjin, the god who makes the rice grow: at his feet are heads of the grain offered on platters.[5] Finally, at the bottom of the picture, I recognized Sarutahiko-Daijin, a bearded old man holding boughs of the *sakaki* tree: he is the god who once guided the descendants of the sun, who came to exercise their celestial power over our Japanese isles.[6]

The other, smaller painting was more recent. Although the ink had faded, I could distinguish in it the Ontake mountain range. Gods, beginning with Kunidokotachi no Ōkami, who created Japan, seemed to be perched like strange birds, on clouds, at twilight.

When I saw these paintings, I recalled how piously Naka had venerated them. She had hung them in the *tokonoma* (alcove), where she would present them with flowers every week, bowing deeply. She often said that the paintings were gifts of the gods. To protect the family, I thought the best thing to do would be to return to these objects, which, having belonged to Naka, must have had a specific power for her. The shame of my negligence filled my heart, and I regretted having gone elsewhere in search of gods when there were such noble ones here in the house.

While I did not know the origin of the small painting, the history of the larger one was known to me. Tomekichi, Tatsuo's father, had received it in his youth. At the time, following the trade of his father, who was a smith, he worked at a gun manufacturer's, where he held the high rank of inspector. So he had a good trade and found he was doing well enough to lend people money on occasion. Once, when one of his friends and debtors was having trouble paying him back, he agreed to take the painting in lieu of cash. He immediately brought it to an antiques dealer, intending to sell it. But the merchant told him that the object was more to be venerated than sold. So he took it home with him and asked Naka to hang it in the *tokonoma*. Some years later, because the fabric was yellowing from exposure to the light, they put it away, to be displayed on formal occasions only. Later, the silk being torn, they put it away in its box, whereupon they forgot about it.

For two reasons, I suspected that the painting had once belonged to the great Yamazaki Ansai. First, I had grown accustomed to the idea that our house had descended from the scholar. Only such an origin could justify our wealth and my success. In the second place, the venerable Sarutahiko, who figured in the center of the piece, was counted among the gods to which Ansai granted particular consideration.

In fact, Ansai was a child of Sarutahiko. His mother had given birth to a first son, who had died. She made a wish at the shrine of Hiyoshi, where

Sarutahiko is honored, for a new inheritor. On the full moon of the following month, the gods of Hiyoshi sent her a marvelous dream: returning from
a pilgrimage, she passed by a cemetery whose entrance was marked by a
Shinto *torii* gate. Next to the *torii* was a bearded old man who was dressed
in an immaculate white robe. He held a white-flowered plum branch before him, which he gave to the woman, telling her to slip it into the left
sleeve of her garment. She obeyed; then she realized that she was pregnant
and gave birth to a son, whom they named Kizaemon. Much later, the son
took the pen name that he would make famous: Ansai. I thought that the
Sarutahiko in the painting must certainly be the old man from the shrine
of Hiyoshi.[7]

In his fifties, Ansai founded a shrine where he venerated the deified form
of his own soul, called Suika, Divine Grace and Protection. He installed
the shrine first inside his house and later in a special building outside. But
the military government, the *bakufu*, which recognized the existence of
living buddhas, would not accept a man praising his own divine nature in
that way. So Ansai had to transfer his soul/shrine back inside the house.
After his death, however, his disciples dedicated a shrine to him, the Suika-
Reisha, the Shrine of the Soul of Suika, where in memory of the respect
of their master for the god-guide, they venerated the great Sarutahiko.[8]

That is the reason the words of Yamazaki Ansai are still found in most
shrines consecrated to that saint and god. One day as I was visiting Tsubaki-
Jinja, the Camellia Shrine that the inhabitants of Yokkaichi in Mie Prefecture built to honor Sarutahiko, I noticed one of Ansai's phrases calligraphed
on a black plaque over the entrance:

Michi wa, Nisshin no michi narite
Oshie wa, Sarutahiko-Daijin no oshie nari.

The Way is the way of the Sun,
Instruction is the instruction of the great god Sarutahiko.

Eager to have even greater certitude about the origin of the rediscovered
painting, I asked the medium of Daiwa, whom I still consulted from time
to time. She confirmed that the Yamazaki ancestors had commissioned it.[9]
I marveled that the gods had thanked Tomekichi for his generosity by re-
storing to him an ancient family treasure. I closed up the two paintings,
truly the bodies of our gods, in the domestic altar. They remain there,
hidden from human eyes, as they should be.

Painting by Kanō Sozan kept as a *shintai*, body of a god, in the miniature
shrine placed on the Yamazakis' Shinto altar (drawing by Shige).

Painting of Ontake-san kept by the Yamazakis (drawing by Shige).

THE HISTORY OF ANSAI

I realized that my task was to learn more about the life of our ancestor Yamazaki Ansai, through books and oracles. I read that the great Confucian scholar had been born in Kyoto in Year 4 of the era called Genna, Primordial Peace (1618) and that he had died in Year 6 of Tenwa, Heavenly Peace (1682). His father, who had been an acupuncturist, had quickly tired of this intelligent but difficult child and placed him in a monastery on Mount Hiei, intending that they make a monk of him. From there, the young man left for the region of Tosa, where he was revealed to be but an uninspired Buddhist: one of his favorite games was to trip the young monks as they walked along. I don't know whether that story is true or not, but it is certain that he had little reverence for the buddhas. Nevertheless, he came to the attention of a noble of those parts by one day bringing him tea that was neither too hot nor too cold, but the perfect temperature for drinking. That man, who was called Tani Jitchū, spoke to him about Confucianism. Fascinated by the rigors of his philosophy, Ansai threw himself into the study of the thought of Shushi.[10] He cast off his monk's robes and returned to lay status.

That high-spirited conduct, however, displeased the local lord, Yamauchi Chūgi, who had him banished from the fiefdom. So the young scholar went back to Kyoto, where he began to teach Confucianism. He taught many students there, until one day he left for Edo (Tokyo).

There, again a simple unknown, he lived in destitution. He rented a room next to a bookseller's, from which he borrowed the books he wished to read. He was living in that way when the noble Lord Hoshina Masayuki of the fief of Aizu heard tell of his intelligence, which was said to be livelier than the morning light. That lord took Ansai under his protection so that he might assist him in his political policy making.

After the death of Hoshina, the scholar went once more to Kyoto, where he taught, to thousands of students they say, a religion called Suika Shinto, a Shinto purged of all foreign beliefs, a religion of absolute purity. According to the very high moral teachings of Suika Shinto, men must pray to the gods, receive the benefits they grant through the grace of prayer with honest hearts, and put the gifts thus received into practice with rectitude. It was also deemed fitting that the sublime power of the emperor be revered.

On the night before his death, Ansai called his favorite disciple to him and said, "Take the three *kakemono*, hanging scrolls, that are in the antechamber and put them in their boxes." Those were his last words.

Learning of this history, I found it wonderful that the gods had chosen to reveal to me our ties with Ansai through the scroll paintings. Of course, the paintings I had rediscovered were not those of which Ansai had spoken in his last breath. Tradition reports that what he venerated in that way were *sanja takusen*, paintings bearing calligraphies of the oracles of Amaterasu, Hachiman, and Kasuga, which he had received from his father.[11] In his childhood, his father had told him that every morning he should wash his hands and rinse his mouth before offering salutations and bowing respectfully to the scrolls. His family, moreover, was so pious that he had performed the pilgrimage to Ise, residence of the great sun goddess, at a very young age.

HEREDITY

Through the piety of Ansai, I came little by little to understand my own religious nature and the strangeness of my destiny. The house of my birth had originated near Aizu, where Ansai had lived for a time, and, like him, I had wandered before finding my true faith. But because of those hesitations, which led me from sect to sect, I had at last learned enough to comprehend the teachings of my ancestor. Like him, I had studied the Way of Yin and Yang. That allowed me to understand clearly the meaning of his thought when he claimed that the laws of nature are the principles that must govern the acts of men. Had I not been convinced, long before, that the only moral conduct is that which identifies itself with the rules of nature?

The traditional education dispensed by the Ochanomizu school and the chance accidents of life had also created ties for me with the Court, which permitted me to appreciate the importance of the Imperial Family and the care with which I, like all Japanese, must watch over the emperor so that Japan might continue to exist for eternity.

The postwar period (when we Japanese, remembering the sting of defeat, valued Western culture more than our own) was not yet over when, to please Yamazaki Seiko and Nobuko, the founders of the Ochanomizu school, I wanted to present a show of the costumes and hairstyles of past nobility to the public. Thanks to a doctor I knew who had an entree in the Department of the Imperial Household, I was able to make an appointment with an *emonja*, a court dresser, named Aoki. That is how I met this man of noble descent who, as I have said, would serve as a lifelong adviser to me (later he would be promoted to chief of protocol).

He agreed to speak with me on his way to work one winter morning on the Benkei Bridge in Akasaka, which spans a branch of the castle moat. The cold forced us to take refuge in a swan hut. Such was the incongruous location where, convinced by my determination and touched by the sincerity of my filial piety, he agreed to help me in my undertaking: the restoration of Japanese culture. He lent me antique costumes, which I presented in an old theater. But, as an irony of fate and a sign of the sad upheavals of the times, my show attracted almost no one but Americans. So I told myself it would take months, even years, before Japan rediscovered its faith in itself.

Later, Aoki instructed me in *Emon-dō*, the Way of Dressing. I learned that princesses of the Court turned their eyes in a yang direction, the south or the east, when they were being dressed in the twelve kimonos of different colors which composed the formal state costume, *jūnihitoe*. The two dressers, always women of noble origin, were themselves subject to strict precautions: the higher-ranked attendant stood to the south or the east, while the princess looked east or south; the secondary dresser was then oriented to the west or north. Therefore, at Court it was not right or left which governed where people stood in relation to one another but the directions of the compass.

Also, when the Imperial Prince Akihito married Princess Michiko, because she was not of noble blood, I, a simple commoner, helped dress the future empress and did her hair in the old *suberakashi* style.[12]

It seemed to me then that the gods had guided my life in a way that allowed me to understand the oft-repeated words of Ansai, based on Shushi: "Someone who stands before the emperor must wear an appropriate garment and hairstyle."[13]

I was capable of applying the strictest discipline to all my actions in the society of men.

In spite of the crime perpetuated by Ansai,[14] for which I never found an explanation, I felt close to my glorious ancestor. I surmised that the family's illustrious heritage was at the origin of my good fortune: only such a predecessor could explain the fact that a girl from the country, in complete ignorance of all science, had been able to discover the marvelous fluid that was a source of beauty. I had always thought that Belle Jouvence was the result not simply of chemistry but of divine virtue. It was therefore with a conviction based on the importance of my mission that I created a motto and calligraphed it on two squares of white cardboard flecked with gold:

> *Omote wa, kami no mizu*
> *Ura wa, kami no michi . . .* [15]

> On the surface, the water of the gods
> Behind it, the Way of the gods.

The motto of Yamazaki Ikue, calligraphed by her.

SHIN TO BUTSU: GODS AND BUDDHAS

The only part of my ancestor's thought that I could not take for myself was his often-expressed hatred of Buddhism. In effect, Ansai felt that only the *kami*, the Shinto gods, were Japanese and that we had no need, on these isles, for those buddhas from the continent. He claimed that the Japanese, born of the world of the gods, must return there after death. He advocated destroying the Buddhist monasteries.

Doubtless his criticisms were not addressed to that true Buddhism which everyone respects in his heart but rather to the dark Buddhism practiced in secret by evil monks. Rather than dedicating themselves to ceremonies of offerings, they used the magic powers conferred on them by sacred mantra formulas for unknown ends. While claiming to accumulate merits for people, they were in fact pronouncing *jumon*, the malevolent incantations of sorcerers.[16]

I accepted Ansai's contempt for these evil monks. Still, it seemed to me that in his rejection of Buddhism he forgot that in Japan all the ancestors are buddhas and that no one can deny his origins.[17] While the gods created the country and its geography, it is the buddhas who constitute each of our histories.

According to the myths recorded in the *Kojiki,* the *Records of Ancient Matters,* which tells the history of Japan, the gods made Japan first.[18] At the origin of everything was the god Ame no Minaka Nushi no Mikoto, the Master of the Middle of the Heavens, the God of the Universe. It was he who commanded Kunidokotachi no Ōkami, the great god of Ontake-san, to create Japan. Thereafter, from those primordial isles, they dispatched other gods to make the rest of the world. But Japan, the original country, located at the root of the sun, remains the country of the gods.[19]

Some people say that the Japanese islands were once attached to the continent. But that idea does not conform to the *Kojiki* nor to the conception that presided over the building of our holy places. In effect, two shrines are found at the Imperial shrine in Ise itself: the *naikū*, the inner shrine, is dedicated to Amaterasu and other *kami* of the archipelago, while in the *gekū*, the exterior shrine, everyone may come and venerate the gods who, long ago, were dispatched to other countries.[20]

All Japanese should demonstrate their pride at having been born in Japan.

After the male gods had created the country, women should have managed it. Knowing that men are motivated by ambitions so outlandish that their undertakings inevitably lead to strife, Amaterasu, the sun goddess, agreed to govern the isles. But men, alas, could not resist the attraction of power, so emperors took over from the empresses. From that day on, catastrophes devastated the world. The errors made by men (not the gods) gave rise to the dramas of history.

It's different with the buddhas. They are responsible not for the existence of the country as a whole but for that of individuals only. The character of each person and his destiny are the present consequences of acts performed by his ancestors. Therefore, no one can dispense with honoring them, with gratitude.

In any case, the buddhas entered our house a long time ago, so long ago that we honor their cult. I really don't see how that could be stopped now.

THE FAMILY TOMB

We, the Yamazakis of Bunkyō, are only a separate house, a *bunke*, because Tatsuo is descended from a younger brother.[21] In our family's book of the past, the *kakochō*, kept in the temple of Kichijō, in which the posthumous names of our dead are written, only one generation is included. When we leave this world, Tatsuo and I will become the second-generation buddhas. And Mitsunobu will be the third.

It's fifteen years ago now since our family acquired a plot in the cemetery of the temple in Kichijō. I would have preferred that we be placed next to the elder branch of the family, in a monastery of the Zen school of Sōtō, located in the center of Tokyo. But there was no more room.[22] So I bought a tomb in Kichijō, in a monastery of the same school. Because the cemetery was a recent one, I was able to choose a favorable placement, to the east, which would have been impossible in the crowded confines of the city. I scrupulously followed the advice of the geomancer. It cost me a lot of money, because land for the dead is sold by "cemetery *tsubo*":[23] an area the size of half a tatami mat, called *tsubo* in this instance and sold as such. In hopes of having many descendants, we bought fifteen cemetery *tsubo*.

At present, only Tatsuo's parents' ashes are there. But I had a *shoentō*, a votive tower, dedicated to all those who have ties with the family: customers and employees who have passed on and others. I had it built to give a testimony to my gratitude to those who have helped me and to facilitate their enlightenment.

With our heirs, we go to the cemetery at least four times a year: before the New Year, for the feast of *O-Bon*, and for the two equinoxes, as well as for anniversaries of deaths. We move a bit of the red earth; then we offer water, flowers, and incense of excellent quality. Then we sprinkle Tomekichi's stele with a *shō* of sake, because he dearly loved to drink. While he pours the alcohol from this large bottle, Tatsuo tells our grandchildren stories about his father's escapades and concludes by saying, "I, too, am a drunkard. Don't forget to pour me a drink when I am dead!" And everyone laughs.

Every morning I render brief devotions to the altar of the ancestors. I care for the flowers, arrange the offerings, light the candles, and say the Hannya Sutra, along with Shinto prayers, which are more suited to the origins of our family than Buddhist texts: the *Senzo Mitamaya no Norito*, the Prayer for the Repose of the Souls of the Ancestors, and the *Sobyō no Norito*, the Prayer for the Souls of the Ancestors. Both express our respect as well as our gratitude.

Unlike Ansai, I have never considered breaking our ties with the monastery. Those monks perform their duties with great care. They always tell me in advance when the day is coming for the ceremonies we must offer to Tomekichi and Naka. One month before the date, the parishioners' office sends us a letter to remind us of the memorial so that we are not in danger of forgetting, thereby allowing the dear departed ones to become *muen*, without ties, which would cause all kinds of problems. Because both my in-laws died in February, he on the seventh and she on the twenty-ninth, we venerate them together, which is easier for everyone. In ordinary years, we just have a little celebration with the children, but for the big anniversaries we invite the relatives, near or distant, and friends, too. We feast together at the monastery, where the monks prepare a special menu without animal flesh.

I really don't see what harm these practices can do. It's not rational to set the gods and the buddhas too clearly in opposition to one another. The dead are close to us, whereas the gods are invisible and far away. Anyway, who really knows whether the buddhas are not in the world of the gods? It's impossible to know before one's own death.

Moreover, I noticed one day that Ansai himself has an old funerary monument in a Buddhist monastery in Kyoto, a stele erected by a man he had saved. And I feel sure that, in spite of our belonging to a Shinto house, it's okay for me to venerate our dead, the buddhas. Are not all the cults good, so long as the heart is sincere?

In fact, I no longer fear anything, neither sages nor imbeciles. Neither the rich nor the poor can frighten me. I have the pure blood of those who conform to the will of the gods, and I will live, I am sure, to a very old age. My own mother lived to be ninety-seven. In any case, I do not fear death any more than life, since, for a long time now, I have been in communication with spirits who inhabit the beyond.

The Brotherhood
of Sangū

犬
も
歩
け
ば
棒
に
あ
た
る

Inu mo arukeba bō ni ataru.
Even a dog out walking will encounter a stick.

Okagesama de yo-no-naka no koto mo . . . Through my efforts to understand
the world and life, I came to the idea that all traditions are good, to the
extent that one respects them from the bottom of one's heart. In that way,
by the grace of the gods, a new medium appeared in my entourage: a *miko*
named Takabayashi Takeko.

MIKO: A FEMALE MEDIUM

The Takabayashi family owned a large fish store directly across from the
Ochanomizu school, and Naka had always been close to them. Because
they had a business, the doors of the house were always wide open, and
one could see in all the way to the back. Naka knew, as everyone did, that
the Takabayashis had problems. The eldest son—there were five boys—
was a depressive. He was given to fits of violence that terrified his family.
He would take all the fish knives and hide them, and no one knew whether
he was planning to kill himself or someone else. They had to keep the
knives out of his sight in order to avoid scenes. He had been hospitalized
at Tokyo University, where he had been given electroshock therapy, but it
hadn't helped matters at all. Naka told Mrs. Takabayashi that the best thing
to do would be to entrust the problem to the gods; then she herself took
the unfortunate young man to Ontake-san.

During the early pilgrimages, the son was so ill he could not speak properly; he was incapable of saying even one prayer. With time, and thanks
to Naka's offerings, his condition improved so that he could perform the
rites by himself. That was what saved him: one day when he was lighting

261

the candles before the gods, he set fire to the *gohei*, symbolic folded strips of paper, and he experienced such fear that the shock cured him. That same year he married, and the next year a child was born. Learning of that strange recovery, Naka murmured that the Takabayashi family could not be an ordinary one.

Amazed by the power of the gods, Mrs. Takabayashi joined the brotherhood of Ontake-san. In fact, she wished to ask a second favor of the sacred mount: she had had only sons and wished to know the sweetness of a daughter. Her wish was soon granted. In spite of her advanced age, she gave birth to a girl. With that event, anyone could see that children received from the gods are not like others: the girl was a dwarf, so small that one wouldn't have thought she would live. But she was never sick. They called her Takeko, Bamboo Child, in memory of the marvelous princess of the old tale, discovered in a bamboo stalk by an old man.[1]

She was a sweet but timid child. She sometimes said that the gods spoke into her ear. Her parents, rejecting destiny, would only gently shrug their shoulders. Still, everything pointed to the fact that she was different. She gained weight and took on a baroque ugliness, with red cheeks and narrow eyes, but with admirable hands, as fine as those of a goddess. Even though they had five sons, her parents adopted a son-in-law for her, and, in spite of her size, she had no trouble giving birth to children, a girl and a boy, both perfectly normal. People said that her deformity would have made this unthinkable were it not for divine intervention.

Takeko was still a child, or nearly so, when, to amuse her, I took her to Daiwa. There, the priestess looked at the horrible little dwarf and said to her, "You must serve the gods." This did not please Takeko, who did not go there again.

However, when her parents gave her a piece of land in the suburb of Tsurugashima as a dowry, she found herself in distress. Her husband, an architect, wanted to build on it, but neither of them had any money. Because my success attested to the efficacy of my beliefs, she went to consult the gods of the priestess of Daiwa. They told her not to worry, to go ahead with the project, that the money would come soon. In fact, several days later, her husband received a commission that would cover the expenses. Nevertheless, Takeko, who was ill at ease in the presence of the gods, did not return to Daiwa.

Two years later, one of her brothers decided to build a house himself. The workers caused so many problems that he too called on the priestess of Daiwa. She declared that he must bury *tama*, spirits, and hold a festival for the appeasement of the ground.[2] However, on the appointed date, the priestess could not come and sent a substitute. Could it have been that the substitute was less talented? Or, for some unknown reason, less acceptable to the gods who were being venerated that day? Whatever the case, the gods refused to appear through her and took over the body of the dwarf instead. As soon as the priestess began to read the Prayer of the Festival for the Appeasement of the Ground, Takeko collapsed, mumbling in a cavernous voice that a terrible anger was torturing her. The professional medium stopped, overcome with surprise. Then she engaged the spirit possessing Takeko in a dialogue:

"Which god are you?" she asked.

"I am the god of the ground," answered Takeko.

I was very distressed, because the dwarf's behavior struck me as terribly rude to the specialist who had come all the way from Sendai for the ceremony. When I scolded Takeko, after she recovered her senses, she remembered nothing.

Time passed, and, since the young woman behaved normally, people forgot about the incident.

Three years later, when Mrs. Takabayashi was supposed to go to Sendai for a formal rite in honor of her ancestors, she caught a bad cold. Takeko agreed to go in her place, with me. We left from Ueno Station together. But it began to rain so violently that the train had to go slower than usual. We didn't arrive until late at night. Even though the priestess had recommended that we pay our respects to the Daikoku-sama, the Great Master of the Country, of the Ōuchiyama Hill that evening, we had to content ourselves with offering our greetings to a statuette of that god in the kitchen of the inn where we were staying.[3] Then, because the ceremony was to begin at dawn, we hastily bathed and went to bed.

That night, Takeko had a strange dream. She saw the little Daikoku-sama of the kitchen come through the window of our room. Once inside, he grew to a gigantic size and walked toward her, his footsteps resounding horribly. He asked her to look into his eyes. When she did so, a blinding light passed from his eyes into hers, three times. She was awakened by terrible pain. She shook me awake and asked me how I could have escaped hearing the god. I told her it must have been a dream. But Takeko was convinced that she had been visited by the little Daikoku-sama of the kitchen. She could not believe it had been an ordinary dream.

She was still in a daze when we arrived at the house of the priestess, who was waiting for us to begin the first prayer. As soon as she heard the sound of the ritual drum which beat in time to the recitation of the sacred words, Takeko collapsed, trembling and growling like an animal. I shook her by the elbow and pinched her arm to bring her back to herself, to no avail. That time, too, I was embarrassed in front of the priestess. But, very quickly, the latter began to interrogate the god who had possessed Takeko's body:

"What is your name?"

"I am the Great Master of the Country," answered the god through the dwarf's mouth.

The priestess invited me to ask the questions. And so I asked, "Who was I in my previous life?"[4]

"You served at Court," answered the god.

He then explained that there was a bond between the Takabayashi and Yamazaki families that, even if broken, could not be undone. And he commanded Takeko to bring back with her his *misugata*, or sacred form, a statue before which she was to say the Prayer of Great Purification every day.

During the day that followed that extraordinary night, we bought a gilded statue of Daikoku for 15,000 yen, which we brought back to Tokyo. As required by the Great Master of the Country, every day Takeko recited before it the Prayer of Great Purification, and every day she collapsed in a trance, at which time she spoke in very antiquated language, in a raucous voice that frightened her husband. She also began to make purchases, quickly diminishing her savings to acquire offering platters, bronze candleholders, and other cult objects. When her husband asked her to stop these extravagances, at first she seemed to listen to reason. But barely an hour passed before the dwarf gave way to the will of the Great Master of the Country. She took the subway to Asakusa, near the temple of Sensōji, where they sold religious objects. Finally, her husband became truly frightened, and telephoned to ask me to come to their house and beg Takeko to stop. But I was so busy that week I couldn't do it.

It was then that the Great Master of the Country made it known to Takeko that I must have a ceremonial garment made for her: in his service, she would from then on wear a violet-colored *hakama* (large skirtlike pants), with a white *kosode* (an underrobe) and a large violet kimono with a chrysanthemum design. Accompanied by her husband, Takeko came to tell me the news. In reality, she was tempted to deny her vocation, because she was afraid. Her husband encouraged her. This perplexed me, because I well understood that it is not easy for a man to see his wife possessed by the gods. I told her it was useless to try to escape one's destiny, but, before making any decisions, she must return to Daiwa to consult the professional priestess. I would accompany her, because, in any event, I wanted to ask where I could have the violet kimono made. (A fabric of imperial color, printed with the imperial chrysanthemum motif, would certainly not be found commercially.)

The priestess told Takeko that she understood her hesitation, because no one can dedicate himself to the gods so simply. Takeko would have to study with her for three months. Then she would acquire the title of *kyōshi* (teaching master), which would authorize her to exercise the gift that heaven had granted her.

But, knowing she was rebellious against any form of discipline, Takeko addressed herself directly to the Great Master of the Country, who said, "That instruction will exhaust you, it will ruin your health. Do not go to Daiwa, but come directly to me, to the mountain of Ōuchiyama. I will teach you what you need to know."

I went back to Tokyo with Takeko and told Mrs. Takabayashi what the god had said. She was afraid that those trials would kill her daughter, whose health had suffered from the frequent trances. Very distressed, I decided to ask Takeko to give it up. But the dwarf answered me with a majesty that she had never before manifested. She said that my concern was in vain, for she had decided to serve the gods. "Last night," she explained, "the Great Master of the Country placed a part of his soul in my body. From now on, I am invulnerable."

As it turned out, Takeko spent only three days at Ōuchiyama. Her mother and I accompanied her. Every morning she went into the snow-covered forest. She turned her face to the tops of the immobile trees among the clouds of winter, then prostrated herself on the frozen ground. She rubbed her cheeks in the snow until they were purplish red, murmuring strange words. Then, her ascetiscm ended, she went back down to the shrine. There, for three days of tears, trances, and stupors, which more than once terrified her mother and me, the Great Master of the Country taught her the entire art of mediums. She learned how to cut paper into sacred symbols;[5] how to make charms for safety, happiness, and prosperity; how to purify herself to perform the rites: before filling the *furo* (bathtub), she would sprinkle it, first with sake, then salt, to the north, east, south, and west. While the tub was filling, she would say the Prayer of Great Purification three times. According to the season, she would throw in peach blossoms, irises, or chrysanthemums. She would wash herself very carefully, not forgetting to rinse her mouth. Then she would dress in her costume with its imperial motif and ask me to do her hair in a chignon in which I would entwine peach blossoms, irises, or chrysanthemums.[6] Everything had to be ready for the month of May, when Takeko would celebrate the birth of herself as a *miko*, divine child—that is, a medium.[7] After that, she could exercise her powers.

When these explanations were over, the Great Master of the Country spoke to Takeko. "Leave," he commanded. "I will go with you. Go quickly, as I have put my entire soul in you, and my life is in danger here."[8]

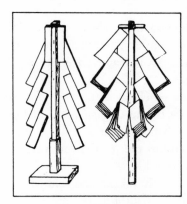

Gohei; sacred symbols.

FAMILY PROBLEMS

As the ceremony ordered by the Great Master of the Country drew nearer, nervousness and impatience got the best of me. The extraordinary complexity of the preparations disrupted the usual order of daily life and exasperated those close to me. Adopting a morose expression, Tatsuo sighed, speaking very low, saying that I was decidedly as crazy as the autumn winds. And, wondering what chain of causes and effects had given rise to my strangeness, he began to frequent temples that specialized in the fetus cult. (Like most Japanese mothers, I had had at least five abortions.[9])

Motoko tried, through prayer, to bring me back to the ordinary cult of Ontake-san. Mitsunobu complained every morning that all these devotions were overdone: "There are lots of gods in the house," he said. "This legacy is too much work." Ryōko, our younger daughter, suddenly attached herself (to provoke me, I'm sure) to a universalist sect that reduced all religions to a day-to-day morality that prohibited killing and stealing.

Distressed at having caused so much trouble with my family, for an instant I considered calling off the celebration. But Naka, my late mother-in-law, spoke to me through Takeko. She said, "Human beings never accept the demands of the gods easily. I see how great the sadness is. But know that perseverance will reduce your pain to nothing. Time will allay your suffering." Since those were Naka's first words since her death, I could not but bow to them.

Nevertheless, my piety was gravely compromising the peace in the family.

Mitsunobu and his wife, Kyōko, had lived with us since their marriage, but my relations with my daughter-in-law had never been easy. While Kyōko, in conformance with her obligations, obeyed me in everything, her eyes sometimes betrayed a flaring of extreme hostility or, worse yet, indifference, which frightened me.

One day when Kyōko was making the rice for lunch, the *miko* Takeko and her two children stopped by without warning. Without thinking, I asked my daughter-in-law to serve them something to eat. She did so, but, through the entire meal, she never once opened her tightly closed lips— not to greet the *miko* or to say anything else. After lunch, Kyōko went out, taking her children. They did not return that evening, nor the following day.

Panic seized my heart. That evening, after sunset, I heard the lugubrious cawing of a crow, and I was gripped by a bad presentiment: I feared that Mitsunobu would follow his wife and abandon the house.

In the Kobayashi family into which she was born, Kyōko was the last of four girls; there were no boys. After the first three girls had married, her parents had expressed their hope of keeping their youngest with them and adopting for her a son-in-law, whom they would make their heir. But their plans came to nothing when Kyōko met Mitsunobu, who was himself an heir: both were young, good-looking, and shy. They had barely caught sight of each other before they were in love. With regret, the Kobayashis let their last daughter go, but I knew that they would welcome her joyously if she decided to go back to them. Then it would be we Yamazakis who would find ourselves without an heir. My work, my ascension in the world, would have been for naught.

In order to avert this peril, I summoned the *miko* to the house in Bunkyō and, desperate, questioned the gods.

Naka appeared for the second time. She explained that it was not right to hate Kyōko: if the girl led a selfish life, it was because an *innen-goto*, a bad fate, weighed on the house of her birth, making it inaccessible to all forms of piety. Was I not aware that Kyōko came from an impious family, who kept no altars, neither for the gods nor for the buddhas? Heaven had decided to marry Kyōko into the Yamazakis, in the hope that the dead ancestors of the Kobayashis would finally enjoy descendants who would pray for their repose. Naka said, "You must make offerings to the Kobayashi dead." And she went away.

At that moment, I heard footsteps on the stairs: Kyōko, having secretly come back for a change of clothes for her son Masashi, had heard the divine message that cast aspersions on her origins. Exasperated, she ran away, like a wounded dog pelted with stones by a blind man.

Saddened by the persistence of this discord in the family, I asked the gods for consolation every day. Since those prayers changed nothing, I tried to remedy things through the world of men. I told Mitsunobu how regrettable I found the situation, vain as a battle fought by clouds in the sky. I stated that in this affair, as in all affairs, there were wrongs on both sides.

"When Kyōko comes back," I said, "she will have to be made aware of the suffering for which she is responsible."

With these words, Mitsunobu, usually so calm that people think him apathetic, had a fit of anger, violent and quick, and flat out refused to speak to Kyōko in that way. I asked Tatsuo to intervene, but he didn't want to mix himself up in what he called women's stories. In fact, since he had become attached to the cult of dead fetuses, the color had returned to his cheeks, which had paled for a while because of the domestic quarrels. His newfound energy prompted him to spend more and more time roaming around Tokyo, so we barely saw him in Bunkyō anymore.

Several days later, though, Kyōko came back, and life resumed as it had been. At least in appearances, because her flight, accomplished without tears or any kind of outlet, continued to poison the air in the apartment at the top of the building.

One morning Kyōko appeared to be in a lighter mood, and I took advantage of it to speak to her directly. I called her into the kitchen and said, "I'm not angry with you. It's not your fault—it's the result of an *innen-goto* of the Kobayashis. I will pray for your ancestors for as long as it takes."

"Don't overdo it, Mother. The mother of the house of my birth would certainly not want you to go to so much trouble on our account. And, besides, if you pray for the Kobayashis, no doubt she will have to participate in the rites."

"No, she needn't bother, since you belong to the house of Yamazaki now. We are sufficiently tied to your ancestors through you."

"If that's what's troubling you," retorted Kyōko, whom until now everyone had thought to be a sweet person, "I can very well leave." She went out, slamming the door behind her.

I felt that I would have done better to have said nothing. I was afraid that, if this continued, Kyōko and Mitsunobu really would go away. I would have to be prudent.

That evening, I summoned the two of them for a talk. "You have been called on to accept the succession of the house of Yamazaki, and you will inherit the business as well as our gods. Even if there are problems between us, we must surmount them by placing the gods at the center of our relations."

Kyōko and Mitsunobu declined my suggestion.

As the months passed, I noticed that the grandchildren were changing. Hitoe, the girl, did badly in school, and Masashi no longer laughed. One day, arguing that their room was too small, Kyōko and Mitsunobu announced brusquely that they were moving to a modern apartment on the top floor of a building in the neighborhood. That very afternoon, the moving men took their things away, and that night they stayed in a hotel.

Contemplating their empty room, I told myself that I must put an end to this disagreement, at all costs. Again I summoned my son and daughter-in-law and opened my heart to them. I turned to Kyōko. "For you, things are fine, since you are lucky enough to have married the man you love. But your children will not find happiness through money alone. They need the affection of everyone. We must get along, putting the children at the center of our relations."

Listening to these words, for the first time since her entry into the house, Kyōko wept a little, her tears filling her eyes without falling. As soon as I saw that, I knew that order would return. I placed my hand on her shoulder in a gesture that signified that she would always belong to our family, and I felt compassion for her.

In fact, our relations became so harmonious that the gods did not hesitate to ask that Kyōko participate in the celebration of the transfer of their shrine from the Japanese-style room to the room she had formerly occupied with Mitsunobu. They insisted that she be the one to sew the names Mitsunobu, Tatsuo, and Ikue on the collar, the belt, and the hem of the ceremonial kimono of the *miko*. I wondered for a moment if that divine order would not revive our dispute, but Kyōko agreed without a complaint or a murmur. Then, she participated in the rites with the entire family and said nothing about it, whatever she thought in her heart.

In gratitude, I have honored more than ever the gods who watch over us since we moved the shrine to my son's old room. But I felt alone, since there was no longer anyone under my roof to whom I could give orders. To console me, the gods granted me the fervor that devours anguish, and I prayed every day to the supernatural spirits, the dead and the gods.

DIVINE MANAGEMENT

As always happens when a *miko* is sincere, the faithful gathered around Takeko, forming a pious community. Only a few weeks had passed since the birth of the *miko*, when twenty or thirty of the faithful were assembling regularly at her house in Tsurugashima. Luckily, Takeko's husband had had the foresight to build a large veranda around the house, and one had only to remove the partitions to create a vast room perfectly suited to the service of the gods. It was there that the first rites celebrated in honor of the Great God of the Country took place, the god being evoked by the statuette of Daikoku-sama we had brought back from Ōuchiyama, installed on a provisional altar.

But, with the approach of the full moon of autumn,[10] the oracles asked that other *kami* be installed next to him: Amaterasu (She Who Illuminates the Sky), Tsukiyomi no Mikoto (The Lord Who Counts the Months), and Ame no Minaka Nushi no Mikoto (The Master of the Middle of the Sky) were to share the altar from then on. They agreed that the first two could be represented by simple paper charms purchased in great shrines but demanded that a pure gold statue be made for the Master of the Middle of the Sky: it was to be five inches high and would represent the divinity in a seated position; it would have the muscular back of a man, the chest of a woman, the face of a young girl, and the hair of an old man. In that way it would symbolize both male and female, youth and age—that is, the totality of the universe.

The oracles also commanded that a ceremony in their honor be performed every full moon: the altar, located in the northwest, was to be decorated with branches of *sakaki* cut at dawn near the house of the *miko*; the dew could not be washed from them; they were simply to be tied with a hemp rope, then placed in the four corners.

Once the statue was finished, paid for by the offerings of the faithful, the gods commanded that their residence be entirely paneled in *hinoki*, white cypress, so that a real shrine would finally be established in the home of the *miko*.

Every full moon, Takeko would offer on it the products of the three regions that make up the world: the mountains, the sea, and the countryside. From the sea came sea bream, who swim with their tails in the air, and seashells, in which the sea murmurs. From the mountains came wild vegetables, which change with each season, and, from the countryside, the seven kinds of tubers, delight of the gods. She also offered sake, water, washed rice, salt, and fabric, too—two or three pieces of lustrous silk— and seven pieces of dark green *konbu* seaweed, contrasting sharply against the immaculate paper on which the offerings were prettily arranged.

The participants in the ceremonies were mostly hairdressers associated with me, because I had made known to them the great merits of the new *miko*.

I had told the members of the Yamazaki Research Association about the solitary ascetic period the dwarf had spent on Ōuchiyama and reminded them, as a proof of her effectiveness, of my own success in business. To the World Beauty and Health Association I gave as examples my own flourishing health and the sumptuous beauty of the hair of the *miko*, who used Belle Jouvence with remarkable results. I told everyone, "Belle Jouvence is a natural product created by the chemistry of the gods, and not by men."

Charmed by the miraculous effects of that beauty lotion, women joined the new sect in droves. It was an amazing wonder, probably a sign of the goodwill of the gods, that, as the religious community grew, so did sales of Belle Jouvence.

Finally, I enjoined the employees to attend our rites.

For a long time, I had consulted oracles before opening a new shop or hiring an employee. Now, since the gods had granted me the great favor of placing a *miko* by my side, I thought the moment had come to let all those close to me profit by it. Indeed, only the veneration of supernatural powers can give people sufficient conviction in daily life.

I decided to hold a big festival once a year at the Toyama Kaikan, a building where we often rented rooms for events, which would assemble all the employees from the seven salons. Thanks to the *miko*, everyone would be able to freely interrogate the gods on their problems of the moment.

I announced this decision to my nephew Endo. He feared that this obligation would offend the young employees, but I explained, "If I invite them to family rites, it's because I consider them my own children. Of course some of them could care less, but there are others whom this will help. As for those who don't like it, surely they will find other jobs."

When Endo questioned them about this new obligation, the employees replied, "If the Yamazakis are good bosses, perhaps it is thanks to their beliefs. We don't see what harm it can do."

In this way, the annual gathering was instituted.

Later, as business prospered even more, I dared to question the gods on a subject which concerned me more gravely each day—that of my succession.

Seeing the tensions among the three cousins—Hirotoshi, Endo, and Mitsunobu—grow year by year, I worried that my death might transform them into rivals rather than allies. I knew that no legal decision can establish among men the harmony that is indispensable to their success, and I feared that the youngest of the three, my son, would come out the loser in this absurd war.

I asked the *miko* to meet with the cousins once a month, along with two longtime employees, Yoshida Chieko and Fujita Shunshō, who had for some time been administrators. I hoped that the gods would grant them counsel as to the attitude they must adopt in conducting their lives.

As the months passed, the gods revealed their opinions. They told Endo to stop taking on jobs he could not do and to learn to trust others. They suggested to Hirotoshi that he place himself in the foreground a bit less and push another before him, declaring that only in that way would his success be enduring. To the loyal Yoshida Chieko, who had worked ten years for my house but who sometimes stayed out later than she should drinking beer, they suggested she act more feminine. They told Fujita Shunshō, our disciple of twenty years' standing, to continue to conduct himself in the future as he had in the past. For a long time, they refused to speak to Mitsunobu. Finally, when I reached my seventieth year, they incited him to open up to others.

These words reassured me, because I thought that no one would dare to infringe on the directives of the gods after my death. As was common with young people of the fashionable quarters, Hirotoshi claimed to believe in neither gods nor devils. But he also said that one must never go against the will of the dead. He hoped that his own children would venerate his cult after he left this world and was even thinking of marrying for that reason.

So I was able to say to myself every morning: "When my son is dead, his children will direct the house. I am ready to die when the gods will it. I will go to see Naka, Seikō, Nobuko, and the rest. Together, we will watch over the happiness of our loved ones. The world will go on in this way eternally."

KŌ: THE BROTHERHOOD

In fact, the new religion proved so effective that the numbers of the faithful burgeoned. One year after its inception, a gathering of the followers would probably have included close to a thousand people. Besides the hairdressers, many of the group from Daiwa, disappointed in that master, came to consult the dwarf Takeko; charmed by the beauty of her oracles, they stayed with us.

The gods decided that the moment had come to form a real organization, a *kō*, a brotherhood.[11] They gave Takeko the rank of *naka-za* (she who sits in the middle) and described anew the standards she was to uphold in order to serve them. For the most formal occasions, she must wear two *hakama*, one over the other, one dark purple and the other white, with an immaculate robe. She would wear her hair fixed on the top of her head with a precious comb, so that it cascaded, rustling, down her shoulders. For small ceremonies, dressed in a red *hakama* with a white one over it, she would let her long black hair fall freely. They also granted her a new name, Ichi, She Who Possesses Knowledge. That name came from Ichiyo, a female descendant of Queen Himiko, who, in the ancient times before Japan had a name, had governed the realm through the performance of rites.[12]

Then, the gods named me *mae-za*, she who sits in front. Placed between the dwarf and the faithful, I would be in charge of transmitting to her their prayers and would comment on the divine messages. On those occasions, I would wear a white robe. Additionally, the gods said that the two of us were as inseparable as yin is from yang, that Takeko was the yin and I the yang.[13]

Finally, they chose two hairdressers from among the followers, Mrs. Seki from Hiroshima and Mrs. Nomura from Sapporo, and designated them *shiten*, that is, assistants to the dwarf and myself.[14] While she was in trance, they would sit a few feet away and recite prayers and formulas that would ward off danger. And on ceremony days, they would come to the *miko*'s house in advance to prepare the offerings and the cult instruments. Like me, they would be entirely dressed in white.

The gods next explained that they had chosen women to serve them because women are, as a rule, more courageous than men.

MANGETSU-SAI: THE FESTIVAL OF THE FULL MOON

The following autumn, more than three hundred people came to the *Mangetsu-Sai*, Festival of the Full Moon. We put up a great red-and-white-striped tent in the garden in Tsurugashima, purified in all four directions with sake and salt. A temporary altar of white wood was installed there, but no statue was placed on it because the back of the tent opened onto nature, which is the essence of the gods. However, it began to rain so hard that we had to close the canvas door.

As the members of the brotherhood (mostly women) trickled in, they made a detour into the dwarf's house, to the bathroom, where they washed their hands and rinsed their mouths. Then each one prepared her offering: a five-thousand- or ten-thousand-yen bill in an envelope tucked under her belt. When the time had come, the faithful removed their shoes at the door of the tent and filed in, in one silent, long line. They sat down on the canvas-covered ground. I began a slow reading of the prayers, while our two *shiten* collected the offerings.

Barely ten minutes had passed before the *miko*, seated before the altar, entered into trance. She sank lightly down and began to speak quickly, at times in a sharp, high voice, and at others in a raucous voice, short of breath like an old man. Periodically, I translated the messages from heaven into clearer language. The gods of water spoke first—they said that they were very angry and had made the rain fall for that reason. Next it was the Counter of Months, who watches over the souls of the dead. He wailed, "I am sad because the dead souls, incensed by the impiety of men, are agitated in the world below. I will not show myself."

It was true that fog and clouds had gathered in a way that was not ordinary for the season, and the moon, although celebrated that day, remained invisible.

"What must we do to remedy it?" asked a group of believers.

The gods replied, "A delegation of the brotherhood will make a pilgrimage to Izumo, the place to which, in ancient times, the Great Master of the Country withdrew. Next they will go to Ise, where She Who Illuminates the Sky resides, then to the isles of the south, where so many unhappy souls met their deaths in the last war."

Then the gods took individual questions from those who were beset with problems of money or health, and for each they prescribed offerings and prayers. On some of the devotees, they conferred the right to acquire an image of the Great Master of the Country to install and venerate in their own homes. One tall, skinny woman who had just lost her husband, realizing that she did not figure among the list of lucky beneficiaries, stood up, waving her black sleeves like wings. She let out a single strident cry before falling. Somewhat annoyed by this sudden uproar, I said to her, "Do not worry. The gods will soon authorize you to address a private cult to the Great Master of the Country. I am sure of it." Reassured, the woman sat down.

SEKAI HEIWA: WORLD PEACE

For the *hatsu mairi*, the first pilgrimage of the next new year, I accompanied the delegation, including the *miko* and about twenty of the faithful, to Izumo, to the shrine of the Great Master of the Country, who, after having pacified Japan, left it to the descendants of the Sun.[15]

There, the god agreed to reveal to us for the first time the reason for our mission. As we were bowing before the altar, the priests of the place having purified us, the members of another brotherhood, who were making the same pilgrimage, asked us, "What is the name of your sect?"

I answered that we didn't have a name, but that our representative was called Takabayashi Takeko. A second group, and still another, questioned me in the same way, so that I thought that it would indeed be a good idea if we had a name that would permit everyone to identify us easily. I consulted the Great Master of the Country on the subject. And, through the mouth of the *miko*, he answered that he would give us the name Sangū, Three Empresses.[16] Then he explained the significance of the name.

"At the beginning of the world," said the Great Master of the Country, "there were three gods. At the center of the world was Ame no Minaka Nushi no Kami, the Master of the Middle of the Heavens, who is indivisible; beside him, as noble as himself, were Takamimusubi no Ōkami, the Great God of High Production, and Kamimusubi no Ōkami, the Great God Producer of Gods. And the latter two divided themselves in half, which made five divinities, corresponding to the five elements that compose the universe. Next, through a series of successive divisions, in exactly the way the cells of the human body divide, they engendered the seventy-five gods who are the inhabitants of the world of celestial gods over which She Who Illuminates the Sky, Amaterasu, reigns. In parallel fashion, in the world of shadows which is ruled by her brother the Counter of Months, the seventy-five gods that reside in the world of the dead were formed.

"The rites that you perform serve to promote harmony in the three worlds: the heavens, the earth, and the shadow world. The souls who died in the Second World War and other conflicts are agitated with such frenzy that they keep the light of the celestial gods from shining on the earth. You will appease them by your prayers. Then, the divine light will be resplendent in the world, preventing all wars. Finally, when peace has come, the Way of Beauty will have accomplished its task.

"If you neglect the rites, the troubles stirred up by those souls in despair will drag the world into a third war. Men and women will die before their time. And, driven into the land of shades, they too will trouble the living."

That evening, to celebrate the great news, we stayed in a luxury hotel where crabs and shellfish from Cape Miho were served to us in abundance.[17] Once we got back to Tokyo, we had our brotherhood registered as a legal entity.

The following spring, the devotees who had received this instruction from the gods flew to Saipan, where so many innocents had perished in the Second World War. High on a cliff, in the name of the entire brotherhood, we said the Prayer of the Great Purification three times. On the waves that had once washed over dead bodies, we cast our offerings—pages of square cardboard on which we had calligraphed our prayers. They headed out to sea in a long line, against the current. We understood by this strange sign that the dead had accepted our rites.

Then the Great Master of the Country spoke to us again: "A third world war is once more threatening the world. Japan must remain strong enough to serve as mediator between the countries of the East and those of the West. For Japan to remain strong, the virtue of its emperor must be strong. Go to Ise and venerate the ancestors of the Imperial Family."

At the beginning of summer, we visited the gods of Ise. We purified the earth, the sea, and the sky, that the gods might watch over the perpetuity of the sovereign line.[18]

RELIGION AND POLITICS

Up until then, I had troubled myself very little with politics. I belonged to the generation raised before the war, during the time when *danson johi*, men exalted, women scorned, was the rule. I was born into a world where the mere expression of a political opinion was thought unseemly for a girl.

After the war, when the Americans decreed the equality of men and women, I thought for the first time that perhaps there was something useful about politics after all. But the defeat convinced me at the same time that the politicians were nothing but arrogant, stupid liars. They had dragged us into an imbecilic war and duped us, claiming over the months and years that we would be the victors.

As for our leaders today—the ministers, secretaries, and elected officials—they're all corrupt. They go from scandal to scandal like birds from branch to branch. They buy votes, distribute gifts to force the poor to vote as they want them to, and promise the moon and the stars![19] Our political parties are worthless. On the right, their only interest is money; on the left, they might as well not even be Japanese. Not to mention those members of the Kōmeitō or the militarist parties, who do nothing but religious "business."[20] They use the name of the emperor to gain respectability and draw crowds. But they, who are themselves incapable of living, want to drag the entire world into war, chaos, and death. They are flies, dirty flies of summer that should be driven from the earth or at least from its spirit. No one attributes their behavior to the system. However, it was men, not the gods, who invented politics.

What would I ask of our politicians? Only that they show themselves to be truly proud to have been born in Japan. These days, simply hoisting the flag, singing the national anthem, or making a pilgrimage to the shrine Yasukuni Jinja, the resting place of the souls of our dead soldiers, prompts accusations of "Militarism! War!"[21] The poor soldiers, dead for their country, and we're ashamed to thank them!

No doubt things would go better if women held the power. Although none of that is of great importance, since the emperor guarantees the existence of our country, which—the gods have told me—will bring about peace in the world.

Our emperor has nothing to do with those contemptible politicians. I asked Aoki, the chief of protocol of the Imperial Household, about this, and he put it well: "The emperor is not a man of politics. He is a god. The language we use to address him, and the rites we offer him, prove that. No human being could be treated like that."

So it is of little consequence that the politicians lie, amass the people's money, and then waste it. That will not change one bit the destiny of the world, which depends not on their unscrupulous dealings but on the wisdom in the hearts of the living, on the appeasement of the rancor in the hearts of the dead.

The wisdom of the living might take the form of building an airport in the Northern Islands, which Japan has claimed for many years.[22] They belong to no one, no more to us than to the Soviet Union. Since we are rich, we could build an airport there that would profit all nations. In exchange, we would ask nothing, or perhaps just fishing rights. And the people of the entire world would thank us!

Wisdom would be to understand that the peoples of the world complement one another. The gods have endowed Japan with intelligence and skill. To other Asian countries, they have given raw materials. We would educate them, and they would allow us to buy the products we lack for a good price.

The greatest of wisdoms would be the disappearance of hatred. That end to evil passions is the affair not of politics but of religion.

In order for the world to live in peace, first of all the souls of those who have died unjust deaths since the beginning of time must be delivered from their sufferings. For that to happen, we must pray and pray again, that their ferocious spirits be appeased and the light of the gods shine at last on the earth.

One evening, when I was staying in a hotel on the Izu Peninsula, I offered a few grains of white rice out my window for spirits without ties. I immediately had a marvelous vision: the sun was setting over the sea, coloring the waves with eight hundred colors. It suddenly looked as if the rays of light were gently moving, as if millions of little things were sliding down the light toward me. It was so beautiful, I wanted to cry out. I looked closer and saw tiny beings of light traveling from sky to earth. After they disappeared in the rays of the sun, I had the impression, I don't know why, of having witnessed the descent of the gods to earth.

When, back in Tokyo, I described the scene to the *miko* Takeko, she said that the gods had appeared to me to thank me for my efforts in their behalf and to announce that my dreams of peace would soon be realized.

BETRAYAL

In fact, as we continued to repeat our rites in the great shrines and the places where war had caused the unjust deaths of innocents, East and West began a rapprochement. One day, I read in the paper that they had decided to destroy their armaments.

I wanted to telephone Takeko immediately to announce the marvelous news. But because her line was continually busy, I called an old friend of Mitsunobu who sometimes drives for me and asked him to take me there. We left around five and arrived well after the dinner hour. Since the doors of the house were wide open, I walked in, calling out: "It's me, Yamazaki! Sorry to bother you!"

No one answered, so I went through the rooms one by one until I got to the kitchen, where a bright lamp was on. I opened the door, apologizing, and found the *miko* lolling with her head on the table. A man who was not her husband was seated next to her, half drunk. He shook the dwarf, who winced slightly when she recognized me. On the table, I saw a jumble of empty sake bottles and discarded skewers from a meal of broiled chicken.

I murmured a terse apology and left without fanfare. My driver was such a chatterbox that he didn't notice I was unusually quiet. I thought, "I've been fooled again. She has betrayed me."

In fact, I already knew that: it is difficult for anyone to remain a good *miko* for long. To perform that function, the gods choose women who are so burdened with fates, with *innen-goto*, that they can do nothing in half measures. They can only be very good or extremely bad. Also, these women's heads are turned by the exhaustion of performing the rites, the money, and the compliments of men charmed by the mystery that surrounds them.

That evening, I didn't think it out to that extent. I just told myself that my worst forebodings seemed to have been well-founded: she wanted to drive me away—I, who had helped her so much—and replace me with a man who would take over as *mae-za*, mediator to the faithful. In great anguish I asked myself whether greed and lust had not overtaken her, and this filled me with desperation.

I went to bed early. The next day, so as not to betray my inner turmoil, I took unusual care with my makeup. I used a pale green foundation to hide the sallow tones of my skin, then over that a dusting of pink powder. I blackened my eyebrows dramatically and lined my eyes with India ink. I gave my hair, which I wore very short, a quick brushing. Then I looked in the mirror. "I look like I always do," I thought. "It doesn't show." But what was it that didn't show? I didn't know exactly. My age, my sadness, my fatigue, no doubt. I realized that fate, the gods, or the demons were once again laughing at me. And what if the *miko* since the beginning had lied? What if it were impossible that the dead, or even the gods, could speak to us? What if all religions were nothing but charlatanism? Endo had once told me that there were as many sects legally registered in Japan as there are hairdressers. Frightened by my thoughts, I turned away from the mirror. I put on a red dress that made me look young, and I walked out to the landing of the apartment. I had a painful cramp in my calf. I gritted my teeth and went down to the salon on the ground floor.

When I opened the door of the shop, I was met with a volley of joyful greetings: "*Ohayō gozaimasu!* Good morning!"

The pink, perfumed figures of the employees performed a comforting symphony of bows. I greeted them in turn. I commanded them, "Cancel all appointments with Takabayashi Takeko." And I had them do my hair.

I put on a plastic smock and sat down. My thoughts were scattered, my dreams crushed. When I felt the nimble fingers of the young woman touch my head, a wave of hope filled my breast. I felt like crying. So I repeated to myself, "I am happy. I'll never be hungry again. I have succeeded."

And as these words brought me gently back to serenity, I thought, "Besides, who knows—perhaps I really did save the world."

No one, truly no one, will ever be able to prove the contrary. A smile floated to my lips. I began to drowse, enveloped in the warmth of the hair dryer.

Epilogue

My last interview with Yamazaki Ikue took place in Paris. We met at the Hotel Intercontinental, where she had come with her son, the eldest of her grandsons (Motoko's child), and about twenty of her disciples in the Way of Beauty. During their three days in Paris, the conclusion of a two-week tour of Europe, she refused to take part in any of the sightseeing jaunts planned for the group, preferring to stay in her room to answer my final questions.

On the evening before her departure, we met for a ceremonial dinner in a restaurant on the ground floor of the hotel. As is the custom in Japan, the meal was punctuated by speeches. Everyone told something of what he or she had learned from the trip. Some said how they appreciated the peaceful rhythm of life in France, where people take the time to enjoy meals together; they expressed their resolution to adopt that convivial custom. Others stressed the importance of mastering foreign languages, without which no one can feel at ease in the world. One young woman confessed she had come to find a European husband but had failed in her quest. Everyone sipped the white wine, laughing and applauding. Yamazaki Ikue herself announced that I was writing a book in which the story of her life would be told.

As the coffee was being served, she turned to me and asked, "What will you call the book?"

"I don't know yet," I said. "I'll decide that with the director of the series."

"There is a better way. Write down, right now, on a piece of paper, the titles you are considering. I will question the gods to find out which one they consider appropriate."

I proposed three titles: *Madame Yamazaki*, *The Yamazaki Family*, and *The House of Yamazaki*, explaining the connotations of each.

281

We parted.

The following week, I received a telephone call from Tokyo. The *miko* who had been consulted, a woman whom Yamazaki Ikue had only recently met, had questioned the gods for me. They had declared that *The House of Yamazaki* was the best of all possible titles.

Thus I understood that Yamazaki Ikue had recovered her confidence in the gods and their mediators in this world. I knew that she was once more traveling the path of serenity, certain that she would, one day, find happiness.

Afterword:
How This Book Came to Be

I met Yamazaki Ikue on January 15, 1970. With my first husband, François Berthier, I had taken the Trans-Siberian Railroad across vast stretches of snowy forests. When the boat docked at Yokohama, I disembarked for the first time in my life in Japan, where the Yamazakis waited to greet us. Berthier had interpreted for that couple during their first trip to France. Yamazaki Tatsuo; his wife, Yamazaki Ikue; and their daughter Ryōko had come to welcome us and to let me know that we would soon be friends.

I had studied a little medicine, Arabic, and ethnology, but as yet I spoke only a few words of Japanese. Although our first conversations were difficult, the Yamazakis amazed me—as much by their indulgence and their patience, put to the test by my foreigner's ignorance and clumsiness, as by the love they evinced for the culture of their country. Yamazaki Tatsuo soon initiated me into Japanese cuisine (as well as sake), while Ikue told me about the beauty of Japan and the ancient roots of its history. She also unwrapped for me the treasures that she kept hidden in closets: hair ornaments, ancient engravings, and paintings. Their children—at the time only Motoko, the eldest, was married—helped me settle in and taught me Japanese. When, fascinated by so much kindness and simplicity, I expressed aloud the seductive hold Japan was beginning to have over me, they looked at me with somewhat astonished expressions and asked, "But how can you love Japan? There's no space; the disorder is horrible!" Then they took me to visit places dear to them.

During the three years I lived in Tokyo, I saw them nearly every week and soon felt that I'd acquired a sort of family. After I moved to Kyoto, they came to visit me only once, but I saw them whenever I was in Tokyo. When I left Japan in 1975, Yamazaki Ikue gave me a pearl necklace, slipped

into an envelope which bore her own calligraphy: "To Roransu (her pronunciation of my name), my French daughter."

It was during my return trip the following spring that Yamazaki Ikue let it
be known, very indirectly, that she would like me to write the story of
her life.

After a family dinner in the *dainingu kichin* at her house in the Bunkyō
ward of Tokyo, she described the strange malady that had overcome her
after the death of her mother-in-law. I told her how astounding I found
this story. She looked at me fixedly for a moment and then said, "It's true,
I've had a strange life. I even know a writer who would like to make a
novel of it. But no doubt the pure truth would be more interesting." From
that day on, she seemed to confide more and more of her secrets to me.

Because I was writing my thesis then, I could not respond to her suggestion. But another chance presented itself in 1981, when I applied for a
research grant from the Foundation for the Study of Japanese Language
and Civilization (sponsored by the Fondation de France) with which to
pursue my studies. I soon received an unofficial, incongruous response: I
would definitely get the grant if I proposed research in an urban setting;
up to then I had worked essentially with rural Japanese society. I must add
that a terrible quarrel between ancients and moderns was then raging
among French "Japan" scholars. Deciding to find a subject that would
demonstrate the structural role of tradition even in the midst of modernity,
and then show the absurdity of this dispute, I acquiesced. I wrote to ask
he Yamazakis if I could come and study their history and that of their
normously successful hairdressing business.

After Yamazaki Ikue responded that she was flattered by my proposition,
I returned to Japan to interview her. Almost every morning of that extremely hot summer, we met in the *dainingu kichin*, drinking coffee prepared by her husband. We chatted in a rambling way, vaguely touching on
the themes I hoped to broach. Then we took refuge in the antechamber
of the room reserved for the gods, on the top floor of the house. We talked
for hours, a small tape recorder between us, interrupted from time to time
by a servant who would bring us scalding hot tea or some strawberries.

At first reticent and agitated, Yamazaki Ikue seemed to take a growing
interest in these intimate times. Little by little she forgot that she was speaking for others, for posterity, and seemed to take pleasure in her confidences.
She canceled appointments to stay and work with me. She railed against
the telephone, sometimes refusing to answer it; it is nothing important, she
said. At the end of one of our first conversations, she had looked at me
suspiciously and said, "You certainly know how to make people talk!" Now
she was admitting the sweet nostalgia she felt in evoking the past.

The rest of the family, however, showed some irritation at our growing complicity. The men accused Yamazaki Ikue of letting the business go; the women wondered what we might be talking about. In the hope of shrinking the gulf that had grown up between the family and the two of us, I asked each of them to give me a few hours of interview time to complete my information. Thus I was able to speak (almost always alone) with children and nephews as well as veteran employees, and I had the chance to participate in some parts of the business.

While everyone took my inquisition with good grace, Yamazaki Ikue, in turn, began to show signs of disquiet and of wanting to monopolize me again. She met with me more and more, to the point where her work did begin to suffer. Finally, one morning as we sat drinking our coffee, her husband, Tatsuo, asked me, with a somewhat worried look, "When are you going back?"

"Next week," I answered.

"Already?" said Ikue. Then she gave a long sigh and murmured, "In the end, I suppose it's better this way."

From that day on, our dialogue became difficult. She suddenly decided that we would have to go to her home village, Asaka—which we did, on the day of a typhoon. Upon our arrival, we learned that the grape harvest had been completely destroyed. She consoled her brother and her nephew: "Luckily, you hadn't put the bags on yet! Then all that work would have been for nothing!" (To protect the grapes, two or three weeks before the harvest the bunches of grapes are individually wrapped in plastic bags.)

The following night, as we slept in the same room, she woke me up around one o'clock, saying she felt like talking. I groped in the dark for my tape recorder. For two or three hours, she told me about her beliefs in the good gods who protected her, because she was just and deceived no one.

When I left for Paris, I carried with me close to two hundred hours of tape recordings and about fifty sheets of paper on which Yamazaki Ikue had jotted down phrases to underscore what she was saying, explanatory charts, and the like. At the beginning of our interviews, we had decided to cover events in chronological order. However, that plan quickly fell by the wayside, as Yamazaki Ikue was guided by her current concerns more than her memories. When I tried to return to the plan, I realized that my questions—even when they concerned mere details (for example, I would press her to name objects or notions that, in her mind, had not needed naming until then)—influenced the content of her narrative. One day I asked her the name of the brotherhood she had formed around the medium Takeko. She answered that it didn't have a name, but that a lot of people had asked the same question, and she would certainly have to give it one. The next day, the oracles revealed the future name of the brotherhood. Disturbed by this obviously not fortuitous coincidence, I determined not to ask questions, leaving Yamazaki Ikue to her somewhat disjointed monologue. I decided to save points of clarification for later, thinking that, in this first phase, it was better to preserve the spontaneity of her speech as much as possible.

The night before I departed, the oracles announced that it would soon be possible to open a Yamazaki salon in Paris.

Back in France, I transcribed all the tapes and established a sort of repertoire of themes, in order to reconstitute both a sort of chronology and thematic subsets. Then I quickly wrote about a hundred pages in which I summed up Yamazaki Ikue's ascension, described the organization of her enterprise, and tried to explain how the business incorporated traditional Japanese work relations.

This report eventually reached Augustin Berque, academic director of the School of Higher Studies in the Social Sciences (EHESS). He said it reminded him of the first months of his own stay in Japan, when he had found lodging with a hairdresser. He put me in touch with a colleague at the school, Jean Malaurie, who wished to publish a book on Japan in his Terre Humaine series. That is how a second adventure began.

My report immediately interested Jean Malaurie. What remained was to finish the work, to give it the coherence of a book and make it readable. The first step was to find the right form, and this proved extraordinarily difficult, since three radically different possibilities suggested themselves: I could write my own personal view of the history of Yamazaki Ikue; I could tell her story in an "objective" third-person narrative; or I could report her story in the first person, in her own words.

Each approach had its strengths and weaknesses. On the one hand, having known the heroine since 1970, I had witnessed a number of the recent events of her life, on which I felt inclined to give my point of view. On the other hand, virtually everything I knew about her childhood was limited to what she had told me. For the period from her arrival in Tokyo in 1934 until January 1970, I had, besides her own testimony, that of people close to her. Furthermore, the goal of the book was to provide the richest possible information on Japan, but my knowledge of the country was gained only partially through the Yamazaki family.

I tried each approach in succession; I even briefly considered adopting a different form for each part of the book. After I submitted these to Jean Malaurie, he encouraged me to let Yamazaki Ikue tell her own story, in her own words. Writing from the point of view of Yamazaki Ikue had the advantage of making her appear to the reader as a person rather than a character. This is the approach I have taken.

This choice, however, posed new difficulties. From the start, the free nature of my interviews with Yamazaki Ikue had left many points of detail imprecise or implicit. I realized that, in order to write from her point of view, I would have to gather additional material. I went back to Japan in the summer of 1983.

Yamazaki Ikue gladly lent herself to my questioning. In addition, from that visit on, the entire family was favorably disposed to this enterprise, and all of them were happy to cooperate. In fact, they had in the meantime learned of the contents of our interviews.

Because her business was growing wealthy in an era when, overseas, accusations of selfishness were beginning to be leveled at Japan, Yamazaki Ikue wanted to "do something good" for Southeast Asian refugees. Her children suggested that she publish a promotional album, to be sold to employees and customers, the profits going to the refugees. This luxury book would trace the life story of Yamazaki Ikue and include the best family photos. At their request, I sent the Yamazakis my original tapes to use in writing the text. Before they were returned to me, the children had heard all or part of the tapes.

That had a double effect. First, it allowed a sort of "tabling" of the conflicts that had strained family relations. It especially contributed to the amelioration of Kyōko's relations with her mother-in-law. She understood her desire for harmony and recognized the inanity of a quarrel she herself did not enjoy. Kyōko ceased to resent Yamazaki Ikue's authoritarianism and agreed to work in the business once her children were old enough for her to work outside the home. Second, the divulgence of our interviews dispelled any mystery and reassured the entire family about the substance of my inquest.

A new set of difficulties appeared, however.

Three years had passed since our first interviews, and certain contradictions arose between the new and the old narratives. These contradictions all seemed to go in one direction; they attested to the fact that Yamazaki Ikue's growing professional success had conferred on her enough self-confidence to acknowledge difficulties and mistakes. In general, she embellished her past less. For instance, the reason for her leaving the Ginza salon, at first explained by the fear of a band of thugs sent by the competition, became a simple employee matter since, as she then said, "I have never been afraid of anything." I generally opted for the second version of the facts.

Another problem concerned the origins of the Endo family. My curiosity had led to a revival of Yamazaki Ikue's. A very positive woman, oriented toward the future rather than the past, she had been satisfied with the simple belief in the ancientness of her native house; in addition, she was more preoccupied with the rank of her family by marriage. Now, suddenly, she began to interrogate her sisters in Kōriyama. In turn, multiple versions of the Endo family history were presented to me. Here, too, I retained the last one given—the one that my narrator judged to be more "true."

A further complication occurred when her daughter Ryōko began to do her own research and found a document left by her mother's eldest brother; in addition, an Asaka resident gave me still other versions of the facts. By that point, it seemed to me that the essential elements of this labyrinth would have to be clarified—if not conveyed—through notes, which I have since added.

On the management of the business, especially the number of employees, in several instances I found Yamazaki Ikue's version differed from the figures given me by Endo Muneo. Except where the problem was obviously the result of involuntary error or forgetfulness (corrected after consultation), I used Yamazaki Ikue's version, deciding that her representation of reality was at least as important as reality itself.

During this entire period, Jean Malaurie regularly suggested trails to follow, new questions to ask that would help clarify the portrait of Yamazaki Ikue. Our relationship was by this time so trusting that my inquest had become an occasion for introspection. Back in Paris, I sent Yamazaki Ikue long letters, asking for her opinions on such subjects as the rise of women in Japanese politics. Or would she mind, one more time, drawing me a plan of the house she grew up in (for she had already given me three slightly different ones)? She fell into the habit of responding with long recorded monologues, with which she included charts.

Another major difficulty in writing the book was to find the right tone. Yamazaki Ikue speaks standard Tokyo Japanese (with a slight Tōhoku accent), and she sometimes uses patois terms for which it would have been absurd to seek equivalents. From what French regional speech could I have chosen them? More characteristic of her mode of expression, it seemed to me, was her taste for imagery and a precise, often careful lyricism, which made her shift between storytelling and oration. She has a talent for the discovery—whether scientifically true or false was of little import—of the etymology of words and characters, which conferred on her commentaries an often unexpected weight. I should observe that she was quite conscious she was speaking for a book, so she often adopted a more careful tone than the one she used in daily life.

From the point of view of style, the difficulties were compounded: I first ran up against the problems posed by any translation, which are obviously all the greater with a language as far from French as is Japanese. To cite just one example among a thousand, it is impossible to render the expression *yamato nadeshiko*, used by Yamazaki Ikue to describe the grace of her elder daughter, in French. *Yamato* designates the province of Japan in which ancient Japanese culture developed. *Nadeshiko* is defined in Japanese-French dictionaries as the flower *oeillet de Chine* [literally, "Chinese Pink," but known in English as sweet John]. Taken together, they denote the classic Japanese ideal of female beauty. This floral image, exotic in French, is a cliché in Japanese, but the use of clichés in Japanese poetics is a sign of culture and refinement, whereas in French it merely betrays a lack of imagination and real poetic sensibility. So the problem is inextricable.

Over these difficulties in the translation of individual words and phrases, larger problems loomed: could I keep using "I," the equivalent of *watakushi*, a four-syllable word that is rarely used in Japanese? (The spoken language usually dispenses with pronouns.) Could I state unequivocally that "protect" is equivalent to *mamoru*, a word full of *m*'s that make a sort of cocoon and that evokes the Japanese words for eyes and seeing (*me* and *ma*)?

Even trickier were the usual pitfalls in going from spoken language to written. In a written text, it is unthinkable to use numerous repetitions of words or phrases, linguistic tics, or aberrant syntactic gaps. In the same vein, it was hardly imaginable to render the intonations or facial expressions that always accompany the speaking of a phrase and are an integral part of its meaning. For a moment, I considered noting expressions or intonations in the margins, but that very quickly struck me as overly fastidious.

Here's a simple example, where boldface type denotes spoken emphasis:

> *Inaka nante nē, shōgakkō no undōkai ni nattara, mō mura no* **dai**gyōji *desu kara . . . mura no daigyōji desu kara ne . . . gakugei-kai to ittara, sorekara undōkai to ittara, mō mura* **daigyōji** *desu kara, seito no gyōji yori mo . . . mō mura no okāsan ya nanka wa o nigiri wo mottari mō nani shitari shite, goshisō wo* **ippai** *tsukutte, mō mushiro wo kakaete kite, soko he shiite, soshite jindotte . . . Anone, sorega tanoshimi da kara ne.* **Taisetsu** *na toki nan desu ne. Sakura no hana ga mankai na toko de yaru wake desu yo ne. Yokkatta desu yo!*

Literal translation:

> In the country like that, when it came time for the primary school sports event, because it was a big festival for the village . . . um . . . because it was a big festival for the village . . . um . . . whether it was a cultural gathering or a sports event, because it was more a big festival for the village than an elementary school pupils' festival . . . the mothers of the village and others brought *o nigiri* and also, well, they made all sorts of delicious things, and they came with *mushiro* in their arms,

they spread them out, and took their positions. Because it was an out-ing, it was fun. It was a very important time. We did it when all the cherry trees were in full blossom. It was great!

Final translation:

In a country area like ours, the entire village got involved in the annual sports festival. Like cultural or other gatherings, this festival was of far more concern to the villagers than to the students. So the mothers of the village and the other women prepared rice balls and all kinds of good things on which to feast. The ladies came, under their arms their rush mats, which they would spread out to make a camp. This affair was both a pleasure and an important time. The cherries were in blossom. All was right with the world!

Over the course of the project, I had the feeling of working on raw material, and the fear of remolding a character often stopped me. The selection of facts and the importance I granted them had necessarily to do with the way I myself looked on them—as well as on the life of this woman who, speaking not a word of French, could have no access to the manuscript save what I told her about it. My various attempts at writing convinced me that there could be no totally faithful witness: the only exact witness is that of experience, which, by definition, is not transmittable. Any telling of an event implies a redefining of it, an artificial carving up of time and ideas—one that is, at best, an interpretation and, at worst, a betrayal. In addition, to render that telling readable, I had to fashion a complex amalgam of diverse raw materials. To be sure I was not fooling myself, I translated some passages back into Japanese (without referring to the transcriptions of the tapes). I gave these to Yamazaki Ikue, who declared that she readily recognized herself in them.

Extract from an Interview

LC: Your mother-in-law, Naka, prayed fervently every day, you've told me. In that, was she very different from your mother?

YI: Yes, Mother was not very pious. And also, at the Endos' no one was exceptionally fervent. We wouldn't have had the time.

LC: But still, the altars in your native house were very big?

YI: It wasn't due to piety, but more because we were rich. They raised the prestige of the house. And Mother respected customs, those of men as she did the rites for the gods.

LC: What did she offer to the gods? Rice and water, I think . . .

YI: She offered rice, water, and the time for prayers. She didn't think one could give any more than that to the gods and ancestors in the other world.

The manuscript was more or less finalized when Jean Malaurie was invited to Japan on business in the winter of 1990. I had to go back to thank the Yamazakis for their long collaboration, to tell them about the upcoming appearance of the book, and to verify a few last points of detail. During dinner in an old Tokyo restaurant, Malaurie explained to them the importance of the Terre Humaine collection in which their history was to appear. He asked Yamazaki Ikue a few questions, especially about her political opinions, which he hoped she would elaborate on later with me. We also looked through the Yamazakis' family photo album and made a first selection of photos to appear in the book.

So this work, begun between Yamazaki Ikue and myself, had evolved not only into a concern of the entire family but into a matter of international relations.

Here I would like to thank those who have helped me. The Yamazaki family, of course, but also their employees, who always welcomed me with great kindness, especially Shige, who did several of the drawings reproduced in this book. Jean Malaurie, without whom this work would never have seen the light of day and who sustained me through all those years. Harmut O. Rotermund, who was so kind as to reread the entire manuscript for me. Bernard Frank, who made extremely pertinent suggestions, as did Simone Mauclaire, and, particularly, Miho Moto and Patrick Beillevaire, who contributed to the perfecting of the text.

Finally, I would like to thank Paul De Angelis, who is entirely responsible for the conception of the American edition of this book. May he find herein the expression of my admiration for his lucidity, and my gratitude for his immense kindness.

Letter from Yamazaki Ikue

May 26, 1990

To Monsieur Jean Malaurie, Director of the Terre Humaine series:

Twenty years have passed since I first met Laurence Caillet.

Only three months after that young woman came to live in Japan, she was able to speak Japanese to the point that she no longer had any difficulties communicating with us, which stupefied me. She is that extraordinarily gifted.

Whatever she once studies, she never forgets. I am certain that it is that capacity of assimilation that, along with her warm and human character, has allowed her to become the scholar she is today.

Because she is someone with very rich and very human sensibilities, my family and I feel that there is no difference between us, and the intimacy and trust which unite us are those which unite the members of the same family.

As she is a part of our family in that way, I hereby wish to state that I place my total confidence in her judgment as regards the publication of this book.

When she first spoke to me about her plan to write a book on the Yamazaki family and asked for my help, I was in complete agreement.

As a Japanese woman, I was all the more pleased that it was a woman who so quickly understood the Japanese spirit and who adapted herself so well.

I hope that, thanks to this book, many people, or even just one, will be able to understand both the true nature of the Japanese and my researches into methods of conserving health and youth. My particular hope is that the readers will come to understand, even if only a little bit, the Japanese people's way of thinking and that thereby the circle of those who want to live without war, in peace and happiness, might be enlarged.

For all these reasons, it is with joy that I authorize the publication of this book, which faithfully reflects what I have said—my words, my way of thinking, and my ideas. Being entirely in agreement with its contents, I state my wish that the Terre Humaine series, issued by the publishing house Plon, which is publishing this book in French, use our real family name, Yamazaki, and that that also be done in any editions to be published in languages other than Japanese. This is also the wish of all the members of my family. However, in order not to cause discomfort or inconvenience to others, I have asked Laurence Caillet to change the names of all those who are not members of the family.

293

In addition, my wish is that this book not be published in Japanese in its present form while my husband and I are still living.

Last, I authorize Plon to make use, free of charge, of the family photographs, documents, drawings, and so on, with which I have provided Laurence Caillet. The same applies to any future editions of the book in other languages.

I pray for the success of this enterprise.

Yamazaki Ikue (Nami)

The letter is countersigned by Yamazaki Tatsuo, Yamazaki Mitsunobu, Yamazaki Kyōko, Yamazaki Yasunobu (Yasuo), Yamazaki Tomiko (Motoko), Tanaka Teiichirō, Tanaka Ryōko, Endō Muneo, Yamazaki Hirotoshi.

TRANSLATOR'S NOTE

I was doubly pleased when asked to translate this book—as a translator, my two languages are French and Japanese. Odd though it may seem that we have translated the autobiography of a Japanese woman from the French, the fact is that the book does not exist in Japanese.

Ideally, a translator works from the language in which material originates; each subsequent translation implies the possibility of further distortion. In this regard, Laurence Caillet's liberal use of Japanese terms, phrases, poetry, proverbs, and so on, was of great help to me; with a few exceptions, I translated all Japanese elements directly. But for the bulk of the text, my translation problems were compounded by the divergent implications of a vocabulary historically developed to express the concerns of French society having been used in the service of a Japanese context. It was my task to make English of it (to make it "neutral" to English readers). In this and in matters of culture, my experience with the Japanese language and my time spent in Japan were invaluable.

Many thanks to Laurence Caillet for her detailed answers to our queries. Thanks, too, to Paul De Angelis for his kind support on this and other projects.

Last, I wish to join Mrs. Yamazaki in her hope that this (English version of the) book will add to the world's understanding and appreciation of the Japanese people.

Megan Backus
New York, NY
July 1993

Notes

Prologue

1. The blackberry lily (*Belamcanda chinensis*) is a wild perennial of the Iridaceae family cultivated for its decorative orange flowers. Its seeds are an intense, shiny black.

Chapter 1: Origins

1. The word *kami* designates all supernatural entities of the indigenous Japanese religion called Shinto (Way of the Gods); it includes both gods and long-deceased ancestors.

2. The term "powerful house" (*gōka* in Japanese) implies luxury. Contradicting herself, Yamazaki Ikue later declares that it was during her own childhood that her family was at the height of its wealth. Japanese people often "valorize" their origins in order to legitimize present success.

3. Kōriyama, a city of around 300,000 inhabitants, is the major railway hub of Fukushima Prefecture.

4. The old Japanese names for the "barbarian" fisher-gatherer population living in the north of Japan were Emishi or Ezo. It is unclear whether these people were Ainu or Japanese. The campaign to subdue them began in the ninth century, after which the term *sei-i tai-shōgun* (great general charged with the pacification of the barbarians), coined by the emperor in the eighth century, fell into disuse. It was taken up again, however, by Minamoto no Yoritomo (1147–1199), founder of the military government based in Kamakura, the *bakufu*, in reference to himself, after he relegated the emperor to second-rank status.

The poem on the wall of Nakoso associates the ephemerality of flowers with the destiny of young warriors killed in combat.

5. Nōin-Hōshi (988–?), poet-monk who made a pilgrimage to Ōshū, the "province at the end of the world"—that is, in the north.

6. This is the title of a famous haiku composed by the poet Matsuo Bashō (1644–1694) during a trip through the north of Japan.

7. At the end of each summer (mid-August according to the old Japanese calendar), the souls of the dead return to the houses of their descendants, who offer them dances and food in hopes of improving their own fate in the next world and benefiting from their protection. The ancestors use a variety of vehicles to travel back to their villages: wildflowers that are cut in the mountains, horses and oxen which children make out of cucumbers and eggplants, and dragonflies which have a red spot in the form of a saddle on their backs. The most beautiful insects, especially dragonflies and butterflies, are also sometimes considered forms of reincarnation favored by the dead—as are rare flowers.

8. Linguists propose three interpretations for the word *ubu-suna*. Written with the characters for "childbirth" and "sand," it would mean "land of one's birth." It could also be written with the characters for "childbirth" and "place of habitation," which lends it the meaning "place of birth," most often one's place of residence. The third interpretation, broken down into "childbirth," "root," and "action," would mean the energy of spontaneous growth that is at the origin of all things.

This god of the land of one's birth is often confused with *uji-gami*, a divinity conceived of as ancestral, to whom the inhabitants of a place are attached through a genealogy (whether factual or not). This confusion reflects the overlapping of territorial and blood ties, which, in religious terms, underlies a tendency to consider humanity and nature as one.

9. *Records of Ancient Matters* was compiled by imperial edict in 712 and is about fifty pages long. It relates the genesis of the archipelago, the mythic founding of the state of Japan, and the reigns of the first sovereigns.

10. While it means "body," the word *mi* is written with the character 身 , which represents a pregnant woman. When *mi* denotes "fruit," it is written with 実 , which shows valuables under a roof. The common origin of the two words is not in doubt among etymologists.

11. Even though births take place in hospitals today, the custom of conserving the umbilical cord continues. It is placed in a case and given to the mother.

12. This reference to ancient mythology is erroneous. According to *Records of Ancient Matters*, silkworms were born from the head of the goddess of food, rice from her eyes, millet from her ears, azuki beans from her nose, *mugi* (wheat and barley) from her vagina, and soy from her anus. But the *Nihonshiki* (the *Annals of Japan* [720] presents versions very close to those of Yamazaki Ikue. Her speculation reflects the metaphorical confusion between agricultural cycles and human reproduction, which is the basis of all the variants of the myth.

13. Kannon (or Kanzeon) is the Japanese name for Avalokiteśvara, the bodhisattva of compassion, who, along with Seishi (Mahāsthāmaprāpta), the bodhisattva of wisdom, is seated next to Amida (Amithāba), the buddha of the Pure Land or Western Paradise. Kannon resides on Mount Fudaraku (Potalaka), which is in the sea to the south of India. Nyoirin Kannon is represented with six arms. Kannon was first feminized in China. For a time in Japan, s/he was even assimilated by the Christians with the redemptive Virgin.

The principal Buddhist entities and certain particularly popular Shinto gods all have their days of connection, on which prayers addressed to them are more easily answered. These days, *ennichi*—a distortion of *enichi* or day of gathering (for Buddhist teaching)—have been replaced today by small fairs held outside shrines. The atmosphere often recalls a European village fair.

14. Koyasu, whose name means "makes children easy," is a god who facilitates easy childbirth, a god of fecundity and painless education, often identified with the goddess Kono Hana no Sakuya Hime, mythical wife of the first celestial emperor on earth. But in certain cases the word *koyasu* may also designate appeals to other dieties, notably Kannon and Jizō. The latter, known as Kśitigarbha in Sanskrit, is the bodhisattva who watches over the six paths of rebirth and protects dead children.

15. The celebration of the maternity band is most often held in the fifth month of pregnancy, but in certain regions it takes place in the third or seventh month and furnishes the occasion for announcing the coming birth publicly. During the Edo Period (1603–1867), in which infanticide was common, it was forbidden to practice abortion after the celebration of this ceremony.

16. The *nando*, used as a bedroom for the master of the house or the eldest son, or (as in the Endo house) a storage room, is often located in the most sacred corner of the house, in the auspicious northwesterly direction. It may also house a small altar consecrated to the god of the rice paddies.

17. Until 1945, a village birthing hut was still in use in southwestern Japan. New mothers stayed there for thirty days after giving birth (as opposed to fifty at the turn of the century); they then moved to another, more spacious, cabin, the *fujō goya*, or cabin of impurity, for twenty days (twenty-five at the turn of the century). At the end of those fifty days of seclusion, women purified themselves by throwing salt on the ground before returning to their homes. Today, in Mie and Kagawa prefectures, some villages provide modern *ubu-ya*, considered resting houses for new mothers, who are obligated to stay in them.

18. Tatami mats, the traditional floor covering of Japanese homes, are six feet long (about the length of a man lying down) by three feet wide. The area of a traditional Japanese room is indicated by the number of tatami covering the floor.

19. The lunar-solar calendar, Chinese in origin, is based on the calculation of new moons, solstices, and equinoxes. The months, which have either twenty-nine or thirty days, last from new moon to new moon. The harmonization of the lunar calendar with the solar calendar necessitates the insertion of seven supplementary months over a nineteen-year period. These thirteenth months are called intersert months.

20. Even today, most women return to their native homes for the birth of a first child.

21. Like most divinities linked to metal, Hachiman was a god of war. According to one tradition, Hachiman was a legendary emperor. As his cult—of a god who soon became the protector of all warriors—spread across Japan, his name was eventually conferred on the most diverse gods.

22. Under the effect of physical or moral suffering, notably jealousy or fear, or else at the new year or the change of seasons, the soul, or *tama*, has a tendency to leave the body. Therefore, rites must be performed to allow the soul to reestablish itself in the body. Various techniques may be used: the garments of the endangered individual (or a substitute for them) are shaken; the presiding professional strikes the feet of the patient noisily against the ground; or the *tama no o* (the string of the soul) is knotted, relinking the spirit to the body.

It is the forsaking of the body by the spirit that provokes death. This is why one of the first funerary rites performed is the *tama-yobai*, or "calling of the soul," an attempt to call back the soul of the deceased.

23. The dead are said to leave the otherworld two days before O-Bon, the feast of the dead that takes place in mid-August. For those who have suffered retribution for their acts, the departure from the underworld is violent: they bellow as they lift the covers of the boiling caldrons where they usually reside, break down the infernal gateway, and so on. This violence, a sign of their dissatisfaction with their lot, justifies the rites of appeasement that are then offered to them.

24. Destiny, or *innen*, "causal bonds," is a Buddhist term that designates the karmic causality constituted by the totality of acts performed in past lives. In a Japanese context, in which reincarnation has never been a unified dogma, this sort of destiny is usually justified by the acts of the ancestors as much as by one's own.

25. Japanese ethnographers and theologians are hardly more precise than Yamazaki Ikue in their definition of the god of birth (*ubu-gami*). This is the god who watches over a woman after she changes her ordinary belt for a maternity band and helps her with labor. It is explicitly affirmed that the god of the land of one's birth (*ubu-suna-gami*), like all the other gods except the god of birth, keeps his distance from pregnant women and flees places where birth occurs because of his horror of blood. Nevertheless, the sand that is sometimes placed at the head of the woman giving birth to aid with her labor comes from the shrine of the god of the land of one's birth, and it is that god whom the mother thanks after she emerges from her confinement.

According to a classic hypothesis, this incoherence results from a confusion of the ancestral god *uji-gami* with the god of the land of one's birth, *ubu-suna-gami*, who, says the theory, would originally have had no fear of the defilement of blood. The amalgam of the two divinities would have provoked the extension of interdictions imposed on the blood to the god of the land of one's birth and, finally, induced the invention of a new god of birth, friendly to blood. The close resemblance of the two gods' names—*ubu-suna-gami* and *ubu-gami*—betrays their common origin.

26. From 1915 to 1920, Japan's population rose 10.1 percent a year (as opposed to 5.0 percent during the years of the Meiji Restoration). In spite of increases in agricultural production, the countryside suddenly seemed overpopulated. As a result, daughters and younger sons, all excluded from inheritance to some degree, flocked to the cities, giving rapid rise to a poverty-stricken urban proletariat.

The life of these workers, divorced from tradition and considered promiscuous, explains in part the development of the agrarian schools of thought that began in the eighteenth century. According to their adherents, it was family farming that furnished the foundations of a state conceived of as a "large family" and that permitted alimentary self-sufficiency, an indispensable condition for the perpetuation of Dai Nippon (Great Japan). Even though immigration to Manchuria was not very successful, these ideas played a considerable role in the militarist politics of the 1930s.

27. It is believed that the vital energy, the *tama*, is transitorily incarnated in the rice of one's birth, *ubu-meshi*. In light of this belief, ingestion of this rice is thought to foster restoration of the mother's strength and help increase the vigor of the child.

28. The milk mother, or *chi-tsuke oya*, is more often chosen without regard to the sexes of the children. Unlike that of a Western wet nurse, her function is purely ritualistic. She gives only a small amount of milk, which is mixed with the milk of the natural mother for one nursing only—the idea being to multiply the newborn's sources of vitality. In all cases, the child retains a lifelong fictive kinship with the milk mother, visiting her for the principal holidays (especially the new year) and receiving small presents on these occasions.

29. Rivers, perceived as fissures in the earth's crust, are considered dangerous areas, affording access to the other world. The crossing of the bridge reiterates the child's coming into the world, while the exorcism of the dangers of water lessens the risk of his spirit's return to the other world.

30. The choice of a first name for a child often provides the occasion for establishing familial relations between the child and a name-giving father, a *na-tsuke oya*. As with the milk mother, these relations are lifelong.

Purely phonetic transcriptions of girls' names were very common until around the mid-1920s.

31. The first pilgrimage to the shrine of the god of the land of one's birth, the tutelary god of the village, marked the beginning of the child's integration into the village community. On that occasion, the baby would be dressed in a costume donated by the maternal grandparents.

32. This cessation of nursing, probably the result of a lack of milk, is unusually early. Nursing infants were not usually cut off until the birth of the next sibling, passing directly from the breast to a normal diet. When a baby was cut off too young for solid food, it would be fed on rice-cooking water.

In the 1940s the government tried to induce mothers to stop nursing around eight months.

Women, who considered breast feeding to be among the greatest pleasures in life, offered a lively resistance to this official propaganda.

Chapter 2: The House of Endo

1. The word *ie*, house (etymologically, "hearth"), which designates the traditional domestic system, is currently contrasted with *kazoku* (literally, "the people of the house"), which applies to the more restricted modern family, especially the *kaku-kazoku*, the nuclear family, which sprang up in the 1950s. This opposition is perceived as an exemplary expression of the contrast between a past, considered specifically Japanese, and a modernity marred by Western influences.

The *ie* is thought of as a perennial entity that includes all the living members of a patrilinear family community (generally excluding collateral spouses), their ancestors, and their descendants yet to be born, as well as those contributing to the practical effectuation of the patrimony, such as servants and agricultural workers who live in.

The Japanese house is characterized by its systematic recourse to adoption in the absence of a male heir. This rule, which authorizes the choosing of an heir who may or may not have living natural parents, allows for the formal observance of the principle of patrilinear continuity, on which the whole social system is based.

In the seventeenth and eighteenth centuries, the house was the essential unit of Japanese society, reaffirming the ultimate model of administrative and political structure. It also served as an all-encompassing framework, preventing the growth of individualism. Abolished as a legal entity in the aftermath of the Second World War, the institution of the house was long criticized for its feudal character. Today, however, it is looked upon favorably, as the matrix of the values of harmony and efficiency which will further the building of the society.

2. Buddhism was introduced into Japan from the Asian continent beginning in the sixth century. This elaborate system of thought, rather than obliterating the indigenous Shinto (Way of the Gods) religion, contributed to a doctrinal reinforcement of that aboriginal animism and promoted the formation of an original syncretism, in which Buddhist and Shinto practices coexist. Today the Japanese adhere concurrently to both religions, as evidenced by the close proximity in many private homes of Buddhist and Shinto altars. The Shinto gods have the exclusive function of assuring happiness and good fortune in this life. Buddhism, while it had to offer tangible, short-term benefits in order to gain popular acceptance, also brought—in its function as a religion of individual salvation—new eschatological developments. Therefore, the principal events of worldly life, birth and marriage, are celebrated according to Shinto rites, while burials and funerary commemorations are within the jurisdiction of Buddhist thought. At the end of a long process of Buddhist purification rites, the deceased will lose his living identity. He may reincarnate in conformance with Buddhist dogma, or—especially if he is the eldest son (inheritor) of a house— he may merge with the ancestral Shinto powers of nature and watch over his descendants. Both fates may coexist, not stringently differentiated in the minds of the surviving family.

The Buddhist altar, a sort of tabernacle representing the chancel of a Buddhist temple, houses the funerary tablets, which bear the posthumous names of the family's recent dead. Each of these remains in place for the duration of the deindividualization process of the person they represent. Ceremonies are performed regularly during this period, which ranges from seven to one hundred years, in order to liberate the soul of the deceased. Once this ritual period is over, the funerary tablet is either destroyed or put aside; thereafter, the deceased is venerated only on the *kami-dana*, a simple platform decorated with Shinto symbols.

The widespread diffusion of domestic altars in the eighteenth century corresponds historically to the affirmation of the house as the archetype of familial organization.

3. The analogy between familial patrimony and national lands is sustained by the political ideology of the Family-State, the *kazoku-kokka*, which was elaborated by nationalist thinkers at the end of the nineteenth century. This official doctrine reinterpreted mythology transcribed in the eighth century, which portrayed the emperors as direct descendants of the gods of the archipelago in terms of Neo-Confucian morality. Identifying loyalty to the sovereign with filial piety, this doctrine also upheld the notion of a common biological origin of the Japanese population and defined the entire nation as a large family placed under the authority of a sovereign father.

4. The development of individualism along Western lines, thought to be founded exclusively on selfishness, is one of the favorite themes of the Japanese when they speak of themselves. It ranks high among the list of evils engendered by modernization. Therefore, the selfishness of businesses is often designated as the primary cause of urban pollution. When this issue arose in the 1970s, the seriousness of the pollution problem contributed to the debate about the benefits of economic growth. Individualism, whose development is tied to the nuclearization of the family, is

also perceived as the principal cause of the solitude of the aged and the sometimes spectacular aggressiveness of the young.

5. Social organization in Japan orders groups and individuals according to principles perceived as primordial, by time and by place, in what is held to be a simple reflection of natural law. The hierarchy that unites locally defined groups or their members is seniority. Just as the emperor is descended from cosmogonic divinities, dominant houses of villages descend from founders, who cleared the sites for habitation, and the leader of a group of houses related either biologically or according to accepted tradition is in principle the elder son of the senior branch.

The traditional subordination of material success to rank conferred by birth, as well as the persistent confusion between nobility of blood and virtue, prompts those who ascend to wealth to attribute valorous ancestors to themselves retrospectively. That is why most wealthy rural landowning families today claim samurai ancestors. By this they indicate that they are descended from the warrior class that dominated the social order during the Edo Period. Additionally, there are many who, via fantasized genealogies, claim descent from legendary heroes of the Middle Ages, nobles related to the Imperial Household, or, going back even further, from gods distinct from their own divinitized human ancestors. In these cases the later demotion of the family is often explained by membership in a clan vanquished in one of the wars that devastated the country until the modern era. The ancestor thus appears in the light of pathetic hero, after whose wanderings a quiet village existence must have appeared a haven of peace and happiness.

Before the Meiji Restoration, only the aristocracy and the families of samurai had last names; therefore, the ancient existence of the name Endo would reinforce the family's thesis about its warrior origins. It could also be supposed that the family were simple *ashigaru*, low-ranking foot soldiers, originally armed with two sabers, and later, during the Edo Period, with bows or firearms.

6. Yamazaki Ikue's version of the quarrel between the two brothers is not historically accurate. Knowing that after his remarkable military successes his brother wanted him dead, Yoshitsune fled to Hiraizumi (in the present-day Iwate Prefecture), a city developed in the eleventh century by a branch of the great northern Fujiwara family. There, Yoshitsune was welcomed by Fujiwara Hidehira (1096–1187), who put lands at his disposal, but upon his death his son and successor, Yasuhira (?–1189) chose to ally with Yoritomo. Besieged, Yoshitsune killed his wife and children before taking his own life. Yasuhira (not Kudo, as Yamazaki Ikue relates) carried his head to Yoritomo. Yoritomo ordered the successor's death as well, then distributed lands of Mutsu to his personal allies.

7. Yamazaki Ikue is correct in stating that the Itō, following the victory of the Minamoto in the northeast, received Asaka as their domain. In fact, the entire prefecture of Fukushima was placed under the dominion of leaders from the Kantō region near Tokyo, most of whom were content to send representatives to the northeast and continued to reside in their region of origin.

8. The designation "Warring States Period" was created by modern historians and covers a century of civil wars (1467–1568) between lords who, cut off from the eldest blood lines residing at court, resorted to uninterrupted battles for the affirmation of their local supremacy and the appropriation of new domains.

9. The Itō were to rule Asaka until around the end of the sixteenth century, but they had to defend it numerous times against more important lords, as well as reinforce their authority among the peasantry. To this end, they made a number of alliances with other local lords. All were defeated, however, by the Date clan, whom they battled on the plain of Asaka in 1589 and 1590. These are most likely the battles in which the ancestors of the Endo family participated.

Date Masamune (1567–1636), a famous warrior who was at one time favorably disposed toward Christianity, was also known as a protector of the arts and sciences. In 1589, he established himself by force of arms in the fief of Aizu, but he soon had to cede that domain to Gamō Ujisato (1556–1595). From the age of thirteen, the latter came to the attention, for his weapon making, of one of the principal contributors to the unification of the nation, Oda Nobunaga, whose son-in-law he became.

10. The three mountains of Kumano, in the Kii Peninsula in the south of Wakayama Prefecture, are among the most sacred locations of Buddhist-Shinto syncretism. Since ancient times, this site has been considered one of the places in Japan from which one can easily accede to the other world, to the paradise of Fudaraku-zan (Sanskrit: Potalaka), residence of the bodhisattva Kannon.

After the Imperial Family made several pilgrimages in the twelfth century, common people began to go there in such numbers that it gave rise to the expression "a pilgrimage of ants to Kumano." At that time, the ascetics of Kumano, called *yama-bushi*, followers of the Way of acquisition of magical powers through asceticism (*Shugendō*), began to travel throughout the provinces, diffusing the cult of the holy mountains.

Ise is also on the Kii Peninsula. Since antiquity it has housed the shrine of Amaterasu, the goddess of the sun. According to national beliefs, her descendants, the emperors, have reigned over the archipelago since 660 B.C.

11. A *koku* is a unit of volumetric measure used for unshucked rice (one *koku* = about five bushels). The *koku* was also employed as a reference in evaluating land tax revenues, which explains Yamazaki Ikue's metonymic use of the word here.

12. Yamazaki Ansai (1618–1682), a Neo-Confucian thinker born in Kyoto, is also known as the founder of a Shinto sect, Suika Shinto. Although it is entirely inspired by Sung Dynasty thought, Suika doctrine paradoxically is strongly colored by a nationalism mistrustful of unconditional admiration for China. This feeling was shared by most of Yamazaki Ansai's contemporaries.

On his eventual ties with the family of Endo Nami's husband, see chapters 16 through 18.

13. The Meiji Restoration of 1868 marked the entry of Japan into the modern world. The upheavals were provoked by lords who reproached the shogunate for its inability to defend Japan against the insistence of Western powers that it open its doors and by partisans of the return of the emperor to the forefront of the political scene. Their plottings, which were at first conservative, would eventually lead to the abolition of the feudal system and the construction of a modern, industrialized state, with a constitution inspired by European legislative apparati, notably French and German.

14. In the seventeenth century, tenant farmers and servants accounted for as much as 60 percent of the population in the poorer provinces. In most of Japan, this system disappeared before the end of the Edo Period, but it continued until the Second World War in more remote areas, notably in Tōhoku.

15. In Tōhoku, houses that were related by blood ties, united by territorial or work bonds, were generally organized into hierarchical groupings known locally as *maki* (groups) and known technically as *dōzoku* (same clan or race). At the center of these was an originating house or *honke* (main house or principal house), which occupied the preeminent position; the other houses, or *bunke* (branch houses or separate houses), had grown out of it for the most part. This new hierarchical structure was largely a consequence of the rule of inheritance through male primogeniture. When the father retired, one of the children—most often the eldest son—inherited primary authority over the family, the house, and the ancestral altars, as well as the greater part of the family's assets.

Although their social position was somewhat higher, the situation of younger sons was comparable to that of tenant farmers, who could also acquire the status of "separate house" and, in that capacity, could assume a place in the hierarchy. Like the younger sons, they were obligated to perform labor for the landholder who was their father or their elder brother.

16. Houses retaining dominant positions are often called *kusa-wake*, those who have "divided the wild grasses," who have cleared the land and made it valuable. The installation of a newcomer in the village and his access to communal holdings (mountains, forests, grazing land, and so on) were subject to the approval of one of the houses considered to be a founding house, with whom the stranger would have to form familylike ties of subordination.

17. It was around this time that the genealogy (based on civil records) established by Yamazaki Ikue's oldest brother, Yoshiki, began. According to this document, the house of Endo in the hamlet of Kitai was founded by one Unomatsu, born in 1806, who received the right to found a "separate house" from Endo Tadaichi, probably his older brother and himself the son of Endo Shinjūrō.

18. In order to resist the imperial army organized in 1867, the Matsudaira levied an army of young men from their fief. They grouped the recruits by age into four brigades, each designated by the name of a mythic animal which represented one of the four cardinal points. The Byakkotai or White Tiger Brigade grouped youths of sixteen and seventeen years; the three other brigades were the Suzaku or Red Bird, the Seiryū or Blue Dragon, and the Genpu, named for a black monster with the shell of a tortoise and the tail of a serpent.

Almost half of the No. 2 White Tiger Brigade died during this defeat. As Yamazaki Ikue indicates, the survivors committed group suicide. In fact, however, one escaped.

In the regions of the north, the civil war ended in the spring of 1869.

19. It may appear surprising, from a Western viewpoint, to make offerings to the soul of an enemy. However, indigenous beliefs affirm that all who died in a state of dissatisfaction—espe-

cially young warriors who died without issue—are likely to haunt those who, whether voluntarily or not, have contributed to their unhappy destinies.

20. Inheritances were as a general rule transmissible only to men. Where the sole heir was a daughter, the custom of adopting a husband for her who would serve as the inheriting son prevailed. This practice is still common.

21. The *tagaku nōzeisha giin* sat in the Chamber of Peers, which also included members of the Imperial Family, nobles, and eminent personages. These rich men were chosen from each prefecture, according to fixed numbers prorated on the taxes paid, from among the large contributors over thirty years of age. Being a candidate for such a post was considered a great honor.

22. Adopted sons-in-law were often considered dowry hunters and consequently found themselves accused of incompetence or dishonesty. In fact, according to the oldest Yamazaki brother, it was the brother-in-law of this man, the founder of a sort of familial mutual bank who died without leaving an account, who was at the origin of the family's ruin.

Furthermore, Yamazaki Ikue's assertion that her grandfather was adopted is erroneous. It is based on her desire to explain both Heizaburō's having married into a higher social rank and his disreputable conduct, which in her mind could only be accounted for by the artificiality of his ties to the house of Endo.

23. The ruin of the Endo family was aggravated by the economic difficulties which developed in Japan following the First World War and the crisis of 1929.

24. Traditional solidarity among the Japanese is not so spontaneous as one is sometimes led to believe on the basis of nostalgic ruminations. While wet paddy rice cultivation required the cooperation of all inhabitants, the communal character of the village was forged above all during the civil wars, when peasant-warriors had to assure the defense of their homes themselves. It was strengthened during the Edo Period, when the Tokugawa government constituted the village as an administrative unit for the tax surveys of assets and required that villagers gather themselves into groups of five neighboring houses, thus establishing a rule of fiscal and penal coresponsibility.

25. On the domestic level, the mistress of the house is the principal priestess of the gods. The master will officiate for more important rites, especially those of the village community, where he represents the house or a group of related houses.

According to Japanese beliefs, a demon is not an evil entity but one endowed with extraordinary power, which he may use for the better as much as for the worse: for example, the grimace of a demon is thought to keep maleficent forces at bay.

The word *oni* (demon), which has the etymological sense of "hidden," appeared in the ninth century; before that, the character employed to write "demon" was *mono*. This latter term literally means a "thing," either tangible or perceptible; it has not changed in meaning over time, and it serves as a euphemism for anything one does not dare refer to directly.

Japanese demonological conceptions, however, were profoundly modified by concepts imported from the Asian continent. In Taoism and the Way of Yin and Yang, demons (in Chinese, *gui*) were evil entities who had to be pacified through rites, while according to Buddhist doctrine demons had to be converted and put to the service of the law. The fusion of these diverse interpretations of the nature of demons has resulted in the essential ambiguity of the Japanese *oni*.

26. In former times, only the roofs of palaces and Buddhist temples were tiled. That covering consisted of a double layer of interlocking round tiles, which formed an extremely heavy roof requiring a very sturdy supporting framework. Even after the invention of simpler tiles in the Edo Period, tiles remained a luxury reserved for noble residences. In addition, according to the sumptuary laws that the Tokugawa shoguns had decreed for each social class, thatched roofs were reserved for landowners, while the roofs of the houses of tenant farmers were covered with shingles, rushes, and so on. Thus, in the 1920s, a thatched roof still bore witness to a certain prosperity.

27. If all goes as planned, the inheritance is transmitted from a living father to an eldest son. This passing on of the powers is effectuated when one of the following conditions is met: the son has children himself; all the brothers of the heir are married; the head of the family reaches the age of sixty, which traditionally marks the beginning of old age (sixty years represents a complete cycle of the traditional Chinese-derived calendar); or there are health considerations or other reasons that make it convenient for the father to step down. Most often, the outgoing head of the family will then retire to a room reserved for him. However, he might move into a separate house, sometimes accompanied by unmarried children; when the family's holdings are extensive enough, he receives a parcel of land that he may cultivate for his own use.

When exceptional longevity coincides with a degree of material prosperity, two retirement houses are provided, for two generations of retired heads of the family. A multiplicity of residential buildings on a property bears witness to the wealth and prestige of the house.

28. Geomancy is based on a theory of the five elements—wood, earth, fire, water, metal— which compose the universe, the varying balance of which determines the destinies of beings and things. In Japan, these techniques of divination were especially widespread among the aristocracy, in educated settings, and in the cities in general; in the countryside, certain of the precepts of geomancy were applied, but without a knowledge of the total system.

29. *Mochi* are steamed cakes of rice gluten, pounded and most often molded into squat balls, sometimes flavored with azuki beans, chestnuts, or other additions. The name of this ritual dish, which is especially associated with the New Year celebrations, probably comes from *mochi-zuki*, "full moon," the high point of a festival. According to another hypothesis, *mochi* is derived from the verb *motsu*, which means "have" or "keep."

30. The village of Azuma is to the south of Kōriyama, not far from the hot springs called Nekonaki, meaning "meowing of a cat."

31. The Buddhist title *hōin*, or seal of the law, is bestowed, especially in Tōhoku, on those religious who have shamanic powers and who are consulted for solutions to problems of everyday life.

32. The Japanese feel that even the domesticated cat has the potential to become dangerous because of its independent nature. Numerous legends relate the presence of cat villages in the mountains, and the existence, in the sea, of isles inhabited solely by cats. For sailors or mountain folk, meeting a cat is an unpropitious omen. Among cats, only the three-colored variety, *mike-neko*, who are said to announce the weather, are considered lucky.

Buddhists say that the cat was the only animal who did not weep over the death of the Buddha.

33. *Tabi* are traditional split-toed white socks.

34. The god of the hearth is represented, near the family fire, by a repugnant mask or by symbols made of cut paper that are placed on a special platform, also decorated with paper charms; the symbols vary locally. This god specializes in the protection of the cooking and heating fires. Because the hearth designates by extension the domestic group, he also functions as a general household divinity.

Like most gods of the people, the god of the hearth travels seasonally between the house and the mountain, between sky and earth, and he shares certain attributes of the agricultural divinities as well as the ancestors: he may be the god of the land or the tutelary divinity of horses. In Tōhoku, under the name Kōjin, "wild god," he is a male god who often is mated with a goddess of agricultural production, O Kama Sama, the hearth. The name Kōjin, undoubtedly of scholarly origin, suggests that the cult was diffused beginning in the Middle Ages by monks and itinerant exorcists.

35. The supremacy of the head of the family, legally mandated only until the end of World War II, found form in a number of privileges that have survived to the present: he has rights to a place near the hearth or in front of the decorative alcove that adorns the main room of the house; he is served a higher-quality diet than the other members of the house; and he is the first to enter a freshly drawn bath.

36. The *Daikoku-bashira* is technically as well as symbolically the principal pillar of the house. Its consecration to the god Daikoku seems to go back to the second half of the sixteenth century, when his cult as a divinity of luck spread to the populace.

Daikoku was originally an Indian god, Mahākāla, Great Black, a warrior god with an enraged expression, possessing three faces and six arms. In China he became an agrarian divinity and protector of dining halls, losing his extra heads and arms. It was therefore as a good-natured god and protector of Buddhist law that he was introduced to Japan, principally through the Tendai school of Buddhist thought. Eventually, as part of the fusionary process, which required of each borrowed divinity a Japanese counterpart conceived of as a "local" manifestation, Daikoku was assimilated into one of the principal divinities of ancient Japanese mythology, Ō-Kuni-Nushi, the Great Master of the Country, whose name, via a play of phonetics, can be read *daikoku*. That no doubt contributed to his being brought from the kitchen to extend his expertise to the entire house and the ground on which it stands.

On the pillar consecrated to him, he is represented by a glued paper charm or by a small statue that shows him in the aspect of a plump personage, carrying rice balls (this statue is placed in a special indentation). The master of the house periodically makes offerings to him.

37. The absence in Japanese homes, until very recently, of collective or individual bedrooms is generally justified by the dearth of space. Although that argument holds for large cities like Tokyo, it seems ill-fitted to rural areas. In farmhouses, which were sometimes extremely large,

there was traditionally very little differentiation between bedrooms and living rooms, and an individual sleeping in a room alone would have been an exceptional event. While the possession of a bedroom was among the prerogatives of the master couple of the house, they would usually share that room with the youngest of their children. In fact, the presence of several small children sometimes obligated the mother and father to sleep separately: the mother would sleep with the youngest child, the father with one or several of the older ones. In addition, relatives or guests would often sleep with one or several of the children of the masters of the house.

Boys and girls are separated before puberty, when possible.

38. This Chinese-derived expression means "a passion for reading."

39. *Mushiro* is the generic term for woven mats, of bamboo, straw, or various kinds of rushes.

40. Residence in an unoccupied retirement house is a privilege of the heir.

41. The use of the graphic shapes of characters from the two phonetic syllabaries of Japanese, *katakana* and *hiragana*, to describe configurations, floor plans, body positions, and so on is common. A square house plan is described as *ta* 田 , the Chinese character for "rice paddy"; the *katakana* サ (*sa*) suggests a rectangular plan, while the *hiragana* さ (*sa*) describes the human body in the fetal position.

42. During the postwar occupation, the Americans believed that agrarian reform was an essential element of democratization. They also were responsive to the wishes of a number of Japanese leaders, especially Communists and Socialists, who saw in the reforms a way of increasing agricultural production. Central to this reform was the abolition of the tenant farming system, which favored the enrichment of parasitic landowners, the *kisei jinushi*, those who neither resided on nor exploited their properties directly.

The reforms were enacted from 1945 to 1947. The state repurchased lands held by nonresident and nonfarmer proprietors; holdings of one *chō* (2.45 acres) or less remained in the hands of nonfarmer residents (in Hokkaidō, this was increased to four chō). The lands ceded to the government were resold to small farmers and former tenant farmers.

But this reform was only partially successful. The large landholders tried to skirt the law. They attributed some parcels to fictitious family members or—with the help of relatives or loyal (or intimidated) tenant farmers—passed themselves off as owner-farmers. This is exactly what happened in the Endo family; they retained close to three acres of farmland, as well as their orchard, which was officially considered a "noncultivated ornamental garden."

Nevertheless, the nonindexation of land prices during that period of uncontrolled inflation was in the end injurious to the big landowners. Finally, the obligation to farm one's own land, as defined by that law, still hampers the rationalization of agriculture; the cost of engaging in farming, especially in rice culture, is very high.

43. Traditionally, villages organized several cooperative groups, their members classed by age (especially the youth), neighborhood, or other factors. These groups performed tasks that had a collective or individual benefit, according to a reciprocal system of mutual aid. For instance, they oversaw the levels of the water supplies used for irrigation, fought fires, maintained the roads, and rethatched roofs. They also organized the rice planting, as well as marriages and funerals.

The decline of these groups after the war contributed to the disappearance of thatched roofs. Today, thatched roofs are making a comeback, albeit at an exorbitant price.

44. The god of the land on which one's house stands is called *yashiki-gami*. He may be considered either an ancestor or a local divinity, reflecting the inextricable character of familial ties and ties to the land. In certain villages, only the principal houses had the privilege of consecrating an altar to this god in a corner of their yards; the related, surrounding houses subordinate to it might be included in the celebration of his cult. Elsewhere, all houses possessed a *yashiki-gami*, or this god protected entire neighborhoods.

45. While the influence of Buddhist art gave rise to some Shinto gods' being represented in human form, that practice remains fundamentally foreign to Shinto. Most often, gods are incarnated either by natural objects with extraordinary forms (forked trees, twisted stones or rocks) or by more or less manufactured objects (cut green branches, bands of paper cut and folded in zigzags, mirrors).

46. Inari, the only rice divinity with a clearly individuated personality, is undoubtedly the most popular god in the Japanese pantheon. Throughout the nation there are tens of thousands of shrines consecrated to Inari and to his messenger, the fox (who is sometimes confused with him). Offerings to this god, more or less identified with the ancestors, are presented on the domestic Shinto altar as well as in the chapel dedicated to the god of built-upon land.

Some Japanese authors suggest that Inari favors the fox because continental cosmology associates the color yellow with the earth element and the fur of the fox is yellow. It would therefore be via the earth that the fox is linked to fertility and to grains. In addition, some myths from southern Japan specifically attribute the origin of grains to an act of theft committed by a fox.

47. The god of built-upon land is often represented by a tree or an outdoor, natural rock. However, especially when he is associated with Inari, a small chapel containing symbols and images of fox messengers is also built to honor him. According to some local traditions, the roof of this enclosure must be remade every year for the harvest festival in September or October. The ninth day of the ninth month originally corresponded to a Chinese festival for obtaining longevity. After being introduced into the Japanese Court, it was transformed in rural areas into a seasonal harvest festival.

The partial reroofing of the chapel, like the periodic reconstruction of the largest public shrines (every twenty years), is carried out to remedy the natural degeneration of beings and things, which are regularly given new life in order to maintain the (supposed primordial) order of the world.

Chapter 3: Childish Knowledge

1. Simultaneously with Western chronology, Japan still uses the names of eras to designate years. This old custom first appeared in the seventh century and was regularly instituted in the eighth. When a new emperor acceded to the throne, or in the event of a calamity of some kind, eminent men of letters proposed names for the new era. These names had to possess the virtue of preventing calamities while expressing the political ideal of the contemporary reign. The emperor made the final choice.

Since the Meiji Era, the names of eras have been changed only for the coming of a new emperor. Although officially abolished by the postwar constitution, the usage of names for eras continued, and it was legally reinstated in 1979.

Today, in the Heisei Era, while postage stamps, for example, are dated according to the Western calendar, money retains the name of the era. In daily practice, reference to the era remains the norm.

2. In the traditional village community, children were assembled from the earliest age into informal play groups, the older ones bringing their younger siblings with them. When they got a little older, children were incorporated into a formal children's group, the *kodomo-gumi*. These were often organized by neighborhood, and in Asaka there was one for the eastern part of the village and one for the west.

3. While the older children, especially girls, usually took care of the younger, sometimes the children of indebted families were taken in as babysitters.

4. Shamelessly misleading advertisements appeared in the poorest villages, promoting employment in the weaving factories and emphasizing that machines did all the work. In fact, these jobs consisted of workdays of twelve hours or more. Escapes by female workers increased until the workshops were surrounded by high walls, barbed wire, or even moats.

The wages due the workers, who were fed and lodged, sometimes were held by the employers until they left their jobs to marry, thereby constituting a nest egg for their dowries. In general, work for wages seemed more acceptable for girls, who would have to leave the paternal home upon marriage anyway, than for boys, in whose behalf much greater efforts were made to assure they stayed at home.

5. This event probably occurred somewhat later. The sale of children developed at the beginning of the 1930s, following the crash of 1929 and the excessively abundant rice harvests between 1927 and 1930, which reduced prices.

6. The *hakama* was the female uniform, worn solely for scholastic ceremonies; Nami wore hers for the first day of school only. The sailor-style uniform, which appeared in the 1920s, was adopted slowly in rural areas, at first only for secondary education.

The boys' uniform was military style, with a high, straight collar and gold buttons, modeled on that of the Prussian Army; it made its appearance in secondary education during the Meiji Era.

The little girl's taunting of Nami for wearing red is surprising—true, red undergarments were often reserved for pubescent girls, but red, orange, and pink were encouraged for little girls' clothes. The schoolmate's remarks may have originated in local custom or an error on her part, or they may have been based purely on jealousy of the wealth displayed in Nami's costume.

Endo Nami's discomfort stems from sticking out from the group, which is, of course, frowned upon in Japan.

7. The sending of portraits of the emperor and empress to the schools goes back to 1889. Ninomiya Sontoku (1787–1856) is remembered as a model peasant. He founded a sect called Hōtoku-Kyō, the Teaching of the Retribution of Virtue. This group, which was simultaneously Shinto, Buddhist, and Confucian, favored the alliance of morality with economic activity and

taught peasants how to avoid poverty based on a just evaluation of their possibilities. As an insurgent who opposed the onerous impositions of landowners and defended the emancipation of the peasantry, Ninomiya Sontoku was idealized during the Meiji Era.

The Imperial Decree on Education (1890), which all children had to learn by heart, was inspired by the ideas of Motoda Eifu (1818–1891). This lecturer to the emperor was already the author of *Elementary Principles*, a book of ethics ordered by the emperor, who worried over the excessive Westernization of mores: the guiding idea was that the moral education of the people and government were one and the same.

8. Beginning in 1880, ethics (practically defined along nationalistic-militaristic lines) figured among the major subjects taught in school. The 1919 scholastic reform made it the principal subject, specifying that it be taught four hours weekly (and that all other education revolve around it). Starting in 1925, personnel from the land army (the most nationalistic branch of the military) were sent to secondary schools to carry out military exercises with the children. A decree on the military education of young workers was carried out the following year.

More generally, in the 1930s, 20 percent of teaching materials had nationalist content. At the beginning of the 1940s, this went up to 38 percent. The teaching of ethics was discontinued after the Second World War.

9. The primary meaning of *manabu* is "imitate," while that of *narau* is "become accustomed to." Therefore, while both terms imply repetition and are usually little differentiated, the second undoubtedly makes a stronger appeal to subjectivity. The original reflections of Yamazaki Ikue are based on a popular etymology of the formation of characters, which in the end accords with the most scholarly analyses.

10. The taboo against certain words, *imi-kotoba* (literally, "words to be shunned"), at sites perceived as sacred—for instance, mountains, sea, and Shinto shrines—is still relatively common. Accordingly, at the shrine at Ise, a highly sacred site of the cult of the sun goddess Amaterasu, ancestress of the imperial line who is thought to hate Buddhism and sickness, tonsured Buddhist monks are called *kami-naga*, "long-haired," dying is "to heal," and blood is called "sweat."

The reason one must not speak of mice in the mountains is that mice seem to come from another world. They become agitated before fires and floods, go out mostly at night, and live under the earth. They are called *yome-sama*, brides, because they enter houses from the outside, like brides.

11. One shō is roughly 1.6 dry quarts.

12. Some form of age groupings was present in most villages, and the hierarchy from high to low was based more on age than social class; the groups were of less importance in communities where social stratification was stronger. Two types of groups coexisted: (1) gender-mixed groups, which included boys and girls of the same age who would retain bonds of camaraderie for their entire lives; and (2) groups of boys (and, more rarely, girls), inclusion in which was a function of age, position in one's household, or social status. The groups were as follows:

> *Kodomo-gumi*: The children's group, a loosely organized neighborhood group with separate boys' and girls' sections, whose internal hierarchy was based solely on age.
>
> *Wakamono-gumi*: The young people's group, boys from age fifteen or eighteen up until when they married. Boys in this group received training in communal tasks such as policing, firefighting, and flood watching. They would have regular interaction with the girls' group, if there was one.
>
> During the Meiji Period, *wakamono-gumi* were transformed into *seinen-dan*, youth groups, inspired by Christian organizations, which rapidly evolved into paramilitary organizations. In 1934, the youth groups became in effect a patriotic militia. The *seinen-dan* that exist today are mostly folkloric organizations or study groups focusing on agricultural problems.
>
> *Musume-gumi*: A group of young girls organized around dormitories. Less developed than boys' groups.
>
> *Chūrō-gumi*: A group for men too old for the youth group who did not yet have head of family status.
>
> *Koshu-gumi*: The group of heads of households; in fact the village assembly, which made decisions on communal works and acted as a tribunal.
>
> *Yome-gumi*: The group of young wives.
>
> *Shufu-gumi*: The group of "mistresses of houses"—women with sons old enough to be married.
>
> *Rōjin-gumi*: The old people's group.

13. *Sai no kami* is the local name for *dōsojin*, the road-ancestor gods. Venerated in China as divinities of roads, they are honored in Japan in mountain passes, at crossroads, and at the limits of villages, from which, barring passage to insects and maladies, they assure the security of the inhabitants.

These border gods, often represented by stelae on which images of couples are incised, or by round or phallic-shaped rocks, sometimes presided over matrimonial unions. They are also encountered in the apparition of the bodhisattva Jizō, who stands between this world and the underworld.

Sai no kami is also venerated in fields where children play. Under his aegis, children perform rites of expulsion of natural pests.

14. *Nenbutsu* means "to think or pronounce the name of a buddha"—most often, of Amida (Amithāba), the buddha who resides in the Western Paradise. Originally a simple concentration technique, the invocation of the name of Amida became, with the development of Amidist schools of thought, a means to automatic rebirth in the Western Paradise.

15. The new year, the most important of all annual festivities, is celebrated at both Buddhist temples and Shinto shrines. The Buddhist observation consists of a nocturnal pilgrimage to a temple, whose bell is rung 108 times to dissipate the 108 evil passions brought on by greed, anger, and ignorance (108 is the sum of the time and weather divisions of the Chinese year).

Domestic rites fall into the Shinto camp. Foods chosen for their propitiousness are offered to a *toshi-gami*, god of the year, and are then consumed ritually. Finally, after the family has exchanged good wishes and gifts and inaugurated, day by day, the principal activities of the house, the god is sent back on the smoke of an outdoor fire, which has the secondary virtue of keeping calamities at bay.

Although the new year is now celebrated on January 1, and only the first three days of the year are generally holidays, some traditional celebrations remain fixed around January 15. The fifteenth, the old date of the first full moon, is called *ko-shōgatsu*, the little new year. Some traditional rites are even deferred until the first of spring (which falls in February). (See page 295, note 25.)

16. Although originally a calendar god according to the teachings of the Way of Yin and Yang, *toshi-toku-gami* became confused with an indigenous god the new year called *toshi-gami*. *Toshi-toku-gami* then became another name for this god.

17. The burning woodshed called *dondo yaki* (the three-legged grill on which firewood is placed) marks the end of the festivities of the "greater new year," January 1. Constructed at the edge of the village for the children by the youth group, it often takes the form of a hut two or three yards high. In former times, as the representatives of the gods, the children slept in the hut the night before it was to be set aflame.

18. The image of a deer traced by melting snow is a traditional reference to the primitive calendar, called the natural calendar, which subsists in partial fashion in sayings in rural areas.

19. Various hypotheses have been suggested for the origins of the term *goō*, which is generally written with the characters for "bull" and "king." According to one of them, the word *goō* designates the historic Buddha, the "bull-like king among men."

Whatever its etymological origins, the *goō* is a paper amulet bearing woodcut-printed figures of crows, perceived to be divine messengers, and magic formulas. Formerly used as paper on which to note the texts of the most sacred sermons, they are today distributed in Buddhist temples to assure easy childbirth as well as for the expulsion of insects.

20. The return of the dead to this world is celebrated four times a year: at the new year, the equinoxes, and above all the feast of *O-Bon*. The rites offered them must pacify the recent dead and attract to their descendants the good graces of ancestors long deceased. The dead come back at the moment the sun sets at the westernmost point, because the most popular Buddhist paradise, that of Amida, is thought to be situated to the west of the world.

21. *Hina matsuri*, the girls' festival, or "doll festival," among the most famous Japanese festivals, follows Chinese custom. An ancient Chinese custom had called for people to go to beaches on the first day of the snake of the third month, for purification and celebration. Because of the importance attached to "doubled days" (see p. 322, note 6), the festival was moved to the third of the month.

Over time, the giving of luxurious dolls on that date became a festival for little girls. This custom spread first in wealthy homes, then, during the Meiji Era, throughout all social classes.

Regional customs attesting to the ancient purifying role of the doll festival nevertheless survive. In the south of Japan, women made pilgrimages to the seaside; anthropomorphic figurines of paper or clay were put out to sea, notably on the Japan Sea coast and in Tōhoku.

A boys' festival is also celebrated, on the fifth day of the fifth month. Today it is a national work holiday called the children's festival.

22. *Yui* are communal mutual aid groups. For more on them, see p. 301, note 5.

The word *kannushi*, literally "master of the gods," is used generally to designate people who preside over Shinto rites, whether professional or not. In antiquity, only the large shrines had professional priests, while in the village shrines the heads of the principal houses would take turns planning and performing the rites. The transformation of Shinto into the state religion in the Meiji Era brought the development of a clergy. Nonetheless, for the annual festivals of village shrines, certain communities still designated a *kannushi* for the year, who officiated jointly with the professional priest.

23. For the rites of *O-Bon*, planned around the fifteenth of the seventh month, families gather to honor the dead. Because of upheavals in the calendar system, today the festival is celebrated in either mid-July or mid-August.

The word *bon* is the common abbreviation for *urabon*, a Japanese version of the Sanskrit *ullambana*, the name of an apocryphal sutra, meaning literally "to be suspended head down": this expression describes the extreme suffering of the dead who have received a bad incarnation. According to legend, a disciple of the Buddha, Mokuren (Mamaudgalyayana), asked him what he must do to help his mother, reduced after her death to the state of a starving demon, a *gaki* in Japanese. The Buddha told him that if he gave alms to monks in the middle of the seventh month, the suffering of his relatives would be relieved for seven generations. In addition, according to a Chinese doctrinal elaboration, the rites of *O-Bon* increase the longevity of living progenitors.

Although its Buddhist origins are unquestionable, three facts bear witness that this Japanese festival is not a mere reproduction of continental rites: (1) the great resemblance of the rites of *O-Bon* to those of the new year (especially the construction of special altars); (2) the welcoming of local divinities along with the ancestors; and (3) the duration of the rites, which take place over one or two days in China, whereas in Japan they spread over an entire month. Since the 1950s, however, the festivities have tended to be concentrated on three days.

24. Only the prayers and offerings of the living, *kuyō*, may deliver the dead from the defilement of death and permit them to accede to their awakening and, eventually, to become gods. Therefore, keeping the ancestor cult is among the principal duties of the living. Those dead without descendants are generally neglected and tend therefore to haunt the world of men in order to avenge their sad fates by provoking catastrophes: for example, *gaki*, starving demons, having fallen onto the worst of the six paths of rebirth, are condemned to wander invisible among humans in quest of food.

25. *Risshun*, or the point of departure of spring, marks the commencement of the first of the twenty-four periods that make up the solar year of the Chinese calendar. Today it is celebrated on February 4, a date close to the moment when the ecliptic is at a thirty-five-degree angle. This first day of spring, rather than the new year, is often used as a reference point for the agricultural and ritual calendars.

The 210th day (or, in some regions, the 220th day) after the beginning of spring corresponds to the beginning of the autumn season of typhoons, of which only the tails brush the Tōhoku area. If, while performing the rites of appeasement of the wind, people claim that the gods inhabit the winds, this is no doubt because the presence of protective entities is thought to be indispensable as harvesttime approaches.

26. On the festival of the young wild boar, *i-no-ko*, celebrated on a day of the boar of the tenth month, and sometimes of the second month as well, children, usually boys, strike the ground to render it fertile as well as to drive away unpropitious forces. They bounce on the ground either a boot made of tightly packed and bound straw (the gun of straw) or a stone encircled with a metal ring to which cords have been attached. These rites coincide with the arrival and departure of the divinity of the rice paddies, who resides in the plain during the time of agricultural work.

27. The choice of any day of the ninth month ending in 9 for the celebration of the harvest results from the Japanese adaptation of a festival of Chinese origin: *chongjiu*, which originated as a sun festival. The number 9 is thought to be the most important of the yang numbers (which are odd). It is therefore associated with the prime yang element, the sun.

The god of the rice paddies moves seasonally between the mountain and the plain: he descends to the village at the beginning of spring, going back to the mountain at the first frost; during the off-season, *yama no kami*, the god of the mountain, takes his place near men. The *yama no kami* is sometimes considered the winter aspect of the rice paddy god.

Still, there are degrees of presence of the gods. Ritual celebrations begin with the welcoming of the divinity, who is then sent back to some other world after the festival is over. Except during the performance of rites, the gods are more potentially than actually present.

28. These games are of ritual origin. Kites, decorated most often with warrior figures, were originally used in competitions between villages or hamlets. The game consisted of trying to hinder the flight of the adversary's kite with the string of one's own. In former times, boys most often flew kites at the beginning of the year and in the fifth month, for the boys' festival. This simulation of war had certain divinitory connotations.

Tops and yo-yos, the movement of which symbolizes the perpetual return of time, are both New Year's toys.

The seventh day of the seventh month, called the Tanabata Festival, is of Chinese origin and celebrates the annual return of two stars, Altair and Vega, the Weaver Girl and the Cowherd. According to the most popular Japanese version of this tale, these two stars, absorbed in their love, failed to perform their tasks: the Weaver Girl stopped weaving clouds, and the Cowherd let his charges graze wherever they liked. To separate them, the emperor of the sky made a river run through the middle of the heavens—the Milky Way. But he allowed the lovers to meet once a year, on the seventh night of the seventh month. That night, so that the Weaver Girl may cross the heavenly river, all the magpies in Japan make a bridge with their wings. And children make wishes that it not rain so the lovers may meet. To help the magpies, they also throw into the river branches of bamboo decorated with multicolored bands of paper on which they have penned poems, through which they ask the stars, in return, to help them become good calligraphers.

Fireworks, perhaps a sophisticated version of the fires of the end of summer, on which the spirits of the visiting dead are sent back home, are thought to be a cooling diversion in Japan, as in China. The noise also drives away calamities and demons, which proliferate in the hot weather.

The end of the feast of the dead is often the occasion for special offerings to the bodhisattva Jizō, who watches over the six paths of rebirth and protects children who die young. Devotees dress the stelae and statues of Jizō in childish clothing, making them up and painting them, while children draw effigies of the bodhisattva on flat stones.

29. Besides the fact that there are a great many variants of the Japanese names for the months, the meanings proposed here are based on disputed etymological interpretations. Over the centuries, Japanese philologists have advanced more than ten possible etymologies for each of these names.

Most of the meanings suggested by Yamazaki Ikue relate to field work and nature. However, two of them have to do with religious beliefs: *kamina-zuki*, the godless month, is the month in which all the divinities of the village, with the exception of the two guardians (the *rusu-gami*), go to Izumo to decide on matrimonial unions for the coming year; and *shiwasu* evokes the readings of the sutras that precede the new year.

30. The Japanese have adopted the Gregorian calendar but not the Western names of the months. January is referred to as first month (*shōgatsu*), February, second month, and so on.

31. Legends attributing the origin of a spring to the famous monk Kōbō (774–835) are found throughout Japan. The plot is always the same: hospitable villagers who have gone far to fetch water for the holy man had springs appear at their feet whereas, in the villages that refused hospitality to Kōbō, the springs dried up.

32. Although they often contrast the benign frog with the evil snake, stories also confirm the sacred nature of that reptile. The snake's nature is as ambiguous as that of the god of water (being responsible for irrigation and floods as well as waterborne epidemics), with whom he is generally associated. The dragon in Japan, as in China, is the king of the oceans and the master of rain.

33. The camellia, which blossoms at the outset of spring and which in addition can reproduce by a mere cutting, is a symbol of renewal. In Japan, its name is written with a character that breaks down into "tree" and "springtime." In China the same character designates a marvelous flower that blooms on a tree whose leaves live eight thousand years.

34. The *hagi* or *yama-hagi* (mountain *hagi*) is *Lespedeza bicolor* Turcz. var. *japonica* Nakai. The name *hagi*, which derives from "tree that grows," evokes the abundant character of this bush, which reaches about two yards high; its old stumps regularly produce new branches. In autumn, the *hagi* is covered with violet flowers, making it one of the seven plants of autumn, the *aki no nana-kusa*.

35. This tale goes back to a myth recorded in the *Records of Ancient Matters* (712). There it is told how a future emperor, a mountain hunter by vocation and an occasional fisherman, married the daughter of the king of the oceans, and how the roads leading from the land to the sea were cut off following their separation.

This myth gave rise in early times to a famous tale, mentioned for the first time in the *Annals of Japan* (720): a young fisherman married the daughter of the king of the oceans and lived with her in the undersea palace for three happy years. Then, recalling his duties in this world, he returned to his village, taking with him a chest, provided by his wife, which she forbade him to open. Because he recognized nothing in his village, he was so stunned he opened the chest, from which escaped smoke, representing his soul. The young man died, because time passes more slowly under the sea than on land.

The story of the nightingale differs in that it ends with the reunion of the lovers and the inception of the wind. The wind appears as a possible link between the world of men and the beyond, either the mountains or the celestial realm.

36. The autumnal voyage of the gods to Izumo, earthly home of the divinities from the beyond, according to the myths, is a variation on the theme of the seasonal displacements of the gods of agriculture; at the end of the harvest, these latter temporarily return to the other world. The relating of this assemblage to decisions about human marriages is supported by the personalities the myths attribute to the principal divinities of Izumo, the first rulers of Japan. Descendants of Amaterasu, sun goddess and ancestress of the imperial line, made a number of matrimonial alliances with divine women from Izumo. Like marriages between mortals, these contributed to the unification of landholdings and supported military alliances.

37. The names of the divinities that remain in their habitual shrines during the divine assemblage vary from village to village, doubtless as a function of the festivals celebrated in the tenth month in honor of one or another divinity before the tradition of the voyage of Izumo was widespread. Most often they are

> *Konpira*: Kumbhīra, one of the twelve followers of the therapeutic buddha, Yakushi.
> *Kamado-gami*: the god of the kitchen range, who sometimes, midmonth, fills in for the god of the kitchen pot, O Kama-sama.
> *Yama no Kami*: the Mountain God.
> *Dōsojin*: or "liminary divinities."
> *Ebisu*: divinity of happiness.

38. Eighth-century literature already attests to a belief in the vital power of the wind: a woman could be impregnated by exposure to the wind; a gust of wind could announce the coming of a lover.

Written with the characters for "wind" and "bad," the word *kaze* means all maladies brought on by the cold, from a simple chill to pneumonia, but also, in an older time, chronic nervous maladies and stomach problems.

39. A *gorintō* is a five-tiered tower of stone, wood or metal, each of whose levels corresponds to one of the five principles that, according to the doctrine of esoteric Buddhism, make up the world. These principles also correspond to the functions, forms, colors, and Sanskrit characters symbolizing seeds (*shuji*, Sanskrit, *bija*).

The symbolic correspondences are

PRINCIPLE	*Earth*	*Water*	*Fire*	*Wind*	*Void*
ESSENCE	Hardness	Humidity	Heat	Movement	Absence
FUNCTION	To hold	To take	To become	To last	To not hinder
FORM	Square	Round	Triangle	Crescent moon	Jewel
COLOR	Yellow	White	Red	Black	Green

Since the Kamakura Era (1185–1333), these towers have taken the place of funerary stelae; more generally, they serve as models for the shape carved into the top ends of epitaph panels which are placed on tombs.

Yamazaki Ikue's interpretation of the Buddhist tower is her own, based on a popular belief that

Shinto and Buddhism are by nature not different religions but rather different approaches to natural phenomena.

40. Frequently, to celebrate the renewing of the year at the beginning of the sixth month, the remainder of the *mochi* cakes saved from the new year are eaten. The association of the molting of the snake makes this midyear celebration the second important time of annual purification (after the new year). One custom no longer practiced is that humans, in imitation of the snake's shedding of its skin, chose this date for changing winter to summer clothes.

The relating of the snake to the mulberry tree (more commonly associated with the silkworm) underlines the physical resemblance between silkworms and snakes, both of which molt and belong to the indigenously defined category of *mushi*, loosely definable as anything creepy or crawly.

Chapter 4: Intimate Memories

1. Language usage in Japanese varies more definitely than it does in French or English, depending on region of birth, social status, and the gender of the speaker. In spite of the spread of "standard" language (generally, Tokyo dialect) through education and television, regional dialects and accents remain strong. Although Japanese from the far north and south still have considerable difficulties communicating orally with those from outside their regions, regional particularities are tending to diminish among the youngest age classes.

2. Children are educated to have an awareness of the rank of their family's house of origin, often exaggerated by family tradition, as well as a sense of duty owed to the house and the ancestors who founded it. The family's training of the eldest son (centered on proper maintenance of the real estate assets and the family cults) is generally more demanding than that imposed on younger brothers. The idea that particular duties come with his status as heir is also inculcated into him, notably in terms of academic excellence and mastery of self. The younger brothers, at the same time, are taught the respect they owe him.

As for girls, although their educations are much more liberal than in most Asian countries, they learn early on that they must not disturb their brothers, whose activities are held to be more important. Although girls often play with boys as little children, the two sexes are brusquely separated (beginning a lifelong de facto gender segregation) between the ages of seven and ten. While in the family it is considered adequate to praise girls for manifestations of coquetry, they are brutally made aware that they will have to devote themselves to the service of men. This boy-girl segregation widens in the course of the traditional education process, so that in spite of the relative freedom granted in premarital sexual relations, the worlds of women and men are definitely separated. Their principal functions as adults remain clearly differentiated—women are linked to family life and men to their salaried employment. This fundamental gender segregation remains in force.

3. This episode, as the wearing of the school uniform attests, takes place after Nami's entry into middle school.

4. The mother traditionally assumes entire responsibility for the rearing and education of the children. Only minimally authoritarian, she tends to prolong the symbiosis that united her to the fetus during pregnancy: she often sleeps with the baby, letting it suck of its own accord, consoles it at the slightest sign of tears, carries it on her back (or more recently on her breast), and generally indulges all its whims (which are not numerous).

Education in cleanliness is gradual, and recourse to physical punishment is rare. Instead, the mother plays on the affection that unites her to the child to obtain what is expected of him. Acts of disobedience lead to denial of love, or the declaration of preference for another child or for a seldom-present father, who is designated both a model of conduct and the dispenser of an authority feared equally by mother and child. The father, although he sometimes voluntarily plays with the child and from time to time carries out acts of authority, above all appears as the representative of the house to the outside.

This situation results in an intense lifelong attachment between mother and child, as well as the fear of being rejected by the social group. The absence of the father encourages sublimation.

The mother-child relationship remains the nucleus of the Japanese family, as opposed to the contemporary Western family, which is more centered on the conjugal bond.

5. In cases of separation, a wife usually had to leave her children, especially her eldest son, with her mother-in-law. This custom, which avoided the interruption of the patrilineage, has not entirely disappeared. However, following a divorce, custody of the children is almost always granted to the mother. The development of the nuclear family would make it difficult, in any case, for the mother-in-law to assume responsibility for rearing her son's children.

6. Murasaki Shikibu wrote the celebrated *Tale of Genji*, or *Genji Monogatari*, which describes life at the Imperial Court around A.D. 1000. She was born in about 978 into a family belonging to a minor branch of the powerful Fujiwara clan.

The literary magazine of the Bluestockings, *Seitō*, a name directly inspired by the Bluestocking feminist intellectuals of London, was published between 1911 and 1916. While it was originally supposed to have the objective of developing women's literature and to encourage the development of "geniuses," in fact it was consecrated to the study of the difficulties women encountered in social life.

7. The architects of the Meiji Restoration made education a priority not only in order to form a new national consciousness but also to furnish the economy with a managerial class.

8. Knowledge of foreign culture has always been considered the highest form of learning in Japan: Chinese writing and the Chinese classics in ancient times, Western languages and sciences in the modern epoch. It is thus easily understandable why translations have flourished since the opening of the country to the West in the 1870s. At that time, translations from the English or from Chinese translations of English texts were especially common.

9. Calligraphy consists of two principal styles: the *kaisho*, printed-type writing, in which the characters, detached one from the other, must each be written in individual squares; and *sōsho*, literally, "grass writing," or cursive style. There is also an intermediary semicursive style, called *gyōsho*. *Kaisho* writing, generally considered masculine because it implies an extensive knowledge of Chinese characters, is deemed a sign of great culture (see below, note 13).

10. The name Tenjin is today used as the divine name of Sugawara no Michizane (845–903), the celebrated poet, scholar, and man of politics. After having been for a time minister of the right (the highest title of office after minister of the left), he was exiled to Kyūshū, where he died. Because of the accidental deaths of several of his old enemies, and a number of calamities that occurred after his death, Michizane came to be considered a malignant ghost. It was in order to pacify his ghost that the court conferred on him the name of the god of the storm and the title *tenjin*, celestial god. Next, through oracles, the god demanded several times that a shrine be consecrated to him, and that it be built in a place called Kitano, in Kyoto. After this, the cult of Sugawara no Michizane spread throughout the country, where, under the name Tenjin, he eclipsed the local storm divinities. In addition, in his capacity as a man of letters, he became known as the protector of calligraphy and the teaching of letters.

11. In the Japanese religious context, an offering only rarely involves a sacrificial act. Instead, it is a way to make objects destined for the common use of men and gods sacred. Food offerings are usually consumed by the faithful, who commune with supernatural powers via that rite.

12. This is a reference to the type of marriage most common in the modern era: *yome-iri-kon*, or marriage where the bride enters into the house of her husband.

13. Japanese writing is of Chinese origin. While the importation of that writing probably dates back to the fifth century, no text known in Japan predates the eighth century. Ancient historic texts imply that it was in the sixth and seventh centuries that massive importation of Chinese writing, along with the entirety of continental culture—Buddhism, calendar science, and so on— took place. Used for their semantic or phonetic value, Chinese characters were very badly suited to transcribing the indigenous language, whose syntactic structure was totally different from Chinese. The difficulties encountered in the transcription of the Chinese grammatical apparatus were reduced by the invention of phonetic symbols, the *kana* (syllabaries), in which simplified Chinese characters were used phonetically; these were used instead of Chinese characters to express Japanese grammatical elements. These phonetic signs took on a growing importance over the centuries, notably in the writing of women, who were usually less well-educated than men, although writing in a more or less bastardized Chinese long remained the mark of culture.

Today, around 1,850 characters are used in journalism. In the school system, learning to write is spread over six years. Obligatory education requires a minimum knowledge of 881 characters.

14. The *hinoki* (*Chamaecyparis obtusa*) is a cypress tree, commonly called the hinoki cypress, the hinoki false cypress, or the Japanese false cypress in English. The *asunaro* (*Thujopsis dolabrata*), or hiba arborvitae, belongs to the same family.

15. This is the most commonly held calligraphic tradition. According to the legend, calligraphy was invented in China by the man of letters Caiyong (133–192), then imported from the continent at the beginning of the ninth century by the Japanese monk Kūkai (774–835), founder of the esoteric Buddhist school of thought, Shingon.

16. Even in the first half of this century, hairstyles, in the country at least, were determined by age. Little girls usually had their hair cut in the *kappa* style, with bangs in front and the hair cut square at the nape. Around the age of nine or ten, girls would let their hair grow in order to be

able to wear it in pigtails, tied back with a ribbon, or in a ponytail pulled up in a tassel over the head toward the front.

Around the age of sixteen or seventeen, young girls wore their hair in the "split peach" style until their wedding day, when they wore the Shimada chignon. This was essentially a very low, loosely tied ponytail, brought up behind the crown into a loose mass and held there with pins, forming a second ponytail. The day after her wedding, a young woman would assume the *maru-mage*, "round chignon," a large, flat chignon that was the hairstyle of respectable married women.

17. The *susuki* (*Miscanthus sinensis*) is actually a reed that grows only five feet high. It is one of the seven plants that symbolize the autumn and the harvest, and it often appears in agricultural rites.

18. This reflection is commonplace among Japanese women, most of whom characterize the later years of their childhoods by the sadness provoked by their brutal rupture with the boys' world and the realization that a destiny of submission awaits them.

19. Middle school education was determined by the career the student was to follow; later changes of program were extremely difficult to arrange.

20. Following German custom, the school year, like the administrative year, began in April. The entrance ceremony consisted essentially of an introduction of the teachers and the students, followed by a reading of the school rules.

21. The old method of calculating an individual's age required that a newborn be assigned the age of one year upon birth; the entire population aged by one more year each new year. So, to cite the most extreme example, a child born on New Year's Eve would be considered two years old on the second day of his life. In the case of Yamazaki Ikue, who came into the world on the second of January, such a calculation is not applicable. Her young age is invoked here only as an excuse.

22. This story is a variant on the theme of the serpent son-in-law. In a mythic context, snakes who resort to ruses to marry beautiful mortal women are usually divinities who, through those marriages, give birth to extraordinary individuals. But folktales more often describe these reptiles as maleficent beings, with whom union puts the human spouse's life in danger or gives rise to the birth of the dreaded "snake's children."

The moral derived from these stories would be that women who do not submit to certain rites of purification, or who simply go against the norms, will give birth to serpents.

23. The sale of children was prohibited several times, starting in the seventeenth century. Therefore, adoption was a way of getting around the slavery law. The adopted child was placed in a family as a loan guarantee. The duration of service was determined by a contract that bound the adoptee for life, until he reached majority, or for one or more years. The salary, specified in the contract, was deducted either annually or at the end of service from his family's debt. The interest on that debt would be scrupulously calculated on a case-by-case basis, which determined whether any salary was actually to be paid.

24. Nine years was popularly considered the appropriate age to begin work. Although the employment of children under the age of twelve in factories was prohibited by law, factory owners argued that children worked from the age of nine in the country. They often recruited nine-year-olds of both sexes, to whom they paid barely half the normal wage.

The analogies relating the age of children to the number of teeth in a harrow and the pillars in the Imperial Palace are examples of the constant recourse among Japanese to metaphor as a demonstrative form.

25. Children who died before the age of seven—that is, before having reached the status of complete human being—were excluded from the usual cycle of reincarnation or attainment of divinity. They were often buried in a special part of the cemetery (see p. 304, note 16).

26. The belief that summer vegetables with spots on them, especially eggplants and cucumbers, are marked out by supernatural powers and therefore not appropriate for human consumption is found throughout Tōhoku and the provinces of the southwest. Those vegetables are usually offered to the god of water, who is considered to be particularly active during the hot weather, or to the ancestors.

27. An 1873 law inspired by European legislation established a national army based on universal conscription of twenty-year-olds for three years. But in fact there was no need for such a large army, and opposition to the law was very strong in rural areas. In response, a lottery system was instituted, allowing for the annual conscription of 10,000 young men.

Around 1930, the ranks of the military were filled mainly from rural areas. Still, because of the limitations on the number of conscripts, the army remained essentially professional.

28. Because rice is grown in water, the water god, *suijin*, cannot be clearly distinguished from

the rice paddy god, *ta no kami*, nor from the mountain god, *yama no kami*, who engenders springs. Whether male or female, the water god is often represented by mischievous spirits called *kappa*. Like all the agricultural divinities, he makes seasonal changes of residence between the mountain and the plain.

This anecdote evokes the tale of the poor man who got rid of a heavy load of wood by throwing it into the water. The water god mistook that trivial act for an offering and gave him a veritable fortune in return.

29. When served as the main dish of a meal, rice was usually mixed two parts to one with barley and was flavored with daikon radish, beans, potatoes, taro, pumpkin, sweet potato, and so on. Buckwheat noodles were principally reserved for Buddhist festival days. Snacks were most often rice balls or potatoes. Fresh fish was rare and meat even rarer, with the exception of chicken.

The word *konbu* designates a family of seaweed to which belongs the *makonbu* or *Laminaria japonica*, which forms a more or less daily component of the Japanese diet.

Miso, still common in the Japanese diet, is a paste of fermented soy used as a soup base.

Chapter 5: Exclusion

1. Journal keeping is still quite popular in Japan, although it rarely takes the form of very developed introspection. Instead, it helps the individual come to terms with his duties toward society.

2. As mentioned in note 5 to Chapter 2, the use of family names by Japanese is not old except in aristocratic settings. According to archaic rules, an individual's first name—often determined by birth order—was preceded by the father's name or an abbreviation of the name of the lineage. The name of the house, *kamei*, could also make reference to the family's place of residence; in addition, a place name reference could be combined with the name of origin to form a new family name. In medieval Japan, houses took the names of their domains, so father and son might be called by different family names if their domains differed. Toward the end of that period, warrior families also chose names to give their vassals. It was not until the modern era that the custom of last names took hold and inheritor branches as well as junior branches of one lineage began to bear the same patronym.

Among the common people, family names were prohibited until the Meiji Restoration; instead, the first names of progenitors or *yagō*, names of residences, were used. At the end of the nineteenth century, these de facto names were usually transformed into true patronyms.

The concept of "house" has been abolished under modern law. Family names are legally considered personal names, but, in fact, the traditional attachment to the reputation of the name of the house remains; the primary task of the head of the family is still to "raise the name of the house"; his supreme error would be to "make the name of the house fall." Maintaining the reputation of the name constitutes an explicit duty common to all inhabitants of the family house, and he who "throws shame on the name of the house" risks being "struck from the family register." It is in such terms that, still today, threats of disinheritance or divorce are formulated.

3. Traditionally, meat eating has not been common in Japan, because of the Buddhist ban on consuming animal flesh. However, as part of its modernization drive, the government began during the Meiji Restoration to encourage the eating of meat to improve health.

4. The geisha alluded to here would have had little in common with those highly cultured courtesans educated in special schools in Kyoto. Even if they did possess some artistic talent, they were simple prostitutes.

The consumption of unusual foods perceived to be virile in nature, usually fatty or strong tasting, and the visit to prostitutes seem to be remnants of old rites of passage to adulthood, which were once celebrated in the family or the age class group.

For girls, the passage to adulthood, formerly celebrated at puberty, rarely was of great importance. Nevertheless, like the boys, girls could establish new, fictive kinship relations, while their aptitude for marriage was marked by the change of hairstyle and especially by the blackening of their teeth with a metallic tincture (*kane-tsuke*), which later became the legacy of married women.

5. The term *yui* designates communal mutual aid groups that include all or some of the houses in one hamlet. These groups, made up of young men and women from the age of seventeen or eighteen, as well as adults, organize agricultural mutual aid (transplanting and harvesting of the rice most notably but also rice husking, and so on) on an egalitarian basis. While some groups may be periodically restructured, they are necessarily permanent when their purpose is the rebuilding of roofs or communal aid for funerals, since these events occur in a given family only infrequently. Repayment of services rendered is indispensable and must include compensation in food or money when it cannot be made in full with a similar service. The inequality of the *yui*

is perceived as contrary to *giri*, the ties of obligation that hold together the relations at the heart of village society, respect for which is the basis of individual honor.

6. In conjunction with the traditional belief in the interdependence of body and soul, skin maladies not only are considered a sort of direct retribution for wrongdoing but also are judged to be faults in themselves.

7. It is usual for the ancestors to be kept informed of the principal events of family life. Daily cult keeping often consists of relating the deeds and circumstances of each family member, especially in times of domestic difficulties. The ancestors, who supposedly participate in the daily lives of their descendants, in some way hold the position of supreme family judges.

8. The situation of the younger sons is traditionally difficult because the eldest son will inherit the greatest part of the family assets. In the poorest regions, a younger son would receive a plot of land only very late (in some cases, as late as age forty), which would force him to delay marrying; in rare instances, a younger son would have to live his entire life in the house of his eldest brother, where he would be called "uncle"—the expression "an uncle's life" being more or less equivalent to "a dog's life." With the development of factory jobs, it was younger sons who, following the daughters, went on to form the urban proletariat.

9. The upbringing of girls—marked by successive ruptures (first, separation from the males of the family and later, by marriage, separation from the entire birth family)—seems rife with contradictions. Although raised to be proud of the social rank of their families, they would be called upon to renounce those families when they married. Even if after marriage they maintained ties with their mothers and sisters that were doubtless closer than is often supposed, they were officially dead to these women.

In addition, the ideals of life that were proposed to them were contradictory. On the one hand, in the traditional rural community, the woman assumed the management of all aspects of domestic life after the retirement of her mother-in-law. She would appear to be mistress of the house in the full sense of the term. However, the Neo-Confucian ideology that developed in samurai families and was diffused throughout urban society as a whole and in all the well-off classes made women into submissive beings; furthermore, bourgeois snobbery preferred a woman to be idle.

10. [In massaging the crown, or occipital lobe, of Endo Nami's head, the physician-monk is attending to the soft spot on a baby's skull, the place that later closes up. This area has important metaphysical connotations.—Trans.]

Moxibustion is practiced by family members or specialists, sometimes clergy but more often actual physicians, for benign afflictions or all kinds of nervous disorders.

The worm, prototypical of the unpropitious category of pests, is often thought to be the cause of childhood maladies (nervousness, meningitis, and the like).

11. The first return to the village of a new bride usually took place a few days after the wedding. Over the following three-year period, she would come back regularly for the principal seasonal holidays and during the transplanting and harvesting of the rice. After that, her visits would be less and less frequent.

12. The word *kakaku* designates the social standing of a house (based on the ancientness of its history, its position in the hierarchy of its kinship group of houses, and its wealth). This recognition of status reinforces the social stratification among landholders, tenant farmers, and live-in servants.

13. Warrior dolls are set up in the interior of the house, often in the decorative alcove called the *tokonoma*, for the boys' festival, in honor of the unmarried males of the family. At that time, a pole is also erected in the yard on which are hoisted wind socks in the form of carp: they evoke the endurance of those fish, which, during that very season, swim back upriver; this is the kind of courage expected of boys.

14. When a woman acquired the position of mistress of the house in a samurai home, upon the retirement of her in-laws, her status was still decidedly inferior to that of men. Among the common people, however, this transfer brought with it real power. The wife was responsible for managing the supply and production of food for the family. The passing of powers from the mother-in-law was symbolized by the transfer of the rice-serving paddle, *shakushiwatashi*.

Chapter 6: The Sages

1. The word *yo*, which originally designated the portion of a stalk of bamboo between two knots, signifies the duration of a year between two harvests, a life, an existence from life to death, or a generation. Other senses in which it is used, deriving from this, are of seeds or of prosperity, longevity, or the length of the life of a sovereign; by extension, it also means the court or the emperor, the latter thought to be responsible for the cyclic renewal of time since the beginning.

2. In spite of their common origin, the five elements to which Chinese and Japanese astrology refer, founded on the Way of Yin and Yang, differ appreciably from the five elements of Buddhism (see p. 297, note 39).

		I	II	III	IV	V	VI	VII	VIII	IX	X	XI	XII
	Duodecimal series / Decimal series	rat	ox	tiger	rabbit	dragon	snake	horse	sheep	monkey	rooster	dog	boar
1	wood elder	1		51		41		31		21		11	
2	wood younger		2		52		42		32		22		12
3	fire elder	13	·	3		53		43		33		23	
4	fire younger		14		4		54		44		34		24
5	earth elder	25		15		5		55		45		35	
6	earth younger		26		16		6		56		46		36
7	metal elder	37		27		17		7		57		47	
8	metal younger		38		28		18		8		58		48
9	water elder	49		39		29		19		9		59	
10	water younger		50		40		30		20		10		60

Table taken from B. Frank, "*Kata-imi et kata-tagae* A Study of Interdictions of Direction of the Heian Era," *Bulletin de la maison franco-japonaise*, new series V: 2–4 Tokyo, 1958, p. 217.

According to traditional custom, days and years were designated by reference to a sexagesimal cycle which combined the ten celestial stalks corresponding to the names of the five elements (doubled by the designation of elder and younger), with the twelve terrestrial branches, which were the animals of the zodiac. Contemporary almanacs detailed, day by day, which activities and movements were propitious or unpropitious, mostly as a function of correspondences.

3. Girls born under the signs of the fire and horse elders are still supposed to be difficult-natured, and female birthrates drop in the years that fall under those signs.

4. Yamazaki Ikue's predictions predated a veritable boom in mineral water sales, which took place in 1987.

5. The ancestor cult usually differentiates between inheriting couples and successive generations of collateral ones. Whether or not they resided in the ruling house or founded separate branch houses, the latter are honored only briefly and less formally.

6. The custom of orienting the head of a dying person toward the north is more often explained by its being the position in which the Buddha himself is said to have died: facing west, the direction of the Paradise of the Pure Land, with his head pointing north. Yamazaki Ikue's interpretation seems to be supported by the custom of placing the pillows of newlyweds on the wedding night to the north (marriage being at once an end and a beginning—especially for the woman, for whom the rupture with her birth house is often compared with death).

7. The age of seven is effectively accepted to mark the transformation of a child into a full-fledged human being. However, funerary commemorations formerly extended over longer periods: of thirty-three, fifty, or even one hundred years (see p. 313, note 23). The contemporary tendency to reduce the period of ritual memorial services for the dead to seven years, or even three, is sometimes justified by the desire to permit the dead to attain the state of buddhahood more rapidly, to become a *hotoke*.

The word *hotoke*, which is written with the character for "buddha," means, in a popular sense, "dead person." The term derives from the verb *hodokeru*, to unbind, and would therefore designate someone who undoes his bonds to the passions chaining him to life and attains the state of awakening. However, the expression "to become buddha" remains ambiguous: it designates death itself sometimes but also the end of the purificatory process, which permits the transformation of a dead person into a benevolent ancestor or his fusion into a divine tutelary entity.

8. The words for day, sun, and fire, undoubtedly of a common origin, are all pronounced *hi*.

A *hijiri* is someone who has the power to manipulate sacred forces: starting with the emperor but including all those gifted with exceptional capacities: monks, ascetics, Confucian sages.

9. As a moral term, *makoto*, which etymologically derives from "true word," or "true act," stems not from the idea of the absolute authenticity or sincerity of the individual but from the goodwill or zeal applied to the rules of loyalty that unite all individuals to their superiors. The "true" man seems to be above all one who is free from selfishness and ignores his personal profit in order to devote himself to another.

The emperor Tenmu (reign: 673–686) considerably reinforced the centralization of the state.

10. The Sino-Japanese word *shūkyō* contains complex layers of meaning. *Kyō* means "teaching." The primary meaning of *shū* is "originary or principal house," but by extension it means "leader," "cult of a leader," "ancestral mausoleum," "the most virtuous ancestors," "community of common blood origin," and "theory, teaching, or school formed from one source." Yamazaki Ikue's proposed etymology for the character *shū* is based on her own speculations.

11. *Miko*—literally, "child of a god," or "child of the emperor" (*mi*: that which is gifted with miraculous power, the gods and the emperor; *ko*: child)—is the term currently used for the regular priestesses of Shinto shrines as well as for mediums. It is rarely used in reference to a man.

Noriwara, a dialect term in use in the southern part of Tōhoku, where the cult of the gods of Hayama is practiced, comes from the combination of *noru*, transmit, and *warawa*, an onomatopoeic word evoking the disorder of a child's loose hair.

Mediums are known as children because like children they are mediators between the world of the gods and the world of men; they are thought to belong more to divine lineages than to those of men.

Hōin, in Sanskrit *dharma-uddāna*, is the miraculous sign that allows for the differentiation between the authentic doctrine of Buddhism and that of other religions. The term also designates the seals used in esoteric rituals and, by extension, a high monastic rank formerly awarded by the Japanese Imperial Court. The term *hōin*, however, also came to designate most masters of exorcism who more or less definitely claimed adherence to *Shugendō*. *Shugendō*, the Way of the acquisition of miraculous powers through asceticism, came out of the fusion of Buddhism with Shinto.

In contrast to the *miko* and *noriwara*, the *hōin*, who are always men, are considered exponents of a scholarly tradition. *Miko* and *noriwara* often acquire their religious knowledge only following a divine revelation of their powers.

Today, many people consult these diviners in cases of sickness or tricky decisions. But, in contrast to the West, recourse to a seer is not socially frowned upon.

12. *Daishizen*, "great nature," refers to wilderness. *Shizen*, "nature," goes back etymologically to the Chinese "that which is as it is, by itself." Paradoxically, the indigenous language of the Japanese, who think of themselves as nature lovers, has no single word encompassing this concept.

13. While the rulers of the Edo Period had made registry of civil status in Buddhist monasteries obligatory, the imperial Meiji government was Shinto-based. First the Meiji government proclaimed that the indigenous mythology of antiquity (which made the emperor the descendant of the divinities) was historically factual. This justified their proclamation of Shinto as a civil and lay obligation. That government then decreed that Shinto and the state were one, and that Buddhism and Shinto must be separated. This division led to an attempt to eradicate the Shinto-Buddhist synthesis that had been Japan's religion for centuries.

Every place of worship was then obligated to declare itself Buddhist or Shinto, provoking the destruction of a number of works of art in the combined Shinto-Buddhist iconography. In addition, state Shinto played a considerable role in the rise of the nationalism that eventually helped push Japan into the Second World War.

14. Mountains—as links between heaven and earth, stopovers for the dead, and the residence of gods on earth—are strictly tied to the activities of mediums and diviners. The importance of mountains in magic is so great that the followers of *Shugendō*, or the Way of the acquisition of miraculous powers through asceticism, are called *yama-bushi*, those who sleep in the mountains.

15. The absence of a rupture between the world of the gods and the world of men makes it easier to relate earthly landscapes with the various regions defined by Buddhist cosmology or Shinto. That is why all sites may be perceived as representations of certain locations in the other world to which their topography, for example, associates them; alternately, local sites act as stand-ins for regional or national representations of these mythic sites.

16. Like those who complete a normal life cycle, those who die in childhood know two forms of afterlife: living close to the gods, according to Shinto eschatology, they are given dispensation from the cycle of purification to which adults are subject and leave again for the country of their ancestors to reincarnate quickly; according to Buddhist doctrine, though, fate condemns them

to reside in a kind of purgatory where they work toward the salvation of their parents. Their destinies, then, appear to be even more rife with contradictions than those of adults.

17. The festivals of spring and autumn, which marked the welcoming and the departure of the divinity of the rice paddies, are theoretically symmetrical. During the off-season, the divinity of the rice paddies is replaced by the divinity of the mountain.

18. The vague natures of these groups of divinities—those of Hayama (the mountain where the ordinary gods of the village community as well as its ancestors are venerated) and those of the Dewa Mountains—characterize a kind of popular religious thought. Gods are considered proliferant beings, vaguely defined in identity and having only minimally specialized functions. They are often designated by generic names and confused with other gods in the rites.

19. The three mountains of the Dewa chain lie in Yamagata Prefecture, north of Fukushima. Since medieval times, they have been one of the most important locations of the syncretic cult of the *yama-bushi*. According to tradition, these mountains were "opened" by a son of the emperor Sūshun (reign: 587–592) half a century before the founding of the syncretic current of thought called *Shugendō*, by a legendary ascetic, En no Gyōja. Exorcists and healers, these recluses sought to obtain magical powers through their ascetic practices, which would allow them to command natural phenomena and evil spirits.

These three mountains are considered to be incarnations of the bodhisattva Kannon and the buddhas Amida and Dainichi (the corresponding indigenous manifestions are, respectively, a rice divinity, the god of the moon, and the mountain god).

Every year, 60 million pilgrims climb Haguro.

20. It is generally forbidden for menstruating women to approach the Shinto gods, who are supposed to despise the defilement of blood. In the past, the fear of menstruation sometimes led to the cloistering of women during their periods, in huts on the peripheries of villages.

The death of a snake in the yard or the house, considered to be caused by some error in the veneration owed to it, is perceived as a source of ill fortune.

21. Fudō-myōō (Sanskrit: Acalanātha) is the most powerful of the kings of wisdom. This personage has an enraged facial expression and extraordinary physical strength. He protects ascetics, serving them and helping them to reach wisdom and buddhahood.

22. The freedom to marry based on personal choice, traditionally very great in rural settings, was restricted in the upper classes of village society, where the necessity to marry someone from a family of equal or (preferably) higher status took precedence.

A good marriage enhanced or reinforced the status of a girl's entire house, which is why their father welcomed Endo Riki's marriage.

23. Ochanomizu, literally, "tea water," so called because of a famous spring located there, is at the center of a vast student quarter, which contains, notably, Tokyo and Meiji universities.

24. *Tōku*, a word of Chinese origin whose usage in contemporary Japanese corresponds to our word "virtue," also designates an individual's material wealth.

Chapter 7: Waiting

1. The *yamabuki* is *Kerria japonica*, the Japanese rose.

2. This is an allusion to the events of 1853: although the country had been closed off to foreigners since the beginning of the seventeenth century, Commodore Matthew Perry entered the port of Yokohama with his "black ships" to deliver a letter to the Japanese authorities in which the U.S. government demanded the friendship of the Japanese, the right to restock his coal supply in Japan, and the guarantee that shipwrecked Americans would thereafter be treated well. He also announced that he would return the following spring with a more powerful fleet, at which time he would expect an answer (in fact, he returned in February 1854, in order to get there before the British).

3. The Chinese character used to write "political party," which originally meant "gang" or "faction," served to strengthen the generally unflattering opinion people had of politicians. Thought of as small groups defending their private interests and disrespectful of the traditional hierarchies, the Japanese parties only rarely enjoyed the support of the people.

4. It was during the Meiji Restoration that the emperor left Kyoto (capital city), where emperors had resided since the end of the eighth century, for Edo, where the shoguns of the *bakufu* had installed their government. At that time the name Edo was changed to Tokyo (eastern capital).

5. The *Hannya Shingyō*, or wisdom sutra (Sanskrit, *prajñā*) is one of the most popular sutras. This short text, only 262 characters, which monks recite for ordinary benedictions of the faithful, explains how the wisdom and discernment of the Way of the Righteous Mean leads to Buddhist awakening.

6. The competition from synthetic fabrics and improved yields has contributed to a continual diminution in sericulture in Japan. It remains an important industry in only five prefectures: Gunma, Fukushima, Saitama, Yamanashi, and Nagano. But as late as the 1930s in a large area of Honshū north of Kantō, sericulture was at least as important economically as rice cultivation.

7. The morphological association, of Chinese origin, between the mouth of the silkworm and a horseshoe is based not only on the shape of the silkworm's mouth but also on the silkiness of a horse's mane and on the commercial equivalence, in ancient China, of silk and horses.

8. If themes of love and marriage are particularly common in the work songs of sericulture, that is because a good wife not only had to be a mother and cook but also had to prove herself capable of clothing her family.

9. The earliest record of this story is from China, where it appeared in the *Soushenji*, a collection of stories of gods, demons, and ghosts from the Jin Era (265–420). Well known to many Japanese today as a miraculous tale from the northern and northeast provinces of Honshū, it also belongs to the repertoire of the *itako*, female blind mediums who, in these same regions, speak for the dead, for the consolation of the living.

The association of silkworms with the dead is partially founded on a tie established by homophony, in China, between the word for mulberry tree, the only food of the silkworm, and the word for death, and partially on the hope that death is finally assimilable with the molting and metamorphoses of the silkworm.

10. The name for India, Tenjiku, the country where the buddhas originated, means in fact "the beyond."

11. *Sōmon*, mulberry gate, is a deformation of *shamon*, a translation of the Sanskrit term *śramaṇa*, which means those who have renounced the lay world. *Sha*, written with the character for "sand," means "sort out small things by putting them in water," "discern," and "reject evil and choose good."

12. The boundaries of Hitachi correspond more or less to those of the contemporary Ibaraki Prefecture.

13. This story associates the four moltings of the silkworm with the four tests to which the princess was put: before giving birth to silkworms, she symbolically crosses the four beyonds, which are, according to Japanese cosmology, mountain, sky, the subterranean world, and the sea.

It was in the reign of Kinmei (539–571), the twenty-ninth sovereign of Japan, that Buddhism as well as a great deal of continental technology was officially introduced into Japan. This is doubtless the reason for this sovereign having been chosen as the father of the goddess of sericulture, which was itself imported from China via Korea.

As for Mounts Tsukuba and Fuji, since antiquity they have been closely associated in the myths, which contrast the fertile greenery of the first with the barrenness of the second.

14. Remember here that the god of the mountain substitutes for the rice paddy god in watching over the village community during the off-season (see p. 295, note 27).

15. The methods of repayment of gifts, in kind or in money, vary according to region and occasion. As a general rule, a wedding present will be returned with something equaling its entire value, while a going-away present will be returned by at least half, and a funeral gift by only half. That is why funerals cost the relatives of the dead almost nothing, while trips, the number of givers usually being fewer, are thought of as costly, and marriages as ruinous.

Chapter 8: Beginnings

1. Strikes intensified during the 1920s, especially in the mills, where women workers struck for the rights to join labor unions and to reside outside the company dormitories if they wished, for the reduction of the workday from eleven to nine hours, and for better food.

Following the crash of 1929, the number of urban unemployed in Japan reached 3 million. Demonstrators then included those asking for work and wage workers protesting cuts in pay. The strikes diminished gradually with the rise of militarism.

2. Originating in the need for monks to remain awake during nights of meditation, *sadō*, the tea ceremony, was developed in the samurai milieu, where it became a ceremony of social communion. Among the bourgeois classes, it came to be viewed as one of the pleasing arts, the elegant mastering of which confers on young women of marriageable age a supplementary virtue.

3. It is customary to address people by adding a term called an honorific to their last (or, more familiarly, first) name; this is only roughly equivalent to Mr. or Ms. The term used is carefully chosen as a function of a hierarchical relationship, based on factors such as degree of acquaintance, social position, and age. The failure to use any honorific signifies the speaker's lack of interest in the status of the party addressed, that he or she is considered in some way insignificant.

4. Senju Kannon (Sanskrit: *Sahasra-bhuja-sahasra-netra*), Kannon of the Thousand Arms, is also called Kannon of the Thousand Arms and Thousand Eyes. This compassionate being prolongs people's lives, erases their errors, and keeps sickness at bay.

5. Women coated their teeth with a blackish substance, made of iron oxidized with tea or vinegar. This custom, which did not die out entirely until the beginning of this century, was both aesthetic and prophylactic.

6. Pine, bamboo, and plum generally symbolize happiness and longevity.

7. The eighth-century *Annals of Japan* record that a man named Tajimamori journeyed to Tokoyo, the eternal country, in search of a fruit of immortality with which to heal Emperor Suinin (eleventh emperor, dates unknown). Returning ten years later, he found Suinin had already died.

8. According to popular beliefs, while horned demons often disguise themselves as women in order to deceive men, an actual woman may also, in the throes of jealousy, transform into a maleficent horned demon. The *tsuno kakushi*, used to hide these horns, was first adopted by the faithful of the Amidist Buddhist school Ikkō-Shū; it later became the headdress of brides.

9. Yamazaki Ikue frequently employs, with obvious pleasure, this expression she discovered several years ago, coined by the writer Tanizaki Junichirō.

Chapter 9: Marriage

1. Yamazaki Ikue's accounts of many important events in her life, such as those leading to her marriage, were often contradictory. The fact that I was unable to elicit a more precise explanation has a clear psychological significance. Like most of us, Yamazaki Ikue is not reconstructing her past along purely factual lines but is offering an inner ordering of events—one that is far more important than the actualities in demonstrating her way of seeing the world. Here, Yamazaki Ikue wants to be both the barely tolerated, poor girl who suffers a difficult youth and the talented apprentice who inspires spontaneous love and becomes the object of demands that she would rather not give in to.

2. The cult of Mount Ontake (literally, "noble mount," it's located on the border of Nagano and Gifu prefectures) is tied to the history of *Shugendō*, or the way of the acquisition of miraculous powers through asceticism, a form of the Buddhist-Shinto syncretism that developed during the Heian Era. The right to ascend the mount, at first reserved for ascetics, was then granted to lay followers and finally, in the eighteenth century, to all the faithful who wished to make the climb.

Pilgrimages to Mount Ontake offer the chance to consult the gods through the oracle. Questions on the most diverse subjects—meteorology, sickness, or the origins of curses—are supposed to be expressed through the mouth of the *naka-za*, a person who occupies the middle seat, who is questioned by the *mae-za*, or person who occupies the seat in front. Both of these are ascetics who have completed seven cycles of ablutions, asceticism, and ascensions of Ontake-san.

The followers, who number around one million, worship a trinity on this mountain consisting of Kuni no Tokotachi no Mikoto, the founder of the universe; Ōnamuchi no Mikoto, the Great Master of the Ground (also known as Ō-Kuni-Nushi, the Great Master of the Country); and Sukunabikona, the Little Master of the Ground. The last two are healer divinities, who, according to myth, initiated Japan's unification as a nation.

A host of secondary divinities are also venerated there, among which are the divinitized forms of the founders of cults and various brotherhoods, as well as those from among the faithful who asked to have some of their ashes placed on the mount: stelae two or three yards high, called *reijin-ishi*, or stone of a marvelous god, are consecrated to them on private land given by municipalities or innkeepers. Kaigen Reijin, literally, "marvelous god who originally opened (the mountain)," whom Yamazaki Naka consulted, was the founder of the brotherhood from Tokyo of which he was a member.

Through the completion of this pilgrimage, the followers hope to find purity of heart, to contribute to the realization of divine virtues in this world, and to aid the stability of the State.

The cult of Ontake is supported by a more general belief in the sacred nature of mountains. It has often been noted that barely 20 percent of Japanese land is inhabited. In explaining the concentration of the population in the valleys, the sacredness of mountains is invoked even more than their steepness. Areas at a higher elevation than springs are considered reserved for the dead and the gods. To this day, mountain hikes often retain the character of a pilgrimage.

Myths recorded in the eighth century reflected the failure of the emperors to master the mountains. As soon as he arrived on earth, the first, divine, emperor—the ancestor of a dynasty that, in theory, remains unbroken to this day—met the daughter of a mountain god and asked for her hand. This mountain god offered him a polygamous marriage with both his daughters: the younger, whose name evokes the beauty of ephemeral flowers; and the elder, an ugly girl whose name evokes the perennial nature of stone. Alas, the emperor rejected the ugly girl in favor of the young beauty. Their union was only partially successful. Emperors thereafter lost the extraordinary longevity personified by the older girl, and they ceased trying to dominate the mountain, the reservoir of life, which remained in part a "beyond" inaccessible to men.

This loss of long life contributed to the transformation of some gods into human beings. In Japan, there is no myth concerning the creation of man: humans—or nobles at least (the only people of concern to the myths)—are portrayed as distant descendants of gods, who lost their divine qualities over time by residing on earth. Not only did the length of their lives diminish but they became incapable of journeying freely between sky and earth, and soon were no longer able to converse directly with their divine ancestors. To do that, humans had to resort to professional priests, ritualists, or mediums.

Mountains, whose peaks climb toward the sky, seem then to be favored areas: a link between this world and the other, the residence of the dead awaiting reincarnation or divinization, a stopping place for gods who have come to sojourn here below, and a favorable site for oracles.

3. According to current dictionaries, the word *giri* is defined as the just path which man must take; the way that man must follow as a function of the relations that unite him to others (that is, honor); the ties analogous to ties of kinship which he establishes with nonrelated persons; and, finally, reason, meaning. According to custom, there are two sorts of *giri*, the debt one owes to one's own name, which entails the necessity of defending its honor; and the debt due to a benefactor, by a vassal to his lord, and by all men to their relations by alliance or even to distant relations when they hold one of their common ancestors to be their own benefactor. In contrast to *gimu* (which designates duty to the emperor, to the law, to Japan, and to one's parents and close relatives, as well as obligations created by work), *giri* is theoretically reimbursable. However, the greater the benefits received, and the greater the hierarchical difference between donor and receiver, the more difficult *giri* becomes to reimburse—to the point, in extreme cases, of its being confused with *gimu*.

4. Despite the strength of the patrilineal system of lineage, women occupied a not inconsiderable place in traditional society. Therefore, because the union of two families of similar status was the essence of any matrimonial alliance, a wife could serve as an instrument in the social ascension of her adopted family when the rank of her birth family was superior to theirs. In addition, she was endowed with the right to transmit and receive property.

In rural settings, women constituted an indispensable part of the workforce.

Up until the contemporary era, marriage was perceived as a contract between two individuals only secondarily. The marriage ritual resembled the adoption of a daughter-in-law—or, more rarely, a son-in-law—by the in-laws. Even today, marriages for love undertaken against the wishes of the parents are uncommon. Conversely, young couples are rarely forced to marry against their own wishes, except in the upper classes. So, although it is difficult to differentiate between forced and freely chosen matches, contemporary statistics indicate that the latter outnumber the former. However, the increased divorce rate since the beginning of the 1980s has given rise among the young to debates over the advisability of love matches.

5. The open cosmology proposed by Buddhism and a systematic respect for established customs encourage the simultaneous practice of several religions. Most men and women educated in Christian institutions vaguely claim to be Christians, even if they have not been baptized. At the same time, a great number of those who have been baptized perform rites of the ancestor cult.

6. Chinese and Japanese see in the moon the image of a rabbit pounding *mochi* cakes.

7. This move does not strictly correspond to the Japanese norm. In fact, Tomekichi, contrary to custom, lived with his wife, Naka, in the house of his older brother, Yamazaki Seikō, until the marriage of their eldest son, Tatsuo. This particular configuration was due to the fact that Naka herself worked in the beauty school. Tatsuo had his own apartment before marriage, after which the family established a more traditional living situation, the elder parental couple cohabiting with their eldest son, his wife, and eventually, their children.

8. An improbable popular etymology associates *koi* with *kou* (to ask), which was written in China, and in Japanese antiquity, with characters meaning "a woman's disorders of the heart." Today the word *koi* refers to anyone's attachment for someone of the opposite sex.

Ai, by contrast, designates love in general, affection for parents and children as well as amorous sentiments. Highly valued in Confucianism, *ai* was decried by Buddhism, which saw in it an egocentric sentiment, encouraging the strong to take advantage of the weak (as opposed to compassion, the Buddhist virtue par excellence). Although now forgotten, this pejorative connotation was once so strong that the first translators of Christian materials hesitated to use *ai* for the notion of Christian love and instead substituted an expression meaning "to treat as something precious."

In describing love, such expressions as *suki desu*, like, or *horeru*, be charmed by, were up until recently more in use than the word *ai*.

9. There are two kinds of readings for (ways to pronounce) most Chinese characters. One is derived from Chinese pronunciation (Sino-Japanese reading); the other is the native Japanese word corresponding to the same meaning.

10. Sometimes, according to ancient custom, a sick daughter-in-law, considered by her in-laws a useless mouth to feed, is sent home to her birth family, either permanently or until she is well again. In any case, the idea that the family that has given a woman is in the position of debtor when she is in poor health remains fairly widespread.

11. The sect known as the House of Progress belongs to the category of new religions, *shin-shūkyō*, or newly emerged religions, *shinkō shūkyō*, that developed on the edges of the major, established religions, Buddhism, Shinto, and Christianity. These sects have appeared, for the most part, during times of social or political strife, notably during the decline of the feudal *bakufu* government and the rise of the imperial Meiji government; between World War I and the 1930s, while the militarist regime came to power; and after World War II. Although they appear to have been formed in opposition to the official religions, they take most of their doctrinal elements from those established systems, old elements coexisting in syncretic fashion with the new.

Taniguchi Masaharu began as a follower and theoretician of the Ōmoto sect, a strongly messianic movement whose prophetic foundress, Deguchi Nao, predicted the total destruction of the world, the "great laundering," and the installation of a paradisiac realm. Under the influence of Nao's principal assistant, Deguchi Kisaburō, the sect veered toward an exacerbated militarist nationalism. It is apparently because of these difficulties that Taniguchi left Ōmoto to create an organization for education and social work; its teachings are close to those of Ōmoto in that they remained messianic, but they make equal reference to Buddhist and Christian dogmas.

The doctrine is also strongly nationalist. Universality is not considered except in terms of Japan, whose superior position is justified by geographic characteristics supposed to confer on it the position of mediator in the world of men (between east and west) and between the gods and men (being at the root of the sun (see below, note 15). This ethnocentric attitude, used even to discredit communism, is deeply inscribed in the political context of the postwar period.

After the founding of a first House of Progress in Kobe in the 1920s, a subsidiary was established in Tokyo in 1932. That became, in 1934, the headquarters of the sect. *Seimei no Jissō* (*The Philosophy of the Reality of Life*) was published in 1935. After the war, in 1949, the sect was officially registered as a *hōjin* (juridical person), a type of legal entity.

12. Reference to the great divinities of national mythology is a constant theme in the new religions, which attempt in that way to lend themselves some of the gods' prestige.

Wakahirume no Kami, the young sun, is a goddess who, according to some mythic variations, is related to Amaterasu, the sun goddess and founding ancestress of the Imperial Line.

13. In Japanese, as in French or English, there are only two halves to any whole; the device of three "halves" contributes to the impression that this is a system unrestricted by mundane laws.

14. The idea that a school of thought or a religion may contain those that have preceded it no doubt finds its roots in the open cosmology, characteristic of Far Eastern thought. Westerners too easily mistake the resulting capacity of syncretism for tolerance. The open cosmology is supported by the esoteric Buddhist doctrine, which holds that all buddhas—past, present, and future—are reincarnations of the one Buddha.

15. The idea that Japan is located at the root of the sun comes from the name of the country, Nihon or Nippon. This name, given to the archipelago by the Chinese, means "the origin of the sun" (that is, east)—hence the expression "empire of the rising sun."

16. The popular women's magazine *Shufu no Tomo* is still published.

17. Following the feast of *O-Bon*, the ancestors, often represented by boats or lanterns, were sent back to the other world: while setting little boats in the water, the descendants would sometimes pray that they not return before the next year's festival, so the worlds of the living and the dead would not be confused.

18. The word *shura* is the common abbreviation for *ashura*, a term of Persian origin that later took on an interpretation in India as "that which is not a god," or "bad god." Anger, pride, and passion are the principal causes of a rebirth in the path of *shura*.

19. In pious families, the rules of propriety demand that gifts received be consecrated to the gods or buddhas before being opened.

Chapter 10: The War

1. Having counted on a short war, the Japanese government took no measures to assure the provisioning of the country. Because of the institution of the wartime quasi-economy, the black market began to develop in 1939. As a result of shortages of both manpower and fertilizer, agricultural outputs regularly declined, while deep-sea fishing was abandoned. Estimates suggest that, toward the end of the war, a million people left Tokyo every Sunday to look for food in the countryside. At the same time, the workers' search for food led to considerable absenteeism in the factories, so that manufactured goods, such as perishable foods, clothing, light bulbs, matches, candles, charcoal, and medicine, gradually disappeared. The government suppressed protest by preaching endurance, the supreme virtue of the fighters on the "front behind the front."

2. This raid was carried out on April 18, 1942, by sixteen B-25s over Tokyo, under Col. Jimmy Doolittle.

3. According to the Japanese press, the naval battles of the Coral Sea and Midway, which marked the turning point of the war in the Pacific, assured Japan's Pacific supremacy. It was only in 1943—after the retreat from Guadalcanal (February), the death of the hero of Pearl Harbor, Adm. Yamamoto Isoroku (April), and the loss of the island of Attu in the Aleutians (May)—that the Japanese people began to worry, without daring to admit it, about the outcome of the war.

4. After the air raid of 1942, the obligatory attire for women taking part in anti–air raid exercises (training in how to extinguish fires, dig out immediate shelters, and so on) consisted of puffy trousers called *monpe*. These were worn with a short jacket of traditional cut.

5. The taking of Saipan was extraordinarily costly in human lives. There were 3,500 dead and 13,000 wounded on the American side. The Japanese suffered 30,000 to 40,000 dead according to American estimates: all the soldiers were killed, and the civilians threw themselves into the sea by the thousands to escape occupation.

6. Ghost stories traditionally count among the pleasures of summer, although very few Japanese today make the connection between the apparition of ghosts and the seasonal return of the dead to this world.

7. Conforming to an ancient custom imported from China, the Japanese ritually contemplate the full moon of September (the eighth month of the old lunar-solar calendar), which is thought to be the most beautiful of the year.

8. In May 1946, food distributed by the Americans constituted about a quarter of the people's ration. This was mostly corn, which, because of lack of cooking fuel, was rarely edible.

9. The Allies evaluated in various ways the emperor's responsibility in the war. The Potsdam Declaration stated that the occupation would end as soon as a government favoring peace could be established (in conformance with the freely expressed will of the Japanese people), but it did not guarantee the continuation of the imperial system. At a meeting called on August 9, 1945, by Hirohito, the government resolved that such a guarantee should be obtained as early as possible. On August 14, the emperor accepted the principle that his authority and that of the Japanese government would be subject to the Supreme Command of the Allied forces and the ultimate form of Japanese government would be determined by the will of the people.

10. In addition to establishing universal suffrage for men and women, the new constitution stipulated that marriage could take place only with the consent of both parties, and that husband and wife were equal under the law.

11. This speech recalls early-twentieth-century Japanese feminist arguments. Citing on the one hand the gender of Amaterasu, the sun goddess and ancestress of the Imperial Line, and on the other a third-century Chinese text that emphasizes the supremacy of a queen over the Japanese realm of Wa, the feminists defended anthropological theories that proposed an original Japanese matriarchy.

Chapter 11: The Death of Naka

1. A *tsubo* is a unit of surface measurement which equals roughly 36 square feet.

2. Geomancy was introduced from China into Japan, along with the calendar arts, around the beginning of the seventh century. It is based on the principles of an astronomic system common to China, India, and the Arab countries that, according to the most accepted hypothesis, was of Babylonian origin.

The Way of Yin and Yang divides the compass card into twenty-four sectors, marked either temporarily or permanently by interdictions which affect all or some people. In the situation Yamazaki Ikue describes, the temporary interdiction on construction is tied to the movements of divinities traveling from sky to earth, as well as across different sectors of the compass card, as a function of a fixed calendar. The definitions of these harmful divinities and the interdictions they determine vary considerably according to which works are consulted.

In choosing a plot of land to build on, geomancy teaches that one must take into consideration not only the wanderings of divinities and the location of the star that presided over the birth of the advice seeker but also the configuration of the terrain. Mixing considerations based on simple common sense with magical intuition, geomancy establishes, for example, that the best lands on which to build are red earth, earth that contains black portions, earth that is plant-covered, and earth that is not very rocky. It discourages building on land facing due north, favors orienting buildings from north to west if on a slight elevation, from south to east when in a depression, and so on.

Because of the multiplicity and complexity of the rules of geomancy, specialists can make fortunes.

3. Formerly, a monk read the sutras at the head of the dead person the entire night of the *tsūya* (the wake), which took place before the body was placed in the coffin. The washing of the dead, *yūkan*, came after the wake, before the body went into the casket. The increase in the number of deaths in hospital settings, however, has led to modifications in the rites.

Since the eighth century, funerals have been performed according to Buddhist ritual, which assumed the primary role in matters of death and the practices relating to it. The dogma of reincarnation did not overshadow the indigenous belief in a progressive divinitization of all dead. Nevertheless, the Buddhist idea of one's fate in the afterlife reflecting the deeds of one's life led to the establishment of some qualitative differentiation among the multiple "beyonds" recognized in Japanese Buddhism. In spite of contemporary tendencies toward simplicity, funerals remain the more traditional rites in contemporary Japan.

4. While custom still requires that the dead person be dressed in a new garment, pajamas are supplanting the traditional *yukata*, which itself supplanted the earlier traveling costume.

5. Generally, death is conceived to be a process entailing multiple stages of separation from the world of the living. It is therefore necessary, at the beginning, to be sure that the soul of the deceased has departed, and then to make that departure definitive. Such is the origin of the delay (today most often reduced to twenty-four hours but formerly lasting from three days up to several months for people of high rank) between death and cremation.

The offering of water to the recently dead also reveals an ambivalence: it is both the water of resurrection and a drink for the other world, where burn the torrid fires of hell.

6. The domestic altar consecrated to the Shinto gods must be hidden because these gods are known to hate the defilement of death.

Shiny objects like mirrors (which are perceived as representations of the soul) have an ambiguous power that is best kept at bay while the departed soul is wandering between the worlds of the living and the dead. In addition, the covering of mirrors is one of the inversions characteristic of funerary ritual.

7. The complexity of the tasks and rites of funerals is largely the reason for the formation of local mutual aid groups for funerals. In both cities and villages, these play an important role in the feeling of solidarity.

However, the development of commercial funeral homes has tended to dissolve these groups; their role is now often limited to participation in the wake.

8. In the past, the bereaved family was sometimes obligated to reside for the duration of the mourning period in cabins constructed far from the village. But today it is considered sufficient to place some flowers and a sign reading *imi-ya*, taboo house, on the doorsill.

Today mourning is observed only on the days of the wake, the funeral services, the burial itself, and any ritual commemorations. Relatives wear either white or black on those days.

9. The presentation of this rice, *makura no meshi*, to the dead, is a widespread custom, although in some regions balls of rice flour are substituted. In all cases, the mode of preparation must be different from that of rice consumed normally: the rice is cooked outside the house, and, once the deceased's rice bowl is filled, not a single grain of rice must remain in the pan. In addition, just as for the rice of birth or of marriage, the sticky grains are formed into a pointed heap; however, in contrast to ceremonies for those propitious occasions, a single chopstick is stuck upright in the mound. Traditionally, this rice bowl was carried by the wife of the inheriting son of the dead person when the cortege left the house.

10. The posthumous name is a monk's or nun's name, the Buddhist form of which should facilitate the salvation of the deceased. It is always chosen with as much care as was the person's living name. Until the fourteenth century, people who felt death approaching could, whatever their age or marital status, become monks or nuns in order to improve their fates in the afterlife.

Today, while one is still living, one may have a name chosen and have it written on the family tomb: it will be calligraphed in red and will fade away with time. Any remaining traces of red will be removed at death, when the name is rewritten in black.

11. For fear of propagating defilement through food cooked on the fire of a mourning family, the neighbors remain theoretically in charge of the preparation of all foods offered to visitors. Today, however, they sometimes prepare the food in the kitchen of the grieving family, and very often they serve only what has actually been prepared by members of the family. There is an increasing tendency to order cooked dishes from outside shops.

12. Regardless of Yamazaki Ikue's opinion on the subject, repayment in cash of half the value of the incense offerings is still current, especially in villages where it is difficult to procure objects of exchange rapidly. As a consequence, the mourning families let the amount they intend to reimburse be known in a semiofficial manner through the members of their funerary mutual-aid group, so that visitors can calculate the amounts of their gifts.

The register of offerings serves, in addition, to determine the gifts one must make in cases of a death in another household. This amount is based on rules of reciprocity.

13. The custom of eating ascetic cuisine for funerals remained the rule until recently. Even today, although fish or poultry is sometimes served, red meat would be completely incongruous.

14. This prohibition against going out by the usual entryway is also applied to the deceased. Traditionally, the undertakers did not take the coffin out by the main door. In some villages, a wall would be purposely broken; to keep the deceased from coming back, it would be rebuilt immediately. There were also a number of magic practices designed to prevent the eventual return of the dead person: the ground would be swept behind the coffin carriers to erase any traces of their passage; a sort of porch made of branches would be erected in the yard and destroyed immediately after the coffin had crossed it; on the road or even at the cemetery, the coffin would be turned three times, to make the deceased lose his bearings.

15. According to a Chinese belief imported into Japan in the sixteenth century, a six-day cycle consisting of propitious and unpropitious days is repeated throughout the entire year. This belief, which was fixed in its current form during the Edo Period, spread through all layers of society around the middle of the nineteenth century.

The first day of the cycle is called *senshū*, the day of victory to those who take the lead. At that time, it is best to tie up urgent problems or to undertake rapidly what one hopes to accomplish. This day loses its propitiousness after 8:00 P.M.

The second day is called *tomobiki*, originally a day on which things stop and draw out. This is a time when everything stagnates and undertakings have but a half chance of success. Because of a homophonic game, which led to writing the word with the characters "friend" and "pull," funerals are proscribed on this day, during which the deceased might be likely to "pull his friends" with him to the services.

The third day is called *senpu*, defeat to those who take the lead. The early part of the day is unpropitious.

The fourth day, called *butsumetsu*, ruin of buddhas, is the most unpropitious of all. Anything one undertakes on this day will be a failure, and illnesses which arise on this day will be prolonged.

The fifth day is that of *taian*, great peace. It is an extremely propitious time and is especially favored for weddings.

The sixth day is called *shakkō*, literally "red mouth," a name sometimes given to *rasetsu*, demons who live on meat and are hostile to Buddhist law. Although they have been converted to the teachings of the Buddha and have become protector divinities of his law, the day that bears their name is still unpropitious, except between 9:00 A.M. and 3:00 P.M.

The majority of Japanese no longer pay much attention to these cycles, except when choosing wedding and burial dates.

16. Traditionally, the wake held more importance than the funeral. But the latter, called *sōgi* or *sōshiki*, has recently acquired such a role that some guests forsake the wake and do not bring their incense offerings until the funeral. Generally, for the death of someone who was not extremely close, one participates in only one of the two ceremonies.

17. The rule against using a hammer for driving in the nail of the coffin can be related to the prohibition on the use of any metallic instrument in cutting the umbilical cord. In birth as in death (times when souls oscillate between the worlds of gods and men), it seems wise to use only primitively manufactured tools, perceived to be possible links between nature and men. In the case of funerals, some Buddhist schools of thought, especially the Zen sects, insist on the use of "natural" instruments only, to facilitate the return of the body to nature.

18. The rule dictating that each of the bones must be grasped at the same time by two people

gave rise to the contemporary interdiction on two people holding a morsel of food in tandem; food must be placed on a plate by one person before another may partake.

19. The thyroid cartilage was usually not entirely destroyed by wood fire cremation. Its common name, *nodo-botoke*, buddha of the throat, is associated with its form, which recalls the silhouette of a seated Buddha.

20. The first week following a funeral is in principle a time of strict mourning, during which the relatives of the dead must present daily offerings to the deceased and agitate his clothing, in order to unbind him from any unfulfilled vows he made in life. This week ends with a new ceremony, during which a monk is invited to read the sutras. But the actual tendency is to shorten the rites by performing the first seventh day just after cremation. The other seven-day celebrations have almost disappeared, with the exception of the last, that of the forty-ninth day, which is frequently chosen for burying the bones. While the closure of the funerary period may be advanced to the thirty-fifth or the forty-second day, it must in no case take place later than the forty-ninth. Generally, only close relatives take part in these rites.

21. The forty-ninth day generally marks the end of the mourning period, *chūin*. Formerly, it was after this date that the close relatives could resume their everyday activities. Offerings of *mochi* cakes on the Buddhist altar consecrated to the dead still mark this definitive separation with the deceased. The cakes, which are presents ordinarily reserved for the gods, signal the hope that the deceased, freed from funerary pollution, has now attained the status of god. Fish is also eaten, to demonstrate the rupture with Buddhist ritualism, which prohibits the eating of flesh. That same day, the Shinto altar is cleared of the white sheets of paper with which it has been covered since the death.

22. The first funerary tablet, of white wood, is generally given back to the Buddhist officiary, who is charged with throwing it away or keeping it in the monastery, according to local custom. But it may also be burned or left on the tomb site.

23. Filial piety urges inheritors to be concerned, after the forty-ninth day, about the destiny met by the deceased in the beyond: the seasonal festivals consecrated to the dead, during the equinoxes or *O-Bon* near the end of summer, provide an occasion to consult mediums, who claim to be able to enter into communication with the dead. The anniversary days of the death are also thought to be favorable for these meetings.

In any case, relations between the deceased and his heirs will not end until his memory is entirely extinguished. Commemorative rites, *nenki*, are performed annually on the date of death, and in a particularly formal fashion for the first, third, seventh, thirteenth, seventeenth (or twenty-third), thirty-third (or thirty-fifth or thirty-seventh), forty-ninth, fiftieth, seventy-fifth, or even, sometimes, the hundredth or hundred fiftieth year. After that, if the deceased is still remembered, the commemorations are repeated every fifty years. The last ceremony marks the moment when the spirit of the deceased has met his ultimate fate. Viewed in the light of Shinto, the deceased is thought to have amalgamated with the tutelary spirit of the village; in the Buddhist view, he will have become buddha (*jōbutsu*) and will experience the liberating awakening from the passions and from life, traditionally marked by planting a living branch on the tomb. The nature of Japanese syncretism is such that the belief in the deceased having simultaneously met both fates is not considered problematic.

At the same time, ceremonies of lesser importance, *meinichi*, are celebrated each month, then each year, on the anniversary of death.

24. The guilt experienced by Yamazaki Ikue resulted not only from her attachment to mediumistic practices but also from the stress provoked by a particularly painful mourning. The relating of ill fortune or difficulties on the part of the living to negligence in the performance of funerary rites is quite common: the complexity of the practices appears to be the foundation of a veritable system of diagnosing illness.

Sotoba, or lathes cut in the form of a five-tiered tower, are offered on the annual commemorations of the death.

Chapter 12: Searching

1. Excessive debt began to constitute a normal avenue of growth for Japanese enterprises, large and small, in the early 1950s.

2. Not until after 1955 (when, for the first time, the rice harvest exceeded the highest prewar levels and the price of rice on the black market fell below the official rate) did the food supply normalize for the entire Japanese population.

3. From the beginning of his term, Prime Minister Kishi Nobusuke courted workers in the tertiary industries, merchants in particular. He hoped to find in them a replacement for the rural

electorate, traditionally loyal to his Liberal Democratic party but demographically on the decrease. In 1957, standards governing the surface area allowable for businesses were set, the prerogatives of the labor unions limited, and the official rates for certain service industries, notably hairdressing and laundries, saw a large increase.

4. Scholars generally agree that the eightieth day represents one of the rare Japanese additions to the great calendar dates fixed in China. Falling around the beginning of May, it marks the end of the frosts and the approach of summer. The choice of this date results from a graphic game relating the figure 88 to the character for "rice." It is a propitious day, as opposed to the twenty-third day of the twelfth month, the winter solstice.

5. These figures cannot be verified mathematically—they are entirely a product of imagination, reflecting the blend of Western and indigenous cultures that governs Yamazaki Ikue's practice of geomancy.

6. The survival in Japan, in spite of widespread Westernization, of conservative ideas which cast doubt on even the possibility of invention—indeed, of progress—can be traced back to ancient Chinese roots.

The concept of invention seems to have been difficult to formulate within the framework of a Japanese philosophy largely subordinate to the influence of Chinese Confucian thought. Ancient Chinese thought held that no individualized power could command nature, whose equilibrium was conceived as the fruit of a spontaneous play of complementary forces. The growth and decline of those forces engendered the seasons. The principal question posed by Chinese philosophy revolved around the nature of man, the order of the universe, and man's place therein. Zhu Xi (1130–1200) held that the principle of *li*, a natural order both physical and moral, was the foundation of social hierarchies. It is easily understandable why the feudal government of Edo Period Japan (1603–1868) granted its protection to the defenders of the ideas of this Neo-Confucian thinker, who prohibited all criticism of the social order.

7. From antiquity, a very centralized State Buddhism coexisted with a popular Buddhism that included more Shinto or Taoist elements. Early in its history, the Imperial Court demonstrated a lively mistrust of those monks and nuns who issued from the popular tradition and were not subordinate to its authority. The latter lived in the mountains in order to become "immortals," according to Taoist custom. The court issued multiple decrees equating them more or less with vagabonds and prohibiting them from retreating to the mountains without the authorization of their clerical hierarchy or from practicing any non-Buddhist form of magic. In addition, it accused these ancestors of the reclusive *yama-bushi*, who lived for the most part on what little they could glean from their activities as healers, of poison making. After the second half of the eighth century, however, the emperors took pains to enlist the most celebrated from among them into their service.

8. The term *shinki* or *jingi* originally meant the treasures granted to men by the gods and, more particularly, the regalia of imperial power: a mirror, a saber, and a "bent jewel," or *magatame*.

9. Benten (Sarasvatī-Devī in India) appears to have begun as a goddess of water. Late in her history, she came to be considered the wife of Bonten (Brahmā), as well as the protector of music, eloquence, and good fortune. In memory of her original nature, she is still venerated in Japan near bodies of water—notably, Lake Biwa.

10. Note that the harmfulness of traditional cold permanent wave products is today well-known to hairdressers: they recommend infrequent use of such products or the use of so-called mild permanent solutions, which are less effective but less dangerous.

11. Yin and yang, the duality born of the One according to Chinese Taoism, are the signs which affect variations in the breath. Yang, profusion, the deployment of an energy that is growing or diminishing, is inseparable from yin, which constitutes its dark aspect.

12. The product called Belle Jouvence, made with a base of thioglycolic acid, seems to have been a prototype of the "mild" permanents which were developed ten years or so after it in answer to the fashion for things "ecological." Because the low acid content makes it more difficult for the permanent to "take," its application requires particular care, notably a prolonged scalp massage, which induces in the client a profound sense of well-being.

13. The New Year is the occasion for a domestic rite in which *waka-mizu* (literally, "young water") is drawn from the usual sources. The water is made "new" by the presentation of supplementary food offerings to the water god, *suijin*, and the filling of a new bucket while pronouncing a propitiatory formula asking for longevity for the family members. This water, first offered on the altar of the god of the new year, is then used to make the year's first tea or the ink for the first calligraphy of the year.

Chapter 13: The Business World

1. Although it is not really the custom except in large companies, lifetime employment is viewed as the norm.

2. Remember that a going-away present has to be returned by about half its value.

3. Ame no Minaka Nushi no Kami (or, "no Mikato no Kami") is the primordial deity of the Japanese pantheon (see p. 321, note 19).

4. *Yamato* evokes Japanese antiquity and the classic grace of Imperial Court culture; *nadeshiko* designates the flower sweet John (*Dianthus superbus*). Taken together, *yamato nadeshiko* refers to an old-style Japanese beauty.

5. *Shichi go san* is today celebrated on November 15. This festival honoring children of seven, five, and three years is a remnant of old rites of passage. With their parents, children wearing traditional costumes make pilgrimages to the shrine of their tutelary god.

6. Most social groupings—political parties, unions, professional associations, schools, universities, gangs, and so on—have a strongly hierarchical mode of organization. As in traditional village communities, the bonds of authority are expressed in terms of kinship. No one can enter such a group without a godparentlike relationship to an *oya-kata*, literally "parent-figure," or an *oya-bun*, "acting parent." The "child," *ko-kata* or *ko-bun*, owes on his part an unfailing devotion.

Chapter 14: Dōzoku-Gaisha: A Family Business

1. Calendar concepts of Chinese origin divide the duration into sixty-year cycles.

2. The vogue for rebuilding wooden houses with longer-lasting materials began in the 1960s, when the nation's prosperity started to take hold.

3. *Iki* (style) is contrasted with the naive crudeness of the provinces, generally in comparison with Tokyo. Still, the talent for living it implies has nothing to do with culture in the bourgeois sense but rather evokes the art of satisfying natural desires with elegance, notably in the domain of sex.

4. Mitsukoshi, one of the most famous of Tokyo's department stores, is known for the expensiveness and luxury of its wares.

5. This is a patriotic, melodramatic song that was in vogue during the war, in which a kamikaze pilot weeps for a school chum who died before him.

6. This image of the Buddha in the form of a baby is particularly dear to the hearts of the Japanese. It evokes for them a relaxed familiarity, as opposed to the formal sculptures found in the temples.

7. The necessity of separating Shinto gods from buddhas is not based on religious dogma but goes back to *kokugaku,* the nationalist school of thought of the Meiji Era, which, in its effort to reestablish an old-type theocracy, tried to dissociate State Shinto from the foreign-originated Buddhism.

8. *Shide* are in fact small *gohei,* white paper symbols of the bodies of the gods. Early in Japan's history, they replaced bands of cloth attached to sticks in place of offerings; they represent supernatural powers.

9. The *Ō-Harae no Norito,* the form of which was fixed in the eighth century, is the best-known popular ritual text of the Shinto tradition.

10. According to tradition, the first doll to be called Hakata style was made in Year 6 of the Keichō Era (1601) by a master tile maker. He is said to have used clay destined for tiles to model a doll, which he offered to the founder of Fukuoka Castle (Hakata). These dolls—which represent beauties, babies, or Nō or Kabuki theater personalities—are characterized by the fineness of their colors.

Wajima, on the Japan Sea, is known for its fine lacquer.

11. *Kokusai-ka,* internationalization, is currently one of the leitmotifs of the Japanese media. Beyond the true internationalization of the economy, it refers to a superficial Westernization of the Japanese way of life—often supposed to be leading in some Japanese to a transformation in their ways of thinking and, in others, to individualism. This is contrasted with a traditional ideology in which the group takes precedence over the individual, whose spontaneous behavior is more or less equated with selfishness.

12. This man who had been in a class ahead of Endo Muneo's at university is a *senpai,* an older classmate who serves as a kind of mentor. Ties between old classmates are perceived to be ties not of friendship but of obligation, on which friendship may be grafted. These relations are defined by a strict hierarchy, which places younger students below older ones.

13. Such a letter obliges its author to make financial recompense to the receiver (in this case

the prospective employer) should the person in question prove incompetent. Although this custom has no legal basis, it is widely followed.

14. The *buraku-min*, people of the (special) hamlets, are the descendants of those who in former times practiced unproductive and/or "unclean" professions. Among these are acrobats, criminals, executioners, and undertakers (*hinin*, nonhumans) as well as those who did productive work having to do with death: meat slaughterers and tanners (*eta*, full of filth). Today they number 2 to 3 million. Although their exclusion from greater society is now illegal, they live in ghettos, and a large number of them continue to exercise "impure" professions, as tanners, butchers, street sweepers, garbage collectors, and so on; they also work in difficult or dangerous jobs, such as construction.

15. A "normal" Japanese would never marry a *buraku-min*, and a "normal" business would never hire one: lists of the names of *buraku-min* circulate illegally in companies so they can avoid inadvertently recruiting them.

16. The comb is featured in ancient beliefs as an instrument of ambiguous magic, associated with not only suffering and death but also the idea of the mysterious (a word that is also pronounced *kushi*). A woman would give a comb to her lover to protect him, or he might take a comb from his own hair in order to transform it into a protective object.

17. Because the characters for "eight 八 , ten 十 , eight," which make up the figure 88 in Japanese, may, via a graphic game, form the character for "rice," 米 the age of eighty-eight years is said to be the age of the longevity of rice. This expression associates the good fortune of longevity with the prosperity symbolized by rice.

Chapter 15: Fate

1. While Inari is venerated all over Japan, his cult as a protecting deity of one's place of residence is especially widespread in the north and east of the country (see p. 291, note 46).

2. For a discussion of Kōjin-sama, the god of the hearth, see p. 290, note 34.

3. The name of *sakaki*, or *Cleyera ochnacea*, means "boundary tree." An evergreen that grows wild in the mountains, it is often planted on the grounds of Shinto shrines, and its branches are used in Shinto rituals.

4. For the explanation of Kaigen Reijin, the gods of Mount Ontake, and the descent of gods into humans, see p. 307, note 2.

5. The importance attached to the science of names, *seimei-gaku*, comes from the influence on individual destiny attributed to personal names. The study of a name is often combined with other techniques for diagnosing destiny: analysis of the date of birth, study of fingerprints, and so on. Most Japanese almanacs include a chapter devoted to *seimei-gaku*.

The combination of several divinitory techniques opens the field to so many possibilities that it is difficult to choose a suitable name without the aid of a specialist, most often a religious.

Although common before the war, this custom is quietly falling into disuse.

6. While most mediums are women—who are thought to have more aptitude for communicating with the dead and the gods—recent ethnographic studies show that a number of men also work in that capacity.

7. These are historic facts. Dazai Osamu (1909–1948) was a famous novelist, on whom the suicide of the celebrated author of *Rashōmon*, Akutagawa Ryūnosuke (1892–1927) made a strong impression. He made a first attempt at double suicide in 1930. Although he survived it, the barmaid who took part in it with him did not. Eighteen years later, he drowned himself in the Tamagawa canal, with Yamazaki Tomie.

Dazai was considered one of the principal representatives of Japanese romanticism. Troubled by the spectacle of a society that he considered decadent, he fell into a despairing nihilism after the war.

8. *Shinjū*, or double love suicide, a relatively common occurrence in Japan, is one of the great themes of the national dramaturgy. It is usually depicted as the tragic result of thwarted love.

9. Suicides are among those dead who are the objects of special rites to assure their deliverance and pacification. See also p. 295, note 24.

10. The contradiction between Yamazaki Ikue's first version of this marriage in chapter 9 (wherein Yamazaki Nobuko contrives to marry her eldest son to her own niece, to the joy of all concerned) and this version (in which the son met his bride in Korea and her foreign background has tainted his filial piety) shows how she tailors the existing facts to support two views—one approving, the other disapproving. The facts are as follows: Yamazaki Seikō and Nobuko's eldest son, Takeshi, married Nobuko's niece Toshiko (some of Nobuko's family had once lived in

Korea). At this time in the narrative (1968), the couple lived in Yokohama. See also note 12 below.

11. Actually, the brothers died fourteen years apart. Yamazaki Ikue's memory was more poetic than factual in this instance.

12. There was indeed a chain of misfortune among young Yamazaki men. Tomie's brothers, Toshiichi and Teruzō, both died of meningitis, the latter while serving in the war. There were seven boys in Seikō and Tomekichi's generation, not six—Yamazaki Ikue doesn't count Tameijirō, who was adopted into another family (and who doesn't appear on the Yamazaki family tree on pp. 344–45). As for the others, the eldest, Masakichi, died at twenty-six; Tsunekichi was adopted as an heir into another family; Kanekichi died at age five; and Tsunejirō died of polio at twenty-one. Thus Seikō became the de facto heir of his father's branch of the Yamazakis; Tomekichi (Yamazaki Ikue's father-in-law) founded a separate branch.

13. Naohi-kyō, literally, "the teachings of Naohi," belongs to the category of new religions (see p. 309, note 11). It was founded by a woman from Ogura (Tochigi Prefecture), Kimura Akahi (1897–1965). At the age of thirty, she created the Experimental Association for the Belief in Protective Spirits of the Country. Later she studied Shinto at Nichidai University and underwent a one-week cycle of asceticisms and purifications at the shrine of Izanaki, on the island of Awaji-shima. At this place, she is said to have "received the spirit of Naohi."

Naohi or Naobi comes from the names of two divinities of antique mythology, the children of Izanaki, the father of the Japanese islands (see note 14 below).

Although they occupy a decidedly secondary place in antique mythology, these respectively malevolent and benevolent divinities were considered by the proponents of *kokugaku* (Nationalist Studies) to have created good and evil for the first time. In the modern era they acquired a considerable importance.

It was following this retreat on Awaji-Shima that Kimura transformed her experimental association into a new religion. The Naohi sect was registered in 1953.

The teachings of this Shinto sect can be summed up in three points:

> —All things are of a common origin and are profoundly identical, even when they appear to be different.
> —All spirits manifest themselves, there being no difference between what appears and what is hidden.
> —The entire world must experience the peace of the gods and buddhas.

This dogma, which like most new religions mixes morality and a Buddhist or Confucian metaphysics with a mythology that is itself Shinto-Buddhist, was principally diffused through a kind of spiritualism borrowed from Western influences.

In the mid-1980s, members of the Naohi sect numbered only 340.

14. Ghosts are primarily those who died without having finished a complete life cycle (young women who died in childbirth, young soldiers killed in war, and so on) but also those who left this world in a state of passion (suicides resulting from insanity or love) or those whose remains, never found, cannot be objects of ritual pacification (especially drowned persons). Yamazaki Tomie, who died young, by drowning, and in the full throes of amorous passion, would naturally be thought to be a particularly formidable spirit.

15. After Izanaki and his wife, Izanami, gave birth to the first Japanese isles, Izanami died giving birth to fire and went to the underworld. Her husband tried to go there and bring her back, but he failed, and, on returning from the underworld, he purified himself in a river. It was during this purificatory bath that he gave birth, first to malevolent divinities, then to benevolent ones charged with remedying the evil doings of the former. The two Naobi gods are the first-ranked among these.

16. A battle took place in July 1582 at a place called Yamazaki, in the old province of Yamashiro (in the south of modern-day Kyoto Prefecture). The warlord Oda Nobunaga (1534–1582), who was working to unify Japan, had died the previous month as his Kyoto palace was besieged by his former vassal Akechi Mitsuhide (1526–1582). Hearing the news of Oda's death, Toyotomi Hideyoshi (c. 1532–1598) met Akechi's forces at Yamazaki. Toyotomi defeated and killed Akechi and by this victory gained control of Yamashiro province. In 1590, he finally achieved unification of the country.

Although this period of civil wars was rife with betrayals of all sorts, there is no written record of the episode recounted by the oracles. In addition, the name Yamazaki, which means "mountainous cape," is extremely common and in no way implies origins in Yamashiro. Also, the explanation for the ill fortune attached to Yamazaki Ikue's family is in direct contradiction with another justification later given by another medium: she attributed the "fate" to Yamazaki Anzai, who lived in the seventeenth century (see chapter 16).

17. The current constitution (1947) was authored by Japanese under the close supervision of the Allied Command. Article 24 stipulates the absolute equality of men and women in legal matters. Under the civil code, widows receive one third of inheritances, the remainder being divided equally among the children of both sexes.

In actual practice, the small size of parcels of land (aggravated by the postwar agrarian reforms) makes any further divisions difficult. A current custom has it that one of the potential heirs, most often the eldest son, asks the others to cede their shares. This maintenance of the traditional form of succession is all the more acceptable in that most young people would prefer to move to the cities. The number of those who return to the country, called *yūtan* (U-turns) remains small.

18. The new religion called Daiwa was founded by Hozumi Hisako, born in the last Meiji years. She was cured of a sickly constitution and morbid temperament at the age of eighteen by an ascetic from a sect called the Religion of Putting Shinto into Practice. After that, she became a follower and began to work to spread its beliefs. She broke with the sect at age twenty-seven, having supposedly received the spirits of the imperial ancestors, who told her to found the new sect, Daiwa.

She married one of the founding members of the flock, bore him six children, divorced, and remarried. In the eyes of the followers, this dramatic personal history conferred on her a life experience useful in her work.

The fundamental dogma of this Shinto sect is that the spiritual force that animated Hozumi Hisako is what makes possible the realization of harmony among the three worlds: the world of the gods, our world, and the spirit world. Its followers are encouraged to find prosperity through the virtue of the Great Master of the Country, alias Daikoku, who watches over their happiness (see p. 290, note 36). The search for harmony and respect for the Japanese gods allow one to lead a moral life, to prepare for the coming of a world without war, and to encourage the growth of beings and things. The five great precepts are peace of heart, gratitude, faith, effort, and practice.

In 1984, the number of faithful reached 55,639.

19. The Western Paradise is the most popular of Buddhist heavens.

20. Shingon is one of the two great schools of thought of esoteric Chinese and Japanese Buddhism. The word *Shingon* is a translation of the Sanscrit *mantra*, true speech, or magic speech, whose temporal and spiritual effectiveness is based on correspondences between sounds and divine powers. Introduced from China to Japan by the celebrated monk Kūkai (Kōbō Daishi, 774–835), the Shingon School distinguishes six degrees of knowledge by which man raises himself to a mystical state of total abstraction; in that way he attains virtue and the happiness of awakening. Along with those of the Tendai school (which had been imported a short while earlier), the teachings of Shingon, which purport to explain the totality of the universe, played a not inconsequential role in the development of Shinto-Buddhist syncretism. The extreme importance placed on ritual in the latter context explains why this school, with its complex dogma, was sometimes thought to make use of magical and dangerous practices. Here, Yamazaki Ikue confuses popular magical practices (over which Shingon rituals formerly exercised a considerable influence) with true Shingon rituals.

21. *Komusō* are monks from a Zen school of thought founded by a Chinese religious called Fuke in Japanese (in Chinese, Puhua; died 860). Their heads hidden under basket-shaped straw hats, swords at their sides, these itinerant, flute-playing beggar-monks traveled all over the country.

22. Marishiten is the Indian Marīci, child of Bonten (Brahmā). In Japan, he is the protecting divinity of warriors. Protection, good fortune, and victory are asked of him.

23. Today, both white, traditional in China, and black are the colors of mourning.

24. *Setsubun* is the day before *risshun* (the first day of spring). This calendar festival is especially notable for its rites of exorcism of unpropitious forces, demons, and malevolent spirits, who take advantage of the change of seasons to flood in great numbers into the world of humans.

Chapter 16: The Gods of Ansai

1. Yamazaki Ansai (1618–1682) is one of the principal representatives of Edo Period Neo-Confucianism. His interest in that current of thought coincided with a revival of Confucian studies in Japan. The study of Confucianism had remained confined largely to the monasteries, which led to an interpretation of Confucian concepts in Buddhist terms. But with the installation

of the feudal Tokugawa regime, Confucianism was given a practical function: the central theme of loyalty to the sovereign was held to be one of the foundations of the rigid and extremely hierarchical social order. In other respects, the birth of a premodern nationalism, which rejected Buddhism as being of foreign origin, led to attempts to harmonize Confucian cosmology with that of Shinto, considered the authentically national religion.

It was in this context that the Neo-Confucianism of Yamazaki Ansai was born. The Confucianism he studied under the direction of Tani Jitchū (1598–1649) was in fact the Neo-Confucianism of Zhu Xi (1130–1200), which was richly metaphysical in spite of its rationalist claims. Despite its inherent nationalism, Ansai's thought originated in the continental philosophies of India and China. His school was characterized primarily by the ambition to make Confucianism a philosophy of justice and rectitude and secondarily by the perpetuation of a metaphysical rationalism that produced a system of rules as valuable in the conduct of everyday affairs as in ontological meditation.

In terms of Shinto, Ansai first studied the Shinto of Ise and then that of Yoshikawa.

Ise Shinto claimed the superiority of the exterior sanctuary of the shrine at Ise over the other, interior one. It inverted the Buddhist theory depicting the Japanese gods as manifestations of the buddhas, insisting instead on the preeminence of the gods.

Yoshikawa Shinto developed from critical interpretations by the Yoshida family in the fifteenth century: under Confucian influence, the Shinto gods were conceived of as spiritual beings without beginning or end, creators of heaven and earth, animating all creatures and the hearts of men. Yoshikawa Shinto reiterated that theory, as did Ansai later, while accentuating Neo-Confucian themes already present in the Shinto of the Yoshidas. It clearly established an equivalence between the Chinese concept of *li* (principle or natural order) and the Japanese god Kuni no Tokotachi (also known as Kunidokotachi no Ōkami-sama), the creator of the universe. Ansai used this theme again in assimilating Ame no Minaka Nushi, the Master of the Middle of the Sky, with *li*. From this, he deduced his theory of the underlying equivalence of Confucianism and Shinto.

On those bases, he in turn founded a sect: Suika Shinto. Along with the Confucian virtues of compassion and loyalty, Suika Shinto insisted on the necessity of an absolute faith in the Japanese gods, and on purity. Only the practice of these virtues, which were to govern relations between men—that is, between vassal and lord, son and father, wife and husband, the people and the divine ancestors of the Imperial Family—could lead to the happiness of all.

Ansai's nationalism was in large part a reaction to the blind infatuation of the intellectuals of his day with China. It contributed in the nineteenth century to the development of the imperial ideology, which led to the overturning of the *bakufu* and the restoration of imperial power.

2. In the organization of village cults, the principal ritual functions were performed by people from the most noble lineages of the village. This equation of superior lineage with greater access to the gods stems from antique mythology, which established the kinship of gods and nobles, depicting the nobles as some form of gods who through residence on earth lost their divine characteristics.

3. Kanō Sozan belonged to the decorative Kanō school of painting.

4. Shocked by his brutality, the sun goddess Amaterasu refused to see her brother Tsukiyomi, the god of the moon and murderer of the goddess of grains, ever again. Out of this quarrel came the separation of day and night.

5. Inao-Daimyōjin is an aspect of Inari, the rice god, associated with the fox (see p. 291, note 46).

6. In antique mythology, Sarutahiko belongs to the category of gods of the country, the first pacifiers of the archipelago, called upon to restore their conquests to the divinities of heaven, who hold the legitimate right over Japan. The loyal divinity par excellence, Sarutahiko went to see the first, divinely descended, emperor to rule on earth, to offer his services as guide. After the celestial gods took possession of the country, Sarutahiko left for the sea—that is, the other world—thereby sharing the destiny of other great divinities of the country, the most celebrated of which is Ō-Kuni-Nushi no Kami, the Great Master of the Country.

His role as guide also qualified Sarutahiko to be assimilated into the *dōsojin*, the border gods who protect the borders of villages on the roads.

Yamazaki Ansai, placing an extreme value on the loyalty of the god toward the emperor, made him his guide in the faith and honored him as a sort of founding father of Shinto.

7. Excepting the aberrant episode of betrayal given by the oracle as the origin of the fate weighing on the family, the principal events of Ansai's life as reported here are attested by his biographers.

The legend attached to his birth must be seen in relation to all the tales that describe the supernatural origins of personages destined for the uncommon. This type of story generally consists of four phases:

    —The mother undertakes a pilgrimage to a Buddhist or Shinto holy site, during which she asks supernatural entities to grant her a child;

    —The mother soon perceives that she is pregnant or finds a child on the way home, or the child is brought to her by an animal;

    —The child, either lost or abducted, is taken in by a religious, a Shinto priest or *miko*. In some variants, the child reveals himself to be of such a nervous or morbid temperament that he is given to a religious to be fortified with prayers and rites;

    —The child becomes a great man.

The celebrity of Ansai and his difficult upbringing in a monastery are sufficient to have given rise to the legend surrounding his birth.

8. Following his time with Yoshikawa Koretaru, founder of Yoshikawa Shinto, Ansai received the name Suika-Reisha, literally, "Shrine of the Soul of Suika." The story Yamazaki Ikue tells of the shrine he erected to house his own deified soul is historically correct.

Just as some Buddhist monks of great virtue may be respected as living buddhas, Shinto devotees, notably the founders of new religions, are thought of by their followers as living gods, *iki-gami*.

9. According to the dedication calligraphed on the painting, it was made by Fujiwara Senki at the age of eighty-one.

10. Shushi is the Japanese pronunciation of Zhu Xi, the Chinese Neo-Confucianist instrumental in the development of the thought of Yamazaki Ansai.

11. The association of these three divinities dates to the erection of a statue of the Great Buddha at Tōdaiji, the Great Eastern Temple, in the capital city of Nara in the eighth century. In order to secure the protection of the indigenous *kami* over these Buddhist buildings, the Emperor Shōmu (701–756) called on a celebrated monk named Gyōki. Traveling to Ise, Gyōki donated a Buddhist relic and consulted the oracles. Through these, the sun goddess was said to accept the offerings and rejoice in the edification of the giant buddha (who was the solar Buddha, Mahāvairocana). The god Hachiman, who resided at Usa in Kyūshū, also declared himself to be in favor of the matter and indicated through an oracle where to find the necessary gold to finish the giant statue. By way of thanks, a shrine was consecrated to him near Tōdaiji, on the Kasuga Hill.

Triptychs or single paintings representing the three divinities were very much in vogue in the fifteenth and sixteenth centuries.

12. The 1959 marriage of Crown Prince Akihito to a commoner, the daughter of a wealthy businessman, scandalized extreme conservatives. At the same time, it was perceived by the young to be a sign of the true coming of democracy and by the people as a whole as a symbol of a new alliance between themselves and the Imperial Court.

The twelve kimonos layered one over the other (*jūnihitoe*) has been the ceremonial costume of noble women since the Heian Era. The *suberakashi*, an upswept ponytail, dates only from the Edo Period.

13. The text of Zhu Xi referred to here has to do with the respect and deference that must in all circumstances be manifested in social relations—notably between subject and lord, father and son, and wife and husband. Ansai adopted Zhu Xi's insistence on discipline and in that sense can be viewed as one of the most rigid Confucians.

Note here the seductive effect on Yamazaki Ikue of an allusion to hairstyling.

14. If Yamazaki Ikue does not wish to elaborate on the subject of Yamazaki Ansai as the murderer of the two messengers, it is probably because she invented that shaky hypothesis before she knew much about it.

15. *Kami no michi* is the Japanese reading of the Sino-Japanese word "Shinto."

16. *Jumon* are magic formulas used in *mikkyō* ("secret teachings" or Tantric) Buddhism and by the ascetics of *Shugendō* and the masters of *Onmyōdō*, as well as fates cast on others by ill-intentioned persons, either religious or lay.

17. The Japanese Yamazaki Ikue used here for "buddha," *hotoke*, designates awakening. *Hotoke* is also a euphemism for any deceased person, no matter what path of rebirth is supposed to have befallen him.

Note that in the popular context, this meaning takes precedence over "buddha of Indian origin." Foreign buddhas are generally designated by their names rather than by this generic appellation.

18. In fact, the *Kojiki* never speaks of Japan being created before other countries—it does not speak of other countries at all.

19. The cosmology of most Shinto new religions is more or less explicitly inspired by premodern nationalism as expressed in the works of Ansai, and even more by the exegeses of National Studies. The National Studies theorist Motoori Norinaga (1730–1801) tried to recover a Shintō that was pure, free from all Buddhist or Confucian influences. His disciple Hirata Atsutane (1776–1843) worked to prove that only Shinto holds truth, which Buddhism had perverted.

Ame no Minaka Nushi no Kami (or, "no Mikoto no Kami") occupied a marginal place in the official and popular cults until the the nineteenth century, when, under the influence of Christianity, Hirata Atsutane and his disciples assigned him a preeminent position: as the representative of "nonbeginning" and "nonending," of "total knowledge" and "absolute power," by which he was made a veritable master of creation. These philosophic readings of his nature went on to influence a number of new sects, which placed this "abstract" divinity at the summit of their pantheon.

20. The shrine at Ise was consecrated, probably in the eighth century, to the ancestors of the Imperial Line. As Yamazaki Ikue says, it is in fact two buildings: the interior, the *naikū*, honors the ancestral goddess of the Imperial Line; the exterior, the *gekū*, is where Toyouke, the goddess of abundant food, is said to reside.

Some ethnologists see in the existence of the two shrines an effect of the influence of Chinese theories on yin and yang, and of a symbolic dualism attributed to the general structure of the universe. But Yamazaki Ikue's idea that the interior shrine is consecrated to Japanese gods and the exterior to foreign gods is, to my knowledge, original.

21. This passage demonstrates the progressive nature of the transformation of a branch, or separate, house into an independent one, possessing ancestors different from those of the original main house.

22. Both Zen schools, Rinzai and Sōtō (or Sōdō), are of Chinese origin, and they constitute the principal currents of Japanese Zen thought. The first was introduced to Japan in the twelfth century by the monk Eisai; the second was founded by Dōgen in the thirteenth. While the Rinzai school, which remained close to its Chinese source of inspiration, emphasizes reflection on koan (seemingly absurd questions without answers), the Sōtō school, strongly Japanified, insists on seated meditation. These techniques permit the "emptying" from the spirit of that which ordinarily fills it (space, time, affirmation or negation, good and evil), in order to come to lucidity, awakening, or satori.

Note that a family's belonging to a Zen temple does not imply its involvement in any particular practices.

23. Recall that the *tsubo* is a unit of surface measure which equals roughly 36 square feet, while a tatami mat is slightly less than eighteen square feet.

Chapter 17: The Brotherhood of Sangū

1. The story of the birth of the dwarf Takeko belongs to a category of miracle stories which are often associated with the births of famous people as well as those having to do with the earthly sojourns of supernatural beings. The *Take-Tori Monogatari*, or "Bamboo-Cutter's Tale," is a famous example of the latter. In this story, which was first written down (probably based on oral tradition) at the turn of the tenth century, an old man discovers a tiny girl child in a bamboo stalk. Once she grows up, she is revealed to be a daughter of the divine inhabitants of the moon.

2. The rites of this festival, *toko shizume no matsuri*, are usually performed before the beginning of construction work, to ask the god of that ground for his protection; they do not usually include the consulting of oracles.

3. Ōuchiyama is the name of a hill near Sendai, the location of a shrine consecrated to the Great Master of the Country, Ō-Kuni-Nushi, also known as Daikoku.

4. This is one of Yamazaki Ikue's rare allusions to the Buddhist dogma of reincarnation. This belief has known little popular success in Japan; it has been largely overshadowed by a belief in the continuity of familial lines, through which are passed not only material inheritances but the conditions of one's current life (based on the conduct of ancestors, rather than that of the individual in a past incarnation).

5. Some lineages of transmitters of the Shinto cult possess special traditions that determine the ways paper must be cut to form symbols, *gohei*, of various divinities. These secret traditions are revealed only to initiates. This knowledge is an important part of the technical expertise of the Shinto priesthood.

6. Peach blossoms, irises, and chrysanthemums are respectively symbols of the third, fifth, and ninth months—and more precisely of the girls' festival on the third day of the third month, the boys' festival of May 5, and the harvest festival of the ninth month. These dates are fixed in conformance with the Chinese ritual calendar, which grants a special importance to yang (that is, odd-numbered) doubled days (dates on which the number of the day corresponds to the chronological number of the month).

In Japan, Chinese rites were grafted onto indigenous seasonal celebrations. During the ritual purification of women that took place both at the beginning of the agricultural work season and during the transplanting of the rice seedlings, peach blossoms or irises were placed in the bathwater; they were thought to magnify the water's regenerative powers. When the gods were thanked at harvesttime, chrysanthemums were floated in the cups of sake men drank to toast the health of the gods.

7. On *miko,* a Shinto priestess or a female medium, see p. 304, note 11.

8. Unlike many lesser *kami,* the gods that constitute the principal figures of mythology are extremely individualized and clearly anthropomorphic. They are also mortal; thus, myths report how the Great Master of the Country was killed in the mountains by his jealous brothers, then resuscitated by his mother.

9. Yamazaki Ikue's lack of precision here shows her desire to banalize the facts in order to minimize their importance. Having had several abortions is normal and freely admittable for a woman her age; abortion is very common in Japan.

The premodern name for abortion was *mabiki,* whose literal meaning is "to thin out [the rice plants]." Eighteenth-century lullabies commonly alluded to abortion, since young women who had had abortions were often employed as nursemaids. Although a birth control movement arose in the 1920s, the government outlawed the spread of birth control information in 1936 as part of its drive to increase the birthrate. Abortion was legalized in 1948. In 1952, the law was revised so that only a physician was permitted to perform an abortion, and then only when the mother's health was in danger. The official figures on abortion reached a peak in 1955, at 1,170,143. However, the actual number of abortions currently performed is thought to be two to three times that; in fact, one out of three married women claim to have had at least one abortion.

The most popular method of contraception today is the condom, followed by the IUD. The government continues to oppose universal legalization of birth control pills, citing their hazardous side effects; they are legal only for therapeutic use. Only 8 percent of women of childbearing age have access to the pill.

As for the aborted fetus, the traditional hope of mothers is that its spirit will pass directly to the buddha state; in other words, abortion is thought to allow the soul to leave the cycle of rebirth more quickly. This requires the intercession of the bodhisattva Jizō, patron of dead children. These beliefs have traditionally served to assuage the guilt caused by abortion and the pain of the death of a child. At the same time, changes in the social structure and the relative weakening of the ancestor cult in Japan appear to go hand in hand with greater concern over the after-death fate of one's children and increasing guilt after abortion, out of which the fetus cult developed in the 1970s. (The influence of Western morality cannot be discounted as a factor in this.)

10. The Japanese adopted the Chinese idea according to which the full moon of autumn, the full moon of the eighth month, is the most beautiful of the year. Yamazaki Ikue's association of the ritual viewing of this moon with the world of the dead, here effectuated through the intermediary of Tsukiyomi, the god of the moon, is, to my knowledge, original. The extraordinary importance granted this rite by Yamazaki Ikue must be tied in with the role attributed by the cosmology of National Studies and numerous religions to this god, sovereign of the world of the dead.

11. The term *kō* (today, "brotherhood") originally referred to a form of Buddhist debate practiced by monks. Between the twelfth and fifteenth centuries, the concept of *kō* was enlarged to include lay groups. As used here by Yamazaki Ikue, *kō* refers especially to those religious brotherhoods that have appeared in great numbers with the rise of new religions. Today the *kō* are the instruments of charismatic leaders who wish to enlarge their audiences. New religious movements that will eventually register as *hōjin* (juridical persons) often begin as *kō.*

12. The story of this queen (whose name is actually Iyo, not Ichiyo) is related in the Wa Chronicles, a short section devoted to Japan in the third-century Chinese classic *The History of the Three Realms.* There it is said that a queen possessed of magic powers governed the country of Yamatai with the aid of her brother, that she was unmarried as well as of advanced age, and that no one had the right to approach her freely. The same text alludes to bloody wars of suc-

cesssion provoked by the coming to power of a king, and the appeasement of the troubles following the accession to the throne of a female descendant of Himiko.

One must not place too great a faith in this single text—brief and often manifestly erroneous—and thereby infer (as have some Japanese historians) the existence of an antique matriarchy. All other records, admittedly of later date, attest to the predominance of the succession of a paternal line.

13. This reflection is an attempt to justify the collaboration of two women. Usually it is a man who holds the role of *mae-za* next to the female medium, the *naka-za*.

14. The *shiten* are in principle four in number, as is attested by the name, an abbreviation of the expression *shi-tennō*, which designates the four celestial guardians, four terrifying figures who, according to Buddhist dogma, watch over the universe. The *shiten* protect the medium in trance through the recitation of prayers or magic formulas.

15. The custom of making a pilgrimage to a shrine or a temple to greet the supernatural entities and attract their good graces for the coming year is very widespread. After this first pilgrimage (usually to a place near one's home and, if possible, a famous one), people may again, in the first days of the new year, visit more distant religious sites, particularly shrines of national renown, such as Ise or Izumo.

16. *Sangū*, which literally means "Three Palaces," designates as a general rule the Three Empresses—that is, the grandmother, the mother, and the wife of the emperor. The imperial connotation may be considered germane to the choice of this name for the sect, since one of its explicit goals is to encourage the perpetuation of the sovereign line.

17. Cape Miho, near the northern extremity of the Izumo peninsula, appears in antique myths as the favorite fishing spot of the son of the Great Master of the Country.

18. The goals advanced by the brotherhood of Sangū are identical with the objectives proposed by most of the new religions: the realization of paradise on earth and nationalism put to the service of a utopia of world peace. The great tenets of its dogma are taken from multiple sects of modern Shinto.

The sole original aspect of this brotherhood consists of its almost exclusive recruitment from hairdressing circles and its professional conception of utopia: the coming of peace will permit the coming of the Way of Beauty—that is, of hairdressing (which entails, of course, the idea of beauty in the world).

19. The corruption of politicians, already bemoaned before the war by both the extreme right and the extreme left, has continued to be common in contemporary Japan. The Lockheed and Recruit Cosmos scandals caused the resignations of two popular and prominent politicians: Tanaka Kakuei as prime minister, and former prime minister Nakasone Yasuhiro as president of the Liberal Democratic party, respectively. In 1993 further scandals brought about the breakup of the Liberal Democratic party.

20. The official connection between the political party Kōmeitō and the Sōka Gakkai sect, which created it in 1964, was broken in 1970, when a scandal arose after an author who had written a book critical of Sōka Gakkai was threatened by the Kōmeitō. But it is generally believed that secret ties between the party and sect remain.

21. Yasukuni Shrine was founded in Tokyo in 1869 for the repose of the souls of soldiers who died in the service of the emperor while fighting in the civil war that led to the Meiji Restoration.

Near the end of the 1960s, conservatives tried to make it the symbol of a strong state. In 1967, they succeeded in obtaining the reinstatement of a festival dating from the Meiji Era in which the mythical founding of the Japanese State by Emperor Jinmu in 660 B.C. was formally celebrated. They then unsuccessfully asked for the nationalization of Yasukuni Shrine.

Today, while custom authorizes chiefs of state to make private pilgrimages to Yasukuni, attempts at officialization of the cult are still met with violent protest from the left.

22. The dispute between Russia and Japan over the northern territories (the islands of Kunashiri, Etorofu, Habomai, and Shikotan; the Kuriles; and the south of Sakhalin) has complicated relations between the two nations since 1955.

Appendix

The Hamlet of Kitai and Village Life in Northeastern Japan

When Yamazaki Ikue was born in 1918 in rural Tōhoku, 80 percent of the Japanese population lived in the country. In her impoverished region, the institutional reforms of the Meiji government, which were aimed at guiding Japan directly from a quasi-feudal state to the restoration of the power of the emperor, led to serious imbalances rather than true modernization.

An 1888 law on the structuring of villages regrouped several hamlets in Asaka, but the hamlet of Kitai remained the entity of reference in daily life. In spite of the development of commerce and industry, the promulgation of obligatory education, and the establishment of military conscription, Kitai, with its small group of houses, remained largely self-sufficient. Dwellings were close to one another, surrounded by dry fields as well as the flooded rice paddies that were fed by a communal irrigation system. Relations with other hamlets or surrounding villages were stained with mistrust. Only the dominant houses, apparently, had the ability to establish relations outside the group, mainly through matrimonial alliances.

The solidarity of the inhabitants, reinforced during the feudal era by a penal and fiscal collective responsibility, was founded on bonds perceived to be familial. Of the nineteen houses that made up the old village, known as the "natural" village, eighteen bore the name Endo. All of them had relations with the main house (or house of origin) as branch houses (junior houses or those of tenant farmers). Marriage further tightened bonds between houses that already considered themselves to have issued from the founding ancestors of the village.

A POOR VILLAGE

Two documents in particular from the archives dated Year 42 of Meiji (1909) lead to the conclusion that the village of Asaka was not rich. These documents record attempts by the heads of houses to put into practice the virtues of economy favored by the government. A sort of sumptuary chart delineates limits on expenditures for festivals and burials: for instance, sake is no longer to be drunk at funeral banquets (unless specifically requested by the deceased), and the neighbors who come to help mourning families will receive no more than a bowl of soup and a "vegetable" (read, one dish). The second text restricts offerings for the gatherings of diverse brotherhoods in honor of the gods of the mountain, the storm, and smallpox; even more tellingly, it limits the raising of fowl which eat grains—no landowner will have the right to raise more than six hens, except during chick-hatching season, and no tenant farmer is to keep chickens at all. All supplementary fowl will be confiscated by the village assembly and used for the needs of the community.

The structure of the hamlet was *dōzoku*, hierarchical groupings of houses locally called *maki*, which characterize the east of Japan (the west is more egalitarian). In fact, social stratification was less marked in Kitai than in similar hamlets and villages, and branch houses in Kitai seem to have held lands as extensive as those of main houses. This is confirmed by the frequency of marriages between first cousins. Since marriages were subject to a certain equality of status between the two parties, such unions imply a weak differentiation in status between main and branch houses.

337

At the same time, a study of tax records places Yamazaki Ikue's forebears firmly in the middle class. The enrichment of Yamazaki Ikue's native house goes back to her father's generation. Through his marriage to a girl with an exceptionally large dowry, as well as through his own military exploits, Endo Keisuke had access to large liquid assets, which he used to acquire rice paddies, dry fields, barren plots, mountains, and forests in Kitai and the surrounding hamlets. In Year 5 of the Shōwa Era (1930), Endo Keisuke's real estate holdings attained their maximum: about twenty-one acres. He was a leading citizen in the full sense of the term: an ardent advocate of education and veteran of the Russo-Japanese War, he was a positive intermediary between the state and the local community; he participated in the government's ideological efforts to form a Japanese identity.

THE VILLAGE SHRINE: A LOCAL AND A NATIONAL UNIT

While archaeological evidence attests that the Asaka plain has been inhabited since before historic times, current residents believe that the virgin land was cleared by common ancestors. Their divinitized spirits are the gods honored in the shrine, which, though semiabandoned today, is the object of many legends.

These legends provide the villagers with valorous ancestors and express and sustain the unity of the community. In addition, they are the sources of the village's legitimacy and its organization, theoretically founded on proximity of origins. This principle is reactualized each generation by the transferral of the house and most of its assets (at least half, according to the Meiji code) to a principal heir, the eldest son.

The legends also point up an important characteristic of the ancestor cult. Two types of ancestors preside over the destiny of village communities made up of their descendants: hero gods of antique mythology, who participated in one way or another in the founding of the early Japanese state, and divinitized human ancestors. Long after their deaths, humans are called upon to become gods or to meld themselves with a divine entity which protects the village and appears to be conceived of as a local manifestation of the cosmological ancestral divinity. This configuration of local pantheons contributed to the development of the theocratic ideology of the second half of the nineteenth century and the first half of the twentieth.

At the summit of this theocracy was an emperor descended from a supreme sun goddess (Amaterasu), more or less clearly related to all the celestial founding divinities of the archipelago. The relatedness of simple human beings with these divinities implied a kinship network among all Japanese, tied to the emperor like children to a father. It supported the concept of the Japanese population as ethnically pure, elected by the gods, and enjoying a sort of oneness with the land. The kinship of humans with divinities made a religious imperative of the two cardinal virtues of Neo-Confucianism, filial piety and loyalty to the sovereign. Thus the state was endowed with spiritual, genetic, and racial dimensions. Through the cult they made of their ancestors, individuals assured not only the continuity of generations but also the perennial continuance of the country. The house became the ultimate link in the national organization, while the state itself was designated by the expression *kazoku kokka*, Family-State.

THE HOUSE

The house comprises all who work toward its maintenance or the expansion of the family patrimony, including the ancestors of the head of the house as well as its future heirs.

In fact, the ideological insistence on the importance of the house corresponded to a definite decline in that system. From 1910 to 1920, the traditional house was weakened by the immigration of the rural population to the cities. The exodus to the cities of a great number of young people, between ages sixteen and thirty-five, loosened the economic foundations of the house, already shaken by land tax reforms. In the cities, the family began to resemble the nuclear family.

This perceptible decline in the traditional house caused conservatives to fear a nascent decline in patriotism. Fear of the development of individualism or even socialism brought on an even more vigorous defense of the house, which conservatives held to be the matrix of the national character.

THE WORKPLACE AS SUBSTITUTE FOR THE HOUSE

Coming from a family that was well-off without being rich and conscious of belonging to the elite, Endo Nami arrived in Tokyo during the influx of peasants to urban areas. Although that move meant a rupture with her old way of life (she changed not only her environment but especially her social status), the structure into which she had to integrate herself was familiar.

The way work was organized in the cities remained close to that of rural society. In spite of rapid urbanization, Japan remained in essence a peasant society. In 1940, while the urban population represented about 40 percent of the total, 80 percent of all Japanese had been born and raised in the country. In a large city like Tokyo, relations among neighbors (at least in working-class neighborhoods) recalled those of the village community. In addition, the majority of enterprises retained familial dimensions; they were often both workplace and residence. In the context of the uniting force of work, everyone labored for the good of the "family." Individual desires were not to exceed the limits tolerable by the group—that is, individuals were never to question the internal hierarchy, because it was believed that questioning would shake its foundations. Customs and authority remained the guiding principles of individual conduct, and the insistence on the necessity for harmony led to conformity.

It was the quasi-familial nature of relations at the heart of the small urban factories that permitted them to survive in spite of the development of larger, modern enterprises. The latter also took the old domestic structure as a model. In fact, early in their development, large enterprises recruited workers who, having formerly worked for small businesses, had been educated in a traditional mentality. Later, faced with a serious dearth of manpower, large firms decided to cement employee loyalty by playing the card of paternalism. They insisted on the importance of the ties that united employers and employees, on the familial and holistic nature of the group. The recruitment of young personnel, the policies of lifelong employment and a salary into old age assured employees' participation in this management method. Enterprises also increased intramural groups, to keep workers from associating with groups not connected to their company. Trade unions were, for the most part, company sponsored and affiliated with professional or national federations.

Paradoxically, there is no doubt that the house was never so structured as it became once it had begun to decline. Originally the locus for the management of familial, religious, and economic ties, the house furnished a reference for the conception of the nation, supporting as it did the national sociopolitical organization; it also surfaced in the production organizations which, from the 1920s to the present, borrowed from it the model of kinship.

Yamazaki Ikue's recourse as a businesswoman to the integrating power of the familial ideology may be viewed as characteristic of personnel management in Japanese enterprises. Furnishing both a strategy and a tactic for growth, that conservative ideology would in the end play a dramatic role in business management.

GROWTH STRATEGY AND FAMILIAL IDEOLOGY

Yamazaki Ikue's objective is not social promotion, which she perceives only as a way of recovering the status that her birth allocated to her and that would accrue to the real or imaginary status of her house by marriage. Wealth is also not a prime objective for her (there is still nothing luxurious about her lifestyle). Considering herself, as do many rich Japanese, the heir of a Confucian morality that prizes the virtue of economy, she readily avows that too much money is useless, because there is a natural limit to human appetites. Instead, her profound ambition is to extend her dominion over a great number of people. To her, success is identified with the ability to feed many employees.

This obsession with growth leads Yamazaki Ikue to take an unusual approach for the size of her business (which she runs like a large corporation). Most indicative of this approach is her frequent recourse to debt. By borrowing to finance expansion, the business can grow faster. As a result, the profitability of the Yamazaki investment increases, even if there is a low return on total capital. For this situation to remain healthy, sales—and therefore profits—must grow faster than the rate of investment.

While large Japanese businesses do not hesitate to indebt themselves, for them debt entails far less social risk than for their Western counterparts. For small businesses, these risks remain more serious in that, not being able to ensure life employment, they must count solely on traditional loyalty to ensure a stable workforce. Finally, in contrast to the large corporations, they enjoy little protection from either the banks or the government. Yamazaki Ikue appears in this light as a superb adventurer.

This desire for growth at all costs is therefore the key to the Yamazaki style of employee management. Rather than implement an actual paternalism (guaranteed lifetime employment) that would be incompatible with her means, she chooses to promote a paternalistic corporate culture, an ideology defined along familial lines, and a style of personnel management that, while in no way exceptional, is definitely conservative.

As in many other businesses, this motivating ideology resides in the language used in defining the corporate culture. Centering on the nature of the group and the kind of work that group does, this culture defines itself by the history of the company but also by its opposition to ideas that are imagined to characterize the West (such as a labor-for-wages contract between employer and employee, who are positioned as antagonists). In theory, the employee who has understood two great rules—first, that work is not an impediment to freedom but rather offers the possibility of self-realization and integration into society; and, second, that wages, while compensating individual efforts, are not the goal of work—will find herself on an equal footing with a serene and harmonious group, among whom all relations are stripped of aggression and marked by friendship. She will benefit from a communal lifestyle, open to society in general, because her work is particularly important to society. That is why she must master the technical skills of her job, which are not a source of profit but rather the reason for the superiority of the Yamazaki enterprise, the source of its past and future growth.

The importance of this affirmation of the worker's worth to society is all the greater because the profession of hairdresser, in Japan as in France, is generally considered mediocre. Conferring dignity on and instilling pride in the workers, this ideology constitutes a real stimulant to industriousness in a profession where a relaxed attitude is more common.

There is no intramural union at the Yamazaki salons. The familial nature of the ties between employers and employees is supposed to render such an organization worthless. Nor is any Yamazaki employee affiliated with an outside labor group. The language used to define the Yamazaki ideology makes it clear that an employee's belonging to an exterior group can make her disloyal to her primary group or create, for the employee herself, unmanageable psychological conflicts. The numerous groups within the enterprise are supposed to take care of the need for professional association.

In Japan today, only 16.0 percent of service sector workers are unionized. Only 13.0 percent of employees in businesses with 100 to 499 employees are union members. More generally, 27.0 percent of all Japanese employees are unionized, including 58.0 percent in large companies (over 500 employees) and 0.7 percent in companies with fewer than 30 employees.

A MESSIANIC CONVICTION

Yamazaki Ikue's religious quest is a part of her need to constitute an identity and a personal dignity. Brought about, like so many religious inventions, by the psychological and intellectual unacceptability of ill fortune, it is motivated not by a metaphysical inquiry into the meaning of life in general but by the need to give meaning to her life and, beyond that, to her country and its position in the world.

In fact, Yamazaki Ikue's recourse to new religions is not exceptional: Japan's new religions today include about a third of the population. These sects have come together especially in times of crisis (notably political ones). A profound malaise concerning national identity underlies their popularity today. For the most part, these new sects do not function in opposition to preexisting religions, and they rarely question the workings of the world. Instead, their messianic perspectives are presented as a form of return to traditional sources or a particularly effective participation in the realization of concrete goals proposed by lay society. Their critical discourses do not differ in content from the editorials that often appear in newspapers; both favor working on the microcosmic level in order to transform the totality of society. Usually conservative while appearing new, they propose a morality founded on the belief in a quasi-imminent chastisement by evil occurrences on earth.

It is in this context that Yamazaki Ikue's abortive attempts to found a new religion must be understood. The ideological certainty provided by such an institution would have served her as a management tool while procuring for her a way of affecting the destiny of the world. That is why, if her nascent new religions occasionally inconvenience her immediate entourage because of the material complications that ensue, they never radically call into question their own foundations. In a more general fashion, the atheism proclaimed by many young people in Japan today simply denotes a vague indifference to questions which may lead to metaphysical reflection.

In fact, these sects propose no transcendence that would oppose the order of the world. In the morality they advocate, individuals are firmly anchored in society, society in history, and history in nature. The realization these sects offer is not of the individual's autonomy (which would endanger group unity) but rather of the accomplishment of a mission in the world. Their only goal is a better world order, believed to be in conformance with a divine or natural order. It is a universal conviction in Japan that paradise, which could be described by the two words "peace" and "prosperity," must be realized on earth. Whether the forces used to gain that be human or divine is, in the final analysis, of secondary importance.

Location of Yamazaki Ikue salons in the Tokyo area

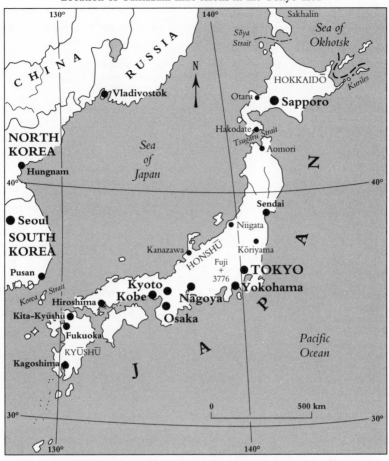

Map: Patrick Mérienne

THE HOUSE OF ENDO

*Based on a genealogy prepared
by Tanaka Ryōko*

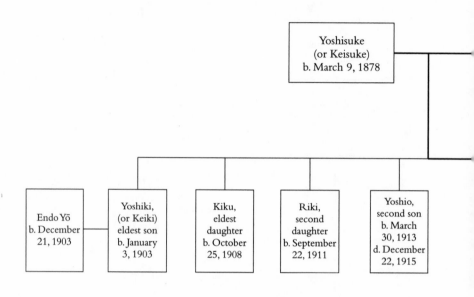

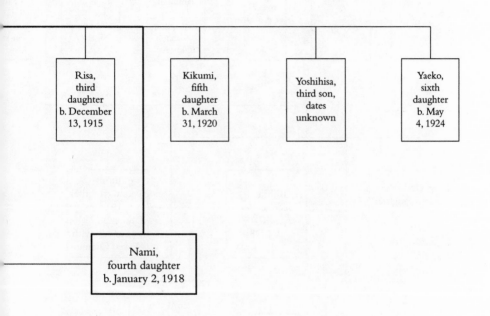

Okabe Mina
b. March 3, 1881

Risa,
third
daughter
b. December
13, 1915

Kikumi,
fifth
daughter
b. March
31, 1920

Yoshihisa,
third son,
dates
unknown

Yaeko,
sixth
daughter
b. May
4, 1924

Nami,
fourth daughter
b. January 2, 1918

THE HOUSE OF YAMAZAKI
Based on a genealogy prepared
by Tanaka Ryōko

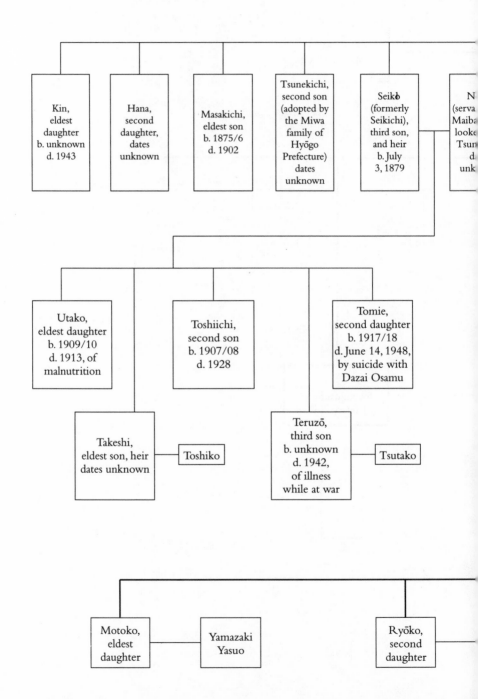

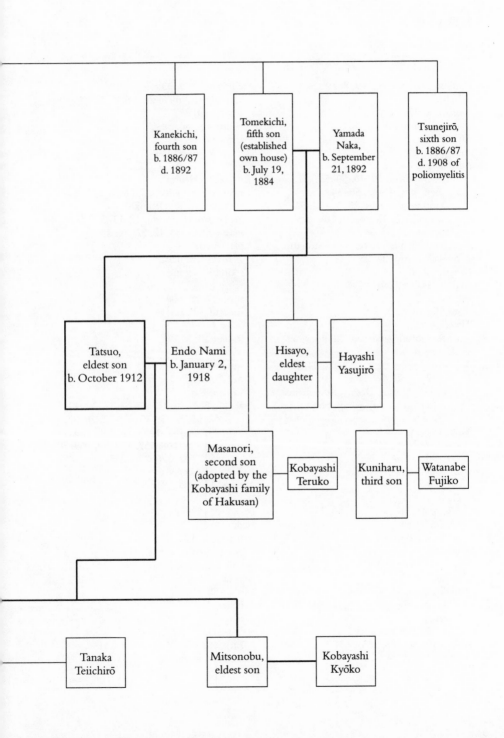

Index